# Mastering Administrative Law

CAROLINA ACADEMIC PRESS MASTERING SERIES
RUSSELL WEAVER, SERIES EDITOR

For other titles, please go to caplaw.com.

**Mastering Administrative Law, Second Edition**
Linda D. Jellum

**Mastering Adoption Law and Policy**
Cynthia Hawkins DeBose

**Mastering Alternative Dispute Resolution**
Kelly M. Feeley, James A. Sheehan

**Mastering American Indian Law**
Angelique Wambdi EagleWoman, Stacy L. Leeds

**Mastering Appellate Advocacy and Process, Revised Printing**
Donna C. Looper, George W. Kuney

**Mastering Art Law**
Herbert Lazerow

**Mastering Bankruptcy**
George W. Kuney

**Mastering Civil Procedure, Third Edition**
David Charles Hricik

**Mastering Constitutional Law, Second Edition**
John C. Knechtle, Christopher J. Roederer

**Mastering Contract Law**
Irma S. Russell, Barbara K. Bucholtz

**Mastering Corporate Tax, Second Edition**
Gail Levin Richmond, Reginald Mombrun, Felicia Branch

**Mastering Corporations and Other Business Entities, Second Edition**
Lee Harris

**Mastering Criminal Law, Second Edition**
Ellen S. Podgor, Peter J. Henning, Neil P. Cohen

**Mastering Criminal Procedure, Volume 1:
The Investigative Stage, Second Edition**
Peter J. Henning, Andrew Taslitz, Margaret L. Paris, Cynthia E. Jones, Ellen S. Podgor

**Mastering Criminal Procedure, Volume 2:
The Adjudicatory Stage, Second Edition**
Peter J. Henning, Andrew Taslitz, Margaret L. Paris, Cynthia E. Jones, Ellen S. Podgor

**Mastering Elder Law, Second Edition**
Ralph C. Brashier

# Mastering Administrative Law

## SECOND EDITION

**Linda D. Jellum**

ELLISON CAPERS PALMER SR. PROFESSOR OF LAW
MERCER UNIVERSITY SCHOOL OF LAW

CAROLINA ACADEMIC PRESS
Durham, North Carolina

Library of Congress Cataloging-in-Publication Data

Names: Jellum, Linda D., author.
Title: Mastering administrative law / Linda D. Jellum.
Description: Second edition. | Durham, North Carolina : Carolina Academic
   Press, LLC, [2018] | Series: Mastering series | Includes bibliographical
   references and index.
Identifiers: LCCN 2017055337 | ISBN 9781611638905 (alk. paper)
Subjects: LCSH: Administrative law--United States. | Administrative
   procedure--United States.
Classification: LCC KF5402 .A83 2018 | DDC 342.73/06--dc23
LC record available at https://lccn.loc.gov/2017055337


eISBN 978-1-61163-978-0


Carolina Academic Press, LLC
700 Kent Street
Durham, North Carolina 27701
Telephone (919) 489-7486
Fax (919) 493-5668
www.cap-press.com


Printed in the United States of America

*For Lee, Chris, and Kaylee:*
*I hope you someday understand why I work so hard*

# Contents

# Table of Illustrations

# Table of Cases

# Series Editor's Foreword

The Carolina Academic Press Mastering Series is designed to provide you with a tool that will enable you to easily and efficiently "master" the substance and content of law school courses. Throughout the series, the focus is on quality writing that makes legal concepts understandable. As a result, the series is designed to be easy to read and is not unduly cluttered with footnotes or cites to secondary sources.

In order to facilitate student mastery of topics, the Mastering Series includes a number of pedagogical features designed to improve learning and retention. At the beginning of each chapter, you will find a "Roadmap" that tells you about the chapter and provides you with a sense of the material that you will cover. A "Checkpoint" at the end of each chapter encourages you to stop and review the key concepts, reiterating what you have learned. Throughout the book, key terms are explained and emphasized. Finally, a "Master Checklist" at the end of each book reinforces what you have learned and helps you identify any areas that need review or further study.

We hope that you will enjoy studying with, and learning from, the Mastering Series.

Russell L. Weaver
Professor of Law & Distinguished University Scholar
University of Louisville, Louis D. Brandeis School of Law

# Foreword

Administrative law is something exotic in the law school curriculum. That is, the subject is unknown to most students. And the field is full of alphabet-soup acronyms and insider jargon. Moreover, most students have had little direct experience with regulatory bodies. All of this can make the subject seem daunting.

But wait! There are two things you need to think about before you become daunted. First, the field is increasingly a vital subject for all lawyers. You can't really function in today's legal world without some introduction to administrative law, so the time you invest learning the subject will not be wasted. And it is an exciting place for a lawyer to be. Administrative law professionals, whether inside or outside government, tend to work at the cutting edge of law. Administering the same policies doesn't usually require lawyers. But when the agency or the client wants to try something new, something different, something innovative, that's when your phone rings.

Answering that phone will introduce you to the variety of roles lawyers play in this field. To agency executives and regulated clients, lawyers are crucial interpreters of the law, specialists on procedural requirements, drafters, critical arbiters of policy analysis, and, of course, advocates in the courtroom and other places. With this skill set, these professionals are usually at the center of the action, including the meetings that really count. For an elaboration of these professional roles inside government, see Thomas O. McGarrity. *The Role of Government Attorneys in Regulatory Agency Rulemaking*, 61 LAW & CONTEMP. PROBS. 19 (1998).

Second, you should know that administrative law is ultimately a practical subject. When one is dealing with really important matters (think of banking regulation, civil rights, labor/management issues, workplace safety, environmental protection, monetary policy, health care, etc.) there is simply too much at stake to allow endless research or infinite doctrinal refinement. Yes, good regulatory policy must rest on solid research and intelligent principles, but the government must also be kept open. Like the experienced administrative lawyer, you should not be paralyzed by doctrinal complexity.

Understand it. But don't let it trap you in a box you can't get out of if more practical resolutions emerge from your thinking. Answers that work are always necessary and usually sufficient.

Finding answers that work may require consideration of multiple perspectives. Effective and workable administrative law doctrines must be consistent with legislative wishes, efficient in the day-to-day work of the executive branch and the independent agencies, sensitive to the attitudes and culture of regulated parties, and ultimately administrable by the courts. These institutions may have different needs and different resources—and finding doctrine that works tolerably well for most of them at a given time is one of the real challenges of the field. It is a challenge worthy of the best minds.

So welcome to the field of administrative law. It is sometimes intellectually difficult but always professionally rewarding. It will, without doubt, be a growth experience for you.

# Preface to the Second Edition

This work is intended for the student or the foreign lawyer in need of a short introduction to the U.S. system of administrative law. Rather than being a contribution to the larger theoretical literature, it attempts to identify central principles in an understandable form and to organize them so that their essential functions are clear. The discussion is accompanied by a number of graphics that should help you visualize important doctrinal relationships.

Three important acknowledgements: I must first thank the author of the first edition, Professor William Andersen who, on retirement, invited me to take on the task of keeping the book current, as to both any new developments I thought relevant and any substantive changes I thought necessary. I appreciate the trust this implied and the freedom that resulted.

Second, I have had tremendous help from a variety of research assistants, including Josh Pico ('17), Moses Tincher ('17), and Jess Lill ('18). They have been patient and helpful as they reviewed each chapter for typos, updated cites, drafted parentheticals for me to rewrite, and researched challenging topics. Additionally, librarian James Walsh has always responded to my research questions, no matter how late at night, with a simple "always happy to help, Linda." And he always is.

Finally, I have been fortunate in having Cherie Jump as my assistant during the manuscript production process. She contributed greatly—with professional skill, grace, and a sense of humor.

> Linda D. Jellum
> Macon, GA
> June 2017

# About the Author

Linda Jellum is the Ellison C. Palmer Sr. Professor of Law at Mercer University School of Law. She teaches Tax Law, Administrative Law, and Statutory Interpretation. In addition to teaching, Professor Jellum is a prolific scholar and has written extensively in the areas of Tax Law, Administrative Law, and Statutory Interpretation. Her numerous articles have appeared in top law journals, such as the *Miami Law Review*, the *Virginia Tax Review*, the *UCLA Law Review*, and the *Ohio State Law Journal*. She has also authored multiple books and book chapters on statutory interpretation.

Professor Jellum has been a leader in legal education. She is currently an officer for the Southeastern Association of Law Schools. Formerly, she served as the Deputy Director for the Association of American Law Schools. In addition, she is an officer for American Bar Association Section's on Administrative Law and Regulatory Practice.

Before joining the faculty, Professor Jellum worked for the Washington State Attorney General's office. While there, she served as lead attorney for the Department of Social and Health Services. Prior to working as an assistant attorney general, she served as a law clerk for the Honorable Paul Yesawich.

Professor Jellum received her J.D. from Cornell Law School and her undergraduate degree from Cornell University. She has the unique honor of having sat for and passed five states' bar exams.

# Mastering Administrative Law

# Chapter 1

# The Role of Administrative Law

---

---

## A. Introduction

Law is instrumental. Law develops in response to identified problems. It is an effort to resolve disputes and provide guidance to people confronting those problems. For example, negligence law allocates the certain kinds of unintended losses; contract law seeks to facilitate private ordering and exchanges; property law seeks to define interests in tangible and intangible things and to facilitate transfer of those interests. Administrative law is no different; it has purposes, functions, and goals.

Understanding the underlying purpose of a set of legal doctrines is not a job solely of interest to a theorist or philosopher. It is essential for all lawyers, including law students. You lay a foundation for deeper understanding of a field of law if you can get a sense of the reason behind that law, meaning a feel for the problems the law was intended to solve. So in a way, this chapter is the most important chapter in the book. If you work through it carefully, you will begin to develop a sense of the underlying rationales of administrative law, a set of perceptions that will pay real dividends for understanding and applying

3

the law. And this chapter will provide you with criteria for critiquing the law, which should be an obligation of all members of a learned profession.

Let's begin with the idea that we are dealing with government and the power that government exercises. We are looking at how government instrumentalities acquire power, how they exercise it, and how they control it. Your courses in constitutional law addressed these issues broadly. Here we look principally at power questions relating to the part of government that is engaged in regulating private conduct.

Whatever may have been the vision of the framers, the subject of regulation today is vast and complex. It touches the daily life of virtually every citizen in seemingly endless ways, from the labels on our food to the air we breathe; from the crops we grow to the security of our financial and banking system; from the television we watch to the safety of our workplaces. In short, the U.S. regulatory agencies have become responsible for standard setting, enforcement, and direct provision of services in a range of activities that includes agriculture, commerce, education, energy, welfare, labor, transportation, environment, consumer affairs, maritime matters, workplace safety, communications, taxation, and monetary policy, to mention just the obvious.

In each of these areas, a body of *substantive* law will be generated (tax law, labor law, securities law, environmental law, etc.) and the typical U.S. law school will have courses in these substantive areas. The typical law school course in administrative law, by contrast, addresses the *procedures* the agencies must follow in carrying out their substantive tasks. In addition, administrative law covers judicial review of agency actions. Judicial review raises especially delicate interbranch issues because the job of the courts is to "police" the other branches, assuring their compliance with the constitution and with any relevant legislative or executive requirements. We will focus in this text on federal administrative agencies, but similar arrangements are made for agencies at the state and local level.

Regulatory agencies in the U.S. come in a bewildering variety of forms. They may be part of the executive branch or free standing. They may be subject to significant executive branch control or somewhat independent of that control. They may carry names such as commission, board, agency, department, bureau, etc. The tasks assigned to them are of many kinds, including planning, research, grant administration, and the provision of direct services, etc. But most of administrative law deals with the regulatory function of agencies, which directly impact individuals and businesses. The statutory systems and mechanisms that empower and control these agencies span an impressive range, and the law that regulates procedure in this area cannot be simply stated. How can we get a handle on this complexity?

We can begin with the history of the process. It is clear today that the framers had no conception of the size this regulatory function would assume. They wrote our Constitution before the industrial revolution — before the growth of communications and transportation had welded our nation (and increasingly our world) into a single interdependent economic unit. They wrote before the principal players had ceased being farmers and small business owners and had become immense corporate organizations whose size and wealth put them beyond the practical power of individual states to control. The framers wrote, too, before the technical complexities of regulation could have been foreseen and before the magnitude of the process could have been guessed. These factors do more to explain the growth of the regulatory process than any changes in political philosophy. National (and increasingly global) economic interdependence explains why so much of the regulatory process was (and is) lodged at the national level. Technical complexity and the volume of regulatory actions explain why regulation was beyond the ability of the legislative branch as well as beyond the ability of a minimally staffed and ultimately political executive branch. Some process had to be invented that could address the increasingly technical and complex issues in a careful, professional manner. Although that process had to be removed from political forces to some degree, it ultimately had to be accountable to those forces.

The development of the administrative state began early. In 1789, the first Congress authorized the president to appoint an administrative officer to estimate import duties. And during George Washington's administration, executive departments were created (War, State, Treasury, Post Office, Attorney General). At first, growth was slow, but after the 1860s, the U.S. added cabinet-level departments such as Agriculture and Labor. By 1887 the first modern regulatory agency was created: the Interstate Commerce Commission (now defunct). Congress gave this agency the power to regulate the new railroad industry. Building on that model, agencies were created over the next 30 years to regulate food and drugs (1906), unfair competition (1914), hydroelectric projects (1920), commodity trading (1922), and radio (1927).

With the economic collapse of the Great Depression in the 1930s, the government began to regulate other specific industries such as securities (1934), wholesale electric power (1935), trucking (1935), airlines (1938), and natural gas (1938). General regulation of labor relations began with the Labor Act (1935), although the Supreme Court declared Presidents Roosevelt's broader attempt to regulate prices and business practices unconstitutional. *A.L.A. Schechter Poultry Corp. v. United States*, 295 U.S. 495 (1935). After World War II, the government moved from regulating business to addressing social and economic problems, in such fields as social insurance, public assistance, health care, farm price supports, and housing subsidies.

In the 1960s and 1970s the government expanded regulation again, moving into such areas as racial and gender discrimination, consumer fraud, health, safety, and the environment. By the late 1970s, the swing of the regulatory pendulum began to slow and, indeed, to move in the other direction. Beginning with the Carter administration and carried forward by later administrations, the government began a process of *de*regulation, especially in the areas relating to airlines, trucking, and railroads. Despite deregulation, the size and breadth of the regulatory process is still immense and continues to expand. No real legislative initiative occurs today that does not require administrative agencies to do the heavy lifting, from the Homeland Security Administration created after 9/11 to the Consumer Financial Protection Bureau proposed by President Obama in July 2009 in response to concerns about banking and credit card practices that injured consumers.

Agencies today make rules that for all intents and purposes have the force and effect of legislative enactments. And as any law librarian can attest, ten times as much shelf space is required for published agency rules as is required for all the enactments of Congress. Agencies today adjudicate cases that for all intents and purposes have the force and effect of judicial decisions. And the number of adjudications is many, many times the number of cases decided by all the federal courts combined.

The growth of the regulatory state has been controversial, and the theoretically minded reader might enjoy some of the academic analyses that has developed, including schools of thought carrying labels like "public choice," "neopluralism," "public interest," and "civic republicanism." One example is Steven Croley's "administrative process" theory, which suggests the importance of administrative procedure itself for an effective and legitimate regulatory process. STEVEN CROLEY, REGULATION AND PUBLIC INTERESTS: THE POSSIBILITY OF GOOD REGULATORY GOVERNMENT (2008).

To keep this text reasonably short, we will focus principally on traditional regulatory agencies. We will not be talking about the governmental organs that take corporate form or whose duties are more operational than regulatory, such as the Public Broadcasting System (PBS) or the Tennessee Valley Authority (TVA). Instead, we will focus on the agencies that regulate private conduct through administrative rulemaking and adjudication. These agencies include cabinet-level agencies (such as the Labor Department), independent executive branch agencies (such as the Environmental Protection Agency), and so-called independent agencies (typically collegial in form, such as the Federal Communications Commission, the National Labor Relations Board, the Federal

Trade Commission, and the Securities and Exchange Commission). The conventional abbreviations for these agencies (EPA, FCC, NLRB, FTC, SEC) give us the storied "alphabet soup" reference to modern government.

Consider the Federal Trade Commission as a typical example. The FTC is a small agency with barely 1,000 employees. It was created in 1914 to regulate a variety of matters, including deceptive and unfair commercial advertising, certain kinds of anticompetitive mergers, and other business practices that restrict competition. In addition, the FTC carries on a significant economic research effort in support of its law enforcement actions. It works with state, local, and international agencies. It conducts hearings, workshops, and conferences for consumers and businesses to develop research and to disseminate information. The FTC is an agency with industry-wide authority. Its authority is not limited to one industry, like the FCC's authority, nor is its authority limited to one aspect of industry, such as the NLRB's authority. To give you a sense of the volume of business done by the FTC, in 2015 the Commission received in excess of three million consumer complaints.

The FTC is headed by a five-person body whose individuals are known as commissioners. All commissioners are appointed by the president and confirmed by the Senate for seven-year terms. No more than three commissioners can be from the same political party. The commissioners' terms are staggered and are longer than one presidential term so that it will take several years for a new president to fill the FTC with "his or her" people. As we will learn later, for independent agencies like the FTC, the president's power of removal may be sharply circumscribed.

The FTC's regulatory work is largely done through rulemaking. Rules adopted through the FTC's rulemaking have the force of law. In other words, they are like statutes enacted by Congress. The FTC enforces its rules through adjudication. In a typical FTC formal adjudication, there will be a trial-type hearing. At this hearing, the guilt or innocence of the alleged violator is determined.

The awkward question is: where in our constitutional structure is there provision for a governmental instrumentality exercising powers of this sort?

## B. The Constitutionality of Regulation

Our federal Constitution identifies governmental powers and invests the various branches of the federal government with these powers. The Constitution separates the powers of these branches. It further imposes limits on the federal and state governments. The growth of the regulatory process has raised important issues about the constitutionality of federal agencies: we will learn how agencies get their power, whether agency structures violate principles of separation of powers, and when agency conduct violates specific constitutional limits, such as those in the Fourth and Fifth Amendments.

Of special concern to us is the separation of powers notion. The Constitution creates the three branches of government: the legislative, the executive, and the judicial branches. The drafters of the Constitution intended to keep the branches separate in important ways. The vesting language in the Constitution underscores the idea of separation. Thus, Article I vests "all" legislative power in the Congress; Article II vests "the" executive power in the president; and Article III vests "the" judicial power in the judicial branch.

There are places, of course, where the branches share a power, where the powers overlap, and where combined action of branches is necessary. For example, the president has a role in the legislative process known as the veto; the Senate has a role in the executive's international responsibilities because it must approve treaties; a court intrudes on the functions of both the other branches when it holds that their actions violate the Constitution. But at the core of their functioning, the branches are separate and disputes regarding separation of powers are often before the courts.

One might think resolving a separation of powers dispute would be relatively easy. One would simply identify the three types of powers, identify the three branches, then ask if a power asserted by actors in one branch was, in fact, a power that had been vested by the Constitution in another branch. If the answer is "yes," we have a violation of separation of powers. Alas, it is more complicated than that. Both the definition of powers (e.g., is it executive or legislative?) and the identification of branches can be difficult characterizations to make.

> The embarrassing secret is that both commitments at the center of separation of powers doctrine are misconceived. The effort to identify and separate governmental powers fails because, in the contested cases, there is no principled way to distinguish between the relevant powers . . . Inquiring about inter-branch balance is incoherent because it assumes that branches of government are unitary entities with cohesive interests, but that is not true. The institutions of the national government are made up of individuals and sub-institutions with varying incentives that do not neatly track the institution [i.e., branches] within which they are located.

Elizabeth Magill, *Beyond Powers and Branches in Separation of Powers Law*, 150 U. Pa. L. Rev. 603, 604–05 (2001).

Still, the framers had something important in mind and we can get a sense of what they had in mind by focusing on core meanings of the words, recognizing that at the margins there will be inexactness. With that objective, core definitions of the respective powers might look something like this:

- Legislative power is used to *promulgate general rules* for the future. These rules affect classes of individuals or events. Article I lodges this power exclusively in the legislative branch.

- Executive power is used *to apply and enforce* legislative rules and includes such functions as administering, investigating, prosecuting, etc. Article II lodges this power in the executive branch.

- Judicial power is used to *resolve individual disputes* arising in the promulgation and implementation of the rules. Such disputes may arise from claims that government action is inconsistent with legislative rules or from claims that the legislative rules themselves are inconsistent with relevant constitutional or statutory provisions. Article III lodges this power in the judicial branch.

If we can agree on these descriptions, we can then ask why the framers thought it so important that the three general holders of these powers be kept separate from each other. The idea of separating the powers has at least three justifications. The first, which was central to the framers, was the need to avoid concentration of too much power in one branch. With the virtually omnipotent British monarch George III in mind, the framers believed that if power were divided among different branches the potential for oppression and tyranny would be reduced. Indeed, the powers were distributed such that one branch can often block action by the other, making control of the whole government by particular interests or individuals much more difficult. Further, officials serving in the respective branches are selected by different methods, serve for different terms, and are responsive to different constituencies. It may seem fanciful to us today to worry about monarchial tyranny, but we do worry that individuals with narrow interests may concentrate their power. Separation of powers prevents this concentration as well.

A second justification for separating powers was simply the obvious point that specialization brings efficiency. While this goal was less important to the framers, the government is more efficient when legislators who are more skilled at legislating legislate, executives who are more proficient at executing execute, and judges who more adept at judging judge.

A third justification for separating powers is of special concern to administrative law. If these powers were not separated, serious problems of fairness would arise. The three kinds of powers are in some ways inconsistent, and combinations can be troublesome. For example, even in the eighteenth century, everyone agreed that those who wrote the laws should not be too deeply involved in their interpretation in individual cases and that those who investigated and prosecuted alleged law violators should not be judges in those cases. For a discussion of the English antecedents to this view of separated powers, see RICHARD PIERCE ET AL., ADMINISTRATIVE LAW AND PROCESS 24–25 (6th ed. 2014). The typical agency, such as the FTC described above, raises concerns about this third justification. All three powers are combined in one agency: the agency writes the rules, prosecutes alleged violators, and judges the guilt or innocence of the alleged violator. It would be difficult to find a clearer example of combined powers and the potential for unfairness is palpable.

Yet the administrative process exists. And grows. Has the Supreme Court been asleep at the separation of powers switch? The Court has never fully resolved this question. Sometimes the Court takes a functional view and concludes that necessity requires some combination of functions. You can find this functional view expressed in *Morrison v. Olson*, 487 U.S. 654 (1988). By contrast, the Court sometimes takes a very formal approach and insists on a strict and literal application of the principle of separation. You can find this formalist view expressed in *INS v. Chadha*, 462 U.S. 919 (1983). As the functionalist/formalist debate continues, a practical compromise has developed that generally permits the administrative process to continue. We will examine this arrangement in more detail in the next section. But a central piece of this compromise is the development of legislative, executive, and judicial principles that minimize the problems of combining inconsistent functions. This central piece of the compromise is what we call administrative law. Administrative law, the law that agencies must follow, is designed in part to address these shortfalls.

## C. Separation of Powers Problems with Regulation

Let's return to the FTC example above. What might the framers have thought of an instrumentality of the federal government holding such powers? There are three ways in which this instrumentality would likely have troubled the framers: its authority, its unfairness, and its unaccountability. The next sections explore each of these three problems and how those problems have been addressed.

# 1. The Problem of Authority

How can any governmental power exist in an entity that was not expressly given that power by the Constitution? Under the usual notion that the federal government is a government of limited and enumerated powers, no entity of our government can exercise a power unless the constitution expressly grants that power to that entity. Under the general definitions we identified earlier, the FTC exercises legislative power when the agency makes general rules. Moreover, the FTC exercises judicial power when it adjudicates. Where did the FTC get those two powers? Certainly not from the Constitution. Some scholars and judges have solved the lack of authority through denial. These scholars and judges have suggested that administrative agencies exercised only "quasi" legislative or "quasi" judicial power. Because the powers are only quasi, not full, the exercise of those powers by those entities not expressly given such powers is constitutional.

Today, most scholars and judges realize that identifying the power as quasi is not satisfying. When the FTC issues a rule identifying a particular advertising practice as misleading, businesses are affected in the same way they would be if Congress had issued the rule; in short, the FTC exercised legislative power. When the FTC then prosecutes a company for engaging in a practice that violates its rule and issues an order requiring the company to cease and desist from violating the rule, the business is affected in the same way it would be if a court of law had issued the order; in short, the FTC exercised judicial power. Given that the framers intended to assign lawmaking power exclusively to the legislature and interpretive power exclusively to the judiciary, why is this divergence from the framers' plan constitutional?

That question is answered today with the concept of delegation. The doctrine of delegation posits that power sharing is constitutional because Congress delegated power to the agencies. But this apparently straightforward answer is overshadowed by something called the nondelegation doctrine. The nondelegation doctrine goes back as far as John Locke and asserts that an agent cannot subdelegate (*delegata potestas non potest delegari*). Nondelegation has no obvious textual basis in the constitution (meaning that the Constitution does not expressly prohibit delegation). Rather, nondelegation is a carryover from the law of agency. Pursuant to the nondelegation doctrine, the legislature, as the agent, may not subdelegate its power to another entity, such as an administrative agency. Agency law does not prohibit an agent from telling its assistants how to carry out tasks, so long as the agent itself remains in control of the basic policy choices.

Using this rationale, Justice Marshall stated that so long as Congress (the agent) decided the important policies, agencies could "fill up the details." *Wayman v. Southard*, 23 U.S. 1, 43 (1825). This holding flowed from an earlier Supreme Court opinion, which had held that Congress could exercise its power contingently, leaving to other entities the task of determining whether facts existed that called the stated policy into operation. *The Aurora*, 11 U.S. 382 (1813). Thus, pursuant to nondelegation principles, Congress can delegate the how-to details so long as it remains in control of the basic policy choices.

How then should a court determine whether Congress has made the basic policy decision? The best answer the Supreme Court has so far offered is that a delegation to an administrative agency is constitutional so long as Congress provides an "intelligible principle" in the statute authorizing the agency to act. *J.W. Hampton, Jr., & Co. v. United States*, 276 U.S. 394, 409 (1928). If there is such a principle in the statute, Congress constitutionally delegates authority to the administrative agency to fill up the details. As understood, the intelligible principle limits an agency's discretion to make policy and allows a court to determine whether the agency is acting within the "limited" authority Congress delegated to it. See Figure 1.1.

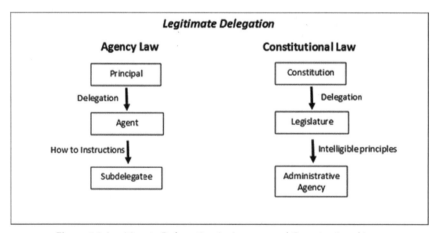

**Figure 1.1** Legitimate Delegation in Agency and Constitutional Law

The delegation doctrine would make perfect sense as the reason agencies make rules and adjudicate cases if one could say with a straight face that the legislature was making policies and the agencies were merely "filling up the details." But this statement stretches the truth. The kinds of intelligible principles that the Supreme Court has accepted as limiting agency discretion are of such cosmic breadth as to leave agencies free to make basic policy choices over a wide range of topics. For example, the Court upheld as an "intelligible principle" that an agency regulate "in the public interest," *see, e.g., National Broad. Co. v. United States,* 319 U.S. 190, 225–26 (1943) and "as requisite to protect public health." *Whitman v. American Trucking Ass'ns., Inc.* 531 U.S. 457, 472 (2001). By providing such little guidance to an agency, Congress effectively delegated its policy-making function. What policy *is* in the public interest or sufficient to protect public health is the question that Congress should be deciding. Such general and non-limiting intelligible principles provide agencies with little guidance to fill up the details and substantial discretion to make policy.

The Supreme Court's refusal to give the nondelegation doctrine any teeth has been controversial. Some judges and commentators have argued that the nondelegation should be stronger to force the legislature to confront and make basic policy choices to assure that it is accountable to the people (a topic addressed below). The current nondelegation doctrine, they argue, insulates Congress from responsibility for its policy choices and shifts the venue of policy debate from the halls of the legislature to the corridors of the agency. *See, e.g., Industrial Union v. American Petroleum Inst.,* 448 U.S. 607, 671 (1980) (Rehnquist, concurring); JOHN HART ELY, DEMOCRACY AND DISTRUST 131 (1980). The Supreme Court, however, has not responded to these criticisms and is unlikely to change its approach to this issue anytime soon.

Nondelegation doctrine aside, if one goal of delegation is to allow for meaningful public participation as policy is formed, the agency rulemaking process may be as good as (or even better than) the congressional process. Public access at the agency level tends to be easier and cheaper than access at the legislative level. And discussions and negotiations among knowledgeable and experienced agency experts may be more useful than debates with generalist legislators. *See* Jerry Mashaw, *ProDelegation; Why Administrators Should Make Policy Decisions,* 1 J. L. ECON. & ORG. 81, 95 (1985).

While the legitimacy of congressional delegation to an agency can be debated, it is well settled today that agency actions must be based on statutory authority that includes some limiting principle (the intelligible principle) and that the courts can and do resolve disputes about the boundaries of those principles. *Compare Massachusetts v. EPA,* 549 U.S. 497 (2007) (EPA *does* have authority to regulate greenhouse gases), *with FDA v. Brown & Williamson Tobacco Corp.,* 529 U.S. 120 (2000) (FDA does *not* have authority to regulate tobacco). The best place to begin thinking about the legality of any agency action is the language of the authorizing, or enabling, statute.

## 2. The Problem of Unfairness

Above, we identified the need to assure fairness and the appearance of fairness in a law's implementation and enforcement as foundational to separation of powers. If one believes that adjudication should be policy-neutral, one might have real concerns if legislative, prosecutorial, and judging functions are combined within one body. Suppose the FTC believes a certain type of misleading advertising practice should be prohibited. Acting in its legislative role, the FTC might promulgate a rule prohibiting this type of practice. Shifting to its role as executive, the FTC may investigate potential violations and decide which violators to prosecute. For those violators the FTC has chosen to prosecute, FTC personnel serve as prosecuting attorneys. The trial of the alleged violator will be before an FTC Administrative Law Judge (ALJ), whose judgment will be final unless a disappointed party appeals. Parties dissatisfied with the judgment of the ALJ can appeal, but the appeal goes to the FTC itself, the very body that developed, investigated, prosecuted, and judged the case from the start. True, any final order of the FTC is subject to judicial review before an independent Article III federal judge, but as we will see in Chapter 6, judges are relatively deferential to agencies regarding their resolutions of questions of policy (should automatic seatbelts be required?), resolutions of disputed questions of fact within the expertise of the agency (do automatic seatbelts save more lives than airbags?), and their interpretations of ambiguities in statutes (does "combination product" include cigarettes?). If the framers wanted powers to be separated to ensure fairness or at least the appearance of fairness in governmental action, they would be astonished to see what happens in a typical FTC adjudication today.

Addressing these unfairness concerns has been a principal task of that body of law we call administrative law. You will see as we work through the ensuing chapters, that administrative law is engaged in correcting some of the separation of powers shortfalls that have emerged from the unexpected development of the regulatory process. For example, when agencies are adjudicating individual cases, we will see procedural requirements that agencies provide notice and an opportunity to be heard, separate employees based on their functions, provide neutral decisionmakers, limit ex parte communications, and base their decisions exclusively on the hearing record.

These protections do not apply in informal agency rulemaking (what is also known as notice and comment rulemaking). Informal rulemaking is a legislative activity; fairness is not of central relevance. Thus, there is no requirement that Congress's decision be based on any discrete "record" compiled during a hearing. Indeed, in the legislative branch, there is not even a requirement that there be a hearing. Nor is there any requirement of a neutral decisionmaker; Congress can be very partisan. And there are no limits on outside communications. In a legislative body, it is expected that many people both inside and outside government will be vigorous advocates of their point of view and that advocacy can be both public and private. Assuring fairness in a basically legislative process is more a matter of expanding rather than constricting communications with decisional officials. As we will see, agency rulemaking procedures, both formal and informal, generally require broader participation by those affected than is anticipated in the legislative world.

Hence, you will discover that through administrative law, we ensure fairness in very different ways depending on the type of activity the agency performs.

## 3. The Problem of Unaccountability

The third constitutional problem we will examine is one that is basic to all representative governments: that of accountability to the citizenry and oversight. We now know that unelected agency officials develop and implement major federal policies with limited congressional direction. What you will learn is that Congress cannot remove these officials, except by formal impeachment, which is difficult to do and thus rarely happens. Even the president cannot remove some agency officials. If the founders presumed that government officials with significant authority would be accountable to the citizenry, then the administrative state seems to frustrate their presumption. However, a variety of formal and informal practices have developed so that the citizenry (at least those affected by agency activity) have an opportunity to impact the regulatory process. While these requirements and practices are not exactly the form of control the framers intended, arguably they offer functionally similar accountability.

### a. Legislative Oversight

Let's start with Congress. The legislature controls agency activities in a variety of ways. First, Congress drafts a statute that creates an agency, defines its powers, provides guiding (intelligible) principles, delineates procedural requirements, and provides for judicial review, if any, of agency activities. Congress may amend an agency's powers at any time; indeed, Congress may abolish an agency entirely, as it did the Interstate Commerce Commission and the Civil Aeronautics Board. Congress may also reorganize a number of existing agencies, as it did when it created the Department of Homeland Security.

Of course, exercising control via legislative enactment is not a practical way to fine-tune the thousands of issues agencies deal with in any given year. So, Congress has, over the years, adopted other methods to control agency behavior. For example, beginning in the 1930s, Congress included legislative vetoes in many statutes. Legislative vetoes allowed one or both houses of Congress to veto an agency decision. However, the Supreme Court held that the legislative veto was unconstitutional. *INS v. Chadha*, 462 U.S. 919, 959 (1983). Congress has since created other methods of control. *See, e.g.*, 5 U.S.C. § 801 *et seq.* (1996). Known as the Congressional Review Act, the statute allows Congress to use an expedited legislative process to disapprove certain new federal regulations by issuing a joint resolution, which the president must sign. The most well-known use of the process occurred in 2001 when the 107th Congress rejected a rule submitted by the Department of Labor relating to ergonomics. Pub. L. 107–5, 115 Stat. 7 (2001).

In addition to enacting statutes, Congress also controls agencies in less formal ways. For example, Congress controls an agency's budget, which is an important way to pressure the agency to take action. Budget pressure, even threatened budget pressure, can dramatically affect agency behavior. Agencies need funding to operate. Congressional approval of agency funding requires two things. First, the agency's enabling statute (or another statute) must provide authorization for legislative appropriations. Such authorizations may be limited by time or purpose, have a ceiling, or be unlimited. Second, each year Congress must approve an agency's budget request. To receive funding, agencies must submit annual budget requests to the Office of Management and Budget (OMB), which the president oversees. These budgets, after any adjustments by OMB, are forwarded to the House and Senate appropriations committees, which then hold hearings and allocate funding accordingly.

Congress also oversees agencies less directly by holding hearings, initiating investigations, and requiring reports. Any congressional committee that has jurisdiction over an aspect of an agency's program may hold hearings and investigate the agency's implementation of its authority. Often, these hearings are publicized to mobilize public and political pressure. These activities can significantly affect agency behavior. For example, in 2012, the House Judiciary Committee held hearings regarding the Bureau of Alcohol, Tobacco, Firearms and Explosives' Fast and Furious Program, which was intended to track firearms that were transferred to higher-level drug traffickers in Mexican cartels, with the hope that tracking would lead to arrests and the dismantling of the cartels. The program was mostly unsuccessful. After a series of public hearings, Congress held Attorney General Eric Holder in criminal contempt for refusing to provide documents to the Committee. President Obama invoked executive privilege to prevent the disclosure.

And, of course, there are many opportunities legislators and legislative staff have to impose informal pressures on the day-to-day operations of the agencies. None of these controls methods is without cost, of course. Some of these methods have been criticized as vesting disproportionate power in key legislative officials and even key staff members or opening private avenues of influence to powerful interest groups. These concerns should be taken seriously, but as anyone who has worked at the policy level in a federal agency will attest, the legislature remains a powerful force to which agencies must give constant and careful attention.

### b. Judicial Oversight

Courts also impact agency behavior. Courts insist that agencies do not go beyond the statutory power delegated to them. When legislative delegation is in vague, amorphous terms, agencies have considerable discretion. But when Congress limits power or where limits develop over time in the course of agency interpretation or practice, courts can ensure that agency rules are consistent with those limits and not ultra vires. Also, and pursuant to the Administrative Procedure Act (APA), Courts are required to set aside agency action that is arbitrary and capricious, that is unsupported by substantial evidence, or that is unreasonable. APA §§ 706(2)(A), (C), & (E). In all, an agency's freedom to wander far from its legislatively granted substantive and procedural boundaries is substantially limited under the doctrine of judicial review. This topic is so important and complex that we will cover it in full in its own chapter (Chapter 6).

### c. Executive Oversight

Finally, the executive branch impacts agency behavior. One way the president impacts agency behavior is through appointment and removal. The president appoints many agency officers, even those in the independent agencies, which gives the executive a significant role in shaping agency policy. Under the Constitution, Congress shares the appointment power with the president in three ways. First, the Senate must confirm presidential appointments of principal officers. U.S. Const. art. II § 2 cl. 2. Second, Congress has the power to vest the appointment power of "inferior" officers in the president, the courts of law, or in heads of departments. Id. Third, Congress has some power to establish the qualifications for agency personnel. Pursuant to this third power, Congress has imposed bipartisanship qualifications for membership in most of the independent agencies. A picture of the appointment process as delineated in the Constitution can be seen in Figure 1.2.

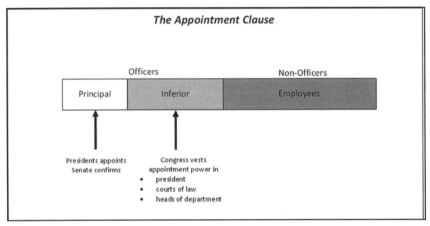

**Figure 1.2** The Appointment Process

What are the differences among principal officers, inferior officers, and employees? Unfortunately, the Supreme Court has not offered clear and consistent guidance on this question.

The difference between principal and inferior officers was litigated in *Morrison v. Olson*, 487 U.S. 654 (1988). At issue in that case was the Ethics in Government Act. 28 U.S.C. §§ 49, 591 *et seq.*, which authorized a special division of the United States Court of Appeals for the District of Columbia to appoint an independent counsel to investigate and prosecute high-ranking executive officials. *Id.* at 661. Investigating and prosecuting are executive functions. *Id.* at 691. The issue for the Court was whether the independent counsel was an inferior or principal officer. The Court concluded that because the independent counsel performed only limited investigative and prosecutorial work for a set period, the officer was only an inferior officer, not a principal officer. *Id.* at 671–72. Justice Scalia dissented in *Morrison*.

Nine years later, in *Edmond v. United States*, 520 U.S. 651 (1997), Justice Scalia, now writing for the majority, rejected *Morrison's* multifactor test for determining whether a government employee was an inferior officer. In *Edmond*, the issue for the Court was whether military trial judges were principal or inferior officers. The Court concluded that these judges were "inferior officers," because "[g]enerally speaking, the term 'inferior officer' connotes a relationship with some higher ranking officer or officers below the President:

whether one is an 'inferior' officer depends on whether he has a superior." *Id.* at 662. Further, the Court reasoned that exercising "significant authority" on behalf of the United States is "the line between [an] officer and non-officer." *Id.* In an earlier case, the Court had identified how courts should determine whether individuals exercise significant authority pursuant to the laws of the United States. *Freytag v. Commissioner*, 501 U.S. 868 (1991). Courts consider a variety of factors, including the manner in which Congress created the position, the appointment process, the responsibilities of the position, the tenure and duration of the position, the amount and manner of pay, the level of supervision, and the identity of the supervisor. *Id.* at 880–82. No one factor is determinative.

As with the distinction between principal and inferior officers, the Supreme Court has not yet clearly defined the difference between an inferior officer and an employee. The Court has said that employees do not exercise significant authority; officers do. *Id.* at 881 (*quoting Buckley v. Valeo*, 424 U.S. 1, 126 n.162 (1976)). The Supreme Court's most relevant case in this area is *Freytag*, mentioned above. In *Freytag*, the Court held that Tax Court special trial judges ("STJ") were inferior officers, not employees. *Id.* at 881–82. The Tax Court is an Article I court with judges who are appointed for limited terms. Congress authorized the Chief Judge of the Tax Court to appoint STJs to hear specific tax cases. The government argued that the STJs were merely employees, who did no more than assist the regular Tax Court Judges in taking evidence and preparing proposed findings and an opinion. *Id.* at 881. The justices unanimously rejected this argument and held that the STJs were inferior officers.

To find that STJs were inferior officers and not merely employees, the Court considered multiple factors. First, the Court noted that the office of special trial judge is "established by Law" and that the statute lays out the "duties, salary, and means of appointment for that office." *Id.* Second, the Court noted that STJs "exercise significant discretion" when carrying out their duties. *Id.* at 882. Third, the Court added that "[e]ven if the duties of [STJs] were not as significant as . . . we have found them to be," there are circumstances where "they exercise independent authority," and they cannot be "inferior Officers" for some purposes and not others. *Id.* Fourth, and almost as an aside, the Court pointed out that STJs were authorized to decide cases *in some instances,* even though in others the regular Tax Court judge rendered the final decision. *Id.* at 886–87.

The *Freytag* Court specifically rejected the government's argument that officials who "lack authority to enter into a final decision" must be employees and not inferior officers because that argument "ignores the significance of the duties and discretion that special trial judges possess." *Id.* at 881. Despite the Court's rejection of this factor as determinative, the D.C. Circuit subsequently relied on this factor alone to conclude that ALJs working for the Federal Deposit Insurance Corporation were employees, not inferior officers. *Landry v. FDOC*, 204 F.3d 1125, 1133–34 (D.C. Cir. 2000).

The distinctions between (1) principal officers and inferior officers, and (2) inferior officers and employees are relevant not only to appointment issues but also to removal issues. Because the Supreme Court has not definitively established three distinct categories of agency personnel, appointment challenges and removal challenges often occur together.

While the Constitution explicitly provides for the appointment of principal and inferior officers, it is less clear about removal. The Constitution contains only one removal provision, which provides that "all civil officers of the United States [may] be removed from office on impeachment for, and conviction of, treason, bribery, or other high crimes and misdemeanors." U.S. CONST. art. II, § 4. The impeachment process is seldom used, yet officers are removed regularly. How is that possible? The answer is that the Supreme Court held long ago that the Constitution vests removal power in the president *implicitly*. The president has the power to remove executive officers because that power was not "expressly taken away" from the president in the Constitution. *Free Enterprise Fund v. Public Co. Accounting Oversight Bd.*, 561 U.S. 477, 492 (2010) (*quoting* Letter from James Madison to Thomas Jefferson (June 30, 1789), 16 Documentary History of the First Federal Congress 893 (2004)). Further, the Constitution provides that "[t]he executive Power shall be vested in a President of the United States of America." U.S. CONST. art. II, § 1, cl. 1. As Madison stated on the floor of the First Congress, "if any power whatsoever is in its nature Executive, it is the power of appointing, overseeing, and controlling those who execute the laws." 1 Annals of Cong. 463 (1789).

In *Myers v. United States*, 272 U.S. 52 (1926), the Supreme Court, led by former President Taft, struck down a statute that required the president to obtain the advice and consent of the Senate prior to removing the postmaster general. *Id.* at 106–18, 176. The Court rejected the government's argument that the removal power flowed from the Senate's ability to advise on and consent to appointments. *Id.* at 126–27, 164. The Court reasoned that if executive appointees were beholden to members of the legislature for their livelihood they would cease to be an independent executive officer. *Id.* at 131. Given Justice Taft's former profession, the holding likely is unsurprising, but the broad holding of this case soon gave way.

Nine years later, in *Humphrey's Executor v. United States*, 295 U.S. 602 (1935), the Court upheld a provision in the Federal Trade Commission Act that permitted the president to dismiss a commissioner of the Federal Trade Commission (FTC), also a principal officer, only for "inefficiency, neglect of duty, or malfeasance in office." *Id.* at 620 (*quoting* The Federal Trade Commission Act, c. 311, 38 Stat. 717; 15 U.S.C. § 1). The Court distinguished its holding in *Myers* by noting that the postmaster general performed purely executive functions and had to be responsible to the president while the FTC member performed quasi-legislative or quasi-judicial powers and had to be independent of the president. *Id.* at 627–28. The Court limited the *Myers* holding to "all purely executive officers," noting that its holding did not apply to "an officer who occupies no place in the executive department, and who exercises no part of the executive power vested by the Constitution in the President." *Id.* at 628. The Court reasoned that Congress intended the FTC and its Commissioners to be independent of the president and provided that their tenure would be limited. *See also Weiner v. United States*, 357 U.S. 349, 350 (1958) (limiting the president's ability to remove a commissioner of the War Claims Commission, which had only a three-year existence, even though the relevant statute was silent regarding removal because Congress intended to insulate the Commission from presidential interference).

Pursuant to this *Myers/Humphrey's* distinction, a president has unlimited power to remove purely executive principal officers, but limited power to remove tenured quasi-legislative or quasi-judicial principal officers. Under this approach, the functions the officer performs dictate the validity of any restrictions on removal. Congress can limit the presidential removal power, a fundamental executive power, when officials have tenured, or limited, terms and when the officials must be free to act without presidential interference.

After *Humphrey's Executor*, there is little question that Congress can limit a president's power to remove some officers, but the exact limits on the removal power are unclear. *Cf. Bowsher v. Synar*, 478 U.S. 714, 726 (1986) (holding that Congress cannot reserve for itself the power to remove executive officers).

However, *Myers*, *Humphrey's Executor*, and *Weiner* all involved principal officers, who were appointed by a president with the advice and consent of the Senate. These cases did not address the removal of inferior officers, who may also be appointed by and, therefore, be removed by the heads of department and courts of law. *See Ex parte Hennen*, 38 U.S. 230, 259 (13 Pet. 230) (1839). The question that remained was whether Congress could impose limits on a president's removal power in the case of inferior officers.

In *Morrison v. Olson*, 487 U.S. 654 (1988), the Supreme Court addressed this issue and upheld a for-cause removal limitation on a "purely executive" inferior officer. In the relevant statute, the Ethics in Government Act, Congress created the position of an independent counsel, whose function was to "investigate and, if appropriate, prosecute certain high-ranking government officials" involved in criminal activity. The Act provided that the attorney general, a principal officer, could remove the independent counsel, an inferior officer, only "for good cause." The Court acknowledged that the independent counsel was purely an executive officer. *Id* at 671. Under the *Humphrey's Executor* and *Myers*, the removal limitation would have been invalid were the independent counsel a principal officer.

Rejecting the *Myers/Humphrey's* distinction as determinative in this case, the Court said, "the determination of whether the constitution allows Congress to impose a 'good cause'-type restriction on the President's power to remove an official cannot be made to turn on whether or not that official is classified as 'purely executive.'" *Id.* at 689. Acknowledging that the type of functions an officer performs is relevant to the analysis, the Court reasoned that the most important question is whether the removal restriction "impedes the President's ability to perform his Constitutional duty" to ensure that the laws are faithfully executed. *Id.* The Court then reasoned that because the independent counsel (1) was an inferior officer, (2) had limited jurisdiction, (3) did not have tenure, (4) lacked policymaking power, and (5) did not have significant administrative authority, the for-cause removal provision was a reasonable restriction on the president's removal authority.

This case left open, however, the question of whether more than one level of for-cause removal would be constitutional. In 2010, the Supreme Court answered this question in the negative in *Free Enterprise Fund v. Public Co. Accounting Oversight Bd.*, 561 U.S. 477 (2010). The Court framed the issue as whether "the President [may] be restricted in his ability to remove a principal officer, who is in turn restricted in his ability to remove an inferior officer, even though that inferior officer determines the policy and enforces the laws of the United States?" *Id.* at 483–84. The answer, the Court held, was "no." *Id.* at 484. Dual for-cause removal provisions are contrary to Article II's vesting of executive power in the president, for the president cannot "'take care the Laws be faithfully executed' if he cannot oversee the faithfulness of the officers who execute them." *Id.* Minimizing the potential effects of its holding, the majority simply severed "the unconstitutional tenure provisions . . . from the remainder of the statute." *Id.* at 508.

While most high-level executive branch officials (purely executive principal officers) can be dismissed whenever the president chooses—no Secretary of State will ever have much job security—the presidential removal powers are less robust than appeared after *Myers*. See Figure 1.3.

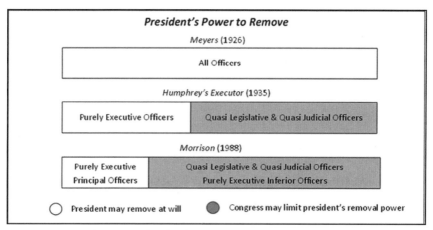

**Figure 1.3** The Shrinking Presidential Removal Power

In addition to appointment and removal, the president also controls agency budget requests. The Office of Management and Budget (OMB) is a part of the office of the White House. This agency reviews all agency budgets. Presidents have used this control of budgets to impact agency policy. We will return to the question of presidential control of agency rulemaking in Chapter 2.

Agencies also act in ways that increase accountability. For example, when agencies make rules, they are required to seek public comment. But agencies set their own rules on how they obtain and respond to the comments. In this day of electronic information flow, access to the comment system is usually easy and convenient. And the right to comment is exercised regularly; the volume of public comments agencies receive on a major rule today can be staggering— sometimes those comments number in the thousands. If you believe that accountability requires that elected legislators make important policy choices, you might consider that agencies can, in some circumstances, be more responsive and accessible to the public. As we have said, citizen access to the regulatory system is probably easier and cheaper than access to the legislature. Moreover, Congress may give more weight to the political clout of a contributor to the process than to the quality of the contribution. In contrast, we will see that under current standards of judicial review, agency decisions must have plausible factual support, must be adequately responsive to public comments, and must be rational. These criteria are more demanding than the criteria used to judge statutes. STEVEN CROLEY, REGULATION AND PUBLIC INTERESTS 135–36 (2008).

In sum, the problem of agency unaccountability does not look quite the same on the ground as it looks in theory. In practice, agency discretion is cabined at many places by the public, by the industry agencies regulate, by the courts, by the legislatures, by the president, and even by agencies themselves. The avenues of accountability and the linkages of key players do not show the straight lines of the civics books or the official organizational chart. But those experienced with the process usually smile at the wag's observation that the administrative process is a "headless fourth branch." Whether agencies are *too* accountable to inappropriate influences may be the true problem, but that is a subject for another day.

# D. Administrative Law Defined

We have, then, an immense regulatory system that dramatically and comprehensively impacts the daily lives of citizens. This system is open to plausible charges that it is unauthorized, unfair, and unaccountable. It would be comforting to hear that there have been developments in the principles of constitutional law or amendments to the Constitution itself that would bring these institutions into harmony with the intent of the framers. Unfortunately, this cannot be said. What can be said is that a series of accommodating arrangements and practices have developed. These practices seek to lessen the severity of the problems and to carry out the underlying purposes the framers intended in separating the powers. This accommodation may be the best we can hope for in a structure needing to satisfy conflicting demands of stability over time and to respond to the emerging needs of the administrative state.

How far and how legitimately these accommodations succeed is a matter of continuing controversy. But central to the question is a body of law through which judges are equipped to deal with problems of authority, accountability, and fairness so far as judicial instruments can be sensibly employed for that purpose. That body of law is what we call administrative law. And because courts apply this law there will be inevitable "rule of law" threads woven into the fabric. Think of the administrative law field as having three distinct but overlapping functions:

(1) Doctrines of administrative law require agencies to take seriously the various statutory and constitutional procedural requirements imposed on them in aid of values such as authority, accountability, and fairness.

(2) Doctrines of administrative law ensure that when these requirements are enforced by courts, enforcement occurs within acceptable standards of judicial competence and legitimacy.

(3) Doctrines of administrative law insist on important rule-of-law considerations, such as predictable, principled, and reasoned decision making.

As you work through administrative law doctrine, keep these functions in mind. Insist that every doctrine you examine address these functions frontally, support compliance with statutory and constitutional requirements, impose on courts only tasks that are within judicial competence, and honor the values of the rule of law. Examining the doctrine through these perspectives will help you understand the doctrines better, apply them more effectively and, finally, ground your professional critique.

---

## Checkpoints

- The administrative process today is varied, immense, ubiquitous, and touches every aspect of American life.

- The constitutional doctrine of separation of powers seeks to prevent the concentration of power in a single branch, to avoid tyranny, and to ensure fairness in decision making.

- Agencies exercise what are effectively legislative and judicial powers in many of their activities; courts have generally permitted delegation, despite nondelegation objections, so long as Congress provides an intelligible principle.

- In many agencies, legislative, executive, and judicial functions are combined in a single agency; courts have usually permitted agencies with such combined powers despite separation of powers objections.

- The problem of unfairness in combining functions is dealt with by a series of legislative and judicial measures that attempt to keep the hearing process fair and the decisional process objective. Most of administrative law serves these goals.

- The problem of unaccountability is dealt with by significant legislative and executive control over agencies and by judicial review, all of which help assure that people affected by agency action have meaningful opportunities to participate in the development of those actions.

- The three central functions of administrative law are (1) to facilitate procedural conditions on agency action in aid of such values as authority, fairness, and accountability, (2) to assure that this is done within acceptable standards of judicial competence and legitimacy, and (3) to insist that certain fundamental rule-of-law values are honored.

# Chapter 2

# Rulemaking

---

---

## A. Why Agencies Use Rulemaking

Let's begin with one of the foundational concepts of administrative law, which you'll need to be very familiar with as we proceed. Leaving complicating details for later, consider that there are two general ways that policy can be developed in the administrative context: (1) through individualized decisions, and (2) through general rules.

## 1. Individualized Decision Making

Law can be developed as part of the resolution of individual disputes. Thus, in the common law of negligence the law concerning the level of due care needed to avoid tort liability is decided on a case-by-case basis. To use a familiar example, in 1928 a court had to identify due care requirements in the context of an accident at the Long Island Railroad Company's station that injured Helen Palsgraf. *Palsgraf v. Long Island R.R. Co.*, 162 N.E. 99 (NY 1928). Technically, the *Palsgraf* decision was binding only on the named parties, but later courts applied the law developed in the case to other disputes, extending and elaborating this law in light of the facts of the new disputes. In this model, law (also policy) is formulated as a specific case is decided, but that law can impact similar cases in the future.

As a student of the common law (as opposed to civil law), you already know some of the advantages of this way of developing law. Developing law to resolve individual disputes builds on past cases; the process allows law to be developed bit by bit as the decision maker feels his or her way in new areas; it permits law to fit the particulars of the case in dispute, taking into account special settings or novel situations; and it permits incremental change, the slow, careful evolution of law to match new needs and changing circumstances. As you will see in the next chapter, Congress may authorize administrative agencies to develop and apply law in a case-by-case manner known as *adjudication*. When agencies act in this way, the "law" they develop is furthered by these advantages.

But developing law by individualized decisions has some disadvantages as well. To begin with, this way of developing law makes law uncertain. Before Judge Cardozo's opinion in *Palsgraf*, the railroad had little way of knowing when its handling of its equipment would subject the railroad to liability. And even after the decision, the law was not much clearer; Cardozo's opinion may be a model of elegant judicial rhetoric, but it is not a detailed inventory of specific steps to be taken to reduce future liability. Moreover, there is a retroactive aspect about individualized lawmaking. The principle the court applied in *Palsgraf* applied to the railroad's past acts. Given the uncertainty of the legal standard, these acts may not have been fault-worthy. In addition, lawmaking through individual decisions can lead to problems of uneven treatment, as potentially irrelevant differences (was Ms. Palsgraf a sympathetic or unsympathetic litigant?) lead to different outcomes in what are essentially similar cases or in which different judges appraise similar facts differently. Still further, those who may be affected in the future by a law fashioned in an individual decision have no opportunity to participate in the formulation of that law. Finally, there is the problem of cost. Litigating a series of individual cases can be a very expensive and time-consuming method for developing law.

## 2. The Use of General Rules

The noted inadequacies of lawmaking through individual decisions have produced in most legal systems a second way of making law: the use of general rules. A carefully drafted, prospective general rule defining the way railroad equipment should be secured might have given the Long Island Railroad advance notice of appropriate conduct and thus might have avoided uncertainty. Indeed, such a rule might have avoided the accident itself. Being prospective, such a rule would not have penalized the railroad for past behavior; would have applied consistently to all railroads; would have been formulated with the input of other railroads, businesses, passengers, and customers; and would surely have saved a great deal of money in litigation and related expenses.

Courts are our model for making law through individual decisions; when agencies make "law" through individual cases we call that process *adjudication*. Legislatures are our model for making law through general rules; when agencies make "law" through general rules we call that process *rulemaking*. Add these two words into your administrative law vocabulary. We will be referring to these two categories of administrative action throughout the rest of this text. It is important for you to know the difference. The different actions require agencies to use different procedures. Hence, correctly classifying any given agency action is an essential skill. Usually, you will have little difficulty identifying the correct category; however, sometimes this determination will be more difficult. When in doubt, you should begin with the idea that if the action is more like what a court does, then the action is adjudication. If the action is more like what a legislature does, it is rulemaking. Then confirm your categorization by consulting the relevant statutory definitions in the Administrative Procedure Act (APA), 5 U.S.C. § 551.

## B. Rulemaking and the Rule of Law in a Democracy

In the case of ordinary legislation, members of Congress write the laws, and the president enforces these laws. The members of Congress and the president are directly elected by the people, which enhances legitimacy. But agency officials are not directly elected. How, then, do we get legitimacy in a system where rules are written by unelected administrative officials? We touched on the answer to this question in the last chapter when we examined how administrative agencies are created and empowered and how agency officials are appointed and removed.

You will recall that agencies operate under a grant of power from the legislature that comes from a statute. The statutes creating and empowering agencies are written by elected legislators and signed by an elected president. Further, agencies are managed by principal officers who have been appointed by an elected president and confirmed by an elected Senate. Accountability to elected officials is clearest for principal officers who serve at the pleasure of the president, but we have seen that even those officers who have more secure tenure face a range of formal and informal mechanisms through which elected officials seek to conform agency action to political preferences. Indeed, there is often criticism of this political control. Specifically, agencies sometimes appear to critics to be too accountable, too political, or too beholden to narrow interests that may have influence in the political arena.

But it is not possible for the president and members of Congress (nor their staff) to attend in detail to all the numerous and highly technical activities of the modern regulatory agency. Administrative law's functional response to this difficulty is a series of procedural requirements that seek to ensure that agencies carefully consider rules, formulate those rules on sound factual foundations, and allow those the rule will affect meaningful opportunity to participate in the rule's formulation. These three limitations form the basic structure of what we call "notice and comment rulemaking." This rulemaking process is described with appealing simplicity in section 553 of the APA. Excerpts from the APA are set out in the Appendix. Here is a quick summary:

> (b) General notice of proposed rulemaking shall be published in the Federal Register ... [t]he notice shall include ... the terms or substance of the proposed rule ...
>
> (c) After notice required by this section, the agency shall give interested persons an opportunity to participate in the rulemaking through submission of written data, views, or arguments ... after consideration of the relevant matter presented, [the agency will issue its rule].

APA § 553.

The drafters of the APA believed that public notice and the opportunity for public comment served both to improve the technical quality of rules and to meet legitimacy and accountability concerns. Note that the requirements for public participation go well beyond what the public gets in the legislative process. In the legislative process, there are no legal requirements for notice, hearing, or consideration of public views.

## C. The Components of Modern Rulemaking—A Case Study

Federal agencies make thousands of rules each year and for the vast majority of those rules the procedures in the Administrative Procedure Act work well. There are also times, however, when the process has been more complicated, cumbersome, slow, and expensive than the APA drafters likely anticipated. We will examine the causes of this problem below, but it will be useful now to get a feel for the complexity of one of these examples. Understanding the example will make it easier for you to understand the procedural debates and their resolutions.

The story that follows involves the Environmental Protection Agency (EPA) and its struggle in the past few years to set a standard for smog, specifically rules relating to the National Ambient Air Quality Standards (NAAQS) for ground-level ozone. If you would like more details of this story, see STEVEN CROLEY, REGULATION AND PUBLIC INTERESTS: THE POSSIBILITY OF GOOD REGULATORY GOVERNMENT 163–179 (2008) or Craig Oren et al., *Whitman v. American Trucking*, in ADMINISTRATIVE LAW STORIES 7 (Peter L. Strauss ed., 2006).

The EPA has both the authority and the obligation under the Clean Air Act (1) to identify air pollutants that threaten human health, and (2) to write rules prescribing acceptable standards. 42 U.S.C. § 7401. Measurement questions vastly complicate these issues, and there is considerable scientific uncertainty about what levels of these pollutants are safe. The Act requires the EPA to review and, if necessary, revise these standards every five years. Standards for the kind of pollutants that produce what we call smog were established in 1978 (ozone standards). Four years later, in 1982, the agency began its five-year review of the standards, but the EPA never actually revised the standards. Twelve years later, the American Lung Association filed suit in federal court to force the EPA to act. The court ordered the EPA to review and, if necessary, to revise these standards as required by the Clean Air Act. *American Lung Ass'n v. Browner*, 884 F. Supp. 345 (D. Ariz. 1994).

During the next several years, the EPA staff and outside advisors drafted multi-volume studies and book-length analyses. The process involved both industry and environmental groups actively participating. Afterward, the staff finally recommended a rule that would reduce the current standard for smog-producing emissions from 0.12 parts per million (ppm) to 0.08 ppm. This difference was highly significant; one study, for example, showed that the reduction of the standard from 0.09 to 0.08 ppm would have measurable effects on the health of 16,000 children. Once a draft rule was finally ready, the EPA started the notice and comment process for public participation.

In 1996, the EPA issued its notice of proposed rulemaking (generally known as an "NPRM") and invited public comment on its revised ozone standards. The proposed rule followed the staff recommendation that emission of smog-producing chemicals be reduced from 0.12 to 0.08 ppm. Along with the proposed rule, the EPA made available to the public the many scientific studies the agency had considered in formulating its standards. Since the EPA's last standards revision, thousands of such studies had been published. In support of its proposed rule containing the new ozone standards, the EPA estimated that the tighter standards would prevent 15,000 deaths annually, would lead to significant increases in children's health, and would save between $50 and $120 billion in hospital costs. These benefits were just a few of those the EPA identified. The EPA also estimated industry compliance costs at between $6 and $9 billion.

If the scientific aspect of the rule was not complicated enough, federalism added still more complexity. Congress drafted the Clean Air Act with federalism in mind. Hence, the EPA does not directly enforce its clean air standards. Instead, the EPA's role is to work with the states to develop adequate "state implementation plans." There was wide disparity around the country regarding the degree to which state plans were adequate. And an interesting geographical divide emerged: manufacturing in the Midwestern states seemed to be the source of much of the pollution, while the adverse effects from this pollution fell mainly on Northeastern states because of prevailing westerly winds. This divide would become important once Congress entered the controversy.

Under the provisions of APA § 553 set out above, the EPA's proposed rule had to run the gauntlet of notice and public comment. In response to the publication of the proposed rule (notice), the EPA received about 55,000 written and oral comments, along with 14,000 phone calls, and 4,000 emails, which were something of a novelty in 1996. In addition to the comment process, the EPA voluntarily held public meetings, regional workshops, and two national telecasts to answer questions about its proposed rule containing the new ozone standards. The APA does not require public hearings for notice and comment rules, so these additional public participation steps were done by agency choice. In addition, Congress created a panel of distinguished scientists to discuss and evaluate the proposed rule and its standards.

Opposition to the proposed rule came from those on whom the immediate costs of compliance would fall: large chemical plants, construction operations, oil refineries, automobile manufacturers, and power plants. Collectively, this group of opponents was powerful and aggressive. In addition, the National Association of Manufacturers, the small business community, and the U.S. Conference of Mayors opposed the proposed rule. These opposition groups spent millions of dollars to lobby and publicize their opposition, which challenged both the scientific basis for the proposals and the accuracy of the EPA's calculation of both benefits (said to be overstated) and costs (said to be understated). Congressional lobbying was especially heavy, and, as a result, some members of Congress became highly critical of the EPA's proposed rule. A number of legislative hearings were held, during which witnesses and some members of Congress attacked the knowledge and credibility of EPA officials.

The Clinton White House was initially ambivalent about the proposed rule, largely due to congressional opposition, although numerous interagency and interoffice meetings were held during this time period, seeking some resolution. Even future presidential politics played a role as environmentalists criticized Vice President Al Gore, who was even then a confirmed environmentalist, for not leading the fight for the White House. Environmental groups sought to enlist the support of Representative Richard Gephart, who was Gore's rival for the 2000 Democratic presidential nomination. This action forced Gore to choose between his environmentalist sympathies and his need for support from the Midwest states, where the proposed rule was unpopular. The Vice President finally supported the EPA's proposed rule, getting President Clinton on board. The EPA adopted the proposed rule in its final form in 1997.

Of course, nothing is ever fully or finally settled in politics. Congressional opponents quickly responded with bills to impose a four-year moratorium. These bills were popular with legislators. Some had more than 200 sponsors, but none passed probably due to the vigorous, if late, presidential support for the proposed rule. But congressional opposition to the proposed rule created uncertainty, including questions of funding. By 1998, a bipartisan compromise bill was enacted. This new law allowed the agency to implement the new standards, but modified those standards for some specially impacted groups (e.g., farmers), provided some funding for state monitoring efforts to comply, and extended the implementation dates. Transportation Equity Act for the 21st Century, PL 105-178, June 9, 1998, 112 Stat. 107.

After the legislative and executive battles led to this uneasy settlement, the opponents turned to the courts to renew their attacks. Most of the material you read while studying administrative law will be court opinions and the APA, but do not forget the rest of the iceberg. Most of these judicial opinions have been preceded by a complex and long-running story, such as this one.

Opponents of the EPA rule were initially successful in the D.C. Circuit Court of Appeals. That court held that the EPA rule was based on an unacceptable interpretation of the Clean Air Act. *American Trucking Ass'n v. EPA*, 175 F.3d 1027, 1052 (D.C. Cir. 1999). However, the Supreme Court reversed. *Whitman v. American Trucking Ass'n*, 531 U.S. 457 (2001). On remand, the D.C. Circuit rejected all the remaining legal challenges. *American Trucking Ass'n, Inc. v. EPA*, 283 F.3d 355 (D.C. Cir. 2002). The remaining legal challenges focused on whether Congress could delegate such broad discretionary functions to an administrative agency (it can), whether the EPA followed the correct rulemaking procedure (it did), and whether the final rule was arbitrary or capricious (it was not). We covered the first issue, delegation, in Chapter One; we will cover the other issues at a later time.

Five years had now passed since the EPA's proposed rule with the ozone standards had been "finally" promulgated. But even the end of this litigation did not lead to immediate implementation of the rule. There was still the problem of determining where in the nation the new standards were not being met. This question was plagued by continuing debates regarding the accuracy of measurement methodology. After the so-called "non-attainment" areas were identified, the EPA had to ask states to develop and put in place implementation plans, because the EPA had no authority to act directly. By 2006, it was estimated that the EPA had identified more than 400 U.S. counties (in which 160 million people lived) that were not yet in compliance with the new standards. In 2008, the EPA issued a new rule requiring even lower limits, from .08 to .75 ppb).

In 2014, the EPA issued a new rule lowering the standards again, this time to .70 ppb. During the public comment period, a wide range of industry groups, state and local chambers of commerce, state governments, and members of Congress, urged the EPA to retain the current .75 ppb standard to no avail. On October 1, 2015, under a court-ordered deadline, the EPA finalized the ozone NAAQS standard at .70 ppb. On October 26, 2015, five states sued, challenging EPA's new standard: Arizona, Arkansas, North Dakota, New Mexico, and Oklahoma. Utah, Wisconsin, Kentucky, and Texas subsequently filed lawsuits challenging the new standard. Some industries did as well. And with a new president in office, the saga continues. The EPA most recently (October 27, 2017) denied a petition from the Northeastern states to add Midwestern states to the Ozone Transport Region because these states significantly contribute to violations of the 2008 Ozone National Ambient Air Quality Standards. As you can see, major administrative rulemaking in the United States is not for the faint of heart.

One final observation on this story: In thinking about agency rulemaking, we sometimes assume that the accountability mechanisms, such as executive appointment and coordination, congressional funding and oversight, etc., is a static process made up of a fixed group of players. But note that in the time period recounted above (1978 to 2017) there were 16 EPA administrators (including acting administrators) who had been appointed by seven presidents (four of them Republicans and three of them Democrats) and there had been numerous changes in Congress. Rather clearly, the complexities of the regulatory function will take place in a rapidly moving governmental and political environment, which is another important dynamic to understand.

Whether the notice and comment rulemaking process, in fact, provides the hoped-for foundations of wisdom and legitimacy will always be debated. The sluggish nature of modern rulemaking is disappointing. There are critics today who believe the rulemaking process has become "ossified" and cumbersome. *E.g.*, Thomas O. McGarity, *Some Thoughts on "Deossifying" the*

*Rulemaking Process*, 41 DUKE L. J. 1385 (1992) (arguing that notice and comment rulemaking "has not evolved into the flexible and efficient process that its early supporters originally envisioned."); Mark Seidenfeld, *Demystifying Deossification: Rethinking Recent Proposals to Modify Judicial Review of Notice and Comment Rulemaking*, 75 TEX. L. REV. 483 (1997); JERRY L. MASHAW & DAVID L. HARFST, THE STRUGGLE FOR AUTO 9–25 (1990). *But see* William S. Jordan III, *Ossification Revisited: Does Arbitrary and Capricious Review Significantly Interfere with Agency Ability to Achieve Regulatory Goals Through Informal Rulemaking?*, 94 Nw. U. L. REV. 393 (2000) (disputing the ossification claim).

Further, while the costs of allowing the public access to the process may be negligible in this day of the Internet, the costs of preparing the kinds of technical and scientific studies needed for many rules may be huge. The result is that the principal players in modern rulemaking will often be dedicated and resourceful interest groups, rather than members of the general public. That may create some bias in the system, though dedication and resources can be present in many types of associations, including those representing consumers, environmentalists, civil rights advocates, etc.

Within the agencies, one thing is clear: the cost, delay, and procedural complexity of today's agency rulemaking create strong pressures for agencies to find cheaper and quicker ways to create general rules. Agencies may use interpretive rules or policy statements that, as we will see, do not require this notice and comment process. Or agencies may state a "rule" in the adjudication of a particular case that — *Palsgraf*-like — may influence future cases.

In the discussion of rulemaking to follow, we will consider most of the elements shown in our story. In most rulemakings the following steps are generally present:

(1) Initiation of the rulemaking process, by internal initiative or external pressure;

(2) A phase of study to determine if a rule is necessary and, if so, which available solution seems best. In this phase, various internal and external players will participate;

(3) Intra-executive branch coordination and clearances;

(4) Publication of the proposed rule;

(5) Public comment on the proposed rule;

(6) Agency consideration of and response to these comments;

(7) Revision of the proposed rule into a final rule and, ultimately; and

(8) Judicial review of the final rule for both procedural and substantive compliance.

All along the way, politics inevitably play a role.

# D.  The Legal Framework for Rulemaking

To engage in rulemaking, agencies must comply with a complex scheme of statutory, judicial, and executive requirements. We will hold off on our discussion of judicial constraints until Chapter 6. After a few preliminary points, here, we examine the most important statutory and executive constraints, including the following: (1) the Administrative Procedure Act (APA); (2) an agency's enabling statute, in which Congress authorizes that agency to act; (3) other statutes that impact agency rulemaking in important ways; and, finally, (4) executive branch controls.

## 1.  Preliminary Questions

The first legal question you should consider in evaluating the legality of an agency rulemaking is the question of whether the agency had authority to act at all. Agencies have no inherent power, so every exercise of power by an agency must be supported by a statutory grant of authority from Congress. If an agency has no statutory authority to promulgate rules, the agency cannot promulgate rules. Such rules are ultra vires, meaning outside of the agency's delegated authority. When litigants challenge agency rules, claiming that the agency lacked power to act, do courts defer to the agency's conclusion that it had that power? We will learn in Chapter 6 that courts sometimes do defer to agency interpretations of their enabling statutes regarding the boundaries of the power delegated to them. Arguably, judges should not defer to an agency's interpretation of a statute regarding its jurisdiction and power to act. *See e.g., FDA v. Brown and Williamson Tobacco Corp.,* 529 U.S. 120 (2000) (holding that despite the agency's contrary interpretation of its statute, the FDA does not have power to regulate tobacco). However, the Supreme Court has more recently rejected this argument. *Arlington v. FCC,* 133 S. Ct. 1863, 1870 (2013) (holding that an agency's interpretation of the scope of its authority to act was entitled to *Chevron* deference).

After you ask whether an agency *has the power to* make rules, you should consider whether there are ever circumstances when an agency *must* make rules through one or another process. Suppose Congress gave the Federal Aviation Administration (FAA) general statutory authority to promote air safety and to use both rulemaking and adjudication to carry out this mandate. The FAA might promulgate a rule requiring 20/20 eyesight for commercial pilots. In a later adjudication, the FAA might revoke Pilot Green's license because her eyesight is not 20/20. Alternatively, the FAA could forego rulemaking altogether and, under its authority to proceed by adjudication, directly revoke Green's license by proving that her eyesight threatens air safety because it is not 20/20. Could Pilot Green challenge the revocation of her license, arguing that the FAA should first have promulgated the eyesight rule first? She might point out that a rule would have been fairer because everyone affected by the rule would have had advance notice of it and would have been able to comment on the proposed rule.

Sadly, for Pilot Green, the answer is "no." Unless Congress has foreclosed an agency's choice of procedure, the choice about whether to proceed by rulemaking or adjudication "lies primarily in the informed discretion" of the agency. *SEC v. Chenery*, 332 U.S. 194, 203 (1947). Thus, a federal agency that is authorized to proceed either by rulemaking or by adjudication is usually free to choose how to proceed. Courts have agreed that new rules should be announced in advance before individuals can be penalized for acting inconsistently with the rule. *E.g., NLRB v. Wyman-Gordon, Inc.*, 394 U.S. 759 (1969). Occasionally, a court will find a due process violation when an agency decides individual cases without "ascertainable standards." *Holmes v. N.Y. Housing Auth.*, 398 F.2d 262 (2d Cir. 1968). But even though federal judges understand the advantages of rulemaking, they still generally leave the choice of how to proceed to an agency.

At the state level, a few state administrative procedure statutes require (or encourage) rulemaking. *See, e.g.*, Fla. Stat. Ann. § 120.54(1) (Harrison 1999) (requiring some rulemaking); Wash. Rev. Stat. 34.05.220 (2003) (encouraging some rulemaking). And an occasional state judicial opinion may require rulemaking. *E.g., Megdal v. Oregon State Bd. of Dental Exam'rs*, 605 P.2d 273, 274 (Or. 1980).

## 2. The Administrative Procedure Act

We turn now to the most important constraint on agency rulemaking, the federal Administrative Procedure Act (APA). In 1946, Congress enacted the APA. With this Act, Congress delineated basic procedural requirements for federal agencies. Notably, the Act has been amended very rarely.

The Act was the culmination of years of debate over the burgeoning administrative state created during the New Deal era. Opponents of the New Deal wanted to confine and limit the power of federal agencies. To limit that power, opponents tried to force agencies to follow traditional judicial procedures, which would protect individual rights in the way that judicial procedures did. In contrast, supporters of the New Deal sought to liberate agencies from these traditional judicial procedures, regarding the procedures as inflexible, cumbersome, and, ultimately, as protectors of the status quo. While fights involving administrative procedure rarely become matters of national debate, the time was apparently right. In 1940, Congress passed a general administrative procedure act, but it was vetoed by President Roosevelt.

By the end of World War II, opponents and supporters had reached an accommodation. The APA, as passed in 1946, shows the compromises of the contesting interests. On the one hand, the provisions on adjudication reflect the views of those who wanted agencies to adopt judicial-type procedures. Read through Sections 556 and 557 of the Act and see how familiar they sound. On the other hand, the provisions on rulemaking are almost wholly free of detailed procedures. Section 553 seems to require little except that the agency publish a draft of a proposed rule and consider public comment on it. The agency can then issue the rule after considering the comments and explaining its choice in a "concise general statement of basis and purpose." APA § 553(c). Thus, as originally envisioned, rulemaking was meant to be a relatively quick, painless, procedure-less process. However, as we saw in the case study above, the process has become much more complex today, complicated by a combination of legislative, executive, and judicial requirements.

The APA applies only to agency action. It defines an agency as "each authority of the Government of the United States . . . not includ[ing Congress, the courts, state governments, etc.]." APA §§ 551(1), 701(b)(1). For purposes of the APA, the term "agency" is defined to include all governmental authorities including administrations, commissions, corporations (e.g., the Federal Deposit Insurance Corporation), boards, departments, divisions, and agencies. This definition is very broad. Most recently, the Supreme Court held that Amtrak is a governmental entity because of the government's oversight of and involvement with the corporation. *DOT v. Association of Am RRs.*, 135 S. Ct. 1225, 1231 (2015).

There are a couple of things to note about the APA's definition of an agency. First, it is very broad and, notably, does not define the term "authority." Second, the definition lists specific exclusions but does not exclude the president. Is the president an agency? Surprisingly, the issue of whether the president is considered an agency subject to the APA did not come before the Supreme Court until 1992, when the Court held that the president was not an agency. The Court rejected an *expressio unius* argument that the president should be considered an agency because the executive was not specifically excluded in the definition while Congress and the judiciary were. *Franklin v. Massachusetts*, 505 U.S. 788, 796 (1992). Despite the strong statutory interpretation argument, the Court held that the president was not an agency due to concerns regarding separation of powers.

### a. The APA Definition of Rule and Rulemaking

Before we can discuss the specific APA rulemaking requirements, we must first determine whether the agency action involves rulemaking, and, if so, what kind of rulemaking. The APA defines rulemaking as the "agency process for formulating, amending, or repealing a *rule*." APA § 551(5)(emphasis added). Section 551(4) defines a "rule" as follows:

> "[R]ule" means the whole or a part of an agency statement of general or particular applicability and future effect designed to implement, interpret, or prescribe law or policy or describing the organization, procedure, or practice requirements of an agency and includes the approval or prescription for the future of rates . . . .

APA § 551 (4).

The definition of "rule" is especially critical because it is part of the definition of "adjudication," which we will examine later. Outlining the definition is helpful. A rule is

An agency statement

1.  Having applicability, and
    a.  General, or
    b.  Particular (as identified in 4)
2.  Having future effect, and
3.  Designed to, or
    a.  Implement law or policy,
    b.  Interpret law or policy,
    c.  Prescribe law or policy, or
    d.  Describe
        i.  Agency organizational requirements,
        ii.  Agency procedural requirements, or
        iii.  Agency practice requirements
4.  Including approval of
    a.  Rates,
    b.  Wages,
    c.  Financial structures,
    d.  Prices, and
    e.  Practices

The APA's rulemaking requirements apply only to agency actions that meet the Act's definition of *rule*. So we must understand the definition. There are several things to notice about it. First, the definition is broader than the ordinary meaning of a rule. The definition includes actions that have "particular" applicability, which we would not ordinarily think of as a rule. The APA drafters likely thought this language was necessary because the definition includes such actions as ratemaking, which often involve only a single regulated party. Read the definition to get a general sense of its meaning. Ignore the "or particular" language; we do not use this aspect of the definition often in this course.

Second, there are no subject matter limits here. The definition covers *all* rules dealing with law, policy, or organization. The APA drafters intended a very inclusive definition, then provided for specific exceptions and exclusions, which we will see later.

Third, a rule is "of future effect." This quality of a rule fits with our sense of legislative actions, which are also usually prospective. However, often we have to distinguish between rulemaking and adjudication to determine the correct procedures. Many adjudications have a kind of future effect as well. The *Palsgraf* case is one good example.

Similarly, an adjudication that leads to a license revocation or results in a cease-and-desist order will have future effect as well. Sometimes it is said that the reference to future effect in the rulemaking definition results from a rule's effort to shape *future* conduct while an adjudication relates principally to *past* conduct of a party. This explanation is tempting, but do not trust it too far. The fact is that all rules are in some sense based on past events. Agencies do not promulgate rules changing the law without an underlying reason. And most adjudications have some future effects (as in the examples cited above). Perhaps the most we can say is that the main objective of rules is that they lay down standards for future conduct, while the main objective of adjudications is to assert something about the legality of past events.

Finally, stay flexible: the APA's rule definition is broad enough to cover a lot of things that will not look like rules. An agency statement designed to implement policy could come in the form of a memo, an email, a bulletin, or even a luncheon speech. If the agency statement meets the definition, it is a rule for APA purposes.

### b. Formal and Informal Rules

Once an agency decides to promulgate a rule, there are four procedural tracks the agency may follow. See Figure 2.1. Section 553(c) shows three of these: an *informal* track (essentially the notice and comment process we will examine below), a *formal* track (requiring use of the more formalized provisions of sections 556 and 557) and a hybrid track (meaning either of these processes supplemented by additional procedures added by Congress, the president, and the agency. See Section 3). Incidentally, the words "formal" and "informal" do not appear in the APA, but judicial opinions and commentary regularly use these terms. Also note that the words "formal" and "informal" do not have their ordinary meanings. The elaborate EPA case study we examined earlier followed section 553 notice and comment process and was, despite its complexity and length, an example of "informal" rulemaking. The third track, the *hybrid* track, is followed where other statutes or rules add procedural requirements to the procedures otherwise required by section 553's informal rulemaking process. To be fair, there are few, if any, purely informal rulemakings these days, but we will learn the traditional informal, or notice and comment, process the APA outlines. There is a fourth track, the *non-§ 553* track, for those rules entirely or partially exempt from section 553's process. This track is omitted from Figure 2.1.

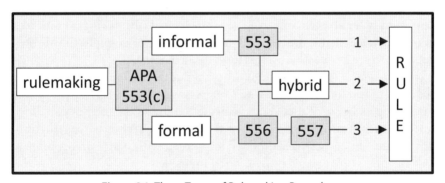

**Figure 2.1** Three Types of Rulemaking Procedures

How do you tell which track an agency must follow in any particular rulemaking? Section 553(c) governs an agency's choice of procedure. The last sentence of that subsection provides as follows:

> When rules are required by statute to be made on the record after opportunity for an agency hearing, sections 556 and 557 of this title apply instead of [subsection 553].

APA § 553(c).

The agency must read its enabling statute to determine whether formal or informal rulemaking is required. Did Congress require its rules to be on the record after a hearing? If Congress were always clear about which type of rulemaking it wanted when it authorized an agency to issue rules, our lives would all be much simpler. Unfortunately, Congress is often unclear. Suppose Congress authorizes an agency to promulgate rules "after a hearing." Does this trigger the formal provisions of sections 556–557? The answer today is "no." The Supreme Court took a literal approach to interpreting the APA's language in *United States v. Florida East Coast Ry.*, 410 U.S. 224 (1973). In that case, the Court held that enabling statutes that merely require an agency to issue a rule "after a hearing" do not trigger formal rulemaking. *Id.* at 238.

Was this a bad holding? As we will detail in the next chapter, sections 556–57 require judicial processes such as cross-examination, discovery, and a decision based on a closed record. These procedures are less beneficial for creating rules. Rather, rulemaking works best when it is handled like legislative action. Does this mean that formal procedures are never used in rulemaking? Not exactly. There are some advantages to formal rulemaking (fuller deliberation, full participation by parties, more objectivity in decision making, etc.) so Congress occasionally requires it. *See, e.g.*, Marine Mammal Protection Act, 86 Stat. 1027, § 103 (d) (requiring the regulations be made "on the record after opportunity for an agency hearing"). While formal rulemaking is quite rare at the federal level, it is more common in the states; for example, the Minnesota legislature frequently requires formal rulemaking.

In sum, *Florida East Coast Railway* teaches us that before an agency can be required to use formal procedures, Congress will have to be very precise in expressing its wishes: Rules are to be made "on the record after opportunity for an agency hearing." In the absence of such "magic language," you can usually assume an agency has authority to proceed with notice and comment rulemaking, as augmented by hybrid requirements.

### c. *"Nonlegislative Rules" (Interpretive Rules, Policy Statements, etc.)*

There are many ways in which agencies can express general policies. Notice and comment rulemaking is one method (and formal rulemaking is another). But suppose an agency wishes to advise regulated parties about a policy that the agency wishes to implement quickly without the delay and expense of the notice and comment process. Alternatively, suppose an agency wishes to issue a policy that will not have a broad enough impact to justify full-scale notice and comment proceedings? Or, what if the new policy is still in the formative stage and needs more experimentation and flexibility than a final notice and comment rule would provide? Finally, what if the policy is one that the agency is not anxious to publicize widely? Can the agency express its policy in a statement issued without notice and comment, for example, in a press release, in a bulletin, in an email statement, or in a notice posted on its web page?

You might begin by noticing that the APA definition of a rule is broad enough to cover all these policy statements. In other words, they are all *agency statements* of future effect designed to implement policy. Hence, the agency must use at least notice and comment procedures, right? Actually, no. Section 553(b) exempts some types of "rules" from notice and comment procedures: policy statements and interpretive rules. Section 553(b) of the APA uses the phrases "interpretative rules" and "general statements of policy." The section explicitly exempts such statements from the notice and comment requirements, although it still requires that these rules be published. APA § 552(a)(1)(D). Hence, these types of rules are sometimes called "publication rules." Peter L. Strauss, An Introduction to Administrative Justice in the United States, 222–24 (2d. ed. 2002). Other nonlegislative rules (such as bulletins, manuals, staff instructions, press releases) are exempt from the notice and comment process and from publication requirements.

Let's examine *why* these types of rules are exempted before we examine *what* they are. When deciding whether notice and comment procedures must be used in formulating these kinds of rules, it is useful to think of rules in two broad categories that we label *legislative* and *nonlegislative* rules. Legislative rules have legal effect; they are similar to statutes. Violation of a legislative rule can earn your client license revocations, fines, and in some cases even criminal penalties. They are "law" in almost every sense of the word. Sometimes these rules are called "substantive" rules. For legislative rules, an agency must follow notice and comment (or formal) procedures. Promulgating a legislative rule is classic rulemaking and results in binding rules.

Nonlegislative rules are more difficult to describe. As suggested above, they come in many shapes, sizes, and forms. When an agency wishes to notify its own staff about preferred enforcement tactics, when it wants to inform outside parties about its views as to the meaning of its statute, and when it wants the public to know about the policies it intends to follow, the agency may communicate its views in interpretive statements, policy papers, bulletins, memos, manuals, letters, press releases, and even speeches. Some courts and scholars have come to describe these expressions under the generic title "guidance documents." As you might expect, agency guidance documents are much more numerous than legislative rules. They can also be extremely valuable, both to regulated entities seeking to anticipate agency action and to agencies themselves seeking appropriate and consistent enforcement by agency staff.

So to sum up what we have learned so far, (1) when an agency issues a legislative rule it must comply with all of the notice and comment (or formal rulemaking) procedures; (2) when an agency issues a nonlegislative interpretive rule or policy statement, the agency need not follow the notice and comment process of section 553 but must publish the rules under section 552(a)(1)(D).

Now the harder question: what is a legislative versus a nonlegislative rule? Unlike legislative rules, non-legislative rules do not have independent legal effect. Rather, any legal effect they have comes from preexisting legislative rules (whether from Congress or the agency). Non-legislative rules are exempt from the formal and notice and comment procedures. 5 U.S.C. § 553(b)(3)(A). The APA identifies two types of non-legislative rules, or guidance documents: (1) interpretative (or interpretive) rules, and (2) general statements of policy. *Id.* Interpretive rules are self-describing; they are rules interpreting language in an existing statute or regulation. In contrast, policy statements are statements from an agency that prospectively advise the public and agency personnel on the way in which the agency plans to exercise discretionary power in the future. Agencies may issue policy statements to announce new duties the agency plans to adopt by future adjudication or rulemaking. Note that there is no such thing as an "interpretive statement" or a "policy rule." Terminology is important.

Agencies use non-legislative rules for many reasons. For example, assume that after an agency has enacted a regulation, questions arise about how the agency will interpret that regulation. Lower-level administrators may seek guidance from senior-level administrators about how to implement the new regulation, or regulated entities may seek clarification about their responsibilities under the new rule. In response, agency administrators may develop a list of "frequently asked questions," update an agency manual, or provide guidance in some other form. To illustrate, the Corps of Engineers maintains Regulatory Guidance Letters, which are issued to field personnel to interpret or clarify existing regulatory policy. Similarly, the Internal Revenue Service issues letter rulings, which are written statements issued to taxpayers that interpret tax laws. There are many different ways that an agency might issue a non-legislative rule. Because agencies do not go through a procedurally prescribed process, such as formal or notice and comment rulemaking, when they issue these rules, the rules are easily modifiable and non-binding.

Non-legislative rules play a legitimate and important role in agency policymaking. They help agencies apply law consistently across field offices by affording guidance to both the public and lower-level agency personnel. Non-legislative rules ensure greater and faster compliance than legislative rules alone, because legislative rules may lack specificity and clarity. Finally, non-legislative rules also help agencies develop a flexible policy quickly and easily, while still giving the regulated entities and the public advance notice of new policies. From an agency's perspective, non-legislative rules are "law" in a practical sense, because they influence the conduct of regulated entities and, thus, regulate behavior. But legally, non-legislative rules are not truly "law," because they are not legally binding. If an agency wants a rule to legally bind regulated entities, the agency must use formal, notice and comment, or, in limited cases, publication procedures.

### d. Section 553 Exemptions

There are also rules that are exempted from section 553 procedures entirely. Rules that involve (1) military or foreign affairs, and (2) (a) agency management or personnel or (2) (b) public property, loans, grants, benefits or contracts. APA §§ 553(a)(1) & (2).

Courts have narrowly interpreted the subsection (1) military exemptions. And some agencies that would be otherwise excused from following section 553 procedures have adopted policies requiring notice and comment procedures for some rules (e.g., the Department of Defense). The foreign affairs exemption is used for rules bearing directly on such things as international agreements and import quotas. *See, e.g., American Ass'n of Exporters & Importers v. United States,* 751 F.2d 1239 (Fed. Cir. 1985); *Nademi v. INS,* 679 F.2d 811, 814 (10th Cir. 1982).

Subsection (2)'s exemption of agency management and personnel functions permit an agency's internal operational functions to be conducted without the need for public involvement, which is generally a sensible idea. However, the subsection also exempts rules involving public property, grants, benefits, and contracts. This exemption is more troublesome because rules on these issues can impact people outside the agency. For this reason, courts have interpreted these exemptions narrowly. *See, e.g., Texaco, Inc. v. Federal Power Comm'n,* 412 F.2d 740, 743 (3d Cir. 1969; *see generally,* Arthur E. Bonfield, *Public Participation in Federal Rulemaking Relating to Public Property, Loans, Grants, Benefits and Contracts,* 118 U. Pa. L. Rev. 540 (1970).

The Administrative Conference of the United States ("ACUS") is an agency authorized to promote improvements in the efficiency, adequacy, and fairness of the procedures by which federal agencies conduct regulatory programs, administer grants and benefits, and perform related governmental functions. ACUS has recommended that these exemptions be eliminated altogether and that, until that time, agencies comply with section 553 notice and comment procedures when issuing rules relating to these issues. ACUS Recommendation 69-8, Elimination of Certain Exemptions from the APA

Rulemaking Requirements, 1 ACUS 29, 38 Fed. Reg. 19,782, 19,784-85 (July 23, 1973). A number of agencies have followed this recommendation, but others have chosen not to. GAO-13-21 (stating that from 2003–2010, agencies did not publish an NPRM for 35 percent of major rules and 44 percent of non-major rules).

In addition to the rules exempted from section 553 completely, some rules are exempted from parts of that section. Specifically, the provisions of the section that require notice and comment do not apply to the following:

(A) interpretative rules, general statements of policy, or rules of agency organization, procedure or practice, or

(B) when the agency for good cause finds . . . that notice and public procedure . . . are impracticable, unnecessary, or contrary to the public interest.

APA § 553(b).

Subsection (A)'s exemption of interpretive rules and policy statements has already been discussed. Subsection (A) also exempts from notice and comment requirements rules dealing with "agency organization, procedure or practice." This exception would seem to be a fairly straightforward exemption of internal housekeeping rules, similarly to the exception for rules relating to agency management and personnel in section 553(b)(3)(A). However, the APA does not define "procedural rules." Courts have defined procedural rules as the "technical regulation of the form of agency action and proceedings . . . which merely prescribes order and formality in the transaction of . . . business." *Pickus v. United States Board of Parole*, 507 F.2d 1107, 1113 (D.C. Cir. 1974) ("This category . . . should not be deemed to include any action which goes beyond formality and substantially affects the rights of those over whom the agency exercises authority."). Courts distinguished between procedural rules and other rules based on whether the rule had a *substantial impact* on the rights of people affected. *American Hospital v. Bowen*, 834 F.2d 1037, 1061–62 (D.C. Cir. 1987); *Batterton v. Marshall*, 648 F.2d 694, 708 (D.C. Cir. 1980) ("The critical question is whether the agency action jeopardizes the rights and interest of parties, for if it does, it must be subject to public comment prior to taking effect."). Using this substantive impact test, a court examined the impact of the rule, rather than the substance of the rule. If the proposed procedural rule has a substantive impact, then the agency must promulgate the rule through notice and comment rulemaking. However, even if a rule is a "procedure or practice rule," then the agency must still follow the APA's publication and 30-day delayed effective date requirements. APA § 553. 5 U.S.C. § 553(b)(3)(A).

The D.C. Circuit has since rejected the substantive impact test because even rules that are clearly procedural affect substantive rights. For example, a statute of limitations prevents people from bringing a lawsuit, thus substantially impacting rights. But such a rule is still procedural. In its place, the D.C. Circuit adopted the following test: when procedural rules encode a substantive value judgment and substantially alter the rights of the parties, then notice and comment procedures are necessary. *See JEM Broadcasting Co., Inc. v. FCC*, 22 F.3d 320, 328 (D.C. Cir. 1994) (holding that a rule governing the content and timing of case filings was "procedural"). In sum, the test examines whether the rule is the agency's way of telling a regulated entity that if it changes its behavior, the agency will then approve or disapprove the action. In other words, the "critical feature" of the procedural exception "is that it covers agency actions that do not themselves alter the rights or interests of parties, although [the rule] may alter the manner in which the parties present themselves or their viewpoints to the agency." *Id.* at 326; *see, e.g., National Whistleblower Ct. v. NRC*, 208 F.3d 256 (D.C. Cir. 2000) (holding that the Nuclear Regulatory Commission's rule relating to the timing of submissions in support of motions to intervene was procedural).

Let's turn to subsection (B). Under section 553(b)(3)(B), when an agency has good cause to believe that notice would be impracticable, unnecessary, or contrary to the public interest, notice and comment rulemaking may be avoided. This useful provision eliminates the need for notice and comment procedures when the time required for such procedures would threaten more important values (e.g., airline safety) or where the comment process itself would not be useful (the issue is narrow, technical, or not in dispute). However, the agency must include the basis for the good cause exception in its final rule. Note that while some states, such as Oregon, require agencies to use notice and comment procedures after the rule has been implemented, the federal APA does not.

Concerns about the overuse of the good cause exemption spawned a couple of alternatives. One such alternative goes by the oxymoronic name, "interim final rules." To issue an interim final rule, an agency with a defensible case for a "good cause" exemption puts the rule into effect without notice and comment but voluntarily agrees to receive comments later. If later comments convince the agency that the rule should be dropped or modified, the agency will do so, ultimately issuing a truly final rule. In the meantime, the interim rule remains in effect. As Professor Michael Asimow said:

> Interim-final rules adopted under the good cause exemption strike
> a compromise between a perceived need for immediate adoption of a

rule and the values of public participation and regulatory analysis. When it adopts an interim-final rule, an agency captures some, but not all, of the benefits of pre-adoption public comment. It also captures some, but not all, of the cost and time savings of adopting a rule without any public participation or regulatory analysis at all.

Michael Asimow, *Interim-Final Rules*, 51 ADMIN. L. REV. 703, 710 (1999).

Alternatively, an agency may skip good cause and issue a so-called "direct final rule." With a direct final rule, the agency promulgates a rule that will go into effect within 30 days unless the agency receives significant adverse comments. If such comments appear, the agency withdraws the rule and proceeds with normal notice and comment process. The use of direct final rulemaking gives members of the public more opportunity to comment than they would get if the agency successfully used the good cause exemption, and this process provides a streamlined process for non-controversial rules.

Even though the rules identified above do not need to go through section 553 procedures, Congress has the power to add additional procedural requirements, and it sometimes does. We will note examples as the discussion proceeds.

### e. Starting the Process — The Rulemaking Petition under APA § 553(e)

There are as many ways to begin the rulemaking process as there are to begin a legislative proposal. The process may be initiated wholly within the agency, as when staff studies or inspector reports identify a problem that can be addressed with a general rule. The process may be initiated by pressure from the legislature, whether formally by a statutory command or informally through a congressional expression of dissatisfaction with existing agency policy or conduct. Or the process may be initiated by pressure from the executive branch in the form of a "prompt letter" from the Office of Management and Budget (OMB), from informal discussions with executive branch officials, or as part of the president's regulatory planning process itself. The process may be initiated in response to recommendations from other government agencies, advisory committees, states, or regulatory beneficiary groups. Sometimes, rulemaking may be required as part of a judicial settlement. *See* James Rossi, *Bargaining in the Shadow of Administrative Procedure*, 51 DUKE L. J. 1015 (2001).

Citizens can also petition for a rulemaking. Section 553(e) allows a citizen to petition an agency to issue, amend, or repeal a rule. Section 555(e) requires the agency to provide a prompt explanation if the agency denies the petition.

In addition to section 555(e), provisions in an agency's rules, in other statutes, or in OMB requirements may affect the manner or timing of an agency's response to a citizen's petition, such as a requirement that the agency ask for public comment before denying petitions or a requirement that the agency publish the reasons for denial.

What might an agency do to respond to such a petition? Because filing a petition is a matter of right, *Massachusetts v. EPA*, 549 U.S. 797 (2007), the agency cannot ignore a petition. Rather, the agency can (1) grant the petition and begin a rulemaking proceeding, (2) deny the petition, or (3) delay ruling on the petition, perhaps setting the petition aside for further study.

If the agency grants a petition for rulemaking, those opposed to the rulemaking taking place cannot challenge this decision. Rather, those opposed to the rulemaking initiation will have to wait to challenge the rule after it has been promulgated. Once a rule has been promulgated, there is "final agency action" within the meaning of APA § 704, which is required for judicial review. We will return to the topic of judicial review in Chapters 5 and 6.

If the agency denies a petition for rulemaking, there has been "final agency action" within the meaning of APA section 704, because there is no further action for the agency to take. "Agency action" includes an agency's "failure to act." APA § 551(13). Hence, the agency's denial is "final agency action" and, thus, judicially reviewable under section 704. Typically, courts sustain an agency's decision to deny a petition unless the court finds that decision to be arbitrary and capricious. APA § 706(1)(A). A decision is this context is arbitrary and capricious when the agency either fails to adequately explain the facts and policy concerns, or the facts the agency relied on have no basis in the record. *Arkansas Power & Light Co. v. ICC*, 725 F.2d 716, 723 (1984). If Congress has required the agency to issue a rule, however, judicial review of the denial may be more demanding. *See, e.g., Massachusetts v. EPA*, 549 U.S. 797, 497 (2007) (reversing the EPA's decision to refuse to act in light of the statutory direction to the agency to act).

If the agency neither grants nor denies a petition for rulemaking, but instead simply delays acting on it, judicial review may be available. Section 555(b) of the APA requires the agency to respond within a reasonable time. "Prompt notice shall be given of the denial in whole or in part of a written . . . petition." Section 706(1) provides for judicial review when an agency has responded with an unreasonable delay. When is delay unreasonable? In *Telecommunications Research & Action Ctr. v. FCC*, 750 F.2d 70 (D.C. Cir. 1984) ("*TRAC*"), the DC Circuit developed the "rule of reason" test for determining when agency delay is unreasonable. The court identified four factors to evaluate whether an agency's delay was reasonable: (1) whether Congress provided a timetable for the agency action; (2) whether the delay negatively affects human health and welfare; (3) whether expediting the delay would lead to negative effects on issues of higher priority for the agency; and (4) whether the nature and extent of other interests were unduly prejudiced by the delay. *Id.* at 80. The court was clear that it need not find that the agency acted inappropriately to find that the agency had delayed unreasonably. *Id.* Because courts balance the *TRAC* factors on a case-by-case basis it can be difficult to predict which way a court will decide any particular case. Importantly, there is no bright-line rule on how long is too long. Therefore, it is important to look at previous cases to see how courts have resolved this question.

One example is *International Union v. Chao*, 361 F.3d 249 (3rd. Cir. 2004). In this case, a union filed a petition for rulemaking with the Occupational Safety and Health Administration (OSHA), asking the agency to promulgate a rule to protect workers from certain kinds of machining fluids. *Id.* at 250. Ten years later, OSHA had not responded to the petition, so the union filed suit, claiming the agency's delayed response to its petition was unreasonable. *Id.* OSHA responded by officially denying the petition, explaining that in its view that the fluids were not especially dangerous and that in any event it, OSHA, had limited resources that were being used to deal with what it considered more serious issues. *Id.* at 252. The Third Circuit accepted OSHA's reason for the denial and the delay, not wanting either to interfere with OSHA's decision on the merits or its judgment about priorities and resource allocations. The court said that that the Union "would have us intrude into the quintessential discretion of the Secretary of Labor to allocate OSHA's resources and set its priorities. . . . This is a step we are not prepared to take." *Id.* at 256. The court did, however, throw the union a bone. It lectured the agency: "we trust that we will not again see delays such as were seen here." *Id.* at 256. Victory for the plaintiff in an unreasonable delay case is rare. William Luneburg, *Petitioning Federal Agencies for Rulemaking*, 1988 WISC. L. REV. 1 (1988).

When a court does find that the agency unreasonably delayed a decision on a petition, the court will not order the agency to grant the petition; rather, the court will provide the agency with a timeframe within which to respond to the petition. *See, e.g., Norton v. South Utah Wilderness Alliance*, 542 U.S. 55, 65 (2004). Furthermore, the Supreme Court has also established that agency rules still maintain the force of law, even when they are promulgated after a statutory deadline. *Barnhart v. Peabody Coal Co.*, 537 U.S. 149, 155, 171–72 (2003). Therefore, a court's only remedy for an agency's unreasonable delay is to impose a new deadline on the agency.

## f. Notice & Comment Procedures

Most proposed rules are issued only after a long process of research, including legal and political analysis and discussions with stakeholder groups, executive branch officials, and legislators. When those discussions are concluded, the proposed rule is ready for public comment. Public comment has many purposes, including assuring legitimacy, rationality, and public acceptance. Further public comment may inform the agency about potential enforcement problems. Comment on proposed rules is, of course, only one part of the full public participation process. For major rules, the process may include investigations, conferences, consultation, advisory committees, oral and written communication to agencies, and hearings of varying levels of formality. When the APA was written, the drafters identified notice and comment procedures as the minimum, leaving the parties, the agencies, and the legislature to require more process when necessary.

Under APA § 553(b), the agency must publish the proposed rule in the Federal Register, although today most people use the Internet to learn about and comment on proposed rules. In addition to the Federal Register and the Internet, many agencies today provide information about proposed rules in press releases, trade publications, looseleaf services, trade association publications, etc. While the APA is silent regarding the length of time the comment period must remain open, agencies must publish final rules at least 30 days prior to their effective date. APA § 553(d). Congress has at times mandated a comment period. E.g., 42 U.S.C. § 300g-1(b)(2)(B) (requiring a 60-day comment period).

The requirements of section 553 are straightforward:

> (b) General notice of proposed rulemaking shall be published in the Federal Register ... The notice shall include—
>> (1) a statement of the time, place, and nature of public rulemaking proceedings;
>> (2) reference to the legal authority under which the rule is proposed; and
>> (3) either the terms or substance of the proposed rule or a description of the subjects and issues involved.

APA § 553(b).

The text of section 553 identifies the minimum of what an agency must include in its notice. Again, the drafters of the APA anticipated relatively short notices with information accessible to the public. However, most agencies today include a final draft of the proposed rule and statements showing their compliance with the requirements imposed by other statutes and executive orders.

Should the agency include information it has supporting its rule? The legislative history of the APA states that the notice must be "sufficient to fairly apprise interested persons of the issues involved, so that they may present responsive data or argument." H.R. Rep. No. 1980, 79th Cong., 2d Sess. 2, reprinted in Legislative History of the Administrative Procedure Act, S. Doc. No. 248, 79th Cong., 2d Sess. 200 (1946). Given this purpose, the D.C. Circuit Court held that agencies must include in the noticed of proposed rulemaking all the scientific data and methodology on which the agency relied. *Portland Cement Ass'n v. Ruckelshaus*, 486 F.2d 375, 394 (D.C. Cir. 1973). Yet this requirement is contrary to the actual language of section 553 and may be invalid under a later Supreme Court case, *Vermont Yankee Nuclear Power Corp. v. Natural Resources Defense Council, Inc.*, 435 U.S. 519, 524 (1978). In *Vermont Yankee*, the Court held that courts could not impose rulemaking procedures on agencies beyond those in the APA and other statutes.

The drafters of the APA probably believed the public comment process was intended to inform the agency about how the rule would impact regulated entities. Today, the notice requirement seems more to function as a way for the agency to inform (a) the *public* about the factual bases for the agency's views so that those bases can be understood and, if need be, challenged, and (b) the reviewing *courts* about the reasons for the rule because the courts must rule on legal challenges. Here is a more contemporary judicial attitude:

> To allow for useful criticism, it is especially important for the agency to identify and make available technical studies and data that it has employed in reaching the decisions to propose particular rules. To allow an agency to play hunt the peanut with technical information, hiding or disguising the information that it employs, is to condone a practice in which the agency treats what should be a genuine interchange as mere bureaucratic sport. An agency commits serious procedural error when it fails to reveal portions of the technical basis for a proposed rule in time to allow for meaningful commentary.

*Connecticut Light & Power Co. v. NRDC*, 673 F.2d 525, 530–31 (D.C. Cir. 1982).

With this shift in the purpose for the notice and comment process, the simple rulemaking model described in section 553 of the APA no longer mirrors current practice.

Perhaps the easiest way for you to get a sense of the current practice is to take a break from your reading, turn on your computer, and take a look at www.regulations.gov. Enter a search word (e.g., "smog" or "drugs"), then narrow the search by choosing an agency (e.g., the Food and Drug Administration or the Environmental Protection Agency) and entering your choice in the box on the left, and then narrow your search further by choosing "proposed rules." Now take a look at some of the proposed rules and some of the public comments on them. (Incidentally, you are free to comment yourself on those proposed rules. It is easy to do — just type in your comment or attach a previously written document.)

Pick a proposed rule of interest to you, and examine the text of the notice. At first glance, you will probably see a myriad of technical details, mysterious acronyms, a long development history (which may include legislative action and judicial interventions) and the elaborate documentation the agency will almost always include or refer to in its notice, in response to judicial attitudes such as that noted above. This material contains the scientific, economic, and other studies on which the agency relied in deciding on the proposed rule. Do not be intimidated by the elaborate profusion of this arcane material. In practice, experienced players in this field (soon to be you!) will usually have been involved in the development of the proposed rule and will be familiar with these details long before the notice of proposed rulemaking is even published.

Any "interested person" can comment on a proposed rule. APA § 553. However, while this language might suggest some limits on who may comment, essentially anyone can comment. The phrase is very broadly interpreted to further the purpose of notice and comment rulemaking. While the idea of public comment has a populist ring to it, the opportunities for lone individuals alone to have major impact — the Ralph Nader model — are rare. If you spent a little time on www.regulations.gov, you will quickly see that dealing effectively with contemporary rulemaking requires financial resources, technical expertise, and the ability to mobilize others. As a result, most comments received today come from organized interest groups. Comments address such matters as the cost of industry compliance, the time for industry compliance, the quality and accuracy of the information on which the proposed rule is based, the proposed rule's clarity, and the agency's authority to issue the rule.

Interested persons may submit written comments only. APA § 553(c). Oral comments are generally not allowed; however, oral presentations may be available at the option of the agency. Some enabling statutes, agency rules, and agency practices may provide more opportunities for oral presentation. Much comment today, of course, arrives in electronic form. For a summary of the prospects and problems of electronic rulemaking, see Gary Coglianese,

*E-Rulemaking: Information Technology and the Regulatory Process,* 56 ADMIN. L. REV. 353 (2004).

Notice is inadequate if it does not give fair notice of the rule as finally promulgated. For this reason, the agency cannot propose rule *A* and, after the comment period, promulgate rule *B*. But if the purpose of the comment period is to allow the agency to change a proposed rule to address legitimate concerns raised during the commenting process, then the proposed rule need not be the final rule. Otherwise, the public comment process would be pointless. Similarly, if every minor difference between a proposed rule and the final rule required reopening the comment period, the rule would never be promulgated.

The courts have tried to reach a compromise. At the practical level, courts have sought to assure that the final rule is close enough to the rule as proposed as to make the opportunity to comment meaningful. If the final rule can be characterized as a "logical outgrowth" of the proposed rule, notice was adequate. *Chocolate Mf. Ass'n v. Block,* 755 F.2d 1098 (4th Cir. 1985). But this test is not of much practical help. The final rule will in some sense always be a "logical outgrowth" of the proposed rule. Final rules do not, after all, come from left field. A more usable articulation of this test is that the final rule should have been *foreseeable* from examining the proposed rule. In other words, what matters is not the logical connection of the proposed and final rule, but whether the proposed rule put all parties on notice about the issues that were "on the table" as the agency worked its way toward a final rule. As the D.C. Circuit put it, "Notice [is] inadequate when the interested parties could not reasonably have anticipated the final rulemaking from the draft." *National Mining Ass'n. v. MSHA,* 116 F.3d 520, 531 (D.C. Cir. 1997). What the agency must avoid is what the D.C. Circuit colorfully called a "surprise switcheroo" in the final rule. *Environmental Integrity Project v. EPA,* 425 F.3d 992, 997 (D.C. Cir. 2005).

Some courts have found adequate notice when an issue that appeared in the final rule was drawn from public comments on the proposed rule. *United Steelworkers v. Schuykill Metal,* 828 F.2d 314 (5th Cir. 1987). Alternatively, the agency's long-standing practice can serve notice as to what issues are or are not "on the table." *Chocolate Mf.,* 755 F.2d at 1107 (finding that the agency's long-standing practice of including chocolate milk as an allowable food was misleading).

The agency is, of course, always free to begin a second cycle of notice if comments received on the first NPRM show the need for substantial modification of its proposed rule. And if there are clear alternative solutions to the problem, the agency might publish those alternatives with its proposed rule, inviting the public to comment on them. Then, no one can claim surprise.

For more discussion of useful agency strategies, see Jeffrey Lubbers, A Guide to Agency Rulemaking, Part 3 Chapter 3 (5th ed. 2012).

### g. Agency Consideration of Public Comment — Drafting the Final Rule

#### (1) The Administrative "Record"

After the comment period, the agency must "consider" the public comments and draft the final rule. APA §553(c). What does it mean to "consider" what can be a mass of material? To answer this question, let's remember the difference between the judicial and the legislative models. In a judicial proceeding the material received in the hearing (transcript of the testimony, exhibits, etc.) form the "record," and a court is bound by what is in that record. A court cannot consider information that is not in the record and cannot "find" facts unless there is competent evidence of those facts in the record.

In contrast, legislative hearings produce an enormous volume of material (testimony, documents, reports, etc.) but it is not a "record" in the same way that the judicial record is, because the legislative record does not bind the legislature when making its final decision. The legislature is free to consider anything else it chooses, and the legislature can pass a law even though all the views expressed in the record are opposed to the law.

During rulemaking an agency acts more like a legislative body; however, the agency is not free to disregard the information developed in the rulemaking process. The agency, much like courts, is bound by the rulemaking record. The idea of a rulemaking "record" first emerged in the APA's legislative history. That history is clear that "the agency must keep a record of and analyze and consider all relevant matter presented prior to the issuance of rules." H.R. Rep. No 1980, 79th Cong., 2d Sess. 259 (1946).

Courts have struggled with defining what materials the agency must consider and the reviewing courts must examine when assessing the legality of a rule. In 1971, the Supreme Court considered this question after an agency conducted an informal adjudication. *Citizens to Preserve Overton Park v. Volpe*, 401 U.S. 402 (1971). Because the adjudication was informal, there was no "record" in the judicial or even rulemaking sense. The Court remanded the case to the district court to determine whether the agency's decision was arbitrary and capricious in light of "*the full administrative record* that was before the secretary at the time he made his decision." *Id.* at 420 (emphasis added). At the time, no one really knew what a "full administrative record" was, but the term stuck. Building on that perhaps unwise choice of words, lower courts have slowly developed an expectation that agencies will review "a body of material — documents, comments, transcripts, and statements" against which "it is the

obligation of [the] court to test the actions of the agency for arbitrariness. . . ."
*Home Box Office, Inc. v. FCC*, 567 F.2d 9, 54 (D.C. Cir. 1977). That "body of
material" has become known as the rulemaking "record," although more
appropriately it is the rulemaking "docket" or "file." Whatever the name, the
APA requires the agency to consider the full record.

Several important questions have arisen about rulemaking records; two of
them are of interest to us. First, what must be included in the record? This is
a difficult question, because the ideas of a closed record and a legislative-like
process do not fit comfortably together. And there are many aspects of agency
expertise, experience, and insight that are vital to the final decision about a
rule, yet simply cannot be encapsulated in documents or reports. The best
answer comes from the Administrative Conference of the United States, which
suggested that the rulemaking record should include the following: all rulemaking notices, copies of all written factual material "substantially relied upon
or seriously considered" by the agency, and all written comments submitted.
ACUS Recommendation 93-4, 58 Fed. Reg. 4670 (1994).

Second, when someone challenges a rule in a judicial proceeding, is the
agency confined in its defense to material developed during the notice and
comment process? May material that was not in the agency's contemplation
when it decided on the rule be used during judicial review? Courts generally
do not favor "post hoc rationalizations," which include factual information
and arguments appearing only after a rule has been challenged. *Citizens to Preserve Overton Park v. Volpe*, 401 U.S. 402, 419 (1971). As you can imagine,
courts doubt the objectivity of post hoc rationalizations and believe that
the material should have been available to the public for comment and adversarial testing if it were so important. Hence, agencies should compile a record
that is full enough to support any justifications that may be needed on review.

### (2) The Agency as Decisionmaker

When an agency is formulating its final rule, agency decisionmakers are
quite different from judges in a judicial proceeding. Two special differences
are relevant here. First, in our judicial system the judge functions as an individual and makes an individual decision (with help from a clerk, perhaps). An
agency, in contrast, produces a group product, drawing on expert staff, analysts, and policymakers. The agency head who signs the final rule will not be
as familiar with the details of the rule as a judge will be. Rather, much of
what the agency head considers will be drawn from summaries and analyses
provided by lower-level staff. There is simply no other way for an agency head
to handle the number and complexity of issues under the agency's purview.
Thus, the rulemaking decision is said to be "institutional," rather than

personal, and derives from that circumstance much of its technical sureness and policy depth. Institutionalism is one of the strengths of the administrative process.

Second, it will be clear from the foregoing description that while the judge is presumably neutral regarding the outcome of a case, the agency and its staff are committed to a legislative or executive declared policy. Do not expect neutrality from the Securities and Exchange Commission on questions of fraud in investment practices, disinterest from the Environmental Protection Agency on questions of clean water, or indifference from the Federal Trade Commission on questions of misleading advertising. One hopes for objectivity in making first-level factual determinations (who did what, when, etc.). But as the proposed rule moves toward finality, the agency will increasingly depend on inferences, implications, guesses about future consequences, choices among competing policies, and, ultimately, political preferences. We will return to this topic in Chapter 6. For now, just understand that agency personnel will tend to have political preferences, which factor into the final rule.

### (3) Ex Parte Communications

During the agency's consideration of public comment and in the course of making its decision about the final rule, how should courts treat ex parte communications to the agency decisionmakers? Ex parte communications are communications addressed to the decisionmaker outside the presence of the other parties. Again, the judicial and legislative models are suggestive but not dispositive. Ex parte communications are strictly forbidden in judicial proceedings, but they are everyday, bread-and-butter components of the legislative process. How should they be treated in administrative rulemaking?

Ex parte communications may come from any private person (such as those impacted by the proposed rule). In addition to the public, such comments might come from other sources, such as the regulated entities, unions, executive officials, legislators, and individuals in other agencies. Considering these diverse sources and the various motives each individual may have who produced the ex parte comments, the question is, are these communications beneficial or, on balance, harmful?

The public may view these comments quite critically. Generally, the policy formulation process should be transparent, the public should know and be able to participate in all aspect of the agency rulemaking, and a court trying to assess the rationality of a rule should also know about important substantive communications to the agency. Hence, ex parte communications in rulemaking appear concerning. But the agency may find the comments quite useful; indeed, the comments may lead to a better rule. As Judge Patricia Wald has stated:

Informal [ex parte] contacts may enable the agency to win needed support for its program, reduce future enforcement requirements by helping those regulated to anticipate and shape their plans for the future, and spur the provision of information which the agency needs.

*Sierra Club v. Costle*, 657 F.2d 298, 401 (D.C. Cir. 1981).

What are the legal standards? For informal rulemaking, there are no prohibitions. As we will see in Chapter 3, the APA contains important restrictions on ex parte communications in the case of *formal rulemaking* proceedings, APA §§ 554, 556–57. For informal, notice and comment rulemaking, the APA does not forbid ex parte communications. Any such limitations must come either from an agency's own rules or from the agency's enabling statute. *See Home Box Office Inc. v. FCC*, 567 F.2d 9, 56–57 (D.C. Cir. 1977). The risks and appearances of uncontrolled ex parte communications have not been lost on either the legislative or the executive branches. Today, some statutes, some executive orders, and most agency procedural rules will contain provisions limiting such communications or requiring their full disclosure. *See* JEFFREY LUBBERS, A GUIDE TO FEDERAL AGENCY RULEMAKING 308–09 (5th ed. 2012).

One caveat about this rule: due process may limit ex parte communications in informal proceedings where those proceedings involved "conflicting private claims to a valuable privilege." *Sangamon Valley v. United States*, 269 F.2d 221, 224 (D.C. Cir. 1959). This limitation applies only when the parties are essentially arguing about agency action that results in a property-like award, such as a license.

### (4)  The "Concise, General Statement"

Once an agency drafts its final rule, section 553 requires that the agency prepare and publish a "concise general statement of [the rule's] basis and purpose." APA § 553(c). The legislative history of the APA is clear that these adjectives were to be taken literally. The statement accompanying the final rule was to be both concise and general. Today, however, under pressure from the lower courts setting aside rules the courts considered inadequately explained, agencies have acted in preemptive self-defense. They have converted the concise statement into a lengthy and detailed part of the proposed rule, which is called a *preamble*. The preamble includes a review of the evidence, the scientific support for the rule, the alternatives considered, and the weight given to various public comments. The preamble can run for multiple pages.

Many scholars have criticized the judicial attitude that has led to these lengthy preambles. Such complete preambles enormously complicate and delay the rulemaking process, which the framers of the APA intended to be short and simple. Lengthy preambles are one of the chief reasons for the "ossification," mentioned earlier. But neither Congress nor the Supreme Court has curbed this movement. We will examine this issue more fully in the Chapter 6 on judicial review.

## 3. Procedures in Addition to those in the APA (Hybrid Rulemaking)

As noted, the APA provides the minimum requirements for agencies to follow. Additional procedural requirements can come from other sources, including Congress, the President, and even agencies themselves. Generally, courts cannot add procedural requirements beyond those required by these three entities because the U.S. Constitution imposes few limits on legislative-type action. *Bi-Metallic Invest. Co. v. State Bd.*, 239 U.S. 441, 445 (1915). Thus, in *Vermont Yankee Nuclear Power Corp. v. NRDC*, 435 U.S. 519 (1978), the Supreme Court sharply criticized the courts of appeal for adding procedural requirements beyond those Congress had required in either the APA or another statute. However, while courts cannot add procedures in addition to those in the APA, Congress, the president, and agencies themselves can.

### a. Congress

Congress has enacted a number of general statutes that seek to further specific goals or to protect certain interests in the field of regulatory action. Just to mention a few, the Regulatory Flexibility Act (5 U.S.C. § 601 *et seq.*) requires agencies to consider the impacts of significant rules on small business enterprises during rulemaking. The Paperwork Reduction Act (44 U.S.C. § 3501 *et seq.*) requires agencies to minimize the paperwork burden of their regulatory activities. The Unfunded Mandates Reform Act (2 U.S.C. § 1501 *et seq.*) requires agencies to provide adequate resources to subnational governments (including Indian tribes) from the onerous burdens of regulation. The National Environmental Policy Act (42 U.S.C. § 4321 *et seq.*) requires agencies to assess the environmental impact of significant rules. All of these acts require agencies to assess a proposed rule's impact, requirements that can be costly and time-consuming, and surely were beyond anything contemplated by the drafters of the APA rulemaking provisions.

More specifically, in a number of agencies' enabling statutes, Congress has required more formality than the APA requires. We call rulemaking pursuant to such additional procedures "hybrid" rulemaking. Typically such additional procedures are added to notice and comment rulemaking. Theoretically, they could be added to formal rulemaking. Hybrid rulemaking is neither informal nor formal but is something in between. For example, the APA does not require that agencies hold oral hearings. But the Occupational Safety and Health Act (OSHA), 29 U.S.C. §655, the Consumer Product Safety Act, 15 U.S.C.§§2056, 2058, and the Clean Water Act, 42 U.S.C. §7606(d) all require the relevant agencies to hold legislative type hearings. *See also*, 15 U.S.C. §57a (requiring the Federal Trade Commission to allow cross-examination); 15 U.S.C. §78f(e) (also requiring cross-examination). Another example is that Congress required the Department of Energy to include "a statement of the research, analysis, and other available information in support of, the need for, and the probable effect of, any proposed rule . . . ." 42 U.S.C. §7191(b)(1); *see also*, 42 U.S.C. §7607(d) (3) (requiring proposed rules under the Clean Air Act to include "a summary of the factual data on which the proposed rule is based; the methodology used in obtaining the data and in analyzing the data; and the major legal interpretations and policy considerations underlying the proposed rule.").

In 1990, Congress added to the APA sections 561–70, which authorize agencies to accomplish some aspects of the rulemaking process by negotiation. Negotiated rulemaking (*reg-neg* as it has come to be called) involves convening a group of major stakeholders—those parties principally affected by the contemplated rule—to see if a consensus about the new rule can be developed. A draft rule worked out pursuant to this process is published as a proposed rule, and the usual public comment process ensues. Supporters believe that negotiated rulemaking produces technically better rules that more clearly identify the diverse concerns of those the rule affects, leads to simpler enforcement, and results in less judicial review. The concept has, however, generated controversy. Critics worry that some affected interests will not be invited to the party. Others are concerned that the system transfers too much power to the private sector. The debate is reviewed in Jeffrey Lubbers, A Guide to Federal Rulemaking 190–97 (5th ed. 2012).

Finally, one last example: Congress enacted the Congressional Review Act, 5 U.S.C. §§801–08 in 1996. This Act requires that major rules be presented to Congress for 60 days during which time Congress can pass a joint resolution rejecting the rule. Joint resolutions must be signed by the president or passed over a veto. While an earlier attempt at permitting a legislative veto of agency rules was rejected by the Supreme Court in *INS v. Chadha*, 462 U.S. 919 (1983), the Congressional Review Act was carefully drafted to comply with the bicameralism and presentment requirements of the Constitution. Initially, this process was largely ignored. However, use is increasing; in the first half of 2017, the process has been used approximately 15 times by a conservative Congress wishing to reverse the prior liberal administration's end of term rules.

## b. The President

Presidents have issued executive orders since 1789. An executive order is a directive issued by a president to implement or interpret federal law. Presidents have used executive orders to suspend habeas corpus, implement affirmative action requirements for government contractors, slow stem cell research, and authorize citizen surveillance. Executive orders are a popular method of executive control of agency action.

> In contrast to legislation or agency regulation, there are almost no legally enforceable procedural requirements that the president must satisfy before issuing (or repealing) an executive order . . . . That, no doubt, is central to their appeal to presidents. They rid the president of the need to assemble majorities in both houses of Congress, or to wait through administrative processes, such as notice-and-comment rulemaking, to initiate policy.

Kevin M. Stack, *The Statutory President*, 90 Iowa L. Rev. 539, 552–53 (2005).

Although there is no constitutional provision or statute that explicitly permits the president to issue executive orders, presidents assumed this power pursuant to their authority to "take Care that the Laws be faithfully executed." U.S. Const. art. II, § 3, cl. 5. Presidents generally use executive orders to guide federal agencies and officials in their execution of statutory authority. However, presidents use executive orders in other ways as well. For example, presidents may use proclamations, a special type of executive order, for ceremonial or symbolic messages, such as when the president declares *National Take Your Child to Work Day*. Also, presidents issue National Security Directives, which concern national security or defense. Executive orders are printed in the Federal Register.

Executive orders are somewhat controversial because the Constitution gives Congress the power to make law, albeit with the executive's assistance. When a president issues an executive order, it might appear as if the president is making law unilaterally. Often, when a president from one party attempts to influence policy using an executive order, members of Congress who are in the other party accuse the president of exceeding constitutional authority. For example, the Republican Party was highly critical of President Obama's executive orders addressing gun sales, deportation deferrals, and minimum wages. Former House Speaker John Boehner said,

> President Obama has overstepped his constitutional authority — and it is the responsibility of the House of Representatives to defend the Constitution . . . . Congress makes the laws; the president executes

them. That is the system the Founders gave us. This is not about executive orders. Every president issues executive orders. Most of them, though, do so within the law.

John Boehner, *We're Defending the Constitution,* USA TODAY (July 27, 2014), http://www.usatoday.com/story/opinion/2014/07/27/president-obama -house-speaker-john-boehner-executive-orders-editorials-debates/13244117/ (explaining a congressional resolution to sue the president for extending a deadline in the Affordable Care Act).

Is President Obama unique? Simply put, no. All presidents issue executive orders, although they vary in how aggressively they use them. Former President Roosevelt issued the most (3,728) as the country dealt with the Great Depression and World War II. Herbert Hoover issued 995. More recent presidents have issued fewer. Jimmy Carter issued 319 (in only four years); George W. Bush issued 291; Bill Clinton issued 364. In comparison, President Obama issued 276. *See generally,* John Woolley and Gerhard Peters, *Executive Orders: Washington—Obama The American Presidency Project* (November 20, 2016), http://www.presidency.ucsb.edu/data/orders.php. Under President Trump, use of the executive order to implement policy is increasing substantially. He has already issued 51 such orders. *Id.*

Many important policy and legal changes have occurred through executive orders. For example, President Lincoln emancipated slaves; President Truman integrated the armed forces; President Eisenhower desegregated schools; Presidents Kennedy and Johnson barred racial discrimination in federal housing, hiring, and contracting; President Reagan barred the use of federal funds for abortion advocacy (which President Clinton reversed); President Clinton fought a war in Yugoslavia; President Obama closed the "gun show loophole," and President Trump attempted to close our borders to certain immigrants. All of these significant events occurred because of an executive order.

Executive orders are legitimate exercises of executive power. Congress gives agencies considerable leeway in implementing and administering federal statutes and programs. This leeway leaves gaps for the executive to fill and ambiguities for the executive to interpret. When Congress fails to spell out the details of how a law should be executed, the door is left open for a president to provide those details, and executive orders are one way to do so.

If a president deviates from "congressional intent" or exceeds the constitutional powers delegated to the executive, the executive order can be invalidated in court. For example, when President Truman seized control of the nation's steel mills in an effort to settle labor disputes that arose after World War II, the Supreme Court held that the seizure was unconstitutional and exceeded presidential powers, because neither the Constitution nor any statute authorized the President to seize private businesses to settle labor disputes. *Youngstown Sheet & Tube Co. v. Sawyer*, 343 U.S. 579 (1952). Notably, this outcome was unusual. Generally, the Court is fairly tolerant of executive orders. *See, e.g., Korematsu v. United States*, 323 U.S. 214 (1944) (upholding the constitutionality of E.O. 9066, which ordered Japanese Americans into internment camps during World War II); *see generally*, Erica Newland, Note, *Executive Orders in Court*, 124 YALE L.J. 2026 (examining 700 cases from the Supreme Court and D.C. Circuit Court addressing the validity of various executive orders).

Let's look more closely at a specific executive order. In 1980, President Reagan campaigned on a platform of deregulation. Once elected, he issued Executive Order 12291. This executive order directed all executive agencies to perform a regulatory analysis assessing the costs and benefits of any "major" proposed regulation. E.O. 12291, 3 C.F.R. § 127 (1982). One of Reagan's purposes for issuing this executive order was to limit what he considered to be excessive regulation.

Although this executive order came from a Republican president, each president since Reagan has reissued this same order, albeit with slight changes. Former President Clinton issued Executive Order (E.O.) 12866, which mostly mirrored President Reagan's order; however, he changed the term "major rule" to "significant action." Next, former President George W. Bush adopted Clinton's order, but also issued two additional executive orders that slightly amended E.O. 12866; it is importantly to note that one of these orders added non-legislative rules to the order's coverage. E.O. 13422, 72 Fed. Reg. 2763 (2007). When President Obama took office, he repealed the two Bush orders, E.O. 13497, 74 Fed. Reg. 6113 (2009), and amended E.O. 12866 to allow agencies to consider not only monetary costs and benefits of "significant actions," but "human dignity" and "fairness" as well. Today, Executive Order 12866 is a fixture of executive agency rulemaking.

E.O. 12866 provides guiding principles that executive agencies (independent agencies are mostly exempt) must follow when developing regulations that will have an economic effect of at least $100 million. Pursuant to the order, agencies may promulgate regulations only when the regulations are "required by law," "necessary to interpret the law," or "are made necessary by compelling public need, such as material failures of private markets to protect or improve the health and safety of the public, the environment, or the well-being of the American people." E.O. 12866 § 1(a), 58 Fed. Reg. 51735 (October 4, 1993). Pursuant to Executive Order 12866, agencies must follow specific procedural steps when developing regulatory priorities, including the following: (1) identifying the problem the regulation was intended to address, including "the failures of private markets or public institutions that warrant new agency action"; (2) determining whether the problem could be addressed through modifications to existing regulations or laws; (3) assessing alternatives to regulation, such as economic incentives; (4) considering "the degree and nature of the risks posed by various substances or activities" within the agency's jurisdiction; (5) fashioning regulations "in the most cost-effective manner"; (6) assessing the costs and benefits, such that benefits justify the costs; (7) basing decisions "on the best reasonably obtainable scientific, technical, economic, and other information"; (8) recommending performance-based solutions rather than behavioral ones, when possible; (9) consulting with state, local, and tribal governments and assessing the impacts of regulations on these local governments; (10) avoiding duplications and inconsistencies among federal agencies; (11) minimizing the burdens; (12) considering the cumulative costs of regulation; and (13) writing all regulations in language that the general public can easily understand. E.O. 12866 §§ 1(b)(1)–(12), 58 Fed. Reg. 51735 (October 4, 1993).

Most important, in deciding whether regulation is necessary, agencies must assess the costs and benefits of the alternatives, "including the alternative of not regulating." E.O. 12866 § 1(a), 58 Fed. Reg. 51735 (October 4, 1993). "[U]nless [the] statute requires another regulatory approach," agencies must choose the regulatory path that maximizes net benefits. *Id.* Once an agency has completed its analysis, the agency submits the proposed regulation along with its analysis of that regulation to the Office of Information and Regulatory Affairs (OIRA). OIRA is responsible for overseeing the Federal Government's regulatory, paperwork, and information resource management activities and is located within the Office of Management and Budget (OMB). OMB is located within the executive office and is very closely aligned with the president and his or her policies. OIRA will review the agency's proposed rule and analysis to ensure compliance with E.O. 12866; in simple terms, OIRA acts as gatekeeper for the promulgation of all significant regulations.

E.O. 12866 imposes regulatory planning measures. All agencies, including independent agencies, must produce a semi-annual *regulatory agenda* of all regulations under development or review. Pursuant to another executive order, E.O. 12291, the agencies provide their agenda in April and October of each year; a requirement that Congress partially codified in the Regulatory Flexibility Act. 5 U.S.C. § 602(a). Each regulatory agenda includes a summary of the action to be taken, the agency's legal authority for acting, legal deadlines, if any, and an agency contact. E.O. 12866 § 1, 58 Fed. Reg. 51735 (October 4, 1993). An example of the 2012 Department of Health and Human Services regulatory agenda can be found at 77 Fed. Reg. 7946 (February 13,

2012), available at http://www.gpo.gov/fdsys/pkg/FR-2012-02-13/pdf/2012 -1647.pdf.

In addition, pursuant to E.O. 12866, all agencies must produce a *regulatory plan*, which identifies the most significant regulatory activities the agency has planned for the upcoming year. E.O. 12866 § 1(c), 58 Fed. Reg. 51735 (October 4, 1993). While the regulatory *agenda* includes *all* proposed actions, the regulatory *plan* includes only the most important proposed actions. The agency must explain how the action relates to the president's priorities, determine anticipated costs and benefits, provide a summary of the legal basis for the action, and include a statement of why the action is needed. Regulatory plans are forwarded to OIRA on June 1 of every year. OIRA reviews the plans for consistency with the president's priorities, the requirements of E.O. 12866, and the regulatory agendas of other agencies.

OIRA publishes the regulatory agendas and plans together in the Unified Agenda, which is available to the public online: http://reginfo.gov. Each edition of the Agenda includes the regulatory agendas from all federal entities that currently have regulations under development or review. In addition, the fall edition of the Agenda includes the agencies' regulatory plans. The Agenda is an integral part of the federal regulatory process. Its semiannual publication enables regulated entities, the public, companies, and other interested persons to understand and prepare for new rules that are planned or under development. The Agenda provides important information to agency heads, centralized reviewers, and the public at large, thereby serving the values of open government.

Finally, at the beginning of each planning period, the director of OMB convenes a meeting with the regulatory advisors and agency heads to coordinate regulatory priorities for the coming year. E.O. 12866 § 1(c)(1)(F)(2), 58 Fed. Reg. 51735 (October 4, 1993).

While E.O. 12866 is the most prominent executive order requiring regulatory analysis, it is by no means the only analysis requirement to come from the executive office. Over the years, presidents have required agencies to perform many different analyses. *See, e.g.,* E.O. 12630, 47 Fed. Reg. 30959 (1982) (requiring agencies to analyze the impact of proposed and final regulations on state and local governments); E.O. 13175, 65 Fed. Reg. 67249 (2000) (requiring agencies to analyze the impact of proposed and final regulations on tribal governments).

### c. Agencies

Agencies may and often do choose to use procedures in addition to those required by the APA. For example, in our case study above, the EPA opted to have oral hearings, which are not required during a notice and comment rulemaking, unless Congress so provides. Further, agencies by rule often prohibit ex parte communications during rulemaking. Hence, always remember to look at the specific agency's rules as a source of additional procedures.

---

## Checkpoints

- There is a fundamental distinction between rulemaking and adjudication, which is critically important in administrative law.

- Because those affected by agency rules can be meaningful participants in the development of those rules, rulemaking procedures advance sound decision-making and accountable government.

- Agencies that have power both to make rules and to adjudicate cases usually can decide which of these processes to use when adopting new policies.

- There are four types of rulemaking procedures: formal, informal, hybrid, and publication.

- Formal rulemaking is rare and resembles formal adjudication under sections 556 and 557.

- Most rulemaking is informal rulemaking under section 553. This section contains the minimum rulemaking procedures, known as notice and comment procedures.

- Congress is increasingly adding procedures in addition to the section 553 procedures to produce rulemaking that is less than formal but more than informal rulemaking; we call rulemaking with additional procedures hybrid rulemaking.

- Some rules are exempt from section 553. Rules regarding military and foreign affairs functions and internal management activities are exempt from all of the section 553 requirements. Interpretive rules, policy statements, rules of procedure, and good cause excepted rules are exempt from the notice and comment requirements of section 553, but remain subject to the publication requirements.

- While agencies may initiate rulemaking on their own, citizens may also petition an agency to promulgate a rule. If the agency denies the petition or unreasonably delays making a decision on the petition, the citizen may file suit.

- Ex parte communications are not prohibited during informal rulemaking because agency officials are acting more like legislators than like judges.

- Executive orders, other statutes, and an agency's own procedural rules augment the minimal rulemaking procedures in the APA. Under *Vermont Yankee*, courts may not add procedures beyond those that come from these sources.

# Chapter 3

# Adjudication

---

---

## A. The Nature of Adjudication

Adjudication is the second great procedure upon which the APA is based. Adjudication is at once more familiar and in some ways more complex than the rulemaking model we looked at in Chapter 2. Adjudication is more familiar to us because it more closely resembles what courts do. Indeed, many of its procedural requirements will be familiar to law students who have learned about case law in other law school courses (not to mention those who have watched the endless stream of courtroom trials that television and movies provide).

Professor Lon Fuller wrote the classic law review article regarding adjudication: Lon Fuller, *The Forms and Limits of Adjudication*, 92 HARV. L. REV. 353 (1978). Professor Fuller wrote that adjudication is distinct because of the way parties participate. He contrasted participation in adjudication with participation in other forms of social ordering, such as elections (in which we participate by voting) and contracts (in which we participate by negotiating). In adjudication, parties participate by presenting proof and reasoned arguments to resolve a dispute according to a preexisting principle of law. From this perspective, an ideal adjudication system would provide the following five guarantees.

First, an ideal adjudication system would guarantee the parties an agreed set of legal principles that functions as the substantive criteria for resolving the dispute. These agreed principles may be specific, as provided in a statute, or they may be general, as provided by common law doctrines. The parties accept that the principles are correct and controlling (assuming they apply). In addition to serving as substantive criteria for resolving the dispute, the principles identify the issues, shape the discussion of those issues, and define what proof and arguments are relevant to resolving those issues.

Second, an ideal adjudication system would guarantee each of the parties a meaningful opportunity to present proof and arguments to support his or her side of the dispute. Having advocates on either side of the dispute independently present their position, rather than having the decision-maker assemble all of the facts and arguments, guards against what Fuller called "the natural human tendency to judge too swiftly in terms of the familiar that which is not yet fully known." *Id.* at 383.

Third, an ideal adjudication system would guarantee the parties that the deciding official is obligated to listen to and consider the argument and proof presented. The decision-maker in an election (the voter) may sleep through a political speech intended to influence the vote, yet we would not be concerned. But a judge in an adjudicative proceeding must pay attention during the proceeding.

Fourth, an ideal adjudication system would guarantee the parties that the deciding official will resolve the dispute exclusively on the basis of the agreed-upon principles and the proof and argument presented. This guarantee gives real meaning to the phrase *opportunity to participate.* Further, this guarantee minimizes the risk that facts outside the record or considerations beyond the agreed principles will impact the decision.

Fifth, an ideal adjudication system would guarantee the parties that the final decision will be accompanied by reasons. Requiring a statement of reasons disciplines the decisional process itself. Judges have been known to say that a particular decision initially seemed correct but "wouldn't write." A required statement of reasons has three additional benefits: it exposes the decision's rationale to professional critique, it communicates to the parties that their participation was meaningful, and, in a precedential system, the statement of reasons provides guidance for future decisions.

You are no doubt unconsciously aware of these guarantees in judicial adjudication, even if you were not consciously aware of them. Administrative adjudication, like judicial adjudication, also incorporates these guarantees.

In contrast, the legislative process does not incorporate these guarantees. In the legislative process, there is no *ex ante* set of governing principles.

Legislation is based on policy preferences of the legislators and the people they represent. And those policy preferences may change radically from one legislative session to another. Moreover, in the legislative process, there is no guarantee that those interested in the legislation will have an opportunity to present proof or argument. The legislature may hold legislative hearings, but the content of those hearings is wholly at the discretion of legislators and intended more to inform legislators than to allow advocates to speak. Also, in the legislative process, there is no legal obligation on the part of a legislator to consider or weigh any views of the public that may be expressed. Legislators can wholly disregard any presentations made and are free to collect and use information from any source they choose with or without notice or any opportunity to respond. Finally, in the legislative process, there is no need for legislators to explain their decisions. These guarantees are similarly absent in administrative rulemaking, as you learned in the last chapter.

While administrative adjudication is similar to judicial adjudication, it is also different. Three such differences are important. First, there is a difference in volume. Federal agency adjudication takes place millions of times each year, as compared to the thousands of cases courts hear. The pressure from this volume will sometimes require simpler and faster procedures than are typical in courtrooms.

Second, there are many different types of adjudications, and those differences may call for quite different ways of structuring the proof and argument process. For example, consider the procedural design implications of these different types of adjudications:

- An agency is trying to stop what it regards as unlawful conduct by a party.
- An agency is deciding whether to confer or deny a benefit on a party.
- An agency is deciding whether to grant a party permission to engage in conduct.

These different types of adjudications present different problems to resolve. The differences affect whether the parties will be adversarial, whether the disputed issues will focus more on legislative facts or adjudicative facts, and whether the consequences of the decision will affect individuals other than the parties. These differences require different hearing processes.

Third, the person making the final decision in agency adjudication is rarely the neutral generalist judge we expect to see presiding in a courtroom. In some manner, our adjudicatory design must guarantee the parties meaningful hearings and objective decisions while at the same time allowing the agency to bring its technical expertise and political mission into the process.

Despite these three major differences, administrative and judicial adjudications have much in common, including similar goals. An obvious first goal is factual accuracy. Adjudicatory procedures that are too hurried, that rely on inference and impression rather than on reliable evidence, and that reduce or eliminate adversity might affect accuracy. Most of the procedures we will discuss below dealing with evidence, burdens of proof, cross-examination, internal appeals, and the qualifications of the adjudicator have fact-finding accuracy as their principal objective.

But fact-finding accuracy can be expensive, and we live in a world of resource constraints, especially for agencies, which resolve a large number of adjudications. So cost and efficiency must not be sacrificed entirely for accuracy. For example, eliminating or reducing cross-examination in an adjudication will surely lower costs, but it might impede the goal of factual accuracy. Similarly, giving parties the opportunity to appear with counsel increases cost, but its absence may reduce accuracy. The goal in administrative adjudication is to maximize accuracy while minimizing cost. Applying this goal, one would ask whether cross-examination could be limited to situations where the issues in dispute make cross-examination especially useful. Could the participation of counsel be limited to narrowing and sharpening the issues? The effort to seek accuracy at a lower cost is present in many of the procedures we will discuss below.

Accuracy and lower cost do not exhaust the list of factors to be considered. In our culture, procedures must be viewed as fair to those affected. Fairness is a principle deeply embedded in our legal culture. Hamlet's complaint about the "insolence of office" is a palpable concern. People expect officials to deal with parties fairly and openly and to give them meaningful opportunities to participate and to provide rational explanations of the action taken. For a thoughtful discussion of some of these criteria, *see* Roger C. Cramton, *A Comment on Trial-Type Hearings in Nuclear Power Plant Siting*, 58 Va. L. Rev. 585, 592–93 (1972).

We will discuss these competing goals in the discussion below. Consider the degree to which the procedures further each goal.

# B. The Sources of Procedural Requirements in Adjudication

Where does a regulated entity look to find the procedural requirements for agency adjudications? A regulated entity must examine a number of sources, including the APA, the agency's enabling statute, other relevant statutes, the agency's rules, and the due process clause of the U.S. Constitution. In this chapter, we will focus principally on the APA and the requirements it imposes. In Chapter 4, we will examine the due process clause and the requirements it imposes. Do not, however, forget to check whether the agency's enabling statute, other statutes, or the agency's rules require procedures in addition to those required by the APA.

## C. The APA's Requirements

### 1. When the APA's Procedural Requirements Apply

The APA requires an agency to use different procedures depending on whether the adjudication is formal or informal. Let's look at the way that the APA is structured. We examined part of the APA's structure in our discussion of rulemaking in Chapter 2. (See Figure 2.1 in that chapter.) Figure 3.1 expands Figure 2.1 to include both rulemaking and adjudication.

You will notice that there are only four APA procedural tracks: (1) formal rulemaking, (2) informal rulemaking, (3) formal adjudication, and (4) informal adjudication. Hybrid rulemaking is created when laws other than the APA add additional procedures, typically, but not always, to informal rulemaking.

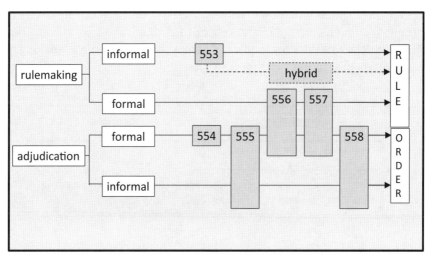

**Figure 3.1** Four Types of Rulemaking and Adjudication Procedures

For formal adjudications, five sections of the APA (sections 554–558) are relevant. (For informal adjudications, only sections 555 and 558 are relevant.) For the procedures in these five sections to apply to an adjudication, two preliminary tests must be met. First, the proceeding must be an "adjudication" as defined in the APA. Second, Congress must be clear in the statute authorizing the agency to adjudicate that the legislature intended for the agency to use these formal adjudication procedures. The next two sections discuss these two tests, starting with the APA's definition of "adjudication."

### a. The APA's Definition of Adjudication

In Chapter 2 we distinguished rulemaking from adjudication. You may recall that section 551(5) defines "rulemaking" as the "agency process for formulating, amending, or repealing a rule." Further, a "rule" is defined by section 551(4) as "the whole or part of an agency statement of general . . . applicability and future effect." APA § 551(4).

Similarly, section 551(7) of the APA defines "adjudication" as the "agency process for the formulation of an order." APA § 551(7). Further, an order is defined by § 551(6) as the "whole or part of a final disposition . . . of an agency in a matter other than rulemaking but including licensing." APA § 551(6). As Figure 3.2 below shows, the APA's definition of "order" is residual; "order" covers every *final* agency action that is not rulemaking.

Note the importance of the requirement that there be a "final disposition." Many agency activities are neither rulemaking nor adjudication. For example, agency investigations, planning, research, legislative activities, and advice to the public about regulatory matters are neither adjudication nor rulemaking. Therefore, the APA does not require an agency to follow either rulemaking or adjudication procedures for these activities.

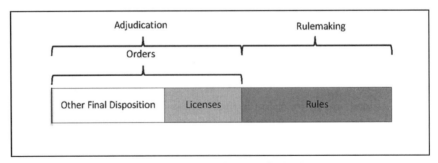

**Figure 3.2** The APA's Definition of Adjudication

Pursuant to the APA's definitions, an "adjudication" is the agency process for formulating a decision of "particular" applicability and "present" effect. You should think of agency rulemaking as akin to a legislature enacting legislation and agency adjudication as akin to a court conducting a trial or hearing. By using rulemaking, an agency crafts a general rule to address a general problem, which will apply to all regulated entities and take effect after the rule's promulgation and publication processes. In contrast, by using adjudication, an agency crafts an order to address a specific problem that will apply to only the specific regulated entities before the agency in the administrative proceeding and has retroactive as well as future effect.

As mentioned, the APA's definition of "adjudication" includes licensing. Licensing is a special kind of adjudication. In it, a citizen or entity asks for permission to engage in a certain kind of conduct. The APA broadly defines "license" to include "an agency permit, certificate, approval, registration, charter, membership, statutory exemption or other form of permission." APA § 551(8). The APA further provides that "licensing" includes the "grant, renewal, denial, revocation, suspension, annulment, withdrawal, limitation, amendment, modification, or conditioning of a license." APA § 551(9).

As we proceed through the sections of the APA identifying formal adjudication procedures, we will see that initial licensing is treated differently in several ways from other licensing proceedings. For example, section 554's separation of functions and *ex parte* communication limitations do not apply to initial licensing proceedings. Also, section 556's requirement of cross-examination is less strict in cases of initial licensing. Finally, section 557's requirements about who may issue an initial decision in an adjudication is considerably more flexible in the case of an initial licensing proceeding.

There are several reasons for these differences in initial licensing proceedings. Unlike a license revocation case, the *parties* to an initial licensing case are not generally adversaries. Because they are not adversaries, there is little need for the kinds of protection that adversarial proceedings require. Additionally, the *issues* in an initial licensing case are more similar to the issues in rulemaking. For example, when an applicant seeks an initial license to operate a nuclear reactor, the main issue may be whether society needs another nuclear reactor, not whether the applicant satisfies the statutory requirements. To resolve the main issue requires general policy analysis and predictions about the future that are better addressed in the rulemaking process, because the issue does not depend upon applicants' technical skills, its financial responsibility, the quality of its equipment, or its history of complying with regulations. These latter issues are classically adjudicatory because they are historical, personal facts about the applicants for which formal adjudicatory procedures are more appropriate.

By exempting initial licensing from some of the formal adjudicatory procedures, the drafters wanted to ensure that agencies would not be prevented from considering the broader policy-based issues. *See* Attorney General's Manual on the Administrative Procedure Act 50–53 (1947).

Thus, for the formal adjudication APA procedures to apply, the process the agency is using must be adjudication. As we will see next, Congress must also intend for the agency to use formal procedures. We look at that issue next.

### b. Congressional Intent to Require Formal Procedures

For formal adjudicatory procedures to apply, not only must the proceeding be an adjudication, as defined in the APA, but Congress must clearly express its intent in another statute that the agency use such procedures. Pursuant to section 554(a), the formal adjudicatory procedures apply only to adjudications required "to be determined on the record after opportunity for an agency hearing." Section 554 provides:

Adjudications

(a) This section applies, according to the provisions thereof, in every case of adjudication required by statute to be determined on the record after opportunity for an agency hearing . . .

In short, the APA itself does not require formal adjudicative procedures; rather, Congress must specify that formal adjudication is required in the agency's statute authorizing adjudicatory powers. When Congress includes such a requirement, then the APA identifies the procedures that are required. So, how does Congress make its intent clear?

We discussed a similar issue in Chapter 2 regarding when formal versus informal rulemaking procedures were required. We learned that the Supreme Court interpreted section 553 literally in *United States v. Florida East Coast Railway,* 410 U.S. 224 (1973). In that case, the Court held that enabling statutes that merely require an agency to issue a rule "after a hearing" do not trigger formal rulemaking. *Id.* at 238. Rather, language similar to the full phrase, "on the record after opportunity for an agency hearing" is necessary to trigger formal rulemaking.

A similar approach applies to adjudication. To determine whether an agency must use formal procedures to adjudicate a case, a court will look at the agency's interpretation of the language in its enabling statute. In doing so, the court will apply *Chevron* analysis (from *Chevron U.S.A., Inc. v. Natural Res. Def. Council, Inc.*, 467 U.S. 837 (1984)), which we will study in detail in the Chapter 6. To apply *Chevron*, a court will determine first whether Congress was clear as to which type of hearing was required (meaning that the court will ask whether Congress used the magic language or its equivalent in the enabling statute), and if not, the court will determine, second, whether the agency's interpretation of the language as requiring or not requiring formal procedures was reasonable. *Dominion Energy v. Johnson*, 443 F.3d 12, 16 (1st Cir. 2006) (overruling an earlier case establishing a presumption in favor of formal adjudication); *Chemical Waste Mgmt, Inc. v. EPA*, 873 F.2d 1477, 1482 (D.C. Cir. 1989) (applying *Chevron*).

Agencies often prefer to use informal adjudicatory procedures because the APA requires so few procedures for informal adjudication. Hence, agencies will likely not find that their enabling statute requires formal procedures absent language close to the magic language. Thus, unless Congress uses words virtually identical to the magic language from APA § 554(a) in the agency's enabling statute, — "on the record after opportunity for an agency hearing" — an agency's decision to use informal adjudicatory procedures will be upheld. For a discussion of cases on the so-called section 554(a) trigger, see William S. Jordan III, Chevron *and Hearing Rights: an Unintended Combination*, 61 ADMIN. L. REV. 249 (2009) (criticizing the use of *Chevron* analysis for interpreting section 554(a)).

As a result of the lower courts' approach to this issue, federal agencies conduct thousands of adjudications annually that do not trigger APA formal hearing procedures because these adjudications are authorized by statutes in which the magic words "on the record after opportunity for agency hearing" or their equivalent do not appear. We will discuss what the APA and other sources do require in Part E, "Informal Adjudication." More importantly, we will explore the Due Process Clause's procedural constraints on informal hearings in Chapter 4.

### c. Exceptions to Formal Adjudication

Section 554(a) identifies six types of formal adjudications for which formal procedures do not apply. These six include "(1) a matter subject to a subsequent trial of the law and the facts de novo in a court; (2) the selection or tenure of an employee, other than administrative law judge; (3) proceedings in which decisions rest solely on inspections, tests, or elections; (4) the conduct of military or foreign affairs functions; (5) cases in which an agency is acting as an agent for a court; and (6) the certification of worker representatives." APA § 554(a).

It makes sense to exclude these types of issues from formal adjudication. For example, an adjudication regarding whether a public employee should retain his or her position is an issue better addressed by special civil service procedures. Similarly, an adjudication involving the strength of an airplane wing (or, for that matter, your qualifications to practice law) may be better handled by test results rather than by trial.

Two things to remember about these exclusions: first, they are narrowly interpreted, as all exceptions to statutes are. Second, even though these proceedings are excluded from formal adjudication procedures, other statutes or agency regulations may impose procedural requirements equal to or more rigorous than the APA's.

## 2. What the APA Requires

Assuming an agency must conduct a formal adjudication, what procedures does the APA require for formal adjudications? The discussion below is organized in the order that an adjudication would typically proceed, beginning with the notice, which is similar to a complaint, and ending with the process for a regulated entity to appeal an adverse agency decision.

### a. Notice

Section 554(b) requires agencies to notify "[p]ersons entitled to notice of an agency hearing" of where and when the hearing will occur. It is important to note that the APA does not define who is entitled to notice; rather, other statutes and the Due Process Clause of the Constitution identify these persons.

Section 554(b) further requires that such notice be timely and identify the matters of fact alleged, the relevant law and legal authority, and the agency's jurisdiction to hold the hearing. Due Process also requires that the notice be adequate. APA § 554(b). Notice is adequate when it is complete enough, or sufficient, to fairly apprise interested parties of an agency action that will affect their interests. *NLRB v. Local Union No. 25*, 586 F.2d 959, 961 (2d Cir. 1978); *Southwest Sunsites, Inc. v. FTC*, 785 F2d 1431, 1435 (9th Cir. 1986). In other words, notice is sufficient when the regulated entity knows what it did wrong and can respond to those allegations. *See, e.g., John D. Copanos & Sons, Inc. v. FDA*, 854 F.2d 510, 521 (D.C. Cir. 1988) (holding that notice was sufficient despite coming "perilously close to . . . denying the applicant a meaningful opportunity to respond" to the agency's allegations).

Section 554(c) requires the agency to give all interested parties opportunity to submit facts, arguments, and offers of settlement so long as time and the public interest permit it; however, the agency need not give notice to such parties. This latter constraint gives the agency considerable discretion: do not be surprised if an agency exercises this discretion to limit participation.

### b. The Presiding Officer

Who presides over an agency adjudication? Section 556(b) of the APA provides that one of three individuals shall preside at the hearing: (1) the agency, (2) one or more members of the body which comprises the agency, or (3) one or more administrative law judges (ALJs). This provision is an important one and represents a compromise dating back to when the APA was drafted.

At the beginning of the nineteenth century, "examiners" presided over most agency proceedings. Agencies hired examiners directly. Hence, these examiners were not independent, in the sense that the agencies for which they worked controlled their assignments, their compensation, their promotions, and their retention. Indeed, some examiners served completely at the pleasure of their superiors and had no job security whatsoever. Hence, judicial "independence" and "impartiality" were not an assured part of the administrative process. *See generally* Russell Weaver & Linda D. Jellum, *Neither Fish nor Fowl: Administrative Judges in the Modern Administrative State*, 28 WINDSOR Y.B. ACCESS JUST. 243 (2010) (discussing the change from examiners to ALJs).

By the 1930s, legal commentators began to raise serious concerns about the status of these examiners, as well as about the examiners' ability to decide cases fairly, independently, and impartially. A central tenet of the criticism was that decisions were being made not by independent life-tenured judges, as in the federal court system, but by agency employees. Even if these employees were "experts," they were neither objective nor independent. Rather, they were viewed by many (especially the bar) as mission-oriented servants of the political appointees at the head of the agency. In 1934, for example, the American Bar Association's (ABA) Special Committee on Administrative Law criticized the fact that some examiners exercised both prosecutorial and adjudicative functions. REPORT OF THE SPECIAL COMMITTEE ON ADMINISTRATIVE LAW, 57 ANNU. REP. A.B.A. 539, 545 (1934). However, separation of functions and status was not the only concern. Even had examiners been functionally separate from their agencies, their decisions were not final and could be overruled by agency superiors.

To respond to the criticism, the drafters of the APA sought balance. On the one hand, they wanted to ensure that agency decisions would be based on employee expertise. On the other hand, they wanted to ensure that when agency proceedings could severely affect the interests of private individuals, those individuals would be entitled to an objective decision-making process.

Their dilemma was how to meet both goals. Figure 3.3 shows three possible approaches, or models, to resolving this dilemma.

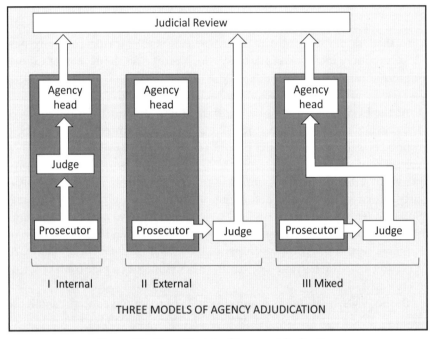

**Figure 3.3** Three Models of Agency Adjudication

With the *Internal* model, the prosecutor, decision-maker, and agency head (who reviews the decision-maker's decision) are all agency employees. The internal model ensures that an agency's political and technical expertise are fully accessible at each phase of an adjudication because all individuals who are involved are agency employees. But while the expertise goal is furthered, the objectivity goal suffers. A citizen whose license is revoked pursuant to this process may feel like a character in a Kafka novel because all phases of the process favor the government.

The *External* model addresses the Kafka problem. With an external model, the decision-maker is not an employee of the agency. Because the decision-maker is not an employee of the agency, the objectivity goal is furthered. This furthering, however, comes with a cost: reduced agency expertise.

Finally, the *Mixed* model is a compromise and the one that the drafters of the APA adopted. In the mixed model, the decision-maker is located outside of the agency to a degree (which we will explore in a minute); however, the independent decision-maker's decisions are subject to agency review. The mixed model furthers objectivity because it insulates the decision-maker from the agency during the decision making process. At the same time, the mixed model retains agency expertise by subjecting the decision-maker's decision to the agency review.

During the debate on enacting the APA, suggestions were offered regarding how to reform the system that was then in effect: the internal model. Some argued that Congress should create an independent federal administrative *court* that would hear only administrative cases. Others suggested that Congress should create an independent administrative *judiciary*—a central panel of judges—to adjudicate administrative matters. Some states, such as Georgia, follow this model. In 1946, with the passage of the APA, Congress ultimately rejected both of these external models and opted for the mixed model instead.

The mixed model Congress adopted included a number of protective components, which will be explored in more detail below. But to summarize them here: First, Congress sought to prevent agency officials from acting as lawmaker, investigator, prosecutor, and jury in the same case. To do so, the APA provided that "hearing examiners" (as they were first called) could not be responsible to, or subject to supervision by, anyone performing investigative or prosecutorial functions for an agency. *See* APA § 554(d)(2). The APA, thus, requires an agency to separate its prosecuting functions from its adjudicating functions. Any agency employee who investigates or prosecutes a case cannot supervise or direct the work of the decision-maker deciding the same case. In addition, individuals who investigate or prosecute a case cannot be part of the decision-making process. APA § 554(d). The APA also restricts some forms of ex parte communications. APA §§ 554(d)(1) and 557(d). With these changes, Congress altered the prior practice to mirror more closely the federal judicial process, but stopped short of adopting that process.

In addition, Congress altered the treatment of hearing examiners to more closely mirror the status of Article III judges. The centerpiece of the APA reform involved strengthening the job protections and status of the ALJs by giving them job protections designed to bolster their independence from the agency. Congress gave the role of hiring ALJs to the Office of Personnel Management (OPM). The OPM is exclusively responsible for examining, certifying, and compensating ALJs. The OPM determines the minimum experience needed for an individual to be an ALJ and evaluates applicants for the position (by conducting interviews, by administering a test to evaluate writing ability, by evaluating the experience of applicants, and by ranking eligible applicants). Despite these changes, however, agencies retained control over the ALJ they selected from the OPM's register and over the ALJ they hired.

Once hired, ALJs enjoy increased job protections and independence vis-à-vis pre-APA examiners. Although the APA did not grant ALJs the life tenure granted to Article III judges, the APA provided that ALJs can be removed only for cause or due to a reduction in the workforce. 5 U.S.C. § 7521. In addition, the APA requires that ALJ compensation be determined based on length of service, rather than on performance evaluations. *See generally* 5 U.S.C. § 5372; 5 U.S.C. § 4301(2)(D). As the Supreme Court later concluded, these changes made a significant difference in the status of ALJs:

> There can be little doubt that the role of the modern federal hearing examiner or administrative law judge within this framework is "functionally comparable" to that of a judge. His powers are often, if not generally, comparable to those of a trial judge . . . . More importantly, the process of agency adjudication is currently structured so as to assure that the hearing examiner exercises his independent judgment on the evidence before him, free from pressures by the parties or other officials within the agency.

*Butz v. Economou,* 438 U.S. 478, 513 (1978).

Today, there are close to 2,000 ALJs presiding over thousands of hearings in federal agencies. The ALJs are employed by the agency over whose hearings they preside, but ALJs have some independence from the agency as noted above. Of course, if agencies were permitted to appoint employees not protected from agency pressure to preside over formal adjudications, the APA would not function as its drafters intended. Hence, section 556(b) requires the agency to assign an ALJ to preside at formal adjudications unless the agency head or heads preside themselves (which happens rarely).

Finally, remember that section 556 applies only to formal adjudications, not informal adjudications. Administrative judges (AJs), who lack the status and independence of the ALJs, preside over informal adjudications; those adjudications are not required to be "on the record after opportunity for agency hearing." *See Conference on Fair and Independent Courts: A Conference on the State of the Judiciary, Appendix I: Tiers of Federal Judges,* 95 Geo. L. J. 1009, 1021–22 (2007).

As noted, ALJs are supposed to be impartial. APA § 556(b). But what if they are not? The process for seeking the disqualification of an ALJ or other agency decision-maker is similar to the process in a federal court. A party files an affidavit asserting personal bias on the part of the ALJ, and the agency (not the ALJ) then decides whether such bias exists. The agency's decision on this issue becomes part of the record for judicial review. Section 556(b) provides in full:

The functions of presiding employees and of employees participating in decisions in accordance with section 557 of this title shall be conducted in an impartial manner. A presiding or participating employee may at any time disqualify himself. On the filing in good faith of a timely and sufficient affidavit of personal bias or other disqualification of a presiding or participating employee, the agency shall determine the matter as a part of the record and decision in the case.

If an ALJ is biased against a party, that bias would be disqualifying. Similarly, if the ALJ has a pecuniary or other personal interest in the outcome of the case, that bias may be disqualifying. These reasons for disqualification are similar to those a party might raise against an Article III judge. However, ALJs are not neutral in the way that an Article III judge is neutral; ALJs are agency employees. And the agency has a substantive mission, which the ALJs must carry out. How do we balance an ALJ's fidelity to the agency's mission with a party's right to a fair hearing from a neutral decision-maker?

For example, a litigant might question whether an agency can be objective when the agency is the investigator, prosecutor, fact-finder, and judge all in one. As we noted in Chapter 1, the framers were concerned about locating these functions within one body. Because of the potential for injustice that might arise, the framers divided these powers among the branches. But the Constitution does not prohibit such commingling of functions in administrative agencies. As the Supreme Court stated in *Withrow v. Larkin*, 421 U.S. 35, 58 (1975), "the combination of investigative and adjudicative functions does not, without more, constitute a due process violation." In its reasoning, the Court presumed that public officials would be honest and recognized the agency's practical need to function effectively.

In addition, a litigant might question whether an ALJ's predisposition to rule in favor of the agency would be sufficient to disqualify the ALJ. These are tougher questions. If, on the one hand, the ALJ's predisposition relates to adjudicative facts, that predisposition may be disqualifying. For example, if Captain Green's commercial pilot's license is being revoked because of her allegedly poor eyesight, an ALJ who had made up his or her mind about the quality of Green's eyesight would presumably be disqualified.

If, on the other hand, the ALJ's prejudgment relates to legislative facts, that predisposition would not necessarily disqualify the ALJ. For example, if the agency has concluded that 20/20 vision is the appropriate standard for commercial pilot licensing, an ALJ who intends to apply that legal standard would likely not be disqualified. Similarly, an ALJ's prejudgment might not be disqualifying if it is about policies. For example, in *FTC v. Cement Institute*, 333

U.S. 683, 690–91 (1948), the Supreme Court reasoned that an administrative agency must study and decide relevant policies. To the potential pilot with 20/30 eyesight, of course, this prejudgment would be fatal to the case, but this kind of line drawing is precisely what Congress expects agencies to do. And ALJs must apply the law their agency promulgates.

Let's assume disqualifying bias exists. In the judicial world, when bias is successfully asserted against a judge, the remedy is simply to substitute another judge. Presumably a biased ALJ could similarly be replaced. But what if the decision-maker is the head of the agency (the administrator of a single-headed agency or the board or commission members in a multi-member body)? There simply is no substitute. If we always required a biased decision-maker to step down, then the public interest may be harmed. For example, if such bias meant that near-sighted Green would get a chance to control a jetliner despite her poor eyesight, the public riding in that plane might be at unnecessary risk. In such a case, the "rule of necessity" would likely be applied. Pursuant to this rule, the agency would be permitted to serve as the decision-maker despite the bias; however, the courts would likely scrutinize more closely any ensuing agency decision. *See generally* Thomas McKevitt, *The Rule of Necessity: Is Judicial Non-Disqualification Really Necessary?*, 24 HOFSTRA L. REV. 817 (1996) (discussing the rule of necessity in both its judicial and administrative forms).

### c. Separation of Functions

As we have seen, the federal Constitution separates the functions of judging, legislating, and prosecuting by placing each function in a different branch. But an administrative agency performs all three functions within one governmental unit. The Supreme Court has held that the constitution does not prohibit this combination of functions. *Withrow v. Larkin*, 421 U.S. 35, 49–50 (1975). But the lack of separation of these functions was one flaw the drafters of the APA tried to address. To provide some assurance that agency decision-making would be objective, Congress included provisions to separate the agency decision-makers from the agency investigators and prosecutors. Thus, section 554(d)(2) ensures that the agency officials who perform investigative or prosecutorial functions do not supervise or oversee ALJs, because these non-ALJs are likely to have a mindset that would be inconsistent with objective decision-making in specific cases. That section provides that an ALJ "may not . . . be responsible to or subject to the supervision or direction of an employee or agent engaged in the performance of investigative or prosecuting functions for an agency." APA § 554(d)(2).

In addition to limiting oversight, this section prohibits prosecutors and investigators from participating or advising the decision-maker in the decision of the case and in the internal review of the case except as witnesses or counsel in the public hearing itself. This restriction applies not only to the specific case, but also to any "factually related" cases, meaning different cases arising out of the same set of facts. Thus, the APA attempts to seal off prosecutors and investigators from decision-makers, unless the prosecutor or investigator is a participant in the hearing itself. *Id.*

The separation of functions prohibition does not apply to three types of adjudications: (1) proceedings involving applications for initial licenses; (2) proceedings involving the validity or application of rates, facilities, or practices of public utilities or carriers; and (3) proceedings involving the agency or a member or members of the body comprising the agency as the decision-maker. APA § 554(d)(2)(A)-(C). This section includes a provision prohibiting ex parte communications *from individuals within the agency* as well, which we will explore below in section C2g. For now, simply note that none of the section 554(d) limits regarding separation of functions and ex parte communications apply to the three adjudications just listed. In contrast, we will see later that section 557(d), which prohibits ex parte communications *from individuals outside the agency*, is *not* subject to these exceptions.

We have already discussed the first exception regarding proceedings involving applications for initial licensing. Such proceedings often turn on general, policy considerations (do we need another nuclear reactor?) rather than on contested facts (is this applicant for a license qualified?). For this reason, the separation of functions and internal ex parte limits are unnecessary.

The second exception applies to proceedings involving the validity or application of rates, facilities, or practices of public utilities and carriers. Because the APA includes ratemaking as a form of rulemaking, section 554(d)'s quintessentially adjudicative protections are unnecessary.

Finally, the third exception for proceedings where the agency is the decision-maker is necessary because of the organizational structure of the administrative agency. When you consider the agency as an organization, you notice that the agency head *is* the prosecutor and the investigator; in other words, those functions are being performed in the administrator's name and with the administrator's delegated authority. To apply the separation of functions provisions of section 554(d) to the head of the agency would not make sense. However, this exception is narrow and applies only to the agency head (e.g., the Administrator in an agency with a single head) or "members of the body comprising the agency" (e.g., the five commissioners of the FTC or the seven board members of the NLRB).

### d. ALJ Powers

Section 556(c) identifies an ALJ's powers to conduct hearings. Notably, an agency may by rule limit these powers. The APA provides that the "employee presiding at hearings may"

(1) administer oaths and affirmations;

(2) issue subpoenas authorized by law;

(3) rule on offers of proof and receive relevant evidence;

(4) take depositions or have depositions taken when the ends of justice would be served;

(5) regulate the course of the hearing;

(6) hold conferences for the settlement or simplification of the issues by consent of the parties or by the use of alternative means of dispute resolution as provided in subchapter IV of this chapter;

(7) inform the parties as to the availability of one or more alternative means of dispute resolution, and encourage use of such methods;

(8) require the attendance at any conference held pursuant to paragraph (6) of at least one representative of each party who has authority to negotiate concerning resolution of issues in controversy;

(9) dispose of procedural requests or similar matters;

(10) make or recommend decisions in accordance with section 557 of this title; and

(11) take other action authorized by agency rule consistent with this subchapter.

These 11 powers are similar to a trial judge's powers; however, there are a few differences. First, section 556(c)(2), concerning subpoenas, does not itself grant authority to an ALJ to issue subpoenas. Rather, that authority must be found in another statute or agency rule, as we will see in Chapter 7.

Second, sections 556(c)(6), (7), and (8) reflect Congress's preference that parties use dispute resolution. In 1990, Congress amended the APA specifically to authorize and encourage the use of alternative dispute resolution techniques. 5 U.S.C. §§ 571–583.

Third, section 556(c)(10) permits an ALJ to make an initial decision or recommend to the agency what that decision should be. We will look at initial and recommended decisions below in section C2i.

Fourth, and finally, it is important to keep in mind that an ALJ has an affirmative obligation to develop the record for the agency's subsequent review. Thus, when individuals are not represented by counsel (as would be typical in a Social Security disability case), the ALJ must act affirmatively to assure that the record contains all the relevant facts. Hence, it would not be unusual for the ALJ to question the parties or the witnesses in such a case. *See* Frank Bloch et al., *Developing a Full and Fair Evidentiary Record in a Nonadversary Setting [disability adjudications]*, 25 CARDOZO L. REV. 1 (2003). Indeed, an ALJ's failure to fulfill this obligation for a private party may violate due process. *Gjeci v. Gonzales*, 451 F.3d 416, 424 (7th Cir. 2006).

### e. The Right to Counsel

The APA addresses the rights of both witnesses and parties to have counsel at an administrative adjudication, whether that adjudication is formal or informal. The first sentence of section 555(b) provides that any person who is compelled to appear in person before an agency is entitled to be "accompanied, represented, and advised by counsel or, if permitted by the agency, by other qualified representative." Section 555(b) thus grants persons compelled to appear the right to counsel. Witnesses who appear in response to an agency subpoena are persons compelled to appear. Witnesses who voluntarily appear are not.

Witnesses who voluntarily appear and testify have no right to counsel under the APA. *In re Groban*, 352 U.S. 330, 332 (1957). Thus, if a voluntary witness has a right to counsel, that right must come from another statute, from the agency's own procedural rules, or from the Due Process Clause of the U.S. Constitution. Generally, witnesses have no constitutional right to counsel in administrative proceedings, but in some situations Due Process may require it. We will explore those situations in Chapter 4. In addition, voluntary witnesses have no right to receive a transcript of their testimony, while compelled witnesses do have that right. APA § 555(c). However, the transcript right is limited to evidence the witness provided. It does not include evidence other witnesses or parties provided. *Id.*

The APA grants only the right to be "accompanied, represented and advised" by counsel. APA § 555(b). These words have different meanings from agency to agency. Some agency procedural rules are quite restrictive. For example, the Federal Deposit Insurance Commission rules provide that "[a] ny person compelled or requested to provide testimony as a witness" is entitled to be represented by counsel in the agency's investigatory proceedings. 12 CFR § 308.148. Counsel may "(1) [a]dvise the witness before, during, and after such testimony; (2) [b]riefly question the witness at the conclusion of such testimony for clarification purposes; and (3) [m]ake summary notes during such testimony solely for the use and benefit of the witness." *Id.* While this rule allows witnesses to have legal representation, the attorney's role is quite limited for both voluntary and involuntary witnesses. The rule does not allow the attorney to object to questions, to make and argue objections for the record, or to cross-examine other witnesses. In the administrative context, these activities are not always understood to be included in the word "represented." *FCC v. Schreiber*, 329 F.2d 517, 526 (9th Cir. 1964); E. Stewart Moritz, *The Lawyer Doth Protest Too Much*, 72 U. Cinn. L. Rev. 1353, 1384–87 (2004).

In contrast, other agency procedural rules are more liberal. For example, the FTC rules permit voluntary witnesses to consult with counsel on each question, permit counsel to object on the record to some issues, to make brief statements in support of the objection, and to request that the witness be allowed to clarify any answers given at the completion of the examination. 16 CFR § 2.9. However, the presiding official retains discretion to regulate the course of the hearing and is specifically authorized to sanction attorneys for any behavior that is "dilatory, obstructionist or contumacious." *Id.* The Administrative Conference of the United States issued a report to encourage agencies to broaden the role of counsel representing voluntary witnesses. *See* Selected Reports of the Administrative Conference of the U.S., Sen. Doc. 24, 88th Cong. 1st Sess. at 223 (1963).

The second sentence of section 555(b) grants *parties* the right to appear in person in an agency proceeding by or with counsel, or to appear by or with another duly qualified representative. APA § 555(b). This provision has two parts.

First, individuals and entities who are parties have the right to appear personally in an "agency proceeding." Note that *agency proceeding* is defined in section 551 to include rulemaking, adjudication, and licensing. This right to appear personally does not apply when other sections of the APA prohibit personal appearances. APA § 555(a). For example, if an entity wishes to personally appear in an informal rulemaking and the agency has limited public participation in that rulemaking to provide written comments pursuant to section 553(c), that entity has no right to appear personally. Moreover, even in a formal adjudication, there may be times when the APA allows an agency to limit evidence to written evidence. *See, e.g.*, APA § 556(d) (providing that "[i]n rule making or determining claims for money or benefits or applications for initial licenses an agency may . . . adopt procedures for the submission of all or part of the evidence in written form.")

Second, the language entitles parties to appear "by or with" counsel or another representative. Presumably, "by" includes an opportunity for counsel to speak on behalf of the party, to examine witnesses, and to make objections. In other words, the section allows attorneys to be attorneys. But note that in informal adjudications, an attorney's role may be more limited. Chapter 4 will explore this issue further.

As for lawyer representatives, the agency has little discretion regarding who may represent a party. Any attorney in good standing can represent parties before federal agencies. 5 U.S.C. § 500. Agencies cannot impose additional restrictions on attorneys' rights to appear absent statutory authority to do so. For example, the Patent and Trademark Office has such statutory authority. *See generally* 35 U.S.C. § 32.

As for non-lawyer representatives, the agency does have discretion over who can practice before the agency. APA § 555(b) (providing that "[t]his subsection does not grant or deny a person who is not a lawyer the right to appear for or represent others before an agency or in an agency proceeding.").

### f. The Hearing

Section 555(b) gives *any interested person*, not just the parties, the right to appear before the agency to discuss any issue involved in a "proceeding," whether that proceeding be an adjudication, a licensing, or a rulemaking. The only explicit limitation in this section is that the person's right to appear may not impair the "orderly conduct of public business." APA § 555(b). Note, however, there is no requirement that the agency notify interested persons of a proceeding; only parties are entitled to notice. APA § 554(b).

Section 556(d) provides that the proponent of a rule or order has the burden of proof. This section puts the burden of proof on the party proposing something, which is generally the agency. For example, in an enforcement proceeding, the agency would have the burden of proof. However, when a private party seeks a license, the private party would have the burden of proof.

Under the federal rules of evidence, the term "burden of proof" can refer either to a party's obligation to produce some evidence on an issue, which is also called the *burden of production* or the *burden of going forward*. Alternatively, the term *burden of proof* can refer to the burden of establishing the issue, which is also called the *burden of persuasion*. For administrative hearings, the Supreme Court held that the phrase *burden of proof* refers to both the burden of production and the burden of persuasion. *Director, OWCP v. Greenwich Collieries*, 512 U.S. 267, 279 (1994).

The federal rules of evidence do not apply in administrative hearings; however, most ALJs have legal training. Hence, the rules are not irrelevant. Many ALJs prefer to follow the rules of evidence even though the APA gives agencies significant discretion. *See generally* Richard Pierce, *Use of Federal Rules of Evidence in Federal Agency Adjudications*, 39 ADMIN. L. REV. 1 (1987). The federal rules of evidence provide a framework for resolving evidentiary questions. For example, section 556(d) provides that "[a]ny oral or documentary evidence may be received, but the agency as a matter of policy shall provide for the exclusion of irrelevant, immaterial, or unduly repetitious evidence." Further, "[a] sanction may not be imposed or rule or order issued except on consideration of the whole record . . . which is supported by and in accordance with the reliable, probative, and substantial evidence." APA § 556(d). The rules of evidence help explain what evidence would be irrelevant, immaterial, unduly repetitious, reliable, probative, and substantial.

Unlike in judicial trials, hearsay is commonly admitted in administrative hearings. Because there is no jury and the ALJ is legally trained or at least experienced, the admission of hearsay evidence is less troubling in the administrative context. As we will see in Chapter 6, the factual findings in an agency's final order must be supported by "substantial evidence." APA §§ 556(d); 706(2)(E).

Hearsay evidence alone can be "substantial evidence" within the meaning of the APA judicial review provisions. First, the Supreme Court in *Consolidated Edison v. NLRB*, 305 U.S. 197, 229–30 (1938), held that there must be at least a residuum of "competent," non-hearsay evidence in the record to support an order. Then, in *Richardson v. Perales*, 402 U.S. 389, 410 (1971), the Supreme Court effectively overruled its *Consolidated Edison*'s so-called residuum rule. In *Richardson*, the Court upheld an order based entirely on uncorroborated hearsay. *Id.* Oddly, the Court failed to mention *Consolidated Edison*. Rather, in *Richardson*, the Court reasoned that there were a number of practical concerns agencies would face if hearsay could not be relied upon. *Id.* at 399. For example, some agencies have to process half a million claims annually based on medical records. *Id.* Relying on hearsay is practically necessary in these kinds of cases. In its reasoning, the Court concluded that the hearsay at issue in *Richardson* was reliable because it included the written reports from standard and routine medical examinations made by trained professionals. An order based on this kind of hearsay, the Court held, would not violate the fundamental fairness Due Process requires. *Id.* at 410.

Not only is hearsay admissible, but there is no absolute right either to cross-examination or to unlimited cross-examination in administrative proceedings. Section 556(d) allows the parties in formal adjudications to present their cases personally, to present rebuttal evidence, and to conduct cross-examination *if necessary*. APA § 556(d). The courts have held that a party seeking cross-examination has the burden to show that cross-examination is required for a "full and true disclosure of the facts." *Citizens Awareness Network v. United States*, 391 F.3d 338, 351 (1st Cir. 2004).

Section 556(d) further limits oral testimony for those claims involving benefits, money, and applications for initial licenses. An agency may, when a party will not be prejudiced thereby, adopt procedures for the submission of all or part of the evidence in these types of adjudications in written form. APA § 556(d). Sensibly, the drafters decided that agencies should be allowed to require written evidence rather than oral testimony to support claims for money or benefits. ATTORNEY GENERAL'S MANUAL ON THE ADMINISTRATIVE PROCEDURE ACT 78 (1947). In addition, when agencies decide cases involving initial licensing, the relevant evidence in support of an application is largely economic, technical, or statistical. Hence, written evidence may well be sufficient.

Additionally and oddly, section 556(d) allows an agency to limit oral testimony in formal *rulemaking* as well. Sections 556 and 557 govern the procedures of formal *rulemaking* as well as formal adjudication. Formal rulemaking occurs less frequently than formal adjudication. As we have seen, the relevant evidence in rulemaking may be economic or statistical; in such situations, agencies should be able to receive the evidence in written form rather than having a witness testify. While evidence submitted in written form cannot be challenged by cross-examination, the drafters did not think cross-examination was of particular value in resolving disputes over rulemaking issues. In any event, agencies must allow oral testimony in all proceedings when a party would be prejudiced otherwise.

### g. Prohibited Ex Parte Communications

As noted earlier, the APA limits ex parte communications in formal adjudications but not in informal adjudications. Section 551(14) defines ex parte communications as communications not on the public record and to which notice to all parties is not given. That section further makes clear that ex parte communications do not include status reports. The status report exception means that the agency can inform Congress, the president, and the public regarding the status of a rulemaking or an adjudication. But it also means that members of Congress and the executive branch can signal their views on a pending case or rule by the manner in which they inquire into the status of the case. *See* APA § 557(d)(2) (providing that "this subsection does not constitute authority to withhold information from Congress").

Two sections of the APA prohibit ex parte communications during formal proceedings: sections 554(d)(1) and 557(d)(1). In section C2d, you learned that section 554(d)(2) addressed the APA's restrictions related to *separation of functions*. Because section 554(d) addresses both separation of functions and ex parte communications, this section can be challenging to understand. However, it is important to grasp the distinctions. Above, we explored section 554(d)(2)'s separation of functions provisions. You may wish to reread it now. Here, we will explore section 554(d)(1)'s restrictions on ex parte communications. After exploring section 554(d)(1)'s restrictions on ex parte communications, we will explore section 557(d)(1)'s restrictions on ex parte communications.

Section 554(d)(1) provides: "an employee may not consult a person or party on a fact in issue, unless on notice and opportunity for all parties to participate." APA § 554(d)(1). This section limits the ALJ's ability to discuss *facts* in the case with any person or party, except in the presence of all other parties. This provision helps ensure that the ALJ's decision is made "on the record" and that any facts asserted by one party can be challenged by the other party. It applies to anyone inside or outside the agency and only to ex parte communications about facts in issue.

Section 554(d)'s ex parte prohibition does not apply to three types of adjudications: (1) proceedings involving applications for initial licenses; (2) proceedings involving the validity or application of rates, facilities, or practices of public utilities or carriers; and (3) proceedings involving the agency or a member or members of the body comprising the agency as the decision maker. APA § 554(d)(2)(A)-(C). Because section 554(d)'s restrictions on internal ex parte communication do not apply when the agency itself is the decision-maker, the agency head may communicate with relevant agency staff when making a final decision. The agency's ability to engage in internal ex parte communications allows the agency to benefit from staff expertise, but this benefit comes at a cost: perceived fairness. The Attorney General Manual suggests that agency heads do not engage in ex parte contact with agency investigators or prosecutors. ATTORNEY GENERAL'S MANUAL ON THE APA 56–57 (1947).

While the ex parte limitations in section 554(d)(1) were an important first attempt to address perceived unfairness, they proved to be insufficient. Section 554(d)(1) prohibited only ex parte communications related to facts. In 1970s, there were a number of cases involving agency ex parte communications with organizations outside of the agency attempting to influence the agency's rulemakings. *See, e.g., Environmental Defense Fund, Inc. v. Blum*, 458 F. Supp. 650, 660 (D.D.C. 1978) (involving an informal rulemaking proceeding); *Home Box Office, Inc. v. FCC*, 567 F.2d 9 (D.C. Cir.) (same), *cert. denied*, 434 U.S. 829 (1997). In 1976, with the Government in the Sunshine Act (Pub. L. No. 94-409), Congress added section 557(d)(1) to cover the perceived limitations of section 554(d)(1). Section 557(d)(1) prohibits ex parte communications regarding the merits of the case to individuals outside the agency, in formal proceedings.

Recall that section 554(d)(1) prohibits an ALJ from consulting ex parte "a person or a party" on a "fact in issue." APA § 554(d)(1). Section 557(d)(1) is narrower than section 554(d)(1) in one sense: section 557(d)(1) prohibits only contact with interested persons *outside* the agency. APA § 557(d)(1). But this section is also broader than section 554(d)(1) in a few ways. First, section 557(d) prohibits communications "relevant to the merits," not just those communications about "facts in dispute." APA § 557(d)(1). Thus, an agency decision-maker may not discuss facts, policy, or law with anyone outside the agency.

Second, section 557(d)(1) prohibits agency decision-makers from having such conversations only with "interested persons." APA § 557(d)(1). Courts have interpreted the phrase "interested persons" very broadly to include not only the parties to the case but also anyone who has an interest in the proceeding that is greater than the interest a general member of the public would have. For example, members of Congress or the White House are "interested persons." *Professional Air Traffic Controllers Org. v. FLRA*, 685 F.2d 547, 570 (D.C. Cir. 1982). Remember that the status report exception still applies, however.

Third, it is important to note that section 557(d)(1) is also broader in application than section 554(d)(1). Remember that section 554's ex parte prohibition does not apply to three types of adjudications: (1) proceedings involving applications for initial licenses; (2) proceedings involving the validity or application of rates, facilities, or practices of public utilities or carriers; and (3) proceedings involving the agency or a member or members of the body comprising the agency as the decision-maker. APA § 554(d)(2)(A)-(C). Section 557(d)(1) is not so limited. Section 557(d)(1) prevents the heads of an agency from having ex parte communications with "interested persons" outside the agency (but not with those persons inside the agency).

Like section 554(d)(1), section 557(d)(1) applies only to formal adjudications and formal rulemakings. Thus, the APA does not limit ex parte communications in either informal adjudication or informal rulemaking. Rather, if any limits exist, they come from another statute, an agency procedural rule, or the Due Process Clause. As noted in Chapter 2, there have been occasional due process limits applied to ex parte communications in informal proceedings when those proceedings involved "conflicting private claims to a valuable privilege." *Sangamon Valley v. United States*, 269 F.2d 221, 224 (D.C. Cir. 1959). Claims involving conflicting claims to a valuable privilege, like a license, more closely resemble adjudication than rulemaking, hence, the Due Process concern.

Because section 557(d) prohibits ex parte communications between an agency decision-maker and interested persons *outside* the agency, section 554(d)(1) is generally understood to apply only to communications between an ALJ and those *inside* the agency. Read in this way, section 554(d)(1) prohibits an ALJ from having ex parte communications with any members of the agency staff on issues of fact. If accurate, then is section 554(d)(2), which prohibits agency prosecutors and investigators from participating or advising in the decision, unnecessary? Or is the *consultation* prohibited in section 554(d)(1) different from the *participation* prohibited in section 554(d)(2)? The section is not a model of clarity.

While ex parte communications appear unseemly in court hearings, they may be less concerning during agency adjudications. You will remember that the drafters of the APA tried to ensure that agency expertise would be part of agency decision-making. And that expertise lies within the agency staff, not within the agency ALJs. What if the ALJ, after a hearing, consulted experts in the agency about the meaning or significance of the material in the hearing record? Would it be better for the parties if this consultation made the ALJ's initial decision more accurately reflect the agency's reasoning, so the parties would be on notice of the issues that had to be addressed on appeal? Or would that consultation unduly taint the decision-making process? The Attorney General's Manual on the APA suggested that section 554(d)(1) prohibits an ALJ from engaging in an ex parte discussion of facts in issue with any person during the *hearing* phase of the proceeding. But during the *decisional* phase, an ALJ can "obtain advice from or consult with agency personnel . . . [such as] the agency heads, supervisors of the [ALJ] and persons assigned to assist the [ALJ] in analyzing the record." ATTORNEY GENERAL'S MANUAL ON THE APA 55 (1947). But note, that is not what the text of section 554(d) actually says.

Unfortunately, neither the Supreme Court nor lower courts have clarified this issue. In dictum, the Court stated that section 554(d)(2) does apply to conferences between an ALJ and "any person or party, including other agency officials." *Butz v. Economou*, 438 U.S. 478, 514 (1978) (addressing qualified immunity of agency prosecutors). However, as dictum, this statement is not binding. And while lower courts have suggested that the ex parte prohibitions are not as strictly read in agency cases as in judicial cases, the question remains unanswered. *See, e.g., White v. Indiana Parole Bd.*, 266 F.3d 759, 766 (7th Cir. 2001).

Because of the lack of clear guidance, academics differ regarding whether ALJs can consult agency personnel during their decision-making stage. For example, one said that "internal [ALJ] contacts with other than prosecutors are not expressly prohibited [by the APA]," CHARLES KOCH, ADMINISTRATIVE LAW AND PRACTICE § 6.1 (3d ed. 2010), while another has said that "because section 554(d)(1) extends to consultations with 'any person,' an ALJ may not have such discussions with other agency personnel, regardless of their duties or lack of involvement in the case." KEITH WERHAN, PRINCIPLES OF ADMINISTRATIVE LAW § 5.1(b) (2014).

Assuming improper ex parte occurs, it should be remedied. The APA does provide a remedy for improper ex parte communications that occur during an adjudication. As a practical matter, the drafters concluded that the APA could not simply order the agency recipient of an unlawful ex parte communication to disregard it. Whether a jury can disregard an improper question is doubtful enough. It is even less likely that an official serving at the pleasure of the president could be asked to "forget" a phone call from the president, for example. In addition, ruling against a party on whose behalf the communication was made may not be realistic if the public interest would suffer.

The APA allows the agency to both cure and sanction. First, to cure the improper ex parte communication, the decision-maker "shall place on the public record" all written ex parte communications and memoranda, including the substance of any oral communications. APA §§ 557(d)(1)(C)(i) and (ii). Cure is effective if the improper activity is discovered before the agency reaches a final decision.

Second, the agency may sanction the violator. Section 557(d) provides: "The agency may, to the extent consistent with the interests of justice . . . , consider a violation of section 557(d) of this title sufficient grounds for a decision adverse to a party who has knowingly committed such violation or knowingly caused such violation to occur." Thus, the agency may rule against a party on the merits of a case where the party made or caused to be made a prohibited ex parte communication. APA § 557(d)(1)(D). Note that ruling against the party must be consistent with the public interest and with the policy of the underlying agency statute. Why? Assume that A and B are competitors for a single television license. Assume further that A is highly qualified, while B is just barely qualified. If A makes an illegal ex parte communication, it would not be in the public interest to disqualify A and grant the license to B. Hence, remedies in ex parte communication cases are difficult; often disclosure combined with an opportunity to respond are the only practical remedies available.

If the prohibited ex parte communication is not discovered until after the agency renders a final decision, then the courts must determine whether the violation was grave enough to void the agency's decision. Courts will consider the following factors when deciding whether the decision should be voided: (1) the gravity of the ex parte communication; (2) whether the ex parte communications may have influenced the agency's decision; (3) whether the party that made the ex parte communications ultimately benefited from making them; (4) whether the contents of the ex parte communications were known to the other side, who would thus have had an opportunity to respond; and (5) whether vacating the agency's decision would serve a useful purpose. *Professional Air Traffic Controllers Org. v. FLRA*, 685 F.2d 547, 565 (D.C. Cir. 1982) (refusing to void an agency decision despite improper ex parte communications).

### h. The Record

As a result of an adjudication, a record is compiled. Section 556 (e) provides that "[t]he transcript of testimony and exhibits, together with all papers and requests filed in the proceeding, constitutes the exclusive record for decision." APA § 556(e). This "exclusive record" provision is close to the heart of what we mean when we speak of an "on the record" hearing. One side of the exclusive record coin assures litigants that all evidence in support of the decision was presented and considered during the hearing with an opportunity for all to participate. The other side of the coin affirms that testimony, exhibits, or other evidence that was not presented in the hearing does not affect the decision.

Court hearings also require exclusive records. In a criminal trial, for example, a judicial or jury finding that a defendant was in Omaha on June 13th would require testimony or documentary evidence in the record to support that finding. Moving this principle from the judicial to administrative setting, however, raises some difficult questions. One strength of an agency adjudication is that the agency brings its expertise into the decisional process. Expertise may be reflected in studies and reports that can be introduced into the hearing record. But beyond that, the agency personnel may also have accumulated judgment, insight, situational sense, and "feel" from its extended experience. This type of expertise may be the most important type of expertise the agency has. If this type of expertise cannot be encapsulated into discrete documents or if it resides in the minds of those for whom testifying at the hearing is not feasible, must the expertise be ignored to avoid violating the exclusive record requirement? The short answer to that question is "no." Let's see why that is so.

Suppose a company advertises that its "charm school" will virtually guarantee graduates positions as airline flight attendants. The FTC believes these advertisements are misleading and seeks to enjoin the company from making them. The FTC holds a formal adjudication during which it is unable to find anyone willing to testify that he or she was naive enough to believe the advertisements were true. Moreover, the company produces many witnesses who testify that they did not believe the ads, considering them to be mere commercial "puffing." With such a record, could the FTC conclude that the ads were misleading under the APA? If the exclusive record requirement were applied too narrowly, the FTC could not so conclude, because there is no direct record support for its conclusion that the ads were misleading. Indeed, the evidence in the record would support the opposite finding.

But query whether the FTC should be allowed to evaluate the evidence that is in the record in light of the FTC's prior experiences. The FTC might have learned over the years that companies do not spend money on advertising unless that advertising persuades some buyers. Or the agency may have learned that while it is relatively easy to find witnesses willing to show their sophistication by claiming not to have believed ads, it is difficult to find witnesses willing to show their naiveté by admitting to having been duped. If the agency's expertise could be used to evaluate the evidence that is in the record, should the agency ignore such expertise under the APA's exclusive record requirement? Again, the answer to that question is no, but perhaps you now understand why.

Thus, the exclusive record requirement in section 556(e) generally permits agencies to use their experience in evaluating the evidence in the record so long as the agency is careful to explain how that experience bears on its factual findings. If the agency does not adequately explain its factual decisions, the agency finding may be reversed on appeal. *See, e.g., Cinderella Career & Finishing School v. FTC*, 425 F.2d 134, 137 (D.C. Cir. 1970) (determining whether the agency provided a jury with relevant and admissible evidence to support a jury verdict). For judicial review, the critical question is whether the agency used its expertise to *evaluate* the evidence or used its expertise to *substitute* for the evidence.

The Model State Administrative Procedure Act addresses this distinction directly. That Act provides: "The presiding officer's experience, technical competence, and specialized knowledge may be utilized in the evaluation of evidence." Uniform Law Commissioners, MODEL STATE ADMINISTRATIVE PROCEDURE ACT §4-215(d) (1981); *see also* Rev. Code Wash. (ARCW), 34.05.461(5) (2013).

In the judicial setting, the Federal Rules of Evidence permit a court to take judicial notice of facts that are "generally known" or that can be readily determined from reliable sources. Fed. R. Evid. 201(b). Such "generally known" facts also exist in the administrative setting. In addition, in the administrative setting there are facts that may not be "generally known," but that are well known to the agency because of its expertise. Section 556(e) permits an agency to take "official notice" of such facts, eliminating the need for evidence of such facts to be developed at the hearing. Section 556(e) provides, "When an agency decision rests on official notice of a material fact not appearing in the evidence in the record, a party is entitled, on timely request, to an opportunity to show the contrary." APA §556(e).

The type of facts an agency decision-maker can officially notice is much broader than the type of facts judges can judicially notice. The Attorney General's Manual provides that official notice can extend to "all matters as to which the agency by reason of its functions is presumed to be expert, such as technical or scientific facts within its specialized expertise." ATTORNEY GEN-ERAL'S MANUAL ON THE ADMINISTRATIVE PROCEDURE ACT 80 (1947). For example, an agency can take official notice of the harmful effects of nude dancing. *Erie v. Pap's AM*, 529 U.S. 277, 282 (2000). An agency can take official notice of a change in the rate on 10-year Treasury bonds. *Union Electric Co. v. FERC*, 890 F.2d 1193, 1194 (D.C. Cir. 1989). An agency can take official notice of whether the lack of binocular vision significantly diminishes a disability claimant's opportunity for certain types of work. *Sykes v. Apfel*, 228 F.3d 259, 261 (3d Cir. 2000).

However, unlike judicial notice, official notice requires the decision-maker to notify the parties that a fact is going to be noticed to give them an opportunity to show that the fact is untrue. The opportunity to show that the fact is untrue need not be oral. For legislative facts (facts about general matters), written opportunity to rebut may be sufficient. However, when official notice is taken of adjudicative facts (facts about the party), written opportunity is likely insufficient. If such facts are capable of being noticed, the opportunity for rebuttal should include oral presentations and even cross-examination in an appropriate case. *See* CHARLES KOCH, ADMINISTRATIVE LAW AND PRAC-TICE 209 (3d ed. 2010). More important, if facts are central to the issue being adjudicated, the facts may not be noticeable at all. Rather, due process likely requires that these types of facts be developed in the record traditionally. *Dayco v. FTC*, 362 F.2d 180, 185 (6th Cir. 1966).

### i. The Initial Decision

Before the APA was enacted, the Supreme Court had held that the administrative official who decides an adjudication must have "heard" the case in some way. *Morgan v. United States*, 298 U.S. 468, 480 (1936). *Morgan*'s holding did not require the head of the agency to personally preside at the hearing. Instead, *Morgan*'s holding allowed a subordinate to preside, summarize the evidence, and recommend a decision. The head of the agency would then "consider and appraise the evidence" to arrive at the final agency order. *Id.* at 481–82. Such subordinates were typically called examiners; indeed, the APA initially used the term "hearing examiners" rather than "administrative law judges" to reflect this arrangement. As these hearing examiners started to play a greater role in adjudication, Congress amended the APA to rename them ALJs.

Assuming an ALJ presided at the hearing, then after the hearing concludes, the ALJ will make a "recommended" or "initial decision." APA §§ 554(d) & 557(b). Typically, the ALJ will both preside at the hearing and make an initial decision. However, if the agency prefers to retain the power to make the initial decision, it can elect to have an ALJ preside at the hearing and make a "recommended" decision. APA § 557(b). The ALJ's initial decision "becomes the decision of the agency" if there is no appeal. *Id.*

An ALJ must rule "on each finding, conclusion, or exception presented." APA § 557(c)(3). All decisions, initial and otherwise, must include a statement of the "findings and conclusions, and the reasons or basis therefor, on all the material issues of fact, law, or discretion presented on the record; and the appropriate rule, order, sanction, relief, or denial thereof." APA §§ 557(c)(3) (A) & (B). This section ensures that the ALJ and agency respond to the parties' arguments so that that reviewing court will know what the initial and final decisions were based upon. The ATTORNEY GENERAL'S MANUAL says agencies can issue decisions in "narrative or expository form" (i.e., without separate sections for each finding and conclusion), so long as a reviewing body is able to find responses to each finding and conclusion sufficient to allow an assessment of the record and legal basis for the decision. ATTORNEY GENERAL'S MANUAL ON THE ADMINISTRATIVE PROCEDURE ACT 86 (1947). In Chapter 6, we will see that reviewing courts today have emphasized the importance that agency explanations be clear.

### j. Appealing the Initial Decision

However, after the initial decision issues, if an appeal is taken, then the agency head resolves the appeal. Neither the APA nor the Due Process Clause require that an agency allow a party to appeal the ALJ's initial decision. *Guentchev v. INS,* 77 F.3d 1036, 1037 (7th Cir. 1996) (noting that "[t]he Constitution does not entitle aliens to administrative appeals. Even litigants in the federal courts are not constitutionally entitled to multiple layers of review"). Commonly, however, agency rules do provide for an appeal of an initial decision when an ALJ, as opposed to the agency head, issued the initial decision. Either the regulated entity or the agency may appeal, depending on who loses. The agency head or an internal body acting for the agency head will resolve the appeal. Appeal procedures vary from agency to agency pursuant to the agency's own rules.

Standard of review is important on appeal. When a trial court judge reviews a jury verdict, the trial judge must defer substantially to the jury on findings of fact but not on findings of law. Similarly, when an appellate court reviews a trial judge's decision, the appellate court must defer to the trial court's findings of fact but not on findings of law.

In contrast, when an agency reviews an ALJ's initial decision, the agency reviews both questions of law and fact de novo. Specifically, section 557(b)

provides, "On appeal from or review of the initial decision, the agency has all
the powers which it would have in making the initial decision." APA
§ 557(b). Thus, the APA allows the agency to give little to no deference to the
ALJ's initial decision. As the Attorney General's Manual explains, "the agency
is in no way bound by the decision of [the ALJ]; it retains complete freedom
of decision—as though it had heard the evidence itself." Attorney General's
Manual on the Administrative Procedure Act 83 (1947). By giving the
agency the ability to reverse ALJ decisions with which it disagrees, accountable presidential appointees, not lower-level employees like ALJs, retain decisional control over policy decisions.

Despite this de novo standard of review, a reviewing court will be less likely
to reverse an agency's final decision that defers to ALJ's findings regarding witness credibility findings, which is known as testimonial evidence. Why?
Because the reviewing court will evaluate the agency's factual findings to see
if there is "substantial evidence" in the record to support those findings. APA
§ 706(2)(E). The ALJ's initial opinion becomes part of the "whole record" that
a reviewing court will examine. *Universal Camera v. NLRB*, 340 U.S. 474, 493
(1951). In those cases where the demeanor of the witnesses is critical to the
outcome, the reviewing court will consider the ALJ's demeanor findings
because the ALJ actually observed the witnesses. U.S. Dep't of Justice,
Attorney General's Manual on the APA 84 (1947) (noting that where the
demeanor of witnesses is important to a case, the ALJ findings may be "of con-
sequence" or may be entitled to "considerable weight" on internal agency
review). When an agency rejects an ALJ's credibility findings without sufficient
reason, a reviewing court may reject the agency's final decision as unsupported
by substantial evidence. *Universal Camera*, 340 U.S. at 497. Thus, while an
agency may reject an ALJ's factual findings and legal conclusions, the agency's success on appeal will be affected by how persuasively the agency explains
its rejection of an ALJ's findings relating to testimonial evidence. *See, e.g., Jack-
son v. Veterans Admin.*, 786 F.2d 1322, 1330 (Fed. Cir. 1985).

Given that an agency has the ultimate decision-making power, should a
lawyer reserve the full development of the case and the best arguments for the
appeal? For a number of reasons, that would be a disastrous way to represent
a client in the administrative world. To begin with, the case must be fully
developed at the hearing because new evidence will not usually be allowed
on appeal. And, under the exclusive record requirement discussed above,
the agency cannot consider evidence that is not in the record.

Further, as a practical matter, most reviewing bodies will grant the initial
decision a presumption of correctness. The agency will consider the ALJ's
efforts over weeks, months, or longer to understand a case and will not be

anxious to redo that work itself. So despite the power of an agency to consider the case de novo and reverse an ALJ's decision, the vast majority of ALJ decisions are affirmed. Thus, the best time to win a case is before the ALJ.

### k. Judicial Review

Assuming the regulated entity is unhappy with the agency's decision, the regulated entity, and only the regulated entity, can appeal the agency's final decision in court. The division of the agency that prosecuted the case cannot appeal the agency's decision, which should be intuitive. We will defer until Chapter 6 a discussion of judicial review of the agency's final decision.

# D. Informal Adjudication

At the federal level, about 90 percent of proceedings fitting the APA definition of adjudication are not required to be "on the record after opportunity for hearing." In other words, they are informal adjudications, which are not required to comply with the formal adjudicative procedures contained in APA §§ 556–557, outlined above. Although many such hearings need not comply with the formal APA requirements, more than half the informal adjudications federal agencies conduct involve notice, a statement of reasons, a neutral decision-maker, and some opportunity for presenting argument. Paul Verkuil, *A Study of Informal Adjudication Procedures*, 43 U. Chi. L. Rev. 739 (1976). Perhaps Congress should amend the APA to include these basic requirements to ensure that the other half of the agencies provide them as well. Some scholars have made such suggestions. Richard Pierce et al., Administrative Law and Process § 6.4.11 (5th ed. 2009); Michael Asimow, *The Spreading Umbrella: Extending the APA's Adjudication Provisions to All Evidentiary Hearings Required by Statute*, 56 Admin. L. Rev. 1003 (2004).

Informal adjudications are not entirely free from procedural requirements. Section 555 of the APA applies to all adjudications, which means that agencies must allow parties to have counsel, must allow all interested parties to appear, and must resolve the matter in a timely fashion. APA § 555. The licensing rules of section 558 also apply. Further, Chapter 4 examines requirements that the Due Process Clause imposes. These requirements are the most significant procedural rules on informal adjudications. Finally, the agency may have its own procedural rules that apply. Beyond these procedural requirements, agencies are free to conduct informal adjudications as they wish.

The 1981 Model State Administrative Procedure Act includes some procedural requirements for informal adjudications, and a few states have included some as well. Uniform Law Commissioners, 1981 Model State Admin. Proc.

ACT § 4-502-505; *see, e.g.*, Rev. Code Wash. (ARCW), 34.05.482-494 (2013). For example, the Model Act provides that in an informal proceeding involving a sanction, the presiding official "shall give each party an opportunity to be informed of the agency's view of the matter and to explain the party's view of the matter," and "shall give each party a brief statement of findings of fact, conclusions of law, and policy reasons for the decision if it is an exercise of the agency's discretion." MODEL STATE ADMIN. PROC. ACT §§ 4-503(b)(1) & (2) (1981). It also provides for some limited internal agency review. *Id.*

---

## Checkpoints

- Adjudication is a form of dispute resolution that involves the presentation of evidence and argument by parties with a decision by a neutral decision-maker.

- Courts apply a *Chevron* analysis to determine whether an agency's decision to apply or to not apply the APA's formal adjudication procedures in sections 556–557 was reasonable.

- The APA uses a mixed model of adjudication in which prosecutors and final decisionmakers are inside agency personnel, while judging is initially done by independent ALJs whose independence is protected by statutory provisions limiting the agency's control over the judge's tenure and salary.

- The federal rules of evidence do not apply to agency adjudications; however, they are still relevant.

- Parties and persons compelled to appear before an agency are entitled to be accompanied and advised by counsel.

- The APA entitles parties to appear in person and, if needed, to cross-examine witnesses.

- The transcript and all papers filed are the exclusive record for decision.

- Ex parte communications from both inside and outside the agency are prohibited in some circumstances.

- When a party appeals the ALJ's initial decision, the agency retains de novo decision-making authority for all but ALJ findings based on demeanor.

- Most adjudications are informal and have limited procedural protection under the APA.

# Chapter 4

# Due Process Requirements for Administrative Proceedings

---

## Roadmap

- Introduction to the Due Process Clause
- Whether due process applies
  - Issues protected by due process
  - Interests protected by due process: property and liberty
  - When due process applies: Pre-deprivation versus post-deprivation
- What process is due?
  - The private interest
  - The risk of error
  - The public interest
  - The right to a neutral decisionmaker

---

## A. Introduction

In Chapter 1, we learned that the federal Constitution provides a general framework for our government. We examined how the Constitution allocates duties to and separates the powers of the branches of the government. We noted that the framers did not anticipate the administrative state in its present scale. We suggested that modern administrative law provides additional protection for the lack of true separateness found in our divided government.

In this chapter, we explore the due process clause contained in both the Fifth and Fourteenth Amendments. You may also cover the Due Process clauses in your constitutional law course; here, we look at their role in the administrative, or regulatory, context. What is *procedural* due process? Procedural due process ensures that governmental procedures are as fair as is practicable: we call this procedural due process as opposed to *substantive* due process.

Let's begin with the text of the Due Process clauses. The Fifth Amendment provides that federal officials cannot "deprive[] [a person] of life, liberty, or property, without due process of law." The Fourteenth Amendment imposes the same limits on state officials. The broad phrase "due process of law" is not defined. What, then, does it mean in the administrative arena?

Let's first be clear. Due process is not a shield preventing the government from ever depriving individuals of life, liberty, or property. Rather, government has the power to deprive individuals of life, liberty, and property when government has a good reason to do so. For example, government may wish to protect the public from unfit airline pilots, from unqualified welfare recipients, from incompetent government employees, and from dangerous criminals. Hence, the government has the power to deprive individuals of life, liberty, and property; however, the government can only deprive individuals of one of these rights when the government provides the appropriate level of process first. As you might imagine, the appropriate level of process will differ depending on the nature of the right and the level of deprivation. For example, when the government deprives an individual of his or her life, government process will need to be at its most protective. Administrative agencies do not typically deprive citizens of life, so we will focus on property and liberty deprivations in this chapter.

To understand what process is due for property and liberty deprivations, you should understand the history of procedural due process. Due process began as a requirement that government act according to procedures provided by existing law. Due process has morphed into a requirement that the procedures used be fair. But fairness is often in the eye of the beholder; litigants generally favor additional and more complex procedures, while the government generally favors fewer and less complex procedures. Litigants want judicial oversight; government wants reduced cost and interference. Finally, the public also has an interest in the cost of government proceedings. Hence, you will see that due process requires that for each procedure, courts balance the fairness to litigants, the helpfulness of the procedure, the agency's need for autonomy, and the procedure's cost.

Because judges, who are lawyers, have crafted procedural due process, you can expect that the kinds of procedures that are required are those associated with judicial proceedings. Hence, due process might require some or all of the following: (1) notice, (2) an opportunity to be present at a proceeding, (3) an opportunity to present orally at a proceeding, (4) an opportunity to confront and cross-examine witnesses, (5) an opportunity to submit rebuttal evidence, (6) the right to be represented by counsel, (7) the right to a neutral decisionmaker, (8) the right to a reasoned decision based exclusively on the record, and (9) the right to judicial review of that decision.

You might wish to review Chapter 3 for a discussion of these procedures in *formal* agency adjudications and rulemakings. Here, we look at due process in the context of informal agency proceedings, because the APA provides more procedural protections than Due Process does. In some cases, agency rules or enabling statutes will similarly provide more protective procedures. Due process is a relatively minor hurdle for the government to clear, assuming it applies at all. Hence, do not view due process as a protective shield. See Figure 4.1 for a humorous approach.

*'For proud Due Process speaks in thun'drous voice*
*Should first we seek, perhaps, some plainer choice?*

**Figure 4.1**  A Useful Reminder in Iambic Pentameter

As we proceed through a discussion of the Due Process Clause, we will address the following questions: (1) Does due process apply at all (what issues and interests are protected)? (2) Assuming due process applies, at what stage of the proceeding does due process apply to (pre-deprivation or post-deprivation)? (3) Assuming due process applies, what process is due? In answering these questions, we will examine the *issues* and the *interests* relevant to due process, the importance of the timing of the hearing, and the *cost* and *benefits* associated with due process requirements.

# B. Question One: Whether Due Process Applies

## 1. Issues Protected by Due Process

If due process requires trial-like protections, then it is fair to ask about the kinds of issues trial procedures deal with most effectively. The trial methods identified above would be most useful in administrative proceedings where the legitimacy of a deprivation turns on disputed issues of fact concerning the individual who is subject to the deprivation. As we have seen, some scholars call these kinds of facts "adjudicative facts." 2 RICHARD PIERCE, ADMINISTRATIVE LAW TREATISE § 9.2, 737–44 (5th ed. 2009). Thus, if an agency revokes an entity's license because of conclusions about the entity's qualifications for the license, we would expect the agency to provide the entity with notice of the decision, a statement of the reasons the action is being taken, and an opportunity to explain or rebut the factual conclusions supporting the action. Providing such procedures can help assure the accuracy of the agency's fact-finding and the neutrality of its law-applying. In addition, these procedures treat those deprived not as helpless victims of government power but as individuals whose dignity warrants an appropriate opportunity to participate in government decisions that especially affect them.

We explored the difference between adjudicative and legislative facts in Chapter 2 when we discussed the *BiMetallic* and *Londoner* cases. You may recall that in *BiMetallic Investment Co. v. State Bd. of Equalization*, 239 U.S. 441 (1915), the Supreme Court held that due process does not require a state to hold a hearing before deciding that the general tax rates should be raised by forty percent. *Id.* at 445. The reason the government was changing the rate was not because of the shape, use, or value of any particular parcels of real property; rather, the government found that local tax assessors had systematically underassessed all the city's property. *State Bd. of Equalization v. BiMetallic Investment Co.*, 56 Colo. 512, 513 (Colo. 1914). The Court could thus resolve the dispute about the government's legal authority to impose such a measure by looking at transcripts from the legislative hearings. Providing individual property owners with the opportunity to present oral testimony and cross-examine the assessors would add nothing but cost and delay and could create inconsistency. In short, due process did not require adjudicatory procedures in that case because the issues involved legislative rather than adjudicative facts.

In contrast, in *Londoner v. Denver*, 210 U.S. 373, 386 (1908), the Court held that due process did require a hearing before the city could levy a special assessment on an individual's property. Because the amount of the assessment was unique to each individual, the agency's decision may have been affected by the value, shape, and use of an individual's particular lot. Hence, both accuracy and acceptability of the government's decision would be enhanced if the property owners were able to present testimony and discuss the issue with the assessors. *Id.* In short, due process required adjudicatory procedures because the issue involved adjudicative facts.

The distinction between adjudicative and legislative facts is not a bright line, but it is helpful to keep in mind as you consider whether process is due. Additional procedure is not cost free. Hence, courts should not impose expensive and cumbersome procedures on government actors unless those procedures will actually increase the accuracy or the perception of fairness. Thus, courts limit due process protections to cases of disputed, adjudicative fact.

Of course, this view of due process offers little solace to the citizen deprived of a government benefit. For example, when the government revokes or fails to renew a taxi license because the government concludes that there are too many taxis, due process is likely unnecessary. Yet the impact on an affected driver may still be catastrophic, and the issue about the correct number of taxis in town may be hotly disputed. However, concerns about accuracy and perceptions of fairness would be largely met by public hearings and written submissions rather than by the considerably more expensive individualized and personal hearings due process requires.

Moreover, in some cases due process does not require individualized procedures even though there are disputed issues of adjudicative fact. As we saw in some of the exclusions from the APA formal hearing requirements (see the discussion of APA §554 in Chapter 3), factual disputes that can more accurately and cheaply be resolved using tests or standards do not require more formal methods. Of course, standards and tests are not perfect, but most people would agree that for some kinds of factual disputes these methods are superior to the use of trial methods. Thus, in such cases, due process requires nothing more.

## 2. Interests Protected by Due Process

Assume, then, that we have identified an *issue* that is appropriate for due process resolution; the next question is whether the *interest* affected is of sufficient importance to warrant due process protection. The Due Process Clause specifically protects "life, liberty, [and] property." How rigidly are these interests defined?

There are many types of interests that the government can restrict, limit, or even terminate. In many of these situations, the consequences for the individual may be very serious. For example, many businesses depend on government licenses, a number of individuals depend on public assistance, all government employees depend on their continued employment, and all public school students depend on a free public education. Because these interests are important and deprivation of them in a specific case would turn on disputed facts, one might conclude that due process should apply. Put another way, if the *magnitude* of the deprivation is severe enough, the *nature* of the interest should not matter.

Indeed, some commentators have suggested that the phrase "life, liberty, or property" should be interpreted as an aggregate general reference to the conditions of life in a political community not as an exclusive list of specific interests that alone are to be protected. RICHARD PIERCE ET AL., ADMINISTRATIVE LAW AND PROCESS 208–209 (6th ed. 2014). Using this interpretation, a court would apply due process protection in *any* case involving serious deprivation caused by governmental action. As we will see, this broad interpretation prevailed for a short time in the early 1970s. *See Goldberg v. Kelly*, 397 U.S. 254 (1970) (applying due process to welfare benefits proceedings).

But this broad interpretation has given way to a much narrower interpretation since then for two reasons: First, text. The interest to be protected must be within the constitutionally enumerated language for which due process is guaranteed: property, liberty, and life. Second, practicality. Due process protections are not free; they are usually not even cheap. Offering a proceeding at all is costly, especially for agencies that resolve thousands of adjudications annually. Moreover, each different procedure, such as the right to counsel, will incrementally increase costs. In addition, because the government generally cannot deprive an individual of a liberty or property interest until after providing some due process protections, costs increase with the delayed termination (think of a disability claimant receiving disability benefits to which she is not entitled during the appeal process). Finally, proceedings place an administrative burden on an agency by interfering with that agency's day-to-day operations. This administrative burden may be especially intrusive for government institutions such as hospitals, prisons, and public schools. For example, if school administrators had to hold full adjudicatory hearings before disciplining students who bring weapons or drugs to school, the education mission would be significantly affected.

As you will see below, courts have rather narrowly defined the interests that due process protects. Determining whether due process applies to an administrative action requires a court to find that the deprived individual has either a "property" or a "liberty" interest. Below, we will explore the courts' definitions of these interests, beginning with property interests.

## a. Property Interest

Prior to 1970, property interests were understood to include only the common law property rights, such as a property interest in one's real property. Property interests did not include "privileges" that the government might grant to a person, such as employment or welfare benefits. At that time, the law distinguished between rights and privileges and granted due process protection only to the former.

However, this rights/privileges distinction protected the rights of the rich, which often came in the form of private property, but not the rights of the poor, which often came in the form of government benefits. Hence, in 1970, the Court explicitly abandoned its rights/privileges distinction in *Goldberg*, 397 U.S. at 254. In that case, a welfare recipient's benefits had been terminated without a pre-deprivation hearing. *Id.* at 256. Surprisingly, perhaps, the government conceded that due process applied. The issue instead was what procedures due process required before the government could terminate welfare benefits. *Id.* at 260. We will talk about what procedures are due in a moment. For now, we need to understand how the Supreme Court defined property interests.

In defining property interests, the Court reasoned that welfare payments were "important" and that the loss suffered from their termination was "grievous." *Id.* at 263. Thus, the Court replaced its rights/privileges distinction with a more generous "grievous loss" test. The Court held that the federal welfare statute created an entitlement that qualified as a "property interest." *Id.* at 263–64.

With this change from the restrictive rights/privileges distinction to the "grievous loss" test, the number of potential Due Process cases threatened to skyrocket. So, two years after *Goldberg*, the Court sharply narrowed the types of property interests due process protected. In doing so, the Court answered the question left open in *Goldberg* of what, other than a statutory entitlement, could qualify as a "property interest."

First, in *Board of Regents v. Roth*, 408 U.S. 564, 573 (1972), the Court rejected an untenured college instructor's claim that he was entitled to due process before the state university could terminate his employment. The college instructor had been hired for a one-year, fixed term. *Id.* at 566. At the end of the term, the university refused to rehire him and gave him no notice of the reasons for this decision, nor a hearing to challenge the decision. The instructor argued that he had a liberty interest in his re-employment prospects, *id.* at 571, but the Court rejected his claim. In so doing, the Court refined its definition of a protected property interest:

> To have a property interest in a benefit, a person clearly must have more than an abstract need or desire for it. He must have more than a unilateral expectation of it. He must, instead, have a legitimate claim of entitlement to it. It is a purpose of the ancient institution of property to protect those claims upon which people rely in their daily lives, reliance that must not be arbitrarily undermined. It is a purpose of the constitutional right to a hearing to provide an opportunity for a person to vindicate those claims.
>
> Property interests, of course, are not created by the Constitution. Rather they are created and their dimensions are defined by existing rules or understandings that stem from an independent source such as state law—rules or understandings that secure certain benefits and that support claims of entitlement to those benefits.

*Id.* at 577. Thus, to have a constitutionally protected property interest, a person must have a "legitimate claim of entitlement" to that interest, and legitimate claims of entitlement are created and their dimensions are defined by existing rules or understandings that stem from an independent source of law, such as state law. *Id.*

Importantly, *Roth* distinguished *Goldberg*: in the earlier case, the "legitimate claim of entitlement" to welfare payments had come from the federal statute defining welfare eligibility. Although an individual has no entitlement to receive welfare benefits initially, once the individual starts receiving those benefits, that individual would be entitled to have those payments continue. *Id.* at 577–78.

In contrast, a government employee who has only a one-year contract with no assurance of renewal has no such right to keep that job any longer than the year. The university authorities had complete discretion to renew or not to renew the contract for any reason other than an unconstitutional one (such as a decision made because of race). *Id.* at 578. In *Roth*, the instructor had only a unilateral expectation, or hope, that his contract would be renewed. The complete discretion over renewal that the university officials had was simply inconsistent with any notion of "entitlement." *Id.* at 577. Because he had no entitlement to have his contract renewed, the instructor's interest was not one that due process protects.

In contrast to the instructor's unilateral expectation of having his contract renewed in *Roth*, the instructor in *Perry v. Sindermann*, 408 U.S. 593 (1972), alleged that the college where he worked had a *de facto* tenure program. Like the instructor in *Roth*, the instructor in *Sindermann* was hired on a one year contract. *Id.* at 594. Sindermann's contract was renewed for four years, then not renewed. *Id.* at 594–95. The college offered him no notice or hearing. *Id.* at 595. Unlike the instructor in *Roth*, Sindermann alleged that he reasonably relied on language in the college's faculty guide, which suggested that there was a *de facto* tenure system:

> Teacher Tenure: Odessa College has no tenure system. The Administration of the College wishes the faculty member to feel that he has permanent tenure as long as his teaching services are satisfactory and as long as he displays a cooperative attitude toward his co-workers and his superiors, and as long as he is happy in his work.

*Id.* at 600. The Court rejected the college's motion for summary judgment because there was a question of fact regarding whether there was an implied contract in this case, an issue to be resolved under state contract law. *Id.* at 603. The Court reasoned that this policy might limit the school's discretion to not renew Sindermann's contract. *Id.* at 601. The Court reasoned that a legitimate claim of entitlement might arise from such "rules or mutually explicit understandings that support [the] claim of entitlement"; hence, Sindermann should have the opportunity to prove he had more than a unilateral expectation, or hope, that his contract would be renewed. *Id.* at 601. It is important to note that *Sindermann* was a summary judgment case; the Court was very clear that a finding of an entitlement would not entitle Sindermann to reinstatement. *Id.* at 603. Rather, such a finding would obligate college officials to provide him due process, like notice and a hearing at which he could be informed of the grounds for his nonrenewal and through which he could challenge their sufficiency. *Id.* Remember that procedural due process only ensures that individuals have a right to process at the time of a deprivation, not a right to keep a government benefit.

Based on these cases, the Court's current definition of a property interest, or an entitlement, seems to depend, in part, on the degree of discretion government officials have over continuing the interest. In *Roth*, the government had complete discretion; in *Goldberg* and *Sindermann*, the government had significantly less discretion. Hence, the Court's entitlement approach has been widely criticized because it gives the government the ability to control in advance whether due process applies. For example, a legislature could in theory grant public officials complete discretion over the continuation of any benefit to ensure that due process would be inapplicable. Indeed, Congress has enacted some statutes giving agencies unlimited discretion. *See, e.g.*, 42 U.S.C. § 601 (1997) (the 1997 welfare reform statutes, which state that "this part shall not be interpreted to entitle any individual or family to assistance under any State program funded under this part."). Yet even when government officials have unfettered discretion to make decisions about individuals, the due process goals of accuracy and acceptability remain; in fact, these concerns may be heightened in such cases.

Finally, even though courts agree that some process is due before an *existing benefit* is terminated, process is generally not due before an *application for a benefit* is denied. *See generally* Sidney A. Shapiro & Richard E. Levy, *Government Benefits and the Rule of Law: Towards a Standards-Based Theory of Due Process*, 57 Admin. L. Rev. 107, 116 (2005) (noting that courts impose more exacting standards for creating an entitlement in the context of applicants). There is nothing at the application stage to which the applicant is entitled, only the possibility that if the applicant's qualifications can be established, an entitlement may be conferred. Yet again, there is no persuasive reason why the goals of accuracy and acceptability do not apply to application cases as well as to revocation cases. Very similar issues about an applicant's qualifications have to be resolved before either determination is made, suggesting that there would be value in some kind of hearing.

In a particularly well-reasoned opinion addressing this issue, the Second Circuit said that whether there is procedure should turn on the amount of discretion the agency has in considering an individual's application. *Kapps v. Wing*, 404 F.3d 105 (2d Cir. 2005). If statutory standards are relatively objective, the applicant's right to due process procedural protections is greater:

> [W]e have explained that whether a benefit invests the applicant with a 'claim of entitlement' or merely a 'unilateral expectation' is determined by the amount of discretion the disbursing agency retains . . . . Statutory language may so specifically mandate benefits awards upon demonstration of certain qualifications that an applicant must fairly be recognized to have a limited property interest entitling him, at least, to process sufficient to permit a demonstration of eligibility.

*Id.* at 115–16. But this case is unique. Perhaps this approach has not gained purchase because there are significantly more application denials than revocations. In addition, the courts tend to be "more solicitous of established relationships than expectations." Peter Strauss, Administrative Justice in the United States 86 (3d ed. 2016).

We turn now from the definition of a property interest to the definition of a liberty interest. Defining a liberty interest has proven to be even more difficult than defining a property interest.

### b. Liberty Interest

Historically, liberty was narrowly defined to mean freedom from bodily restraint and injury, while life was defined to mean, well, life. Thus, the government could not restrain or put to death an individual without providing due process of law.

In 1923, the Supreme Court expanded its narrow definition of "liberty," defining the term more broadly to include "those privileges long recognized . . . as essential to the orderly pursuit of happiness by free men." *Meyer v. Nebraska*, 262 U.S. 390, 399 (1923) (stating that a liberty interest included the right to engage in a profession). Following *Meyer*, the Court held that due process protections apply when the government denies or revokes an individual's license to practice a profession. *See, e.g., Gibson v. Berryhill*, 411 U.S. 564, 571 (1973) (license to practice optometry); *Schware v. Board of Bar Exam'rs*, 353 U.S. 232, 238 (1957) (law license).

In *Wisconsin v. Constantineau*, 400 U.S. 433 (1971), the Court broadened its definition of "liberty" even further to include freedom from reputational harm. In that case, a state law required law enforcement to post the names of "public drunkards" wherever alcoholic beverages were sold. *Id*. at 434. The Court reasoned that "[w]here a person's good name, reputation, honor, or integrity is at stake because of what the government is doing to him, [due process protections are] essential." *Id*. at 437. The Eighth Circuit later explained that "a constitutionally protected liberty interest . . . is implicated where the employer levels accusations at the employee that are so damaging as to make it difficult or impossible for the employee to escape the stigma of those charges." *Shands v. Kennett*, 993 F.2d 1337, 1347 (8th Cir. 1993) (holding that volunteer firemen who were fired for insubordination and misconduct did not have a due process protected liberty interest).

However, the Court soon retreated from this expanded definition of liberty. First, in *Roth*, discussed above, the Court acknowledged that an individual has a liberty interest to "enjoy those privileges long recognized as essential to the orderly pursuit of happiness by free men," such as government employment. 408 U.S. 564, 572 (1972). Further, the Court noted that due process is triggered when "the State . . . has imposed on [an individual] a stigma or other disability that foreclose[s] his freedom to take advantage of other employment opportunities." *Id*. at 573. However, the Court then applied its new stigma test narrowly. Because the plaintiff in *Roth* had suffered no stigma that would prevent him from obtaining future employment, he did not suffer an injury to a protected liberty interest. *Id*. at 574. In other words, stigma alone is insufficient to trigger the Due Process Clause's protections.

Similarly, in *Paul v. Davis*, 424 U.S. 693, 713 (1976), the Court held that when the Louisville police distributed a flyer identifying "active shoplifters" that included the plaintiff's name, the plaintiff had no right to due process. There was no dispute that the plaintiff suffered reputational injury, or stigma. However, the Court cautioned:

> While we have in a number of our prior cases pointed out the frequently drastic effect of the 'stigma' which may result from defamation by the government in a variety of contests, this line of cases does not establish the proposition that reputation alone, apart from more tangible interests such as employment, is either "liberty" or "property" by itself sufficient to invoke the procedural protection of the Due Process Clause.

*Id.* at 701. In short, reputational stigma alone is insufficient to trigger due process; the injury must be more than just reputational. For example, the inability of an individual to find future employment would qualify. The Court distinguished the injury in *Paul* from the injury in *Constantineau*, describing the analysis in that case as one of "stigma-plus." *Id.* at 702. The Court suggested that ruling otherwise in *Paul* would turn a standard defamation action into a constitutional challenge; however, the Court did not convincingly distinguish *Constantineau*.

In any event, to establish a liberty interest entitled to due process protection, a plaintiff must show not only that his or her reputation was harmed (the stigma) but also that the plaintiff will suffer a future harm from that stigma to a "tangible interest" (the plus). Future harm might include the inability to purchase alcohol, such as in *Constantineau*, the ability to obtain future employment, such as in *Roth* and *Sindermann*, or something similar.

The Court, however, did not just narrowly define its liberty test to require "stigma plus." The Court limited when a plaintiff would be entitled to due process protections, even assuming the plaintiff could demonstrate stigma-plus. In 1977, the Court decided *Codd v. Velger*, 429 U.S. 624 (1977). In *Codd*, the plaintiff police officer was fired without any process from his position with the New York City Police Department after an apparent suicide attempt. *Id.* Because he held a probationary position at the time, he had no property interest in his employment. *Id.* at 627. Instead, the plaintiff alleged that by firing him, the City had stigmatized him in a way that would hurt his ability to obtain future employment as a police officer. *Id.* at 626.

The Court held that due process did not apply because the plaintiff did not dispute the facts: "Nowhere in the pleadings or elsewhere has [plaintiff] affirmatively assert[ed] that the report of the apparent suicide attempt was substantially false." *Id.* at 627. In other words, the Court held that due process only applies to *false* stigma plus. The government can harm a citizen's reputation all it wants, apparently, so long as the citizen does not dispute the allegations.

Justice Stevens in dissent pointed out that "a principle basic to our legal system [is] the principle that the guilty as well as the innocent are entitled to a fair trial." *Id.* at 633 (Stevens, J., dissenting). The purpose of a hearing, he noted, is twofold: "First, to establish the truth or falsity of the charge, and second, to provide a basis for deciding what action is warranted by the facts." *Id.* at 634. Query: Is not Stevens correct about this? Regardless, Stevens' dissent has not persuaded the Court to reject *Codd's* holding as erroneous. In *Connecticut Department of Public Safety v. Doe*, 538 U.S. 1, 8 (2003), the Court said in dicta that a convicted sex offender did not have a due process right to have a hearing because he did not dispute the fact that he was a sex offender, which led to his inclusion on a public sex offender registry.

Finally, the Court has narrowed the definition of protected liberty interest even more in the context of prisoner litigation. For example, in *Sandin v. Connor*, 515 U.S. 472, 486 (1995), the Court limited the liberty interests due process protects to deprivations that are "atypical" or "substantial." The state placed the plaintiff in solitary confinement for 30 days. *Id.* at 475. Such confinement would constitute a liberty deprivation under the Court's most restrictive, historical definition. However, the Court held that no process was due because the deprivation was "was within the range of confinement to be normally expected for one serving an indeterminate term of 30 years to life." *Id.* at 487. It is unclear whether this atypical or substantial limitation will be applied in the non-prisoner context. The Court appeared concerned about prisoners bringing thousands of cases a year, claiming protected liberty interests in relatively minor liberty deprivations.

In sum, while the Court appeared to expand the definition of protected liberty interests during the first part of the nineteenth century, the Court quickly retreated. Currently, a plaintiff who alleges reputation injury must show: (1) that the government's action harmed her reputation (stigma), (2) that the harm will negatively affect her ability to do something in the future (plus), and (3) that she disputes the factual underpinnings for the government's actions.

### c. Unconstitutional Conditions

In addition to property and liberty interests, there is another class of interests that is usually protected: one's interest in exercising constitutional rights, such as the First Amendment's right to free speech. Pursuant to the so-called "doctrine of unconstitutional conditions," the government cannot condition a person's receipt of a governmental benefit on the waiver of a constitutionally protected right. For example, a television station cannot be required to refrain from endorsing a political candidate to continue to receive public funding. *United States Agency for Int'l Dev. v. Alliance for Open Society Int'l, Inc.*, 133 S. Ct. 2321 (2013) (holding that a statute that conditioned an organization's ability to receive federal funding on adopting a policy explicitly opposing prostitution and sex trafficking was unconstitutional). This doctrine is developed in more detail in constitutional law classes, but the Court addressed the issue in *Sindermann*, 408 U.S. at 593, as an additional ground for its decision.

In the district court, Sindermann had claimed that the college's nonrenewal was based in part on speeches he had given that were critical of college's board of regents. *Id.* at 594–95. The Court said:

> For at least a quarter-century, this Court has made clear that even though a person has no "right" to a valuable governmental benefit and even though the government may deny him the benefit for any number of reasons, there are some reasons upon which the government may not rely. It may not deny a benefit to a person on a basis that infringes his constitutionally protected interests — especially, his interest in freedom of speech. For if the government could deny a benefit to a person because of his constitutionally protected speech or associations, his exercise of those freedoms would in effect be penalized and inhibited. This would allow the government [indirectly] to "produce a result which (it) could not command directly."

*Id.* at 597 (internal citation omitted). Thus, the college could not fail to renew Sindermann's contract because he had exercised his rights under the First Amendment to criticize his employer. Note that the plaintiff in *Roth* had also claimed that his nonrenewal was punishment for protected speech, but the Court in that case found inadequate factual support for his claim. *Board of Regents v. Roth*, 408 U.S. 564, 575 n.14 (1972). Note how without notice of the allegations and a due process hearing, it might be impossible for an individual to learn the real reason for the government's decision to terminate his employment. *See* Henry P. Monaghan, *First Amendment Due Process*, 83 HARV. L. REV. 518 (1970).

As we conclude our discussion of what interests due process protects, you are no doubt aware that the Court's doctrine is not clear, consistent, or unanimous. Likely, an individual justice's own views about the importance of a particular interest might impact the vote. If the Court were to return to its pre-*Roth* approach — that all interests threatened with serious or grievous loss trigger the clause's protections—then there would be less controversy about whether a protected interest was impacted and more focus on what process will protect against that particular harm. In other words, the Court's doctrine would have been more consistent had it limited the protections available rather than the interests protected. We will return to what protections, or procedures, due process requires after we address when such process is due: pre-deprivation or post-deprivation.

## C. Question Two: When Does Due Process Apply?

Assume that due process applies. Two questions remain: (1) *when* is process due (i.e., before or after the deprivation)? and (2) *what* process is due? The answers to these questions are easy to articulate but more difficult to answer because their resolution depends on the facts of each case. Let's start with when procedures are due.

In 1985, the Supreme Court decided the quintessential case in this area. In *Cleveland Bd. of Education v. Loudermill*, 470 U.S. 532, 538 (1985), the Court considered what pre-termination procedures must be provided to an employee who can only be fired for cause. In that case, the plaintiff security guard lied on his employment application, stating he had never been convicted of a felony. *Id.* at 535. After a routine examination of employment records, the Board discovered his dishonesty and fired him without offering him an opportunity to respond to the allegations or challenge the severity of the sanction. *Id.* at 536.

The plaintiff appealed, claiming that he had believed his conviction was for a misdemeanor rather than for a felony. Despite his claim of ignorance, the dismissal was upheld. *Id.* at 535. The plaintiff then filed suit, alleging that he was deprived of due process because he was not provided with the opportunity to respond to the charges against him prior to his termination. *Id.* at 538. In other words, he alleged that the government had to provide a pre-termination hearing, not a post-termination hearing.

Reasoning that "[a]n essential principle of due process is that a deprivation of life, liberty, or property 'be preceded by notice and opportunity for hearing appropriate to the nature of the case,'" the Supreme Court agreed. *Id.* at 542. Seemingly rejecting *Codd*'s requirement that there be a factual dispute, the Court said, "Even where the facts are clear, the appropriateness or necessity of the discharge may not be; in such cases, the only meaningful opportunity to invoke the discretion of the decision maker is likely to be before the termination takes effect." *Id.* at 543. However, although the Court required pre-termination procedures in this case, the only required procedure was an opportunity to respond to the allegations, coupled with a post-termination hearing. *Id.* at 544. Hence, under *Loudermill*, when the government is able to provide pre-deprivation process, it should do so; however, the process provided may be minimal. *See also Mathews v. Eldridge*, 424 U.S. 319 (1976) (upholding minimal pre-termination procedures when followed by more substantive post-termination procedures).

In contrast, where there are exigent circumstances preventing the government from delaying action, the government may provide few, if any, pre-termination procedures so long as it provides post-termination procedures. For example, prior to *Loudermill*, the Court upheld the government's seizure of misbranded drugs and unsafe food even though the government provided no pre-termination procedures. *See, e.g., Ewing v. Mytinger & Casselberry, Inc.,* 339 U.S. 594, 601 (1950) (misbranded drugs); *North American Cold Storage Co. v. Chicago,* 211 U.S. 306, 320 (1908) (spoiled poultry). Post-*Loudermill*, the Court has held that a statute allowing the federal government to issue a cessation order to mine operators before holding a hearing did not violate due process. *Hodel v. Virginia Surface Mining & Reclamation Ass'n, Inc.,* 452 U.S. 264, 300 (1981) (stating, "deprivation of property to protect the public health and safety is '[one] of the oldest examples' of permissible summary action."). Thus, although some pre-deprivation procedures are generally required, procedures may be minimal, especially when post-deprivation hearings follow. This statement leads then to our next question: what procedures does due process actually require?

# D.  Question Three: What Process Is Due?

After determining whether a pre- or post-deprivation hearing is necessary, you need to determine what procedures due process requires for a particular case. Recall that there are a number of potential procedures due process might require, including some or all of the following: (1) notice, (2) an opportunity to be present at the proceeding, (3) an opportunity to present orally at the proceeding, (4) an opportunity to confront and cross-examine witnesses, (5) an opportunity to submit rebuttal evidence, (6) the right to be represented by counsel, (7) the right to a neutral decisionmaker, (8) the right to a reasoned decision based exclusively on the record, and (9) the right to judicial review of that decision. Not every procedure applies to every deprivation. In some cases, a relatively full formal process will be required, including notice, an opportunity to confront and cross-examine witnesses, and the right to a neutral decisionmaker. In other cases, all that may be required is notice coupled with an opportunity to respond. *See, e.g., Goss v. Lopez*, 419 U.S. 565, 581 (1975) (finding the Due Process Clause, at a minimum, guarantees students facing suspension be given notice, an opportunity to hear the evidence against them, and a chance to deny the allegations by presenting their side of the story). The applicable procedures will vary based on a three-factor test the Supreme Court developed in *Mathews*, 424 U.S. at 319.

In *Mathews*, the government terminated an individual's Social Security disability benefits after determining that his qualifying disability had ended. *Id*. at 324. As part of routine monitoring, the agency sent the claimant a questionnaire, in which he indicated that his condition had not improved and identified his medical providers. *Id*. at 323–24. However, based on the answers to the questionnaire and written reports from doctors, including his own, the agency preliminary determined that his physical condition had improved to the point that he no longer qualified for benefits. *Id*. The agency notified the claimant and allowed him to submit additional information to support his claim that he was still disabled. The plaintiff's ensuing response was not convincing, and the agency terminated his disability payments. *Id*.

The appeal process allowed claimants to request a full evidentiary hearing *after* termination, with any money improperly withheld to be paid retroactively. *Id*. at 339. Instead of appealing the termination through this appeal process, the claimant filed a lawsuit claiming the process violated due process. *Id*. at 325. Citing *Goldberg*, 397 U.S. at 254, the claimant argued that he was entitled to a pre-deprivation hearing just as the claimant in *Goldberg* was. *Id*. Indeed, the two processes in *Goldberg* and *Mathews* mirrored each other: both appeal processes allowed the government to first informally determine whether benefits should continue based on written information. If benefits were terminated, a full evidentiary hearing was provided after termination. *Id*. at 333. In *Goldberg*, the Court had held that a post-termination process was insufficient; you would have expected the same outcome here. You would be surprised.

The issue for the Court was not whether due process applied; all parties agreed that it did. Moreover, the parties did not dispute whether the post-deprivation hearing satisfied due process; all parties agreed that it did. The only issue for the Court was whether the government had to provide a full evidentiary hearing before terminating benefits or whether the informal procedures coupled with the post-deprivation procedures were sufficient. *Id*. at 323. Both the district court and the court of appeals, relying on *Goldberg*, held that a full, pre-deprivation, evidentiary hearing was required. The Supreme Court reversed. *Id*. at 325–26.

The result in *Mathews* is surprising given *Goldberg*'s holding. While the Court attempted to distinguish *Goldberg*, the Court's reasoning is unpersuasive. Rather, the Court appeared concerned about the administrative burden that *Goldberg* would unleash. *Id.* at 347 (claiming the "incremental cost resulting from increased . . . hearings and the expense of providing benefits to ineligible recipients pending decision . . . would not be insubstantial."). Hence, the Court rejected *Goldberg*'s presumption that due process always requires "judicial-type" protections prior to deprivation. "The judicial model of an evidentiary hearing is neither a required, nor even the most effective, method of decisionmaking in all circumstances." *Id.* at 348. Instead, the inquiry is whether those who want to be heard "are given a meaningful opportunity to be heard." *Id.* at 349.

In determining whether individuals are given a meaningful opportunity to be heard, the Court famously developed its three-factor test, now used to assess the adequacy of the agency's procedures under the Due Process Clause:

> [D]ue process generally requires consideration of three distinct factors: First, the private interest that will be affected by the official action; second, the risk of an erroneous deprivation of such interest through the procedures used and the probable value, if any, of additional or substitute procedural safeguards; and [third], the Government's interest, including the function involved and the fiscal and administrative burdens that the additional or substitute procedural requirement would entail.

*Id.* at 334–35. Applying its test, the Court held that the procedures offered pretermination were sufficient in *Mathews*. We will look at each factor in more detail below.

## 1. The Private Interest

The first factor courts consider under *Mathews* is the private interest the deprivation affects. Remember that in deciding *whether* due process applies, courts do not look at how serious the harm is. Rather, courts look only at the nature of harm; the harm must affect either a property or liberty interest. In contrast, when determining *what* process is due, *Mathews* directs courts to consider the seriousness of the harm an individual is likely to suffer from the deprivation of procedure.

For example, in *Mathews*, the plaintiff challenged the timing of the hearing. The Supreme Court examined the "private interest" factor by comparing *Goldberg*'s interest in continued welfare benefits to the plaintiff's interest in continued disability benefits. The Court reasoned that the claimant's interest in receiving disability benefits uninterrupted during an appeal was less important than a claimant's interest in receiving welfare benefits uninterrupted during an appeal because welfare is awarded based on an individual's financial need. *Id.* at 325–26. Even though the claimant in *Mathews* was, in fact, financially dependent on the disability benefits, the Court ignored this fact. *Id.* at 326. The appropriate inquiry, the Court noted, was not whether *this* plaintiff was harmed but whether disability claimants in general would be severely harmed if their benefits stopped temporarily. *Id.* at 344. Welfare benefits, the Court said, are typically a recipient's safety net. *Id.* at 340. In contrast, disability benefits are not essential to survival. *Id.* at 342. Further, when benefits are stopped, disability claimants are less likely than welfare claimants to suffer a year-long wait for a hearing. *Id.* Hence, the private interest, or harm, in *Mathews* was less significant than that in *Goldberg*. *Id.* at 344. The first factor in the *Mathews'* balancing test cut in favor of the government.

## 2. The Risk of Error

The second factor under *Mathews* is whether the procedures available are likely to produce unacceptably high rates of error. In other words, courts will consider whether additional procedures would be likely to significantly improve the accuracy of the government's decision. But courts have been clear that the judicial model is not necessarily the best model for accuracy in administrative proceedings, which do not involve jury trials.

For example, in *Mathews*, the Court reasoned that trial-like procedures would not have been useful to prevent an erroneous deprivation. To reach this finding, the Court focused on the nature of the issues in dispute and the type of evidence necessary to resolve those issues. For example, if the issues involved disputed testimony of witnesses, cross-examination might be useful. If the issues required only written documentation, cross-examination would not be useful. The issues in *Mathews* were technical, medical issues, which could be resolved with "routine, standard and unbiased medical reports by physician specialists." *Id.* Unlike *Goldberg*, in *Mathews*, there were no issues relating to witness credibility. *Id.* Here, allowing a full evidentiary hearing post-deprivation was an error-free enough process to satisfy due process.

Similarly, in *Board of Curators of the University of Missouri v. Horowitz*, 435 U.S. 78, 79–80 (1978), the Court rejected a student's claim that she was entitled to more process before her dismissal from medical school for academic reasons. Without reaching the issue of whether the student had a liberty interest in "pursuing a medical career," the Court held that she had received as much process as would be due. *Id.* at 84–85. She was given notice of the faculty's dissatisfaction with her performance and an opportunity to correct those problems, which she failed to do, *Id.* at 80–81. In fact, the Court found that the school offered more procedure than due process required. *Id.* at 85.

Applying the *Mathews* balancing test, the Court rejected the plaintiff's claim that she was entitled to anything further. Focusing on the second factor, the Court said that the decision to dismiss a student is "not readily adapted to the procedural tools of judicial or administrative decisionmaking." *Id.* at 90. The Court distinguished between the procedures required in disciplinary versus academic proceedings. "Academic evaluations . . . bear little resemblance to the judicial and administrative fact-finding proceedings to which we have traditionally attached a full-hearing requirement." *Id.* at 89. Hence, for academic dismissals, little is necessary other than notice of the deficiency.

In contrast, when a student may be subject to criminal liability from actions addressed in an administrative proceeding, due process requires that the student be able to consult an attorney, at a minimum. *Gabrilowitz v. Newman*, 582 F.2d 100, 107 (1st Cir. 1978). In *Gabrilowitz*, a student, who was criminally charged with assault with intent to commit rape, was required to defend himself in a school disciplinary proceeding. *Id.* at 101. The school prohibited the presence of legal counsel at the hearing, but allowed the assistance of a non-legal advisor.

Applying *Mathews*, the First Circuit held that the student's private interest, the loss of a college degree and possible imprisonment, was substantial in this case. *Id.* at 105. Moreover, the likelihood that legal assistance would "enable [the student] to make an intelligent, informed choice between the risks presented," the second factor, was also substantial. *Id.* at 106. In contrast, the third factor, the public interest in orderly hearings, was not substantial enough to outweigh the other two. *Id.*

It is important to note that the court did not require that the school allow the attorney to fully participate in the hearing; rather, the court held that the student had a right only "to have a lawyer of his own choice [to] consult with and advise him during the disciplinary hearing without participating further in such proceeding." *Id.* at 107; *accord, Osteen v. Henley*, 13 F.3d 221, 225 (7th Cir. 1993) (stating "[e]ven if a student has a constitutional right to consult counsel . . . we do not think he is entitled to be represented in the sense of having a lawyer who is permitted to examine or cross-examine witnesses, to submit and object to documents, to address the tribunal, and otherwise to perform the traditional function of a trial lawyer . . . . The cost and complexity of such proceedings would be increased, to the detriment of discipline as well as the university's fisc. . . ."). In sum, when criminal charges are pending or likely, students should be able to consult with an attorney during a school disciplinary hearing to protect them from further harm. The cost to the schools in such cases is minimal.

The short lesson from these cases is that the Court does not believe that judicial-like procedures ensure error-free decisions, nor that error-free decision making is the standard. Rather, the procedures need only be "good-enough," especially when compared to the cost of those procedures, the final *Mathews* factor.

## 3. The Public Interest

The third factor under *Mathews* is the impact of the requested procedures on the public interest. For fiscal reasons, the public has an interest in agencies working cost effectively. The third factor accounts for this interest.

Developing this third factor in *Mathews*, the Court expressed concern about the increased administrative burden and costs associated with requiring a full evidentiary hearing before the benefits were terminated. *Id.* at 225–226. Monetary costs can be substantial for high volume settings such as disability and social security cases. For example, as of December 2008, there were 7.4 million disabled workers receiving benefits; the Social Security Administration receives 2.5 million new applications each year. If an application gets to the hearing stage, delays can be substantial. In 2008, there were 765,000 cases pending at the hearing level and 53,000 cases pending at the internal appellate stage. The average time to receive an award after hearing was 535 days. *See* General Statistics on Social Security Disability Insurance (SSDI) and Allsup, http://www.allsup.com/about-us/news-room/resources-for-journalists/general-statistics.aspx (accessed June 12, 2017). The cost to pay administrative judges to preside at these hearings is also substantial.

In addition to cost, the Court in *Mathews* focused on the increased administrative burdens from the increased number of hearings that would ensue. 424 U.S. at 335–336. If disability payments continued until a hearing concluded, claimants would have an incentive to sue regardless of the validity of their claim. *Id.* at 346. In other words, why would any claimant not appeal when doing so would mean that the benefits would continue for at least another year and a half? It is true that the statute at issue in the case provided that overpayments could be recouped if the claimant was unqualified to receive them; however, the Court did not view recoupment as likely. *Id.* at 339.

In another case, the Supreme Court applied *Mathews*' three-factor test to uphold a statute that limited attorney's fees in veterans' benefits cases to $10. *Walters v. National Assoc. of Radiation Survivors*, 473 U.S. 305, 334 (1985). Even though the fee limitation frustrated veterans' access to legal representation, the Court gave "great weight" to the public interest factor. *Id.* at 326. The Court reasoned that Congress limited the fee to ensure that the veteran would receive the entire award and to foster an informal, nonadversarial adjudicatory process. *Id.* at 323–24. Given this strong public interest, the Court reasoned, "It would take an extraordinarily strong showing of probability of error under the present system—and the probability that the presence of attorneys would sharply diminish that possibility—to warrant holding that the fee limitation denies claimants due process of law." *Id.* at 326. Although the veterans demonstrated that the value of having an attorney at the proceeding increased a veteran's success rate by approximately sixteen percent, this difference was not significant enough to overcome the public interest factor. *Id.* at 327.

In short, the public interest factor seems to be the most critical factor of the *Mathews* three-factor test, and is often fatal. For example, the Court in *Mathews* seemed skeptical that additional procedures would actually be beneficial and certain that they would be costly. 424 U.S. at 347–48. The Court in *Walters* seemed concerned that administrative hearings would become adversarial judicial events. 473 U.S. at 323–24.

Some commentators have criticized *Mathews. See, e.g.,* Jerry L. Mashaw, *The Supreme Court's Due Process Calculation for Administrative Adjudication in* Mathews v. Eldridge: *Three Factors in Search of a Theory of Value,* 44 U. Chi. L. Rev. 28 (1976). But it is unclear whether that the criticism is warranted. While more process often seems intuitively right to lawyers, the reality is that too much process may be counterproductive and cost-prohibitive. For example, the result in *Horowitz,* 435 U.S. at 90, is surely correct: Schools should not have to provide hearings before dismissing students who fail to meet academic standards. In contrast, when a student may risk criminal liability, some procedure seems appropriate to protect that important right.

While procedures are essential to protect important rights, too much procedure can impede orderly administration and increase government costs. *Mathews'* three-factor test may best balance these competing goals. The test may encourage agencies to develop procedures to reduce the likelihood of erroneous deprivations because *Mathews* encourages agencies to adopt measures such as better training and more effective supervision to keep their error rate low. Lower error rates reduce appeals and litigation and gain public goodwill. Jerry L. Mashaw, *The Management Side of Due Process: Some Theoretical Notes on the Assurance of Accuracy, Fairness, and Timeliness in the Adjudication of Social Welfare Claims,* 59 Cornell L. Rev. 772, 785 (1974).

## 4. The Right to a Neutral Decisionmaker

Above, we discussed what procedures due process requires generally. When considering the question of what procedures due process requires, a lawyer might naturally conclude that litigants must have the right to a neutral decisionmaker. In the last chapter, we explored the APA's approach to this issue as it applies to formal adjudications. Here, we explore what due process requires regarding this issue for informal adjudications and rulemakings.

Prior to the Supreme Court's development of *Mathews'* three-factor test, the Court addressed this issue in *Withrow v. Larkin*, 421 U.S. 35 (1975). In that case the Court noted that "a fair tribunal is a basic requirement of due process." *Id.* at 47 (quotations omitted). Further, a biased decisionmaker is constitutionally unacceptable even in an administrative proceeding. *Id.* In *Withrow*, the plaintiff physician argued that the disciplinary board could not combine functions such that it investigated him, presented the charges, and ruled on those charges. *Id.* at 49–50.

The Supreme Court disagreed. The fact that an agency combines investigative and adjudicative functions does not alone create an unconstitutional risk of bias because administrative officials presumptively are honest and have integrity. *Id.* at 47. In *Withrow*, the Court required the plaintiff to show actual bias, meaning that the mind of the decisionmaker was irrevocably closed on the issue. *Id.* at 54. A decisionmaker's predisposed view of *the law* is not enough to demonstrate bias; rather, bias exists only when the decisionmaker has already decided *the facts*. While it will be rare for a government official to demonstrate factual bias, in one case, the D.C. Circuit found such bias where the Chair of the Federal Trade Commission gave a speech in which he indicated his conclusion that Texaco had violated the law. *Texaco Inc. v. FTC*, 336 F.2d 754, 760 (D.C. Cir. 1964), *vacated and remanded on other grounds*, 381 U.S. 739 (1965). In sum, such bias will rarely be found.

It is important to note that both of these cases were decided prior to *Mathews*. Hence, it is possible today that a court would apply *Mathews'* test to resolved the issue of whether a decisionmaker is biased enough to violate due process. Yet *Withrow* makes clear that the lack of a separation of functions alone will not be sufficient.

# E. Conclusion

We have seen that the first issue a court must address in a Due Process case is whether the clause applies at all. Under current doctrine, courts do not resolve this question by asking about the *seriousness* of the harm to the plaintiff. Instead, courts focus on the plaintiff's interest, asking whether it is a property or a liberty interest. The courts have not consistently or clearly defined property and liberty interests. Moreover, the courts have retreated from broad to more narrow definitions because of the magnitude of the costs that would be incurred if protection were extended to every grievous loss citizens might experience at the hands of the government.

*Mathews'* three-factor test attempts to balance these concerns. Applying it, we see how the level of formality and nature of the procedures required can be adjusted as the private interest, the value of the procedure, and the costs are balanced.

Finally, keep in mind that due process provides only minimal protection to citizens; the APA, the agency's enabling statute, and the agency's own rules often provide significantly more procedural protections. A litigant would do well to start with those sources, and turn to the Due Process Clause as a last resort.

## Checkpoints

- Procedural due process assures basic fairness in process when government action injures individuals.

- The first question is whether due process applies at all.

- Due process applies when there are factual issues in dispute such that a hearing would be beneficial.

- Due process applies when the issues in dispute involve adjudicatory facts and affect an individual's life, liberty, or property interest.

- An individual has a property interest when that individual has a legitimate claim of entitlement to the property under existing law.

- An individual has a liberty interest in being free from reputational injury that impacts future job opportunities or other interests (stigma plus).

- The second question is: when does due process apply?

- Absent exigent circumstances, due process requires the government provide at least notice and an opportunity to respond to allegations pre-termination.

- The third question is: what process is due?

- In determining what process is due, courts apply *Mathews'* three-factor test, which balances the importance of: (1) the private interest that is harmed, (2) the likelihood that added procedure(s) would prevent erroneous deprivation, and (3) the public interest in keeping costs and administrative burdens low.

- One specific procedural protection that may apply is that litigants have a right to an unbiased decisionmaker who has not made up his or her mind about the factual issues prior to the hearing.

# Chapter 5

# The Availability of Judicial Review

---

## Roadmap

- Why judicial review is important
- When do courts have jurisdiction?
- Who is entitled to judicial review?
  - Constitutional standing
  - Prudential standing
  - Statutory standing
- What is subject to judicial review
  - Agency action
  - Express and implied preclusion
  - Committed to agency discretion
- When is judicial review available?
  - Finality
  - Exhaustion of Administrative Remedies
  - Administrative Issue Exhaustion
  - Ripeness
  - Primary Jurisdiction

---

## A. Introduction

In *Marbury v. Madison*, 1 Cranch (5 U.S.) 137, 138 (1803), the Supreme Court famously held that courts have the power to review the constitutionality of acts of Congress. The Court also held that courts have the power to review the constitutionality of acts of the executive. The holdings in this case are important because, without judicial review, citizens would not have the

125

ability to hold members of the legislative and the executive branch accountable. But the availability of judicial review generally does not mean it is available in a particular case. Indeed, Marbury lost his case because the Supreme Court held that it did not have jurisdiction, or power, to hear the case. *Id.* at 138, 175.

This chapter examines the requirements for *obtaining* judicial review, including that a *plaintiff* have standing, that the *court* have jurisdiction, and that the *claim* be suitable for judicial review. Assuming a plaintiff can obtain judicial review, the next question to be answered is what the scope of that judicial review will be. Hence, in this chapter, we will answer the following questions relating to judicial review: (1) *whether* a court has the power to review an agency's action, (2) *who* is able to obtain judicial review, (3) *when* judicial review is available, and (4) *what* claims are subject to judicial review. This chapter will focus on the what, when, who, and how questions related to the *availability* of judicial review. Chapter six will focus on the what, when, who, and how questions related to the *scope* of judicial review.

## B. Why Judicial Review Is Important

Why is judicial review so critical? The answer may not be altogether obvious; after all, if a strict separation of powers were the hallmark of the administrative system, shouldn't we insist that the judicial branch leave the other branches to their constitutionally assigned tasks? After all, the executive and legislative branches are more efficient than the judicial branch, have more resources, are able to innovate, have scientific and technical expertise, and are accountable to the public as elected officials.

Given these advantages, why should we give the judicial branch, whose members are appointed for life, *any* role in reviewing the legitimacy of the regulatory process? Legitimacy is a basic premise of our government. The rule of law requires that all exercises of governmental power be within legal limits. For administrative law, the rule of law means that agencies must stay within the powers Congress and the president assign to them. Moreover, it also means that when Congress empowers agencies, Congress itself must stay within the limits the Constitution lays out.

It is not that judges are pure of heart while executives and legislators are lawless rogues. Executive and legislative officers, just like judges, take an oath to uphold the nation's constitution and laws. And judicial review is not the only way to assure that government officials stay within legal boundaries. Other nations have devised means of controlling their government officials that do not involve judicial review. Our nation, however, has a long tradition of assigning this important role to judges.

Why did our founders choose this system? "[T]here is in our society a profound, tradition-taught reliance on the courts as the ultimate guardian and assurance of the limits set upon executive power by the constitutions and legislatures." Louis L. Jaffe, Judicial Control of Administrative Action 321–24 (1965). We have Lord Coke's seventeenth-century assertion in *Dr. Bonham's case*, 77 Eng. Rep 646 (C.P. 1610); we have John Marshall's opinion in *Marbury v. Madison*, 5 U.S. 137 (1803); we have Madison's insight about the dangers of majority factions in The Federalist No. 10 and Hamilton's follow-up in The Federalist No. 78 that judicial officers are a "barrier to the encroachments and oppressions of the representative body"; and we have America's nineteenth-century frontier experience in which judges were often the most visible embodiments of law and justice in a barely civilized community.

Whatever the cause, the institution of judicial review is firmly settled in our system. We have historically expected courts to serve as one of the important checks on the legitimacy of government action. Thus, there *will* be some type of judicial review of almost all administrative action. It will be a rare legislative delegation that does not contain a specific judicial review provision or is reviewable under the APA. Even when Congress seeks to limit, or preclude, judicial review, the courts must interpret and apply such limits. Given our nation's preference for judicial review, the courts have not been overly generous in interpreting preclusive language.

Asking courts to review the legality of any given action in light of the technical, scientific, and political work of administrative agencies is not easy. How can courts perform their function effectively? Remember that courts are highly specialized entities. Like violins, they are exquisite when performing the job for which they were designed, but almost clumsy when asked to perform tasks for which they were not designed.

Consider the following characteristics of courts. None of these translate well in the context of judicial review of administrative actions:

- Courts are not designed to make general policy or manage large institutions; rather, courts' core function is to resolve individual disputes;
- Courts can provide and enforce only limited types of relief;
- Courts are expected to be neutral tribunals responding to the legal arguments of adversarial parties;
- Courts apply accepted legal principles to reach reasoned decisions;
- Courts employ generalist judges who are not experts in technical, scientific, and political matters;

- Federal judges have life tenure and are not directly accountable to the public; and
- Courts are few compared to the millions of agency actions that might need judicial review.

This topic, the *availability* of judicial review, is very complex and difficult to apply. The doctrines overlap and were significantly narrowed over time as the Supreme Court has moved to limit the availability of judicial review. The doctrines in this area reflect the tension between our notion that judicial review is important and our understanding that it is not an exact fit. The doctrines we will study below attempt to allow courts to contribute what they can to assure the legality and legitimacy of agency actions, without imposing tasks on the judiciary that are fiscally wasteful, functionally infeasible, or politically inappropriate.

As we proceed through this topic, we begin with the most critical issue to address for judicial review, jurisdiction — the issue that handed Marbury his loss.

## C. Whether Courts Have Jurisdiction: The Courts

The first question in every case filed in federal court is whether that court has jurisdiction to hear the particular claim. Jurisdiction is so critical that courts can raise lack of jurisdiction *sua sponte*. *See Steel Co. v. Citizens for a Better Environment*, 523 U.S. 83, 84, 93 (1998) (noting that jurisdictional questions can be raised by a court of its own accord, or *sua sponte*).

Jurisdiction focuses on the courts' power to hear the claim itself. This power must come from a statute other than the APA because the APA contains no jurisdiction-granting language. For administrative cases, Congress may grant federal courts jurisdiction in the agency's enabling statute. For example, the Clean Air Act provides that the federal appellate courts have jurisdiction to review actions taken by the EPA pursuant to that Act. *See, e.g.,* 42 U.S.C. § 7607(b); *see also* 47 U.S.C. § 402(b) (providing for judicial review of Federal Communications Commission orders).

However, even when the enabling statute fails to provide a grant of jurisdiction, the general federal question statute, 28 U.S.C. § 1331, provides federal courts with jurisdiction. That statute provides "[t]he district courts shall have original jurisdiction of all civil actions arising under the Constitution, laws, or treaties of the United States." *Id.* Because the APA is a law of the United States, federal courts have jurisdiction to hear claims brought under that statute. Hence, jurisdiction over a claim is rarely a problem in administrative law cases.

# D. Who Is Entitled to Judicial Review: The Plaintiff

After determining whether a court has jurisdiction to hear the claim, the next question is whether the court has jurisdiction to hear from the specific plaintiff or plaintiffs filing the action. Standing is also a jurisdictional question. The question is whether this specific plaintiff has standing. Standing involves both *constitutional* requirements and *prudential* requirements.

In most administrative law cases, standing is not a problem. When an agency takes action against a particular individual—such as revoking the individual's license—that individual will have standing to seek judicial review of the revocation. But it is a peculiarity of the administrative process that administrative action aimed at one individual may affect other individuals. If there is a plausible claim that the agency's action is illegal, can anyone challenge the legality of the agency's action?

For example, suppose that a private school discriminates on the basis of race. That school seeks a charity exemption from the Internal Revenue Service (IRS) so that contributions to the school can be deducted on a donor's tax return. Assume that the IRS cannot legally grant charitable status to such a school. Who can sue to stop the IRS action? If the IRS grants charitable status, the private school itself would not challenge the action. The school's donors would likely not challenge the action because they, too, would benefit from the decision. Even the parents of students in the school are unlikely to challenge the IRS decision, for their tuition costs may be lowered because of the outside donations. But what about a civil rights organization opposed to discrimination? Could it sue the IRS? Or what about a parent in a *public* school? Could such a parent sue, arguing that the IRS policy encouraged the formation of white-only private schools, which reduce the likelihood of a truly integrated public school system?

If our system is truly operating under the rule of law, one might suppose that these parents could challenge potentially unlawful action. But our standing law is not so generous. Courts have been reluctant to extend the right to challenge alleged unlawful action to those who are not directly affected by an agency's action. Why? The answer to that question involves both *constitutional* limitations and *prudential* considerations. We begin our standing discussion with the constitutional limitations.

# 1. Constitutional Standing

The Constitution restricts the power of the federal courts to hear only "cases and controversies." U.S. Const. art. III § 2, cl. 1. Courts have construed the phrase "cases and controversies" to refer to the kind of disputes that were typical at the time the Constitution was drafted. Thus, for example, there is a case or controversy when the owner of Blackacre disputes the boundary she shares with the owner of adjoining Whiteacre. In this situation, we would expect both parties to vigorously defend their positions in court because they have a personal stake in the outcome. Plaintiffs who do not have a personal stake in the outcome might be less likely to fight so vigorously. Spirited advocacy is very important to the otherwise passive judicial system. Hence, we generally do not let individuals without a personal stake sue.

To be fair, the belief that only those with a personal stake in the outcome of a case will fight vigorously is largely a fiction, given the well-financed and passionately committed views of many interest groups today. Indeed, it would be hard to find a group with a deeper commitment to litigation than the public interest and environmental groups who frequently face standing barriers. But judges continue to give the "stake in the outcome" rationale to support their standing decisions. Judges do not want to deal with hypothetical cases, so they reject claims made by plaintiffs whose interests are not obviously and directly affected. This rationale also reflects the federal judges' historic reluctance to issue advisory opinions. Because the case or controversy requirement is constitutional, Congress cannot open the courthouse doors to anybody with a plausible legal claim. In other words, Congress cannot add a clause to a statute allowing anyone to sue in the case of a violation of a statute.

Let's return to our hypothetical. The public school parents are not as immediately connected to the dispute as the adjoining landowners in the boundary dispute case; hence, a judge would likely find that the parents have no constitutional standing. *See Allen v. Wright*, 468 U.S. 737 (1984) (holding that such parents lacked standing to sue).

How does a plaintiff demonstrate that his or her injury meets the case or controversy requirement? A plaintiff must show three things: (1) injury in fact, (2) causation, and (3) redressability. *Lujan v. Defenders of Wildlife*, 504 U.S. 555, 560–61 (1992). We will examine each element below. As we do so, we will look at the Supreme Court's case law in this area. Do not expect the holdings to be consistent, unanimous, or make much sense. The Court has generously interpreted constitutional standing when it wants to reach the merits of a case and ungenerously interpreted constitutional standing when it does not want to reach the merits. In a moment of rare candor, the Court has said that "generalizations about standing to sue are largely worthless as such." *Association of Data Processing v. Camp*, 397 U.S. 150, 151 (1970). To see two academics debate the Court's efforts to present a principled justification of standing doctrines, compare Lea Brilmayer, *The Jurisprudence of Article III: Perspectives on the "Case or Controversy" Requirement*, 93 HARV. L. REV. 297 (1979), *with* Mark Tushnet, *The "Case or Controversy" Controversy*, 93 HARV. L. REV. 1698 (1980).

### a. Injury in Fact

First to bring a lawsuit challenging agency action, a plaintiff must show that he or she suffered or is about to suffer an *injury in fact*. When a plaintiff suffers an injury directly, such as a fine or loss of a license, that plaintiff suffers an injury in fact. However, there are many other, less obvious types of injuries, such as economic, aesthetic, environmental, recreational, and informational. However, procedural injury alone is not sufficient. *Lujan*, 504 U.S. at 573, n.8.

For example, in *United States v. Students Challenging Regulatory Agency Procedures* (SCRAP), 412 U.S. 669 (1973), five law students from George Washington University sued the now-defunct Interstate Commerce Commission (ICC) after it approved the railroads' request to increase the rate charged for transporting recyclable materials. *Id.* at 670. Their complaint alleged that the ICC failed to follow the National Environmental Policy Act when approving the rate hike. *Id.* But the students could not simply complain about the procedural violation. Thus, they claimed that the higher rates would discourage recycling, which would increase the amount of litter and trash in nearby federal parks. *Id.* at 676. The increased litter and trash would negatively impact their interests in using "the forest, rivers, streams, mountains, and other natural resources of the Washington Metropolitan area and [affect their interests in] camping, hiking, fishing, [and] sightseeing." *Id.* at 678. Thus, these plaintiffs alleged aesthetic and recreational injuries.

In a watershed moment for standing, the majority found that the plaintiffs had standing. *Id.* at 690. Conceding that pleadings "must be something more than an ingenious academic exercise in the conceivable," and admitting that the connection between the agency procedural violation and the alleged harm was "attenuated," the majority found the constitutionally required injury in fact. *Id.* at 688. Although they won the standing challenge, plaintiffs eventually lost on the merits of the case. Remember, standing only gets a plaintiff into court, it does not mean the plaintiff wins the case.

Another generous standing holding came in *Duke Power Co. v. Carolina Environmental Study Group*, 438 U.S. 59 (1978). In that case, the constitutionality of the Price-Anderson Act was challenged. *Id.* at 67. That Act imposed liability limits for nuclear accidents to encourage private companies to build nuclear power plants. *Id.* at 64. The plaintiffs included individuals living near potential nuclear plants who were concerned about the liability limits placed on the plants in the case of a nuclear accident. *Id.* at 67. While none of these individuals had yet been injured as a result of a nuclear accident, the Court found the constitutionally required injury in fact. *Id.* at 60. The Court said that the construction and safe operation of the plants would themselves cause plaintiffs injury, such as increased water temperature in lakes used for cooling the plant and small amounts of radiation that would inevitably be present even in safe facilities. *Id.* at 73. While these injuries were not the injuries about which plaintiffs complained, the Court held that they were sufficient for standing purposes. *Id.* at 80–81.

Some have speculated that the Court in *Duke Power* applied the standing doctrine generously because the Court wanted to address questions about the constitutionality of the Act. After finding that plaintiffs had standing to challenge the Act, the Court held that the Act was constitutional. *Id.* at 84. Thus, like the plaintiffs in *SCRAP*, the plaintiffs in *Duke Power* won on standing, but lost on the merits.

Less generous on standing is the Court's more recent case of *Lujan*, 504 U.S. at 555. In this case, the Endangered Species Act (ESA) was at issue. *Id.* at 557–58. The ESA was promulgated to protect endangered and threatened animals. Pursuant to authority granted to it in the ESA, the Fish and Wildlife Service (FWS) and the National Marine Fisheries Service (NMFS), on behalf of the Secretary of the Interior and the Secretary of Commerce respectively, promulgated a joint regulation stating that the obligations the ESA imposed extended to actions taken in foreign nations. *Id.* at 558. In 1986, the joint regulation was revised, interpreting the ESA to require consultation only for actions taken within the United States or on the high seas. *Id.* at 558–59. The plaintiffs, organizations dedicated to wildlife conservation, filed an action seeking an injunction against the Secretary of the Interior to reinstate the initial interpretation of the ESA. *Id.* at 559. The Secretary moved for summary judgment, citing lack of standing. *Id.*

To establish injury in fact, the plaintiffs alleged aesthetic injuries. They stated that they enjoyed observing certain endangered species in the wild and would not like to see them in captivity. *Id.* at 566. To support their claim, the plaintiffs averred that they might visit countries where threatened animals lived, but they admitted that they had no specific plans or dates for any such visits. *Id.* at 591–92.

The plurality acknowledged that a plaintiff's interest in observing various animal species for purely aesthetic purposes could be an injury in fact;

however, the plurality reasoned that these particular plaintiffs had failed to show that that their alleged injury was concrete and imminent. *Id*. at 572–73. The Court said "such 'someday' intentions—without any description of concrete plans, or indeed even any specification of *when* the someday will be— do not support a finding of the 'actual or imminent' injury that our cases require." *Id*. at 564.

Justices Kennedy and Souter concurred on this issue, but they noted that it would not have taken much for plaintiffs to have established the imminence of the injury. In their view, purchase of airline tickets or the announcement of a date certain for return to the area might have been enough. *Id*. at 579 (Kennedy, J., concurring). All that was required in the concurrence's view was evidence that makes it "reasonable to assume that the [plaintiffs] will be using the site on a regular basis." *Id*.

The outcome in this case shows a Court divided; some justices want a tougher standing doctrine while others prefer a more generous doctrine. If the plaintiffs in *Lujan* had simply purchased airline tickets to Sri Lanka, Justices Kennedy and Souter would have changed their vote on injury in fact and the case would have been heard on the merits. Making a case turn on trivialities like whether the plaintiffs purchased airline tickets hardly seems a triumph of reasoned analysis; yet this is where we find ourselves.

In addition to alleging the aesthetic injury, the plaintiffs in *Lujan* also alleged a procedural injury. Plaintiffs claimed a procedural injury when they alleged that an agency's failure to follow a statutorily required procedure would cause harm. In *Lujan*, the statute specifically authorized "any person" to "commence a civil suit . . . to enjoin any person . . . who is alleged to be in violation . . . of this chapter." *Id*. at 571–72 (quoting 16 U.S.C. § 1540(g)). Such a provision is known as a "citizen lawsuit provision." Although the statute seemed to allow anyone to file suit to force an agency to follow statutorily prescribed procedures, the majority reasoned that the citizen lawsuit provision violated the case or controversy requirement in the Constitution. *Id*. at 573. The plurality reasoned that because the case and controversy requirement is constitutional, Congress could not eliminate it in the statute. *Id*. Thus, the Court rejected the procedural injury as sufficient to constitute injury in fact. *Id*. at 573, n.8. Rather, the Court explained, if the plaintiffs alleged a procedural injury, then the plaintiffs must show that the procedural injury injured them directly, in a concrete and particularized fashion. *Id*. at 560; *compare, FEC v. Akins*, 524 U.S. 11, 19 (1998) (holding that a plaintiff had standing when a statute allowed "any party aggrieved by an order of the [agency]" to file a lawsuit for not receiving requested information).

In a concurrence, Justices Kennedy and Souter argued that Congress could define injuries in a way that would give rise to a case or controversy where one did not exist prior to passage of a statute. *Lujan*, 504 U.S. at 580 (Kennedy, J., concurring). If a statute identified the injury and related that injury to a specific class of persons who were authorized to bring suit, then the statute would be well within Congress's power. However, in this case, Kennedy continued, the statute did not meet these conditions. *Id.* Thus, an agency's failure to comply with statutorily required procedures will be insufficient to constitute injury in fact because of the generalized nature of such an injury. But when the plaintiff is uniquely injured by an agency's failure to follow a mandated procedure (e.g., failure to provide information when specifically and legally requested to do so), the plaintiff would have a sufficient injury in fact for constitutional standing.

In sum, the Court has accepted various types of injuries as sufficient to establish injury in fact, including the following: a reasonable fear of harm, economic injury, environmental injury, recreational injury, informational injury, and aesthetic injury. *Massachusetts v. EPA*, 549 U.S. 497 (2007) (environmental injury); *Friends of the Earth, Inc. v. Laidlaw Envtl. Servs.*, 528 U.S. 167 (2000) (fear of physical harm); *Bennett v. Spear*, 520 U.S. 154 (1997) (economic injury); *SCRAP*, 412 U.S. at 669 (recreational and aesthetic injury); *Akins*, 524 U.S. 11 (informational injury); *Lujan*, 504 U.S. at 555 (aesthetic injury); *Data Processing*, 397 U.S. at 150 (economic injury).

In contrast, the Court has rejected generalized harm and procedural claims. *Lujan*, 504 U.S. at 555 (procedural injury); *United States v. Richardson*, 418 U.S. 166 (1974) (informational injury); *Sierra Club v. Morton*, 405 U.S. 727 (1972) (generalized grievance). Plaintiffs are most likely to meet the injury in fact requirement when they allege injuries that are certain to occur, imminent, specific to the plaintiff, direct, economic, and capable of being described in concrete terms. But even if they allege such injuries, plaintiffs have two more hurdles to overcome: causation and redressability.

### b. Causation

Second, to establish constitutional standing a plaintiff must demonstrate that the injury in fact was *caused by*, or is *fairly traceable to*, the agency action that is being challenged. For direct injuries, like a fine or loss of a license, a plaintiff will have no difficulty establishing causation. However, a plaintiff will have difficulty establishing causation in two situations. First, when the plaintiff alleges that the agency's failure to follow procedure will cause injury, and, second, when the plaintiff alleges that the agency's action has induced a third party to cause the harm.

For an example of a procedural causation case, let's return to *Lujan*. In *Lujan*, you will recall that the plaintiffs sued the Secretary of the Interior to challenge a regulation regarding the geographic area to which the consultation section of the ESA applied. *Lujan*, 504 U.S. at 559. First, the Court found that the plaintiffs did not have standing for their aesthetic injury claim. *Id.* at 570. The Court then addressed the plaintiffs alternative ground: that they suffered a procedural injury and that the ESA had a citizen lawsuit provision allowing anyone to sue any agency " 'who is alleged to be in violation of any provision of the [ESA].' " *Id.* at 572 (quoting 16 U.S.C. § 1540(g)).

As noted above, the Court rejected the plaintiffs' procedural injury claim. *Id.* at 571, 573. However, the Court hypothesized a case in which an individual could successfully bring a procedural injury claim. If an individual lived adjacent to a proposed dam site, that individual would have injury in fact and could challenge an agency's failure to follow procedural requirements, like completing an environmental impact statement (EIS). *Id.* at 572 n.7. The injury would be the building of the dam and its effect on the plaintiff's property (a direct harm); the alleged violation would be procedural. In such a case, there would be no need to show that the procedural injury will cause the alleged harm. Rather, the plaintiff need only show that the agency's final action will cause the harm. *See also, SCRAP*, 412 U.S. at 710 (finding causation where law students challenged the ICC's failure to prepare an EIS before allowing railroads to raise rates); *but see Florida Audubon Soc'y v. Bentsen*, 94 F.3d 658, 672 (D.C. Cir. 1996) (failing to find causation when plaintiffs alleged that their bird-watching activities would be harmed because the agency granted tax credits to manufacturers of fuel additives without first preparing an EIS).

In another case addressing causation, the Court concluded that if the agency's action contributed to the alleged injury in any meaningful way, causation would be found. *Massachusetts*, 549 U.S. at 523. In this case, Massachusetts sued the EPA after it refused to regulate carbon dioxide emissions. *Id.* at 497. Massachusetts alleged that its injury in fact was coastal erosion caused by rising sea levels, a result of global warming. *Id.* at 499. The federal government conceded that carbon dioxide emissions contributed to global warming and, thus, to rising sea levels. *Id.* at 523. The government argued, however, that the contribution from the EPA's decision not to regulate emissions from new cars would be so slight that the EPA's inaction could not be said to be the cause of Massachusetts injury. *Id.* at 524. The Court rejected the argument, saying that any meaningful contribution was sufficient to satisfy the causation requirement. *Id.* at 526.

For an example of a third-party causation case, consider *Simon v. Eastern Kentucky Welfare Rights Organization (EKWRO)*, 426 U.S. 26, 37 (1976). At issue in that case was an Internal Revenue Service (IRS) regulation that allowed tax-exempt hospitals to refuse to provide non-emergency medical care to indigent individuals. *Id.* at 28. EKWRO, a welfare rights organization, alleged that the IRS's regulation would injure its members because tax-exempt hospitals would reduce the amount of medical care they provided to indigent people. *Id.* at 33. Injury in fact was conceded: individuals who could not obtain free medical treatment would suffer direct harm. *Id.* at 40. However, the Court concluded that the plaintiff had not proved causation because it was "purely speculative whether the denials in service specified in the complaint can be traced to the [IRS's] 'encouragement' or instead result from decisions made by the hospitals without regard to tax implications." *Id.* at 42; *see also, Warth v. Seldin*, 422 U.S. 490, 509 (1975) (refusing to find causation where indigent individuals challenged a city's zoning requirements, alleging that the new requirements would limit the availability of low-cost housing).

In another case, the plaintiffs were able to overcome the difficulty of third-party causation by demonstrating that the agency's action would have a coercive effect on that third party, another agency. In *Bennett*, 520 U.S. at 169, the plaintiffs challenged a biological opinion the Fish and Wildlife Service (FWS) issued pursuant to the Endangered Species Act (ESA). *Id.* at 157. The ESA requires the Secretary of the Interior to identify those species of animals that are threatened or endangered. *Id.* at 154. If an agency determines that an action it proposes to take may adversely affect a listed species, the agency consults the FWS, which must provide the agency with a biological opinion explaining how the proposed action can be modified to best protect the species or its habitat. *Id.* After the FWS issued its biological opinion regarding the Klamath Reclamation Project, two irrigation districts and two ranches that all received water filed suit to challenge the minimum water level requirements. *Id.*

Regarding standing, the Court first determined that the plaintiffs' claim that they would receive less water was an injury in fact. *Id.* at 168. Regarding causation, the FWS argued that the cause of the plaintiffs' harm was, as of yet, an unidentified decision by another agency regarding the volume of water that would be allocated to plaintiffs, not the biological opinion itself. *Id.* The Court rejected that argument, saying that while "the Service's Biological Opinion theoretically serves an 'advisory function,' in reality it has a powerful coercive effect on the [other] agency." *Id.* at 169 (quotation omitted).

> The [other] agency is technically free to disregard the Biological Opinion and proceed with its proposed action, but it does so at its own peril (and that of its employees), for "any person" who knowingly

"takes" an endangered or threatened species is subject to substantial civil and criminal penalties, including imprisonment.

*Id.* at 170 (quotation omitted). Thus, the Court concluded, "given [the plaintiffs'] allegation that the [other agency] had, until issuance of the Biological Opinion, operated the Klamath Project in the same manner throughout the twentieth century, it is not difficult to conclude that petitioners have met their burden . . . of alleging that their injury is 'fairly traceable' to the Service's Biological Opinion." *Id.* at 170–71.

Finally, in *Allen*, 468 U.S. at 740, the Court held that parents of African-American children attending public schools did not have standing to challenge an IRS practice that supported racially discriminatory action by private schools. Plaintiff's claimed injury in fact was that the IRS practice allowed private schools to discriminate, which siphoned off Caucasian students who would otherwise contribute to the integration of public schools. *Id.* at 745. The Court conceded that deprivation of the right to attend an integrated school was a legitimate claim of injury, indeed, "one of the most serious injuries recognized in our legal system." *Id.* at 756. However, that injury could not be fairly traced to the action challenged. *Id.* at 757. Rather, the injury "results from the independent action of some third party not before the court." *Id.* The Court concluded that it would be "pure speculation whether, in a particular community, a large enough number of the numerous relevant school officials and parents would reach decisions that collectively would have a significant impact on the racial composition of the public schools." *Id.* at 758.

Justice Brennan wrote a strongly worded dissent. He called the majority opinion "misguided decision making," which shows "a startling insensitivity to the historical role played by the federal courts in eradicating race discrimination." *Id.* at 767 (Brennan, J., dissenting). Justice Brennan defined the causation element more broadly, noting that it would be enough if the plaintiff's interests were "adversely affected" by the challenged action. *Id.* at 774.

In summary, not only must a plaintiff demonstrate a sufficient injury in fact, but the plaintiff must also demonstrate that the alleged injury was caused by or is fairly traceable to the defendant agency's actions. When the alleged violation is procedural or when the entity causing the harm is not the entity being sued, plaintiffs have a more difficult time establishing causation. But again, another hurdle remains: redressability.

### c. Redressability

Third, to establish constitutional standing a plaintiff must demonstrate not only that the injury in fact was caused by, or is fairly traceable to, the agency action that is being challenged, but also that a favorable court decision will likely *redress* that injury. In other words, the plaintiff must demonstrate that if he or she wins the lawsuit, the plaintiff's harm will be remedied.

Often, courts address causation and redressability simultaneously, failing to separate the two elements. Such overlap occurs because when an agency action causes the injury, a favorable court decision will almost always redress the injury. In these cases, courts have little to discuss. Moreover, a plaintiff will have difficulty demonstrating redressability in two situations; and those situations are identical to those mentioned above relating to causation. First, a plaintiff will have difficulty demonstrating redressability when the plaintiff alleges that the agency's failure to follow procedure caused the injury. Second, a plaintiff will have difficulty demonstrating redressability when the plaintiff alleges that the agency's action has induced a third party to cause the harm.

Let's examine redressability in the context of a procedural case. When an agency violates a procedural requirement, any resulting injury comes not from the procedural violation (e.g., the failure to use notice and comment procedures), but from the agency's final action (e.g., issuing a permit to construct a dam). If a court required the agency to start over and follow the correct procedure (use notice and comment procedures), the agency would likely still reach the same result (issuing a permit to construct a dam), which may cause the same injury. Thus, it may be difficult for a plaintiff to demonstrate redressability in the case of a procedural injury because fixing the procedural deficiency will not necessarily change the outcome.

Recognizing this difficulty, the Court in *Lujan* said, "'procedural rights' are special: The person who has been accorded a procedural right to protect his concrete interests can assert that right without meeting all the normal standards for redressability and immediacy." *Lujan*, 504 U.S. at 572 n.7. The Court has not yet explained what this statement means exactly, but the statement suggests that injury in fact and causation may be enough to establish standing in the context of a procedural claim.

Let's examine redressability in the context of a third-party case and, again, return to *Lujan*. This time, we will consider the plaintiffs' aesthetic injury claim. In addition to addressing injury in fact and causation relating to the aesthetic injury, the Court also addressed "the most obvious problem in the . . . case . . . [is] redressability." *Id.* at 568. Like injury in fact and causation, the Court found redressability absent. *Id.* at 571. The Court reasoned that because the agencies funding the projects were not parties to the case, the lower court could provide relief only against the Secretary of the Interior. *Id.* The plurality reasoned that even if the lower court ordered the Secretary to amend the regulation to require agencies to consult on foreign projects, this outcome would not remedy plaintiffs' alleged injury unless the regulation bound the other agencies. Whether the regulation bound the funding agencies was in dispute. *Id*. The Court further noted that because the U.S. funds in question represented less than ten percent of the cost of the projects, the foreign governments might complete the projects even without the U.S. funding, which was another redressability problem for plaintiffs. *Id*. at 571.

Similarly, in *Allen*, 468 U.S. at 757, the Court concluded that redressability was absent. In *Allen*, parents of students in public schools sued the IRS for its decision to grant tax-exempt status to private schools that discriminated. *Id*. at 759. You will recall that the Court did find injury in fact, but did not find causation. Similarly, the Court did not find redressability. The Court reasoned that there was no information in the record about the number of private discriminatory schools in the plaintiffs' communities. *Id*. at 758. If there were only a few schools, then changes in policy would make no appreciable difference in the overall public school integration. *Id*. Further, the Court found it "entirely speculative" whether a withdrawal of the tax exemption for a discriminating private school would lead that school to change its policies. A discriminating private school might continue its discriminatory policy even if it meant the loss of some donor support. *Id*. Finally, the Court found it "just as speculative" that parents faced with an increased tuition at a private school now would decide to enroll their children in public schools. *Id*. In sum, even if the plaintiffs won their lawsuit, they failed to demonstrate that their injury would be remedied.

# 2. Prudential Standing

Even if a plaintiff meets the constitutional standing requirements, courts retain the discretion to dismiss a complaint on prudential standing grounds if the court believes that the action should not be entertained. Because these requirements are not constitutionally based, Congress can alter them by statute.

We will examine two prudential standing issues here: (1) representational standing concerns, and (2) generalized grievance concerns. We will address the zone of interests test below as a *statutory* standing concern; be aware that courts often label it as a *prudential* standing concern.

## a. *Representational or Associational Standing*

Generally, third parties cannot sue to enforce the rights of others. While suits by third parties were not uncommon in either English or early American legal experience, the general rule today is that a plaintiff cannot assert the interests of others who have been injured by an agency's action. Cass R.

Sunstein, *What's Standing After Lujan*, 91 MICH. L. REV. 163, 171 (1992) (noting that prior to 1920, there was no separate standing requirement; if any source of law conferred a right to sue, individuals could do so without showing a "concrete interest" or "injury in fact"). Instead, the plaintiff must be uniquely injured. Thus, if the IRS revoked the nonprofit status of a group like the Sierra Club Legal Defense Fund, the Sierra Club would be directly injured and would have standing. But members of the general public who think the club should have tax-exempt status would have no standing.

Similarly, if the federal government decided to allow Disney to construct a ski resort in the National Forest in California, the Sierra Club would not itself be injured and could not sue. That was the holding in *Sierra Club*, 405 U.S. at 741. In that case, the Sierra Club filed a "public interest" lawsuit alleging that the illegal construction of the Disney resort would lead to irreparable harm to the public interest. *Id.* at 730. Sierra Club did not allege that it suffered a unique, private injury from Disney's ski resort; rather, the club alleged that its historic interest in protecting the environment gave it standing to represent the public interest as a private attorney general. *Id.* at 736. Although it had 27,000 members within driving distance of the forest who would have had an aesthetic or environmental injury, the club did not plead that any of its members used the area and would thus be injured. *Id.* at 735.

Over three strongly worded dissents, the Court dismissed the action for lack of standing. *Id.* at 741. The Court noted that a party's mere "interest in a problem" was insufficient by itself to overcome the "case or controversy" requirement. *Id.* at 739. The majority reasoned that because no interest of the club was affected, the club's challenge came down to an assertion that its general "interest in the problem" conferred standing. *Id.* Allowing the club to sue in this case would lead to a slippery slope problem:

> [I]f a 'special interest' in this subject were enough to entitle the Sierra Club to commence this litigation, there would appear to be no objective basis upon which to disallow a suit by any other bona fide 'special interest' organization [and] . . . it is difficult to perceive why any individual citizen with the same bona fide special interest would not also be entitled to do so.

*Id.* In a unique dissent, Justice Douglas suggested that the trees themselves ought to have standing to sue for their own protection:

> The critical question of "standing" would be simplified and also put neatly in focus if we fashioned a federal rule that allowed environmental issues to be litigated before federal agencies or federal courts in the

name of the inanimate object about to be despoiled, defaced, or invaded by roads and bulldozers and where injury is the subject of public outrage. Contemporary public concern for protecting nature's ecological equilibrium should lead to the conferral of standing upon environmental objects to sue for their own preservation.

*Id.* at 739. After the Court rejected the Sierra Club's assertion of standing, the club amended its complaint to allege that one of its members would suffer an injury from the proposed resort. *Sierra Club v. Morton*, 348 F. Supp. 219, 219–20 (N.D. Cal. 1972). Ultimately, the resort was never built.

Why was the lawsuit allowed to proceed once the individual member's interest was substituted? Interest groups and associations, like the Sierra Club, often bring administrative lawsuits on behalf of individuals and entities who share their interests. Interest groups often have more resources to mount better legal challenges and are more likely to sue in the public interest than individuals. In the last section, we talked about the constitutional standing requirements: injury in fact, causation, and redressability. Yet, when we discussed cases that interest groups, like the Sierra Club, brought we did not look at the standing requirements as they applied to the interest groups. Rather, we looked to see whether one or more of the interest group's members met the three standing requirements. Why?

When it comes to standing, interest groups must show three things. First, they must show that one or more of their members have constitutional standing. In other words, interest groups must show that one of their members could bring the case directly, meaning the member can demonstrate injury in fact, causation, and redressability.

Second, the interest group must show that the group's purpose relates to the issues in the lawsuit, meaning that an environmental group can sue to enforce the environmental concerns of its members while a labor union could not.

And third, the interest group must show that the presence of individual members themselves is not needed in the litigation; meaning, simply, that no monetary relief is sought, just injunctive and declaratory relief. *Hunt v. Washington Apple Adv. Comm'n*, 432 U.S. 333 (1977); *see* Kelsey McCowan Heilman, Comment, *The Rights of Others: Protection and Advocacy Organizations' Associational Standing to Sue*, 157 U. Pa. L. Rev. 237 (2008). As you might imagine, finding a member with constitutional standing is often the biggest hurdle for interest group plaintiffs.

Finally, you should be aware that although a general interest in the agency's action may not get an interest group into court, once the interest group has established constitutional standing, the group can "argue the public interest to support the claim that the agency failed to comply with its statutory mandate." *Sierra Club*, 405 U.S. at 737.

### b. Generalized Grievances

Another prudential concern is that courts should not hear lawsuits addressing injuries shared by many citizens in the same way, meaning non-individualized injuries. For example, an illegal public expenditure injures all citizens because the money comes from a treasury to which all citizens contribute. Additionally, all citizens have an interest in the government's obligation to follow the law in general. Yet courts are reluctant to use such widespread and generally shared injuries as the basis for standing decisions.

Instead, judges require that plaintiffs have suffered or will suffer a concrete and particularized injury. A particularized injury is one that affects the plaintiff in a personal and individual way. Why? Unfortunately, the courts have not been clear about the underlying rationale for this generalized grievance limitation.

Institutional competency concerns may play a role. For example, courts may be concerned that widely shared injuries should be left to the political branches of government to resolve. When agency action affects many people, the legislative branch is often in a better position to respond to these concerns. To the extent that the agency action involves difficult and controversial policy choices, the legislative branch is the more appropriate venue to resolve the issue because that branch is accountable to the public.

Additionally, courts may be concerned that, without this limit, courts might be deluged with cases. As a purely practical matter, courts need to protect their limited resources. Allowing anyone to challenge the legality of agency action could overwhelm the courts.

Appropriateness of the parties may also play a role. For example, courts may be concerned about finding a plaintiff who is uniquely hurt enough to vigorously fight rather than a plaintiff who has a simple ideological complaint. Courts may be concerned that the claimed injury will not occur at all or will not occur in magnitudes worth judicial time.

Constitutional implications may play a role. For example, courts may be concerned about separation of powers. Courts may be concerned that the generalized grievance limitation is constitutionally required. For example, Justice Scalia suggested that the generalized grievance limitation is an Article III requirement that a plaintiff's injuries be concrete, specific, and individualized, rather than abstract and indefinite. *Laidlaw*, 528 U.S. at 203 (Scalia, J., dissenting).

The generalized grievance limitation is somewhat counterintuitive. A mass tort, after all, is still a tort. A recent case addressing this limitation is

*Massachusetts*, 549 U.S. at 510. In that case, the state of Massachusetts sought to force the EPA to regulate greenhouse gas emissions from motor vehicles in an effort to reduce global warming. *Id.* at 497. Because global warming affects every person on the planet, it would be difficult to find a more generalized grievance. Yet the Court held that Massachusetts had standing to raise the issue. *Id.* at 526. The Court said that "[t]o deny standing to persons who are in fact injured simply because many others are also injured, would mean that the most injurious and widespread Government actions could be questioned by nobody. We cannot accept that conclusion." *Massachusetts*, 549 U.S. at 525 n.24 (quoting *SCRAP*, 412 U.S. 669, 687–88 (1973)).

This holding was surprising to many. Perhaps the Court's generous interpretation of the generalized grievance limitation in this case was based on the fact that the plaintiff was a state. Alternatively, Massachusetts had claimed that its potential loss of coastal land represented a particularized injury and, thus, the state was not a plaintiff with a purely ideological concern. *Id.* at 499. Moreover, Massachusetts claimed the EPA had violated a procedural right and that Congress had explicitly authorized the suit. *Id.* at 498; *see* Kimberly N. Brown, *Justiciable Generalized Grievances*, 68 MD. L. REV. 221 (2008) (noting that Massachusetts cited the Clean Air Act's judicial review provision to support its right to bring a procedural claim).

In sum, the generalized grievance concern is still relevant, but exactly how it is relevant is vastly unclear at this point.

## 3.  Statutory Standing: The Zone of Interest Test

In addition to the constitutional and prudential standing requirements, there is an additional standing requirement that we will call statutory because it comes from the relevant statute. You should be aware, however, that courts often speak of the zone of interests test as part of prudential standing

Section 702 of the APA codified this requirement: "a person . . . adversely affected or aggrieved by agency action within the meaning of a relevant statute, is entitled to judicial review thereof." APA § 702. The "within the meaning of a relevant statute" language means that persons who are within the zone of interests of a particular statute may sue. But that simple statement begs the question: who is within the zone of interests a statute is meant to protect? We explore this question next.

Pursuant to the "zone of interests" requirement, a plaintiff must "arguably" be within the "zone of interests to be protected or regulated by the statute or constitutional guarantee in question." *Association of Data Processing*, 397 U.S. at 153 (holding that data-processing services were within the zone of interest of a statute that allowed banks to provide data-process services). In *Data Processing*, the purpose of the relevant act was to ensure the financial stability of banks; and the data processers were not intended beneficiaries of the statute. *Id*. at 158 n.2. Nevertheless, the Court held that the data processers were suitable challengers because of their economic interest: the banks had now become market competitors. *Id*. at 156. The Court said simply, "We think Congress has provided the sufficient statutory aid to standing even though the competition may not be the precise kind Congress legislated against." *Id*. at 155. Thus, the "arguably within the zone of interest" requirement does not mean that the plaintiffs must be one of the entities whom Congress intended to protect. Rather, the zone of interest test merely requires that there be *some* relationship between the injury about which the plaintiff complains and the purpose of the relevant statute.

Like the *SCRAP* case in constitutional standing, the Court in *Data Processing* generously interpreted the zone of interest test. Two other generous zone of interest cases from the Supreme Court include *Clarke v. Securities Industry Ass'n*, 479 U.S. 388 (1987), and *Bennett*, 520 U.S. at 154. In *Clarke*, securities brokers challenged a regulation that allowed banks to compete in the securities broker market. *Id*. at 388. The Court held that the security brokers were within the zone of interest. *Id*. at 403. The Court reasoned that the zone of interest test was "not meant to be especially demanding" and that plaintiffs are only excluded when their "interests are . . . marginally related to or inconsistent with the purposes implicit in the statute . . . In particular, there need be no indication of congressional purpose to benefit the would-be plaintiff." *Id*. at 399–400. Notice that the plaintiffs in *Clarke* suffered economic injury in fact.

Similarly, in *Bennett*, the Court held that ranchers who wished to take more water from a certain reservoir for irrigation purposes were within the zone of interests the ESA protected. *Bennett*, 520 U.S. at 177. The ESA protects plant and animal species from extinction. One requirement in the ESA is that agencies consult with Fish and Wildlife Service before undertaking an action that might adversely affect a species' critical habitat. Pursuant to this process, the Service advised the Bureau of Reclamation that drawdowns of a particular reservoir would jeopardize certain endangered species. *Id*. at 154. The issue for the Court was whether the ranchers were "arguably within the zone of interests" the ESA protects. The plaintiffs brought suit under the citizen lawsuit provisions of both the ESA and the APA.

The Ninth Circuit held that the ranchers had no standing under either statute. *Bennett v. Plenart*, 63 F.3d 915, 919 (9th Cir. 1995). The Ninth Circuit reasoned that the ranchers' interests were not only not within the purpose of the ESA, but were actually "plainly inconsistent" with those purposes because drawing down reserve water could threaten the habitat of endangered species. *Id.* The Ninth Circuit said, "only plaintiffs who allege[d] an interest in the preservation of endangered species fall within the zone of interest." *Id.* As for the APA claim, the Ninth Circuit concluded that because the plaintiffs could not sue under the ESA, the citizen lawsuit provision did not give them standing to sue under the APA. *Id.* at 920. The court's holding makes sense; however, the Supreme Court disagreed.

In a unanimous opinion, the Supreme Court reversed. *Bennett,* 520 U.S. at 179. Regarding the ESA claim, the Court broadly interpreted the zone of interest test because (a) the overall interest of the statute was the environment, in which all have an interest; (b) the statute provided that "any person" may commence a lawsuit (a citizen lawsuit provision); and (c) the statute eliminated the usual diversity of citizenship and amount in controversy requirements and provided for recovery of litigation costs. *Id.* at 165. The Court reasoned that all of these facts suggested that Congress intended judicial review to be widely available and not limited by prudential concerns. *Id.* at 166.

As for the APA claim, the Court similarly found that the zone of interests tests was met: the "Petitioners' claim that they are the victims of [agency officials overzealous but unintelligent pursuing of the ESA's environmental objectives] is plainly within the zone of interests that the [ESA] protects." *Id.* at 177. Like *Clarke, Bennett* involved an alleged economic injury in fact. Notably, Justice Scalia wrote the majority opinion; the same Justice Scalia who wrote the plurality opinion in *Lujan,* which held that plaintiffs who alleged an aesthetic injury were not injured. It would appear that the economic interests of these plaintiffs are somehow more important than the aesthetic interests of the plaintiffs in *Lujan.*

Despite these two very generous approaches to the zone of interest test, the Court usually is less generous. For example, in *Block v. Community Nutrition Institute,* 467 U.S. 340, 341–42 (1984), the Court considered whether milk consumers could challenge an agency order affecting dairy farmers that had the intended purpose of benefiting those producers by increasing the price consumers had to pay for milk. The D.C. Circuit held that the milk consumers had standing: the increase in milk prices would injure them so the consumers were arguably within the zone of interest of the statutory scheme. *Id.* at 344–45.

While this result seems reasonable and consistent with the Court's prior cases finding zone of interest standing when economic injuries were involved, a unanimous Supreme Court reversed. *Block,* 467 U.S. 353. The Court reasoned that Congress intended to restrict judicial review to milk handlers based on the statutory process for raising a complaint. *Id.* at 352–53. The statutory process required the milk handlers to present their complaints to the agency first and then seek judicial review. The Court reasoned that this process assured the agency would first resolve any claims of illegality, which was preferable to allowing consumers to sue directly in court, for the latter process would "severely disrupt this complex and delicate administrative scheme." *Id.* at 348.

Similarly, in *Air Courier Conference v. American Postal Workers Union*, 498 U.S. 517, 530 (1991), the Court rejected the plaintiffs' zone of interest claim. The postal act gave the U.S. Postal Service (USPS) a monopoly on mail delivery. *Id.* at 519. USPS had issued an order permitting private carriers to handle some foreign mail; an arrangement that the postal employees feared would affect their employment. Citing *Clarke*, the D.C. Circuit held that the employees' union had standing to protect their economic interests. *American Postal Workers Union v. USPS*, 891 F.2d 304, 310 (D.C. Cir. 1989).

A unanimous Supreme Court reversed. While the Court concluded that the employees' union had constitutional standing, the Court held that the union did not have statutory standing because the employees' interests were not within the zone of interests that the postal act was designed to protect. *Air Courier*, 498 U.S. at 530. The Court reasoned that the postal act was intended to protect the revenues of the postal service, not the job opportunities of postal employees. *Id.* at 518.

The Court in *Air Courier* also addressed a second issue: specifically, what is the relevant statute for a court's zone of interest inquiry? The Court in *Clarke* had said that "we are not limited to considering the statute under which respondents sued, but may consider any provision that helps us to understand Congress's overall purposes in the . . . Act." *Clarke*, 479 U.S. at 401. Hence, the plaintiffs in *Air Courier* cited labor provisions in the postal act that *did* directly affect employees. *Air Courier*, 498 U.S. at 528. The Court was unpersuaded. It reasoned that the labor provisions were wholly unrelated to the sections challenged, except that they happened to be in the same chapter of the U.S. Code. *Id.* at 529. The Court said "to accept this level of generality in defining the 'relevant statute' could deprive the zone-of-interests test of virtually all meaning." *Id.* at 529–30. Hence, the zone of interest test focuses on the provision of law alleged to have been violated. *Accord, Bennett*, 520 U.S. at 175 (holding the zone of interest test must be resolved based on the particular provision allegedly violated).

Finally, in *National Credit Union Administration (NCUA) v. First National Bank & Trust*, 522 U.S. 479 (1998), the Court found standing for the plaintiff banks to challenge an agency order that expanded the reach of credit unions, essentially creating more competition for banks. In doing so, the Court noted that in both *Data Processing* and *Clarke*, the Court had held that competitors of a regulated entity were within the zone of interest protected by the relevant regulatory statute. *Id.* at 497–98. The Court emphasized that a plaintiff did not have to show that Congress explicitly recognized the plaintiffs' interests in the statutory text or in the legislative history. Rather, Justice Thomas said:

> [I]n applying the "zone of interests" test, we do not ask whether, in enacting the statutory provision at issue, Congress specifically intended to benefit the plaintiff. Instead, we first discern the interests "arguably . . . to be protected" by the statutory provision at issue; we then inquire whether the plaintiff's interests affected by the agency action in question are among them.

*Id.* at 492. Of course, this reasoning merely restates the question: were the plaintiff's interests arguably protected by the statute? But the implication is that the Court will not demand much in the way of a connection between a plaintiff's interests and the statutory scheme in competitor cases. Justice Thomas found the necessary connection in the fact that limiting the reach of credit unions would necessarily affect the plaintiffs' business. He concluded:

> Thus, even if it cannot be said that Congress had the specific purpose of benefiting commercial banks, one of the interests "arguably . . . to be protected" by [the Act] is an interest in limiting the markets that federal credit unions can serve. This interest is precisely the interest of respondents affected by the NCUA's interpretation of [the Act].

*Id.* at 493.

So — how seriously does the Court apply the zone of interest test? It is impossible to say with much confidence. Plaintiffs need to examine the text and the history of the relevant statute, as well as other related statutes, to show that Congress intended some protection for the class of plaintiffs. When a plaintiff alleges an economic injury based on reduced market competition, the plaintiff's case seems strongest. *See National Credit Union Admin,* 522 U.S. at 479; *Clarke,* 479 U.S. at 388; *Investment Co. Instit. v. Camp,* 401 U.S. 617 (1971); *Arnold Tours, Inc. v. Camp,* 400 U.S. 45 (1970) (*per curiam*).

## 4. Standing: A Flow Chart

If you have read this far, you will no doubt agree that standing law is the poster child for a difficult legal doctrine. Figure 5.1 shows a very simple flow chart that includes both the constitutional and prudential standing requirements. At each step, you should ask whether the plaintiff can demonstrate the relevant requirement. If not, the plaintiff has no standing and, thus, no case.

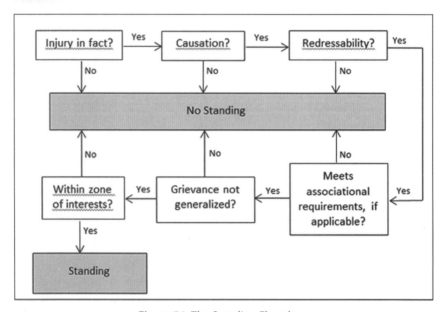

**Figure 5.1** The Standing Flowchart

# E. What Is Subject to Judicial Review: The Claim

In addition to establishing jurisdiction, a plaintiff must have a cause of action, meaning that some statute grants the plaintiff a right to sue. When an enabling statute contains a jurisdictional grant of power, that statute also typically provides the plaintiff with a cause of action. For example, a statute might provide that any person who is adversely affected by the agency's action may file a petition challenging the validity of the agency's action. *See, e.g.,* 29 U.S.C. § 655(f). Judicial review pursuant to a specific grant like this one is called "statutory review" and comes with its own procedural requirements.

For agency actions where Congress has not provided for judicial review in the statute, § 702 of the APA provides that any "person suffering legal wrong because of agency action, or adversely affected or aggrieved by agency action within the meaning of a relevant statute, is entitled to judicial review thereof." APA § 702. Judicial review pursuant to the APA is often called "non-statutory review," although a better nomenclature would be "non-specific statutory review," because the APA is a statute after all.

As we explore the APA requirements for non-statutory review, keep the following in mind. Historically, federal courts were reluctant to intrude on the executive function. At the beginning of the twentieth century, however, and picking up considerable speed in the 1930s, courts became more comfortable in reviewing executive and administrative action. By 1967, the Supreme Court held that *agency actions* were presumptively reviewable. *Abbott Laboratories v. Gardner*, 387 U.S. 136, 140 (1967). To rebut the presumption that agency actions are reviewable, the government had to provide "clear and convincing evidence" of a contrary legislative intent. *Id.* The Court reasoned that the "generous review provisions" of the APA "must be given a hospitable interpretation." *Id.* at 141. We will see that there are two situations when the presumption of reviewability is rebutted: (1) when the enabling statute expressly or impliedly precludes review, and (2) when the enabling statute gives the agency complete discretion to act.

The next sections will explore the requirements for non-statutory review under the APA. The APA has three requirements for a plaintiff to have a cause of action: (1) there must be an agency action, (2) Congress must not have precluded review of that action, and (3) Congress must not have committed that action to the agency's discretion.

## 1. Agency Action

As noted above, "a person suffering a legal wrong because of *agency action*, or adversely affected or aggrieved by *agency action* . . . is entitled to judicial review thereof." APA § 702 (emphasis added). The APA defines an "agency action" as "includ[ing] the whole or a part of an agency rule, order, license, sanction, relief, or the equivalent or denial thereof, or failure to act." APA § 551(13). Generally, a plaintiff can easily meet this requirement because this definition is so broad. However, there have been a few occasions when the plaintiffs were unable to demonstrate that the challenged action was agency action.

First, in *Lujan*, 497 U.S. at 899, the Court held that the Bureau of Land Management's (BLM) decision to reclassify public lands for mining individually rather than collectively was not agency action subject to review. While each individual BLM decision regarding a specific piece of land would be agency action, the Court held that the BLM's choice of considering lands collectively rather than individually was not agency action. *Id.* at 892–93.

Second, in *Norton v. Southern Utah Wilderness Alliance*, 542 U.S. 55, 67 (2004), the Court held that the BLM's alleged decision not to protect wilderness areas from off-road vehicle use was not reviewable agency action. Although the APA defines "agency action" to include an agency's "failure to act," the Court explained that the "failure to act" language applied only to those situations in which an agency failed to take one of the discrete actions in the APA's definition that precede the "failure to act" phrase. *Id.* at 62–63. In other words, agency action includes an agency's failure to issue a specific "rule, order, license, sanction, [or] relief," but does not include an agency's failure to protect the environment generally. *Compare, Massachusetts,* 549 U.S. at 526 (holding that the EPA's denial of a rulemaking petition was reviewable agency action because the statute required the EPA to act).

Even when the plaintiff is challenging agency action, judicial review is not assured. The plaintiff must overcome two other potential limitations: first, that review was precluded, and second, that resolution of the issue was committed to agency discretion. We turn to these two limitations next.

## 2. Express and Implied Preclusion

Article III, Section 2 of the federal Constitution grants Congress the power to regulate the jurisdiction of the federal courts. Hence, Congress can preclude judicial review. The APA recognizes this possibility, noting that judicial review is available "except to the extent that statutes preclude judicial review." APA § 701(a)(1).

Express preclusion cases are relatively rare. However, *Board of Governors, FRS v. MCorp Financial, Inc.,* 502 U.S. 32 (1991), did involve an express preclusion provision. In that case, a bank holding company filed voluntary bankruptcy petitions and then initiated an adversary proceeding against the Federal Reserve System, seeking to enjoin two, pending administrative proceedings. *Id.* at 34. The District Court refused to enjoin the proceedings because the relevant statute *expressly precluded* judicial review. *Id.* at 39. The Court of Appeals disagreed, reasoning that an earlier Supreme Court case, *Leedom v. Kyne,* 358 U.S. 184 (1958), required judicial review of any agency action whenever a plaintiff claimed that an agency exceeded its statutory authority. *Id.* at 43.

The Supreme Court granted certiorari and reversed. The Court distinguished *Kyne,* saying "central to our decision in *Kyne* was the fact that the Board's interpretation of the Act would wholly deprive [the plaintiff] union of a meaningful and adequate means of vindicating its statutory rights." *Id.* at 43. In other words, the union that filed suit in *Kyne* would be unable to obtain any judicial review of the agency's action. In contrast, the plaintiffs in *MCorp* could obtain meaningful and adequate judicial review in the court of appeals "[i]f and when the Board finds that MCorp . . . violated the [challenged] regulation." *Id.* at 44. Thus, because the statute contained express preclusion language and judicial review was available at the conclusion of the administrative process, the Court honored the express preclusion provision. *Id.* at 43.

Congress may also *implicitly* preclude judicial review. The question, then, is when does Congress do so? The cases in this area are somewhat confusing because they generally involve *pre-enforcement* review actions, which are better analyzed under the ripeness doctrine, which we will address below. Pre-enforcement review actions typically involve challenges to agency actions before an agency actually enforces its action by adjudication or court enforcement. As you will see, there is a strong presumption against implied preclusion, but that presumption seems to be weaker in pre-enforcement cases, so long as post-enforcement review remains available.

The most famous implied preclusion pre-enforcement case is *Abbott Labs.* In that case, the Supreme Court adopted a "clear and convincing" standard for finding implied preclusion. 387 U.S. 141. In *Abbott Labs,* the Food and Drug Administration (FDA) proposed regulations that would have required prescription drug manufacturers to include the generic name (Ibuprofen) every time the trade name (Advil) of a particular drug was used in marketing material. *Id.* at 137–38. Before the proposed regulation could go into effect, drug manufacturing companies sued the FDA, challenging this "every time" rule. *Id.* Neither the relevant act nor its amendments expressly precluded review, but the FDA argued that review of pre-enforcement claims was impliedly precluded because the statute specifically allowed other types of claims to be reviewed, but the statute did not specifically allow pre-enforcement claims to be reviewed. *Id.* at 141.

The Supreme Court rejected that argument. The Court stated that "only upon a showing of 'clear and convincing evidence' of a contrary legislative intent should the courts restrict access to judicial review." *Id.* To determine whether there was clear and convincing evidence, a court should ask "whether in the context of the entire legislative scheme the existence of that circumscribed remedy evinces a congressional purpose to bar agency action not within its purview from judicial review." *Id.* Here, no preclusion was warranted.

The Court's clear and convincing test proved too strict; consider whether clear and convincing is all that different from an express provision. Approximately fifteen years after *Abbott Labs,* the Supreme Court substantially revised its preclusion test. In *Block,* 467 U.S. at 340, the Court replaced its clear and convincing test with a new test: whether congressional intent to preclude review was "fairly discernible in the statutory scheme." *Id.* at 349, 351.

Prior to the lawsuit in *Block*, Congress had enacted the Agricultural Marketing Agreement Act of 1937 (Act) to stabilize and increase milk prices. *Id.* at 341–42 The Act authorized the Secretary of the Department of Agriculture to issue milk market orders, which set the minimum prices that handlers (those who process dairy products) had to pay to dairy farmers for milk products. *Id.* at 341. Pursuant to its authority, the Secretary issued market orders under which handlers would pay an additional payment for "reconstituted milk" (milk manufactured by mixing milk powder with water) that was used to make fluid milk products, rather than surplus milk products like butter, cheese, and dry milk. *Id.* at 343.

Three individual consumers and others sued the Secretary in federal district court, contending that the compensatory payment requirement would make reconstituted milk more expensive. *Id.* at 344. The district court held that Congress had intended to preclude judicial review of the Act. *Id.* The court of appeals disagreed, finding that the Act's structure and purposes did not reveal the type of "clear and convincing evidence of congressional intent needed to overcome the presumption in favor of judicial review [under *Abbott Laboratories*' holding]." *Id.* at 345. The Supreme Court granted certiorari and reversed. *Id.*

The Supreme Court restated *Abbott Labs*' presumption favoring judicial review of administrative action, but stressed that the presumption could be overcome with "specific language or specific legislative history" showing congressional intent to preclude review. *Id.* at 349. The Court noted that it had "never applied the 'clear and convincing evidence' standard in a strict evidentiary sense." *Id.* at 350. Rather, the Court said, it "has found the standard met, and the presumption favoring judicial review overcome, whenever the congressional intent to preclude judicial review is 'fairly discernible in the statutory scheme.'" *Id.* at 351.

Applying its new, "fairly discernible in the statutory scheme" test, the Court noted that whether a particular statute precludes review must be determined not only from the statute's express language, "but also from the structure of the statutory scheme, its objectives, its legislative history, and the nature of the administrative action involved." *Id.* at 345. Relevant for this particular case, the Court noted that the structure of the Act evinced congressional intent to preclude review. Specifically, the Act expressly allowed some individuals to obtain judicial review, but not others, because of congressional concern that certain types of lawsuits would interfere with the law's execution. *Id.* at 351.

The Court's next implied preclusion case was *Thunder Basin Coal Co. v. Reich*, 510 U.S. 200 (1994). In *Thunder Basin*, a Wyoming mine brought suit for pre-enforcement injunctive relief, claiming that an order of the Mine Safety and Health Administration (MSHA) violated its rights under the National Labor Relations Act (NLRA). *Id.* at 204. The Tenth Circuit Court of Appeals held that the Federal Mine Safety and Health Act (the Mine Act) precluded district court jurisdiction of pre-enforcement challenges. *Id.* at 206.

The Supreme Court granted certiorari and affirmed. *Id.* The Court identified a two-step test for discerning whether Congress intended to preclude judicial review. Pursuant to this test, a court should determine first whether congressional intent to "allocate[] initial review to an administrative body" is " 'fairly discernible in the statutory scheme.' " *Id.* at 207 (quoting *Block*, 467 U.S. at 351). According to the Court, this part of the test examines the statute's language, structure, purpose, and legislative history. *Id.* at 207. The Court cited *Block* for this part of the preclusion test.

But the Court did not stop there. Even if Congress's intent could not be determined from the statute's language, structure, purpose, and legislative history, a finding of preclusion is not warranted: (1) when such a finding would foreclose all meaningful judicial review, (2) when the federal suit would be wholly collateral to a statute's review provisions, and (3) when the claims are outside the agency's expertise. *Id.* at 212–13. Thus, the Court in *Thunder Basin* added a second step to *Block*'s fairly discernible test. This second step addresses which reviewing body is more appropriate: a court or the agency? Applying its two-step test, the Court concluded that Congress had intended to preclude review. *Id.* at 206.

Unfortunately, the Supreme Court has not clearly articulated how the factors in each of the two steps are to be analyzed. For example, in *Free Enterprise Fund v. Public Co. Accounting Oversight Bd.*, 561 U.S. 477 (2010), the Court applied *Thunder Basin*'s two-step test to hold that a provision in the Sarbanes-Oxley Act did not preclude federal courts from reviewing constitutional challenges to that Act. The Court examined only the text of the statute, ignoring legislative history, structure, and purpose. *Id.* at 489. Additionally, the Court analyzed the second step factors in conclusory fashion, providing little explanation of how the factors were met and whether all were required or whether one factor alone would be sufficient. *Id.* at 489–90. *See also Elgin v. Department of the Treasury*, 132 S. Ct. 2126, 2139–40 (2012) (finding that the Military Selective Service Act impliedly precluded judicial review). Hence, the preclusion standard remains unclear.

Let's summarize the Court's cases. In *Abbott Labs*, the Supreme Court suggested that congressional intent to preclude review had to be demonstrated by clear and convincing evidence. However, the Court soon relaxed this unworkable standard. In *Community Nutrition Institute*, the Court stated that the presumption of reviewability is overcome when congressional intent to preclude judicial review is fairly discernible in the statutory scheme. To determine whether congressional intent to preclude such review is fairly discernible in the statutory scheme, courts consider the statute's language, structure, purpose, and legislative history. Under *Thunder Basin*, even if congressional intent to preclude review is found, then preclusion may still be inappropriate: (1) when a finding of preclusion would foreclose all meaningful judicial review, (2) when the suit is wholly collateral to a statute's review provisions, and (3) when the claims are outside the agency's expertise. These factors help courts identify whether Congress would have intended an administrative agency's actions to be reviewed exclusively through the administrative process or whether early judicial review is appropriate.

## 3. Committed to Agency Discretion

Section 701 also excludes from judicial review agency actions that are "committed to agency discretion by law." APA § 701(a)(2). While § 701(a)(1) might be viewed as a provision requiring courts to defer to congressional intent not to intervene, § 701(a)(2) might be viewed as an invitation to *courts* to decide, as a matter of judicial self-restraint, whether review would be appropriate. *See generally*, Ronald M. Levin, *Understanding Unreviewability in Administrative Law*, 74 MINN. L. REV. 689 (1990).

Section 701(a)(2), which prohibits courts from reviewing agency action that is committed to agency discretion, seems to contradict § 706(2)(A), which allows the court to set aside agency action "found to be . . . an abuse of discretion." When statutes conflict, a lawyer's first step is to try to harmonize them. Doing so, we might begin by noting that for every administrative decision for which judicial review is sought there will be an applicable legal *standard* the agency used to reach its decision. The agency will also exercise some degree of *discretion* when applying that standard to the specific situation. Thus, every agency decision involves *both* the application of legal standards and the exercise of discretion; however, the proportion of the agency's decision that is the result of discretion will vary from case to case. Consider Figure 5.2.

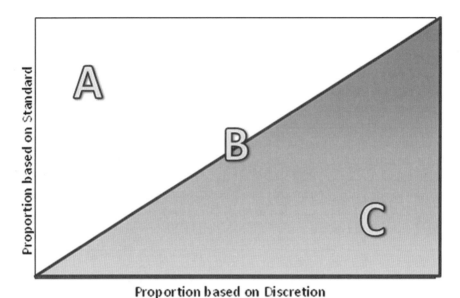

**Figure 5.2** Comparing APA Sections 701(a)(2) and 706(2)(A)

In the cases pictured in Figure 5.2, assume in Case A that Mr. A was dismissed from his job pursuant to a statute that required he pass a proficiency test. Assume in Case B that Mr. B was dismissed from his job pursuant to a statute requiring him to be "reasonably efficient." Assume in Case C that Mr. C. was dismissed from his job pursuant to a statute authorizing dismissal "whenever, in the Secretary's opinion, dismissal is appropriate." The decision in A's case involves a clear standard that requires no agency discretion; the decision in B's case involves a reasonably clear standard, but it also requires more agency discretion; the decision in C's case involves no standard and almost complete discretion.

APA § 706(2)(A) would apply to the decisions in A and B's cases. In these cases, there is a legal standard the agency must apply that the court could review to ensure that the legal standard was met. Part of the judicial review would include determining whether the agency abused its discretion when it applied the relevant legal standard.

In contrast, APA § 701(a)(2) would apply in C's case. Because the proportion of the agency's decision subject to discretion is so high and the proportion subject to the application of standards is so low, the courts would likely find that there is "no law to apply." When Congress confers such broad discretion to the agency, there is no useful role left for the courts. How do courts review the exercise of complete discretion?

The quintessential case in this area is *Citizens to Preserve Overton Park v. Volpe*, 401 U.S. 402 (1971). In that case, a federal statute prohibited the Secretary of the Department of Transportation from financing highways through public parks if a "feasible and prudent" alternative existed. *Id.* at 405. When the Secretary authorized the building of a highway through Overton Park in Memphis, Tennessee, the action was challenged. The Secretary pointed to § 701(a)(2), claiming that his action was not reviewable because the decision was committed to his discretion. *Id.* at 410. The Court rejected the claim. *Id.* After examining the legislative history of the APA, the Court said that review is precluded under § 701(a)(2) only "in those rare instances where 'statutes are drawn in such broad terms that in a given case there is no law to apply.'" *Id.* The Court went on to find "law to apply" in the form of factors the Secretary was to use when exercising discretion. *Id.* at 413. Review was possible, said the Court, because a court could examine the question of whether the agency properly weighed and considered the factors. *See also Lincoln v. Vigil*, 508 U.S. 182, 193 (1993) (refusing to review an agency's decision to discontinue direct clinical services under the Children's Indian Program); *Beck v. United States Dep't of Commerce*, 982 F.2d. 1332, 1339 (9th Cir. 1992) (refusing to review an agency's decision not to appeal); *AAPC v. FCC*, 442 F.3d 751 (D.C. Cir. 2006) (refusing to review an agency's denial of reconsideration).

Despite the Court's pronouncement in this case, however, the APA's legislative history may not be quite as clear as the Court suggested. The Attorney General's Manual identified issues that should be committed to agency discretion to include issues where there was law to apply but for which judicial review would be too intrusive into agency management of priorities and resources. The manual provided some examples: the denial of petitions for rulemaking, the denial of loans, and the refusal to enforce a complaint. H.R. Rep. No. 1980, 79th Cong., 2d Sess. 2, reprinted in Legislative History of the Administrative Procedure Act, S. Doc. No. 248, 79th Cong., 2d Sess. 95 (1946).

There is another limitation to the application of § 701(a)(2). This section provides that review is unavailable only "to the extent that" a matter is "committed to agency discretion." APA § 701(a)(2). This language permits a court to separate the plaintiffs' claims into different issues, some of which are committed to agency discretion and some of which are not. For example, in *Webster v. Doe*, 486 U.S. 592 (1988), the statute authorized the director of the CIA to dismiss an employee whenever the director "shall deem such termination necessary or advisable in the interests of the United States." *Id.* at 600. An employee who was gay filed suit, raising claims under both the statute and the Constitution. *Id.* at 595.

The Court held that the employee's *statutory* claim was nonreviewable because that claim was committed to agency discretion; hence, he was unable to argue that his dismissal was not "necessary or advisable in the interest of the United States." *Id*. at 603. But the Court held that the employee's *constitutional* claim was reviewable. *Id*. at 604. The Court reasoned that any other interpretation would raise serious constitutional questions. In other words, the "committed to agency discretion" provision barred only statutory claims; it did not bar the constitutional claim. *See also Johnson v. Robison*, 415 U.S. 361, 373–74 (1974) (holding that a statute prohibiting judicial review of decisions from the veterans administration did not preclude judicial review of constitutional claims). In a spirited dissent, former Justice Scalia said that the " 'no law to apply' test covers the nonreviewability of certain issues, but falls far short of explaining the full scope of the areas from which the courts are excluded." *Id*. at 608.

In another case, *Heckler v. Chaney*, 470 U.S. 821 (1985), the Court said that the "no law to apply" test precluded judicial review when "the statute is drawn so that a court would have no meaningful standard against which to judge the agency's exercise of discretion." *Id*. at 831. In that case, plaintiffs sought to compel the FDA to enforce a requirement that approved drugs be used only for proper purposes. *Id*. at 823. The Court held that the agency's refusal to enforce the statute was unreviewable because the agency's decision was similar to an exercise of prosecutorial discretion, an action that had historically been unreviewable. *Id*. at 831. The Court said that in such cases, there is a presumption of *un*reviewability. *Id*. Hence, when the decision of whether to enforce a particular law or rule is committed to an agency's decision, the agency's exercise of that discretion is unreviewable.

When evaluating whether issues are committed to agency discretion, courts look at a variety of factors, including the following: (1) how broadly the statute is written; (2) how much agency expertise is required for a sound decision; (3) how "managerial" the decision or its consequences will be, (4) how effectively a court can frame and enforce relief; (4) how important a quick agency resolution is; (5) how many of these decisions are likely to need review; and (6) whether there are other ways of limiting agency abuse other than by judicial action. Harvey Saferstein, *Nonreviewability: A Functional Analysis of "Committed to Agency Discretion,"* 82 HARV. L. REV. 367 (1968).

# F. When Judicial Review Is Available: The Timing

We have now examined jurisdiction, standing, and cause of action requirements: the *whether, who,* and *what* of judicial review. We have yet to examine *when* judicial review can be obtained. There are three doctrines regarding the timing of judicial review: finality, exhaustion, and ripeness.

The finality doctrine respects the right of the agency to complete its work before the courts intervene and use judicial resources that may be unnecessary. The exhaustion doctrine respects the right of the agency to correct its own mistakes before courts intervene. The ripeness doctrine respects the need of the courts to have the issues in the case sufficiently developed for judicial review. We will explore all three doctrines below. A warning first: It would be nice if each of these doctrines had clear boundaries. Alas, that is not the case. Indeed, in *Ticor Title Insurance Co. v. FTC*, 814 F.2d 731 (D.C. Cir. 1987), a panel from the D.C. Circuit all agreed that the court should not hear the case for timing reasons, but disagreed as to which of these three doctrines applied.

## 1. Finality

Courts only review decisions that are "final." Why? Because the function of a reviewing court is to "review" not to "decide" these issues. *See Rochester Tele. Corp v. United States*, 307 U.S. 125, 131 (1939) (explaining that the finality doctrine is routed in Article III's case or controversy requirement). For this reason, appellate courts will not typically review evidentiary rulings and interlocutory orders from trial courts. Those rulings are reviewable only when the case as a whole is appealed. The same principle applies in the administrative context.

For claims brought under the APA (nonstatutory claims), Congress codified this doctrine in the APA. Section 704 provides that "*final* agency action for which there is no other adequate remedy" is subject to judicial review. APA § 704 (emphasis added). As noted above, this finality limitation allows agencies to make a final decision before the courts intervene. *See generally*, Gwendolyn McKee, *Judicial Review of Agency Guidance Documents: Rethinking the Finality Doctrine*, 60 ADMIN. L. REV. 371 (2008) (reviewing the doctrine).

In examining whether an agency action is final, courts focus on two questions:

> As a general matter, two conditions must be satisfied for agency action to be "final": First, the action must mark the "consummation" of the agency's decisionmaking process—it must not be of a merely tentative or interlocutory nature. And second, the action must be one by which "rights or obligations have been determined," or from which "legal consequences will flow."

*Bennett*, 520 U.S. at 177–78 (citations omitted); *accord Franklin v. Massachusetts*, 505 U.S. 788, 797 (1992) (stating that the Court must look to whether an agency has completed its decision-making process and whether the result of that process is one that will directly affect the parties).

Pursuant to *Bennett* and *Franklin*, the first step in the Court's two-step test is for a court to decide whether the agency action the plaintiff is challenging is the culmination of the agency's process or is merely a tentative or interlocutory step. For adjudication and legislative rulemaking, the issue of whether the agency has completed its decision-making process is not commonly in dispute. For example, when an agency cites a regulated entity for violating a law, the regulated entity will have an opportunity to challenge that citation in an adjudication before an ALJ. Until the adjudication is complete and, if appropriate, appealed to the agency head, the agency has not completed the decision-making process. *See, e.g., FTC v. Standard Oil Co.*, 449 U.S. 232, 243 (1980).

For nonlegislative rulemaking, the issue of whether the agency has completed its decision-making process is more commonly in dispute. For example, assume that an association and a local government request clarification from an agency regarding the application of a particular law to a particular situation. Would the agency's responding opinion be the culmination of the agency's process? Two cases from the circuit courts came to different conclusions on this question. First, in *National Automatic Laundry & Cleaning Council v. Shultz*, 443 F.2d 689, 702 (D.C. Cir. 1971), the D.C. Circuit held that the opinion letter was final agency action because the agency head had issued the letter and it applied to an entire industry. In contrast, in *Taylor-Callahan-Coleman Counties District Adult Probation Department v. Dole*, 948 F.2d 953, 960 (5th Cir. 1991), the Fifth Circuit held that the opinion letter was not final agency action because the letter was directed only to a particular local government and not to all local governments. Thus, the breadth of application mattered.

Pursuant to *Bennett* and *Franklin*, the second step in the Court's two-step test is for a court to decide whether the agency's decision will have a direct and immediate effect on the plaintiff or whether legal consequences will flow. Even when the agency has completed its decision-making process, that decision must be one that affects the plaintiff in a concrete way. In *Franklin*, for example, Massachusetts challenged the 1990 census because the state stood to lose a seat in the House of Representatives. *Franklin*, 505 U.S. at 790. Pursuant to the law, the Census Bureau provided the census numbers to the president, who reported them to Congress, which then reapportioned the seats in the House. *Id.* at 791. The Court held that the Census Bureau's action did not cause the reapportionment, rather the president's count caused it; hence, the agency's action was not one that directly affected Massachusetts. *Id.* at 806. Hence, it appears that for non-legislative rules, step two is the critical step of the two-step test. *See also Western Ill. Home Health Care, Inc. v. Herman*, 150 F.3d 659, 663 (7th Cir. 1998) (holding an agency opinion letter to be final action because the entity would suffer direct harm if it ignored the agency's opinion).

Unfortunately, the Court has provided varying articulations of this part of the test, sometimes requiring that legal consequences flow, more often requiring that the plaintiff suffer some direct effect. *See, e.g., Bennett*, 520 U.S. at 178 (test whether "rights or obligations have been determined," or from which "legal consequences will flow"); *Dalton v. Specter*, 511 U.S. 462, 470 (1994) (test whether action "will directly affect the parties"); *Darby v. Cisneros*, 509 U.S. 137, 144 (1993) (test whether there is "actual, concrete injury"); *Franklin*, 505 U.S. at 797 (test whether agency's action has a "direct effect on" the plaintiff): *Abbott Labs*, 387 U.S. at 149 (test whether the "effects are felt in a concrete way"). Because non-legislative rules generally are not ones from which legal consequences will flow, the Court's articulation may differ depending on the type of action being challenged.

In sum, courts apply a two-step test to determine whether agency action is final. The first step focuses on the agencies' actions to see whether the agency has reached the end of its decision-making process. The second step focuses on the impact of that action on the plaintiff—how directly will the complaining plaintiff be affected?

## 2. Exhaustion of Administrative Remedies

Like it had with the finality doctrine, the Supreme Court established the exhaustion doctrine before the APA was adopted, and then Congress codified the doctrine in the APA. The exhaustion doctrine originated from a discretionary rule the courts of equity developed that allowed them to deny a party equitable relief when that party could have obtained similar relief from a court of law. In short, the exhaustion doctrine provides that courts should not review an agency action unless and until the plaintiff has exhausted the remedies available from the agency itself. For example, if a regulated entity loses an adjudication before an ALJ, the regulated entity must appeal that decision. If the entity opts not to appeal, the entity would have forgone an available administrative remedy and, pursuant to the exhaustion doctrine, may lose its ability to appeal the decision in court.

The exhaustion doctrine serves at least two purposes. First, it protects agency authority, allowing the agency to conclude a matter on which Congress has given it primary decisional power. *McCarthy v. Madigan*, 503 U.S. 140, 145 (1992). In addition, the exhaustion doctrine protects the agency's exercise of discretion and expertise. As the Supreme Court said, "exhaustion concerns apply with particular force when the action under review involves exercise of the agency's discretionary power or when the agency proceedings in question allow the agency to apply its special expertise." *Id.* Second, as with the finality doctrine, the exhaustion rule promotes judicial efficiency. The doctrine allows an agency to correct its own errors before judicial intervention. It prevents judicial resources from being wasted on disputes that may become mooted at the agency level. Finally, the doctrine ensures a fuller record for those cases that do ultimately come before the courts. *See id.* at 145–46.

For those actions brought under the APA, § 704 specifically addresses exhaustion of administrative remedies. That section provides:

> Except as otherwise expressly required by statute, agency action otherwise final is final whether or not there has been . . . any form of reconsideration . . . unless the agency otherwise requires by rule and provides that the action meanwhile is inoperative.

APA § 704. This section provides that exhaustion is required in two situations only: (1) when a statute expressly requires exhaustion, and (2) when an agency's own rule requires exhaustion *and* the agency stays its action pending the appeal. *See Darby*, 509 U.S. at 148 (holding that the plaintiff did not need to exhaust administrative remedies because neither the relevant statute nor the regulation required exhaustion). Interestingly, § 704's relatively clear exhaustion provision sat unnoticed for almost fifty years before it was interpreted and correctly applied in *Darby*.

Under § 704, exhaustion is the exception, whereas at common law, exhaustion is required. When a case is not brought pursuant to the APA, the common law doctrine of exhaustion applies. Under the common law doctrine, courts have discretion to require parties to exhaust their administrative remedies. *McCarthy*, 503 U.S. at 144. In determining whether to require exhaustion in a particular case, courts will balance the interest of the individual in getting prompt access to a judicial forum with the countervailing institutional interests favoring exhaustion. *Id.* at 146.

The classic exhaustion case is *Myers v. Bethlehem Shipbuilding Corp.*, 303 U.S. 41 (1938). In that case, the National Labor Relations Board (NLRB) began an unfair labor action against Bethlehem, alleging that in one of its plants the company had engaged in unfair labor practices in violation of the labor act. *Id.* at 43. Bethlehem sued to enjoin the NLRB from proceeding. One of Bethlehem's arguments was that the plant involved was not engaged in interstate commerce, a jurisdictional condition of any action by a federal agency. *Id.* at 47. Bethlehem was not arguing that the agency was wrong in its conclusion about the unfair labor practice; that question had yet to be tried. Instead, Bethlehem argued that, absent an effect on interstate commerce, the federal agency simply had no power over the company. *Id.* at 47–48. In addition, Bethlehem alleged that it would suffer serious harm should it have to defend itself in an illegal forum. Those costs included the loss of time of its officials and the impairment of the good will and harmonious relations that existed between the company and its employees. *Id.* at 50. If, after the hearing, the NLRB issued an order against the company that was later set aside as beyond the agency's jurisdiction, the company could not recoup its costs. *Id.* at 50–51.

Both the district court and the court of appeals agreed with Bethlehem and granted the injunction, effectively stopping the NLRB from further proceedings against the company. *Id.* at 43–44. The lower courts both reasoned that manufacturing was not interstate commerce so the NLRB had no jurisdiction to act, which was an accurate understanding of the law at that time. *Id.* at 50–51.

However, the law soon changed. By the time *Bethlehem* arrived at the Supreme Court, the NLRB's jurisdiction to regulate manufacturers was settled law. Thus, the Supreme Court reversed the lower courts, allowing the NLRB to proceed with its case against the company. *Id.* at 53. In doing so, Justice Brandeis held that the district court did not have jurisdiction to issue an injunction because the statute made the NLRB's decision appealable in the court of appeals, not the district courts. Bethlehem had argued that it was constitutionally unacceptable to force the company to go through an administrating proceeding that might turn out to be beyond the agency's power. Justice Brandeis rejected this argument:

> [T]he long-settled rule of judicial administration [is] that no one is entitled to judicial relief for a supposed or threatened injury until the prescribed administrative remedy has been exhausted .... [The exhaustion rule] has been repeatedly acted on in cases where, as here, the contention is made that the administrative body lacked power over the subject matter .... Obviously, the rules requiring exhaustion of the administrative remedy cannot be circumvented by asserting that the charge on which the complaint rests is groundless and that the mere holding of the prescribed administrative hearing would result in irreparable damage. Lawsuits also often prove to have been groundless; but no way has been discovered of relieving a defendant from the necessity of a trial to establish the fact.

*Id.* at 50–52. In short, Bethlehem had to endure what it considered to be an unconstitutional adjudication before an ALJ, appeal the ALJ's decision to the agency, then appeal the agency's final decision to the federal appellate courts.

Note that if a court dismisses a case because the plaintiff failed to exhaust administrative remedies, that plaintiff may never obtain any form of review, judicial or administrative. Generally, by the time the plaintiff's case is dismissed in court, the time for filing the administrative appeal would have passed. Hence, the plaintiff is simply out of luck.

While the common law exhaustion doctrine can be harsh, there are three recognized exceptions. For a discussion of these exceptions, see *McCarthy*, 503 U.S. at 151. *See generally*, Marcia Gelpe, *Exhaustion of Administrative Remedies: Lessons from Environmental Cases*, 53 GEO. WASH. L. REV. 1 (1984) (arguing that the there are eight exceptions).

First, a plaintiff need not exhaust administrative remedies when the administrative remedy would undermine the ability of the courts to provide effective relief. For example, if the agency action is not stayed during the litigation, the plaintiff may suffer irreparable harm, so exhaustion may not be required. An example is an agency action that has been unduly delayed. *See, e.g., Walker v. Southern Ry. Co.*, 385 U.S. 196, 198 (1966) (finding a possible delay of ten years in an administrative proceeding made exhaustion unnecessary).

Also, exhaustion may not be required when agency relief will be unreasonably delayed or the injury needs immediate relief if any relief is to be had at all. Examples include a delay in a case addressing disability benefits and a case addressing the availability of a defense in a criminal case. *See Bowen v. New York*, 476 U.S. 467, 483 (1986) (disability claimants); *Moore v. East Cleveland*, 431 U.S. 494, 497, n.5 (1977) (determining exhaustion is not required of a criminal defendant when the statute in question did not mandate exhaustion of remedies prior to judicial review).

Second, a plaintiff need not exhaust administrative remedies when the administrative remedy would be inadequate because the agency cannot provide the requested relief. *McCarthy*, 503 U.S. at 156–58 (Rehnquist J., concurring) (stating that exhaustion should not be required when the petitioner sought monetary damages that the agency had no authority to grant); *Moore*, 431 U.S. at 497, n.5 (concluding it would be "wholly inappropriate" to require criminal defendants to exhaust administrative remedies).

Third, a plaintiff need not exhaust administrative remedies when the administrative agency is biased or prejudiced against the plaintiff such that exhaustion would be futile. *Houghton v. Shafer*, 392 U.S. 639, 640 (1968) (stating that requiring exhaustion would be a futile act). This futility exception to exhaustion requires a sufficient showing of bias to overcome the usual presumption of impartiality. *Association of Nat'l Advertisers, Inc. v. FTC*, 627 F.2d 1151, 1156–57 (D.C. Cir. 1979) (holding that judicial review was appropriate because the agency had ample opportunity to explain why a chairperson had not been recused). Hence, it is a rarely applied exception.

While the Court has not yet said so explicitly, it is unlikely that these exceptions to the common law exhaustion doctrine apply to lawsuits brought under the APA because § 704 does not include any such exceptions and because Congress has to specifically require exhaustion.

## 3. Administrative Issue Exhaustion

Closely related to the exhaustion doctrine is the doctrine of administrative *issue* exhaustion. This doctrine prevents parties from raising issues in court that were not raised before the agency. The rationale for administrative issue exhaustion is similar to the rationale for the doctrine that prevents appellate courts from hearing issues not raised at the trial level. *Sims v. Apfel*, 530 U.S. 103, 112 (2000) (allowing a Social Security claimant to raise a new issue before the court because the agency's regulations and forms were misleading about the need to raise all issues before the agency). In short, the parties should fully argue their cases before the agency to best develop the record and to prevent undue surprise. *See, e.g., Paul v. Shalala*, 29 F.3d 208, 210–11 (5th Cir. 1994) (waiving doctrine when agency misled petitioner); *Eagle Eye Fishing Corp. v. United States*, 20 F.3d 503, 506–07 (1st Cir. 1994) (holding that even pro se litigants must raise issues below if a "reasonably well prepared litigant" would have raised them).

While issue exhaustion is applied most commonly in adjudications, occasionally a court will apply it in the rulemaking context. *See, e.g., Southwestern Pa. Growth Alliance v. Browner*, 121 F.3d 106 (3d Cir. 1997) (holding that a party cannot challenge a rule if the challenge was not explicitly raised in the public comments on the rule).

Finally, some state administrative procedure acts have included the doctrine of administrative issue exhaustion in statutory form. *See, e.g.,* Wash. Rev. Statute § 34.05.445.

## 4. Ripeness

Even if an agency action is final and a plaintiff has exhausted administrative remedies, the issues must also be ripe for judicial review. Like the finality and exhaustion doctrines, the ripeness doctrine predates the APA. Unlike those two doctrines, however, the ripeness doctrine is not codified in the APA. Hence, its development and application come from case law.

Before we explore this doctrine, you should be aware that ripeness cases usually involve rulemaking situations rather than adjudication. During a typical adjudication that concludes with a final order, the legal issues are as ripe as they are going to get. Moreover, the hardship to the plaintiffs is real; they must comply with the agency's order or face sanctions.

In contrast, in rulemaking, there may be many steps along the enforcement process that an agency must take before anyone can know how or even whether the rule will impact them. Most of the leading cases on ripeness, therefore, involve attempts to seek judicial review of finalized but, as of yet, unenforced regulations.

The seminal ripeness case is *Abbot Labs*, in which the Supreme Court set out a "simple" two-part doctrinal test. 387 U.S. 136 (1967). In *Abbot Labs*, drug manufacturers sought review of a regulation the Food and Drug Administration (FDA) promulgated. *Id.* at 138. The regulation was final but had not yet been enforced against any drug manufacturer. *Id.* at 139. The regulation required manufacturers to print the generic name of a drug on labels and other printed materials *every time* the manufacturers used the brand name of the drug in such materials. *Id.* at 138. The purpose of the so-called "every time" regulation was to inform consumers and prescribing physicians of the availability of lower cost but equivalent medications. *Id.*

Manufacturers sued to stop the regulation from going into effect. *Id.* The issue for the Court was purely legal: whether the regulation was within the agency's delegated authority. *Id.* at 139. Because there were no facts in dispute, both sides moved for summary judgment. The District Court granted declaratory and injunctive relief, finding that the regulations exceeded the FDA's authority. *Id.* The Court of Appeals reversed, holding that pre-enforcement review was unauthorized. *Id.*

On appeal, the Supreme Court reversed. *Id.* at 156. The Court first described the purpose of the ripeness doctrine:

> [Its] basic rationale is to prevent the courts, through avoidance of premature adjudication, from entangling themselves in abstract disagreements over administrative policies, and also to protect the agencies from judicial interference until an administrative decision has been formalized and its effects felt in a concrete way by the challenging parties.

*Id.* at 148. The Court said that to evaluate ripeness a court must "evaluate both the fitness of the issues for judicial decision and the hardship to the parties of withholding court consideration." *Id.* at 149.

Interestingly, if you reverse the order of these two factors and if you read "countervailing institutional interests" to include protecting the courts from having to decide mooted and unnecessary issues, the analysis is virtually identical to the analysis of exhaustion. However, exhaustion is appropriate when a plaintiff could have tried to address its concerns with the agency directly but chose not to. In contrast, ripeness is appropriate when there was no way for the plaintiff to address its concerns with the agency first, such as when a final regulation is challenged pre-enforcement.

Evaluating those two factors in this case, the majority determined that both factors favored immediate review. *Id.* at 149. The issues were purely legal issues about whether the scope of the regulation was authorized by the enabling statute. *Id.* Resolution of that issue required no further factual development. Similarly, the majority concluded that the hardship to the manufacturers would be significant. *Id.* at 154. The manufacturers faced the choice of complying with the regulation at considerable and potentially needless expense or not complying with the regulation thereby risking "serious criminal and civil penalties for the unlawful distribution of 'misbranded' drugs." *Id.* at 153.

The dissenting justices identified a third concern they believed should be included in the analysis: the public interest. *Id.* at 201 (Clark, J. dissenting). Because pre-enforcement review of the regulation was granted, implementation of the regulation would be delayed for many years. During the delay, the public would be deprived of the benefit of information about lower cost drugs, while the manufacturers had the monetary benefit of "peddling plain medicine . . . for fancy prices." *Id.* at 199. The majority was unmoved and responded to this concern by noting that if immediate implementation of the regulation was necessary to protect the public interest, the agency could have made the regulation effective immediately. *Id.* at 154.

On the same day the Court decided *Abbott Labs*, the Court also decided a companion case, *Toilet Goods Association v. Gardner*, 387 U.S. 158 (1967). In *Toilet Goods*, the Court found a pre-enforcement challenge of a regulation to be unripe. *Id.* at 160–61. At issue in this case was another FDA regulation; this regulation provided that if an entity refused to allow FDA employees access to its manufacturing facilities, the FDA could immediately suspend that entity's certification to use color additives. *Id.* at 159–60. An association of manufacturers of color additives sued to prevent the regulation from taking effect. *Id.* The Court applied the *Abbott Labs* two-factor test.

Regarding the fitness of the issues for judicial resolution (the first factor), the Court conceded that review of this regulation presented a purely legal issue. *Id.* at 162. But the Court reasoned that this factor was still not met because ancillary questions needed to be determined before the full impact of the regulation could be assessed. These ancillary questions included the time and manner of the agency's request for access and whether there were adequate safeguards in place to protect trade secrets. *Id.* at 164.

Regarding the hardship to the parties (the second factor), the Court reasoned that no irremediable adverse consequences flowed from delaying review. *Id.* Unlike the regulation at issue in *Abbott Labs*, the regulation at issue in *Toilet Goods* was conditional and did not affect primary conduct. The regulation only applied if an FDA inspector attempted to gain access to a plant and was subsequently denied. *Id.* at 165. And the ensuing penalty was not as significant as the civil and criminal penalties the manufacturers in *Abbott Labs* risked. *Id* An entity's refusal to admit access would lead to suspension of its certification; however, the entity could promptly challenge the suspension through existing procedures. *Id.* The Court reasoned that the appeal procedures provided an adequate forum for testing the legality of the regulation. *Id.* at 165–66.

After *Abbot Labs* and *Toilet Goods*, courts typically grant pre-enforcement review to agency regulations that require entities to change their behavior to comply with new duties or restrictions. *See, e.g., National Automatic Laundry,* 443 F.2d at 689 (finding a challenge to an agency opinion letter regarding hour and wage requirements ripe). In contrast, when the regulations do not require immediate change, challenges are typically found to be unripe. *Florida Power & Light Co. v. EPA,* 145 F.3d 1414 (D.C. Cir. 1998) (finding unripe challenges to an agency's interpretation of its authority, which were contained in a preamble to a proposed rulemaking).

More recently, the Court has begun its retreat from *Abbott Labs'* pre-enforcement review presumption. Specifically, in *National Parks Hospitality Ass'n v. DOI,* 538 U.S. 803, 812 (2003), the Court found unripe a "regulation" the Parks Service promulgated, which interpreted the Contract Disputes Act of 1978 (CDA). In its regulation, the Parks Service concluded that the CDA did not apply to concessionaire contracts. *Id.* at 804–05. An association of concessionaires challenged the agency's interpretation. *Id.* Applying *Abbott Labs* two-factor test, the majority first acknowledged that the question presented was a "purely legal" question — whether the statute authorized the agency to suspend certification if access were denied. *Id.* at 808. However, the majority did not stop there. As it had in *Toilet Goods*, the majority concluded that "further factual development would significantly advance our ability to deal with the legal issues presented." *Id.* at 812.

Applying the second *Abbott Labs'* factor, the majority found that factor unmet as well. *Id.* at 811. The Court reasoned that the agency had simply issued a policy statement. And because policy statements do not create "adverse effects of a strictly legal kind," such harms do not satisfy the hardship showing. *Id.* at 809. As the concurring and dissenting justices argued in response, when an agency action can cause hardship to the parties, the formality of the agency's action should not be determinative. *Id.* at 814–15.

The Court then reversed *Abbott Labs* pre-enforcement review presumption, making pre-enforcement review the exception rather than the rule. "[A] regulation is not ordinarily considered the type of agency action 'ripe' for judicial review under the [APA] until [there is] some concrete action applying the regulation to the claimant's situation in a fashion that harms or threatens to harm him." *Id.* at 808. The Court conceded that pre-enforcement review is appropriate when a plaintiff must alter conduct immediately because of a "substantive rule," but suggested that such pre-enforcement enforcement was the exception. *Id.* at 810. Thus, *National Parks* represents a step back from *Abbott Labs.*

As we finish our discussion of these timing doctrines, you should keep in mind the following. Finality, exhaustion, and ripeness all began life as common law doctrines, forged from judicial restraint and efficiency concerns. These doctrines attempt to balance conflicting functional goals.

On the one hand, efficiency and fairness may suggest that immediate judicial review is best. Anything that delays a would-be plaintiff from pursuing an immediate challenge requires that plaintiff to endure a long and expensive administrative proceeding that may turn out to be illegal or unwarranted. Moreover, the agency might also benefit from prompt judicial review because a judicial ruling might save it from wasting its time. If a court has all the information it needs to make a ruling regarding the legality of the agency's action, why not allow prompt judicial action?

On the other hand, judicial economy and autonomy may suggest that delaying judicial review is best. Permitting an agency to finish work on a case before subjecting the agency's decision to judicial review allows the agency autonomy to work as the legislature delegated to it and removes those cases from a court's docket that can be resolved at the agency level. For cases that are capable of being resolved at the agency level, the agency can complete its work in a more complete fashion. Thus, a reviewing court will have a record that is more complete both factually and legally. Full development and argument may clarify and narrow legal issues, which will greatly reduce the work for the reviewing court.

As noted earlier, finality, exhaustion, and ripeness are related doctrines. Their resolution turns on the consideration of similar factors; hence, courts sometimes carelessly interchange them. Their focus is different, however. Finality focuses on whether the agency has finished its work so the records will be complete and the judiciary will not waste its time on moot issues. The beneficiary of finality is the court because finality ensures that the court will have a complete record with a non-mooted case before it.

Exhaustion focuses on whether there are means of review or redress available within the agency. The beneficiary of exhaustion is the agency because exhaustion ensures that the agency's internal review processes will be followed before the courts intrude into the process.

Ripeness focuses on the issue to be decided and the degree to which that issue has reached the state of development and refinement that will permit a court to make a decision about its legality. The beneficiary of ripeness is the court because ripeness protects the court from inserting itself into a speculative or abstract question. Thus, these are different doctrines, but their resolution often requires consideration of similar factors.

In sum, the doctrines ultimately affirm the legislature's authority. The legislature gave power to the agency to decide the issues; the judiciary's job is not to resolve the issues but to assure that the agency's resolution is legal and within its delegated authority. As we will see in the next chapter, this delicate and subtle task involves broad respect for the agency's authority, its expertise, and its accountability, all of which are not respected when judicial review is permitted prematurely.

## 5. Primary Jurisdiction

The doctrine of primary jurisdiction is rarely covered in administrative law courses and is not really an availability of judicial *review* doctrine, because no agency decision is available for the court to review. The doctrine arises when a plaintiff brings an action in court and the defendant responds that the case should be dismissed or postponed so that an agency with authority to address the issue can do so first. Only after an agency acts will there be a decision for the court to review.

Nevertheless, the doctrine of primary jurisdiction is closely related to the timing doctrines, so we address it briefly here. This doctrine directs courts to stay out of disputes when the issues in the case fall within the agency's "primary jurisdiction." In other words, the courts should allow the agencies to address the issues first and, if the agency's decision does not resolve the issue, then the court can review the agency's decision later. While this doctrine is similar to the finality doctrine, the finality doctrine is applicable when the agency has already taken some action, while the primary jurisdiction doctrine is applicable when the agency has not yet acted at all.

Why would the choice of forum matter to the parties? It may be simply a matter of geography; a local court may be friendlier to local shipper than a federal agency. It may be a matter of timing; an agency may make a decision faster or slower than court. It may be a matter of cost: one process may be cheaper. Perhaps the most important reason forum would matter is that the law a court would apply may differ from the law that an agency would apply. For example, if a workers' compensation commission is created because of dissatisfaction with the generosity of common law juries, the choice of forum could affect the outcome of an injured worker's case. Consider another example: in the antitrust field competitors that share price information would find courts applying the Sherman Act hostile to such price fixing, but they might find support from an agency that believes cooperative action among competitors is important to the health of the industry.

Primary jurisdiction cases are not about lack of jurisdiction in the usual sense. Both the court and the agency have jurisdiction, for otherwise there would be no conflict. Primary jurisdiction cases are about which entity should exercise jurisdiction first. In *Far Eastern Conference v. United States*, 432 U.S. 570 (1952), Justice Frankfurter identified a list of considerations:

> [I]n cases raising issues of fact not within the conventional experience of judges or cases requiring the exercise of administrative discretion, agencies created by Congress for regulating the subject matter should not be passed over . . . . Uniformity and consistency in the regulation of business entrusted to a particular agency are secured, and the limited functions of review by the judiciary are more rationally exercised, by preliminary resort for ascertaining and interpreting the circumstances underlying legal issues to agencies that are better equipped than courts.

*Id*. at 574; *see also Mashphee Tribe v. New Seabury Corp.*, 592 F.2d 575, 580–81 (1st Cir. 1979) (identifying three factors to be considered in applying the primary jurisdiction doctrine: "(1) whether the agency determination lay at the heart of the task assigned the agency by Congress; (2) whether agency expertise was required to unravel intricate, technical facts; and (3) whether, though perhaps not determinative, the agency determination would materially aid the court.").

The primary jurisdiction doctrine originated in the transportation field when now-defunct federal agencies such as the Interstate Commerce Commission and the Civil Aeronautics Board regulated the rates and practices of airlines, railroads, trucks, and ships. *See, e.g., Texas & Pacific RR. Co. v. Abilene Cotton Oil Co.*, 204 U.S. 426, 441 (1907) (dismissing plaintiff's state common law claim against a railway pursuant to the primary jurisdiction doctrine). On one hand, the federal agencies had authority to determine rates and such.

On the other hand, federal courts had developed a body of common law rules for resolving common carrier disputes. At times the two bodies of law conflicted. Today, these fields have largely been deregulated, but the primary jurisdiction doctrine continues to be relevant when national uniformity is important. *Massachusetts*, 549 U.S. at 508–10 (applying the doctrine in a case involving national emission standards).

## G.  The Availability of Judicial Review: A Flow Chart

In this chapter we learned that many administrative agency actions are not subject to judicial review even though such review is an important constraint on administrative agencies. The purposes of these doctrines are to assure that judicial review is available when it is needed to keep agencies within their legislatively delegated powers and legislatures within their constitutionally delegated powers. But these doctrines also ensure that we do not impose inappropriate tasks on courts or permit them to intrude inappropriately into the executive and legislative spheres. Figure 5.3 summarizes these various doctrines. Notice that the universe of agency actions that might be subject to judicial review becomes smaller and smaller as each of these doctrines is applied. Ultimately, only the most judicially fit cases reach the courts.

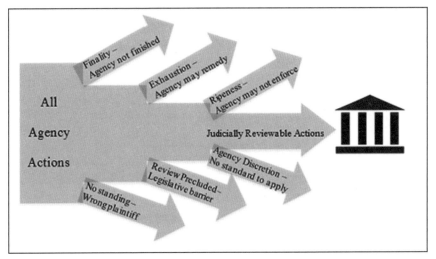

**Figure 5.3** Availability of Judicial Review

# Checkpoints

- Judicial review of agency action helps legitimize the administrative process.

- Judicial review is not always available, due to certain judge-made doctrines.

- Courts must have jurisdiction over the plaintiff's claim. Such jurisdiction comes from the agency's enabling statute or from federal question jurisdiction. It does not come from the APA.

- Courts must have jurisdiction over the plaintiff, meaning that the plaintiff must have standing.

- For a plaintiff to have constitutional standing, the plaintiff must have an injury in fact that is concrete and particularized, that is caused by the agency action challenged, and that is redressable by a favorable court decision.

- Plaintiffs must generally assert their own claims, and those claims must not be widely shared by the public.

- An association may assert claims on behalf of its members if one of its members has constitutional standing, the association's purpose is related to the issues, and the lawsuit seeks declaratory or injunctive relief only so that the individual member's participation is unnecessary.

- Plaintiffs must "arguably" be within the zone of interests of the relevant statute.

- There is a strong presumption in favor of judicial review of final agency actions.

- Congress can preclude review, explicitly or implicitly.

- Congress may grant agencies complete discretion, in which case courts will have no "law to apply."

- Courts only review final agency actions, when administrative remedies have been exhausted (if required) and when the actions are ripe enough to present issues clear enough for judicial resolution.

# Chapter 6

# Scope of Judicial Review of Agency Action

---

## Roadmap

- The Importance of Judicial Review
- Reviewing Agency Determinations of Law
  - Defining Questions of Law
  - Pre-*Chevron*: *Skidmore* and *Hearst*
  - *Chevron*
  - *Chevron* Step Zero
  - Agency Interpretations that Conflict with Judicial Interpretations
- Reviewing Agency Determinations of Fact and Policy
  - Defining Questions of Fact and Policy
  - Substantial Evidence
  - Arbitrary and Capricious
  - De Novo Review
  - The Record

---

# A. Introduction

The last chapter addressed the question of whether judicial review is available at all. This chapter addresses the ensuing question: assuming judicial review is available, what is the scope of that review? As we will see, the answer to this question changes depending on the nature of the issue being reviewed. Scope of review doctrines seek to allocate roles appropriately to the courts and agencies based on their requisite expertise. You will find that judicial review is less exacting when agencies bring their own expertise to the issue and more exacting when courts are equally able to resolve the issue.

# 1. The Importance of Scope of Review

This topic is central to administrative law and is being hotly debated in the legislature as this text goes to press. As we saw in Chapter 1, a major function of administrative law is to correct some of the shortfalls in a form of government that separates powers; shortfalls that have been caused, in part, by the unexpected growth of the regulatory state. One such shortfall is the substantial delegation of basic policy-making power from elected officials (members of Congress) to unelected administrators (agency regulators). While members of Congress are accountable to the public via elections, agency regulators are not. To increase accountability, oversight is necessary to keep agency regulators faithful to congressional preferences. As we have seen, oversight can be done in many ways. One of the most important is judicial oversight in the form of judicial review.

Judicial review is the most visible and, in some senses, the most final oversight mechanism. If agencies lose in court, they generally must start their regulatory process all over again. Moreover, the outcome may serve as a precedent for other agencies and their regulatory efforts. William F. Pedersen, Jr., *Formal Records and Informal Rulemaking*, 85 YALE L.J. 38, 60 (1975) (saying that judicial review "reaches beyond those who were concerned with the specific regulations reviewed. They serve as a precedent for future rulewriters and give those who care about well-documented and well-reasoned decisionmaking a lever with which to move those who do not."). Hence, agency officials understand the potential impact of judicial review and seek to avoid or minimize that impact as they regulate. In other words, the availability of judicial review serves an oversight function even if such review never actually takes place.

When judicial review does take place, the scope of that review is important. As we will see, judicial review is designed to allow courts to police the legality of agency action while simultaneously preventing courts from interfering with congressional delegation and agency expertise. If the scope of judicial review were too intensive, then federal judges would make policy. However, federal judges have neither technical expertise nor political accountability. Instead, if the scope of judicial review were not intensive enough, then agency policies may not sufficiently adhere to congressional delegation and may not sufficiently follow the rule of law. Hence, the scope of review doctrines seeks to find balance.

## 2. Intensity and Scope of Review

Scope of review must be just intensive enough. But what does "intensive enough" mean? We will see that the meaning varies by context.

Let's look first to standards of review in non-administrative law cases. Low-intensity review is review in which a judge is highly deferential to the trier of fact's views. For example, when an appellate court reviews a lower court's opinion for clear error, that is a low-intensity review standard. At the other end of the spectrum, high-intensity review is review in which a judge substitutes his or her own views for that of the trier of fact. De novo review is a form of high-intensity review, perhaps even the highest form. There are gradations in the middle of the spectrum. See Figure 6.1. While the qualities of the various judicial review standards are far too subtle to be captured on a single linear spectrum, thinking about the standards in this way will give us a start on comparing different judicial review standards.

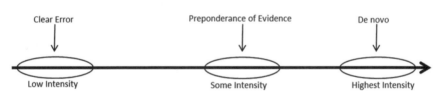

Figure 6.1 The Scope of Review Intensity Spectrum

You should also keep in mind that there is more than one step in the administrative review process. For example, when a court reviews an agency decision reached as part of a formal adjudication process, there are actually three different times when the decision may be reviewed. First, the agency may review the ALJ's decision during an internal review process. Second, a court of appeals may review the final order of the agency. Third, the Supreme Court may review the court of appeals' decision. See Figure 6.2.

This scope of review discussion concerns the second step, where the agency's final administrative order or regulation first encounters the courts. We saw in Chapter 3 that when an agency reviews its own ALJ's order at the first step, the agency's review is very intensive. APA § 557(b) (providing for de novo review). In contrast, at the third step, when the Supreme Court reviews a

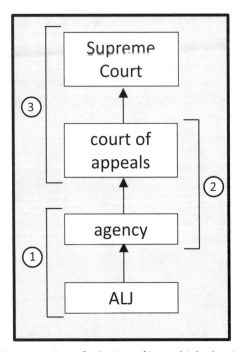

**Figure 6.2** Steps for Review of Formal Adjudication

decision of the court of appeals, that review is often less intensive. The Court has said described such review as follows:

> Whether on the record as a whole there is substantial evidence to support agency findings is a question which Congress has placed in the keeping of the Courts of Appeals. This Court will intervene only in what ought to be the rare instance when the standard appears to have been misapprehended or grossly misapplied.

*Universal Camera v. NLRB*, 340 U.S. 474, 491 (1951). Keep in mind that this substantial evidence standard is not the same one we will be discussing below.

Let's return to the second step. It is unclear whether judicial review of agency action is constitutionally required; however, Congress includes judicial review provisions in most enabling statutes. Moreover, section 706 of the APA contains a default judicial review provision. When you have a question about scope of review, you must first determine whether Congress has provided a specific standard in the enabling statute; only when Congress fails to provide a review standard should you turn to section 706 of the APA. Note that some of these judicial review standards apply to a particular type of case or issue, while others serve a catch-all function. For example, one case-specific provision directs the reviewing court to "[h]old unlawful and set aside agency action, findings, and conclusions found to be . . . unsupported by substantial evidence in a case [involving formal rulemaking or formal adjudication]." APA § 706(2)(E). A catch-all provision directs the reviewing court to "[h]old unlawful and set aside agency action, findings, and conclusions found to be . . . arbitrary, capricious, an abuse of discretion or otherwise not in accordance with law." APA § 706(2)(A).

# B. Reviewing Agency Determinations of Law

## 1. Defining Questions of Law

Let's assume that a regulated entity wishes to challenge an agency's decision. Typically, such challenges involve questions of law, questions of law application, questions of fact, and questions of policy. For now, we will consider the two questions of law categories: pure questions of law and questions of law application.

A pure question of law is one in which the resolution of the question does not require knowledge of the facts. Thus, a statement of law is an assertion about legal effect that can be advanced with no knowledge of the facts in a particular case.

Let's look at a nonagency example. Assume that there was a car accident. During the investigation, the accident investigator noted that the speed limit was 30 mph on the road where the accident took place. This assertion would be a statement of law. The facts relating to the car accident are irrelevant.

Let's turn back to our world of agencies. Agencies must determine the boundaries of their delegated authority and the meaning of the laws within that authority. Questions related to these types of issues are pure questions of law. When an agency resolves a question of law, the facts of an individual case are largely irrelevant. What matters is what the statute or regulation says.

In the section that follows, we will focus on the standard of review that courts apply when agencies resolve pure questions of law. But we must briefly cover another type of question, questions of law application, or a mixed question of law and fact. Let's return to our car accident example. Assume the investigator concluded that the defendant's car must have exceeded the speed limit, given that the skid marks were unusually long. Such a question involves applying the relevant law (the speed limit) to the specific facts in a particular case (the unusually long skid marks) to reach a conclusion (the defendant was speeding).

Let's turn back to our world of agencies. Agencies resolve questions of law application during adjudications when they determine whether a particular law applies to a given set of the facts. For example, are newspaper delivery people employees of a particular newspaper or independent contractors? Would the refusal of an employer to bargain with its employees constitute an unfair labor practice? The facts and the law are both relevant in resolving these mixed questions.

The appropriate standard applicable to mixed questions of law and fact is currently unclear. Some courts accept an agency's resolution of a mixed question if it has "warrant in the record" and "a reasonable basis in the law." *NLRB v. Hearst Publ'n, Inc.* 322 U.S. 111, 131 (1944). Some courts treat the question as a pure question of law, while others treat the question as one of fact. *See, e.g., O'Leary*, 340 U.S. at 507 (treating as a question of fact the issue of whether the death of a federal worker "arose out of and in the course of employment"). Finally, some courts break the mixed question into its component parts of law and fact. To the extent the courts treat the question as a pure question of law, the analysis from the next section applies. To the extent the courts treat the question as one of fact, the analysis from the following section applies.

## 2. Pre-*Chevron*: *Skidmore* and *Hearst*

To understand where the law is today, we must begin with the past. This section will describe two very important cases that predated our current standard of review in this area.

Agencies interpret statutes as part of their day-to-day implementation and enforcement of legislatively prescribed duties. When an agency's legal interpretation is challenged in court, we confront a very complicated intersection of legislative, executive, and judicial powers. Who should make the initial interpretation? Who should have the final say? Judicial review of agency legal interpretations is one of the most challenging, and certainly the most discussed, of all the issues in administrative law.

Again, let's begin our analysis outside of the administrative law context. Typically, appellate courts review questions of law de novo. Appellate courts are experts at law, while trial courts are experts at gathering the facts. When we return to the administrative context, your instinct might be to expect a court to review an agency's legal interpretation de novo. After all, appellate courts are masters of law while agencies are experts at gathering facts and making policy.

The language of the APA would seem to confirm your instinct. The relevant statutory language provides that "the reviewing court shall decide all relevant questions of law, [and] interpret constitutional and statutory provisions. . . ." APA § 706.

The understanding that courts are experts at law interpretation goes as far back as *Marbury v. Madison*, 5 U.S. 137 (1803). Justice Marshall declared that law interpretation is simply what courts do. *Id.* at 177. His declaration was premised on his understanding of the nature of the judicial function and the critical role it plays in our constitutional scheme. Since *Marbury* was decided, it has been difficult to dislodge that notion from our settled traditions and understandings; there is something natural, even sacrosanct, about judges deciding what the law means. Now and then, of course, the Court has taken a more practical and less monopolistic view of the judicial power. *See, e.g., CFTC v. Schor*, 478 U.S. 833, 858 (1986) (holding that an administrative agency may have jurisdiction to hear some state-law counterclaims).

But the view that judges should decide what the law means is deeply embedded in our legal system. Judges are appropriate interpreters of the law because they are trained in legal analysis and statutory interpretation. Legislators and regulators are not. Also, judges are considered more principled, more policy-neutral, and more objective than mission-oriented legislators and regulators. While this latter claim is generally true, there are circumstances in which judicial objectivity could support an argument *against* judicial primacy. Judicial objectivity may mask an insensitivity or even hostility to the underlying legislative purpose behind a regulatory scheme. And it is the legislature, not the judiciary, that has the constitutional power to decide policy.

Consider whether agencies might be better equipped to interpret the laws they administer than the courts. If the meaning of a statutory term should reflect something of the authoring legislature's purpose or goal, the agency may have been "present at the statute's creation," may have had a hand in promoting and drafting the statute, and may thus have a sharper or clearer sense of the legislative purpose than a court considering the statute much later would have. Further, the agency and its staff may be in a day-to-day working relationship with legislators and their staffs and with the regulated parties, which would give the agency additional insight into the practical implications of alternative interpretations.

Moreover, if the meaning of a statutory term should reflect something of the policy preferences of the elected president, agency staff may be in closer touch with such political considerations; they, after all, are recent presidential appointees or people who work for presidential appointees. And, of course, the agency is much more likely than a reviewing court to have technical, scientific, economic, and other expertise, and that expertise may prove critical to interpreting the statutory language.

Finally, there is the important question of which of two alternative inter-preters (courts or agencies) the legislature wished to play the larger role in interpreting a given statute. As we will see, this final question will turn out to be the most central in the development of the doctrine.

In determining the appropriate role for a reviewing court, we might con-sider various ways to take advantage of agencies' interpretive strengths. One option: a judge could examine the agency interpretation to determine whether it was persuasive and, if so, defer to it. The *Marbury* dictum, after all, does not prevent a reviewing judge from having the good sense to rely on experts.

One example in which the Supreme Court took this approach is *Skidmore v. Swift*, 323 U.S. 134 (1944). In *Skidmore,* the Court gave interpretive weight to the views of the Administrator of the Wage and Hour Division of the Department of Labor. The Court deferred even though the Administrator had expressed those views informally rather than in a notice and comment rule-making, and even though the Administrator had no power to enforce the stat-ute itself, but had to go to court to seek an injunction. *Id.* at 139–40. To determine whether to give an agency *Skidmore* deference, as this form of def-erence is known:

> [A court] consider[s] that the rulings, interpretations and opinions of the Administrator under this act ... constitute a body of experi-ence and informed judgment to which courts ... may properly resort for guidance. The weight of such a judgment in a particular case will depend upon the thoroughness evident in its consideration, the valid-ity of its reasoning, its consistency with earlier or later pronounce-ments, and all those factors which give it power to persuade, if lacking power to control.

*Skidmore*, 323 U.S. at 140. While the tenor of this quote is very deferential to the agency, it also protects the principle of judicial supremacy for legal interpretations.

A second option for taking advantage of agencies' interpretive strengths is for a court to determine whether some parts of the interpretive issue are suit-able for judicial resolution and other parts deserve deference to the agency. One example in which the Supreme Court took this approach is *Hearst Publications*, 322 U.S. at 111. In that case, Congress had authorized the NLRB to conduct formal adjudications for the purpose of resolving disputes arising in the labor law field. *Id.* at 130. In such a proceeding, the Board was presented with the question of whether "newsboys" fit within the statutory term "employee." If so, then management was required to bargain collectively with them under the terms of the statute. *Id.* at 113.

The Court separated the issue into two parts. The Court first examined the question of whether Congress had intended to incorporate the common law definition of "employee" in the labor act by using that term. *Id.* at 120. If, on the one hand, Congress had so intended, then the employer would probably not be required to bargain with the newsboys; under normal common law analysis, the newsboys would have been independent contractors rather than employees. *Id.* at 119–20. If, on the other hand, the legislature had intended the word "employee" to be broader than the common law meaning, then the newsboys could be within the statutory term and the employer would be required to bargain with them. *Id.* at 113. The Court concluded that the legislature had intended the word "employee" to extend beyond the common law definition. In doing so, the Court determined de novo whether "there was a reasonable basis in law" for determining that the statutory term "employee" was limited to its common law definition. *Id.* at 131.

To find the meaning of the statutory language, the Court examined the statutory purpose and the practical problems the common law definition would generate in this setting, specifically that there would be different rules for collective bargaining in different states around the country. *Id.* at 124–25. The Court concluded that the legislature intended the word "employees" to cover any person economically related to the newspaper in ways that were relevant to the purposes of the labor act. *Id.* at 129. In its lengthy analysis, the Court did not suggest that it owed any deference to the agency's understanding about the meaning of the statutory word "employees." Rather, using traditional tools of statutory interpretation, the Court decided independently what the legislature meant by the word.

Incidentally, you might be interested to know that the Court in *Hearst* likely got the answer wrong. At its next opportunity, Congress amended the Labor Act to be sure common law independent contractors were *not* included in the definition of "employee." *See NLRB v. United Insurance*, 390 U.S. 254, 256 (1968). Determining legislative intent can be a very chancy business.

In any event, after it determined what the term "employee" in the Labor Act meant, the Court faced a second question: whether the newsboys in this particular case had the kind of economic relationship to the newspaper that would make them employees under this broader definition. 322 U.S. at 130. On this more factual question, the Court deferred substantially to the agency. *Id.* Resolution of this question was highly fact-specific: one must know how many newsboys there were, what their economic situation was, what choices they had about the locations from which they sold papers, what hours they worked, what prices they charged and who set the prices, and how their compensation was calculated. These questions involved matters within the knowledge and experience of the agency and about which the Court had no special knowledge or experience. Accordingly, the Court accepted the agency's conclusion that the newsboys were economically dependent on the newspaper. *Id.* at 131–32. In doing so, the Court limited its role to determining whether the agency's factual determinations "had warrant in the record." *Id.* at 131.

For most of U.S. administrative law's history, these two options for taking advantage of agencies' interpretive strengths were used: *Skidmore* and *Hearst*. Courts either gave agency interpretations persuasive weight if warranted based on the thoroughness of their consideration or the validity of their reasoning. Alternatively, the courts independently established the range within which the agency legal interpretations should fall, then allowed the agency relative freedom to decide whether the facts in a given case fell within that range.

The goal of the two approaches was to allocate appropriate roles to each of the players based on their expertise. Courts and agencies are not competitors, rivals, or players differently situated on some hierarchy of authority engaged in a zero sum contest. Rather, courts and agencies are in a complex system of law interpretation and application. When primary interpretive authority must be allocated to one or the other, the judicial task is to decide (oversimplifying just a bit) when one of the partners will serve as a senior partner and when one will serve as a junior partner or, as Professor Strauss put it, to decide whether the court will play a role as a "decider" or as an overseer. Peter L. Strauss, *Overseers or "The Deciders" — The Courts in Administrative Law*, 75 U. CHI. L. REV. 815, 820 (2008).

## 3. *Chevron*

In 1984, the Court decided *Chevron v. National Resources Defense Council, Inc.*, 467 U.S. 837 (1984), and unleashed a revolution. *Chevron* added a new consideration — congressional preference. Congress has the primary authority to allocate interpretive power (save for constitutional questions). When Congress has expressed an allocation that expression will usually control. The question in *Chevron* was what happens when Congress does not expressly allocate interpretive power.

Fasten your seatbelts; this is going to be something of a roller coaster ride. We have here one of the (thankfully) rare events in our jurisprudence where a single case becomes the occasion for an extraordinary outpouring of citations, law review articles, endless discussion, and sharp division among judges, legislators, and academics at all levels.

### a. The Chevron Two-Step

*Chevron* involved a question about the Clean Air Act. The provision of the Act at issue required plants to obtain a permit when the plant wished to modify or build a "stationary source[]" of pollution. *Id.* at 840. The term "stationary sources" was not defined in the Act. *Id.* at 841. Thus, the Environmental Protection Agency (EPA), the agency in charge of administering the Act, had to interpret the term. The EPA had issued two regulations interpreting "stationary source." The first regulation defined "stationary source" as the construction or installation of any new or modified equipment that emitted air pollutants. *Id.* at 840 n.2. But the following year, after a presidential election, the EPA repealed that regulation and issued a new one that expanded the definition to encompass a plant-wide or "bubble concept" definition. *Id.* at 858. The bubble concept interpretation allowed a plant to offset increased air pollutant emissions at one part of its plant with reduced emissions at another part of the plant. So long as total emissions at the plant remained constant, no permit was required. *Id.* at 852. Not surprisingly, environmentalists sued. The issue for the Court was whether the EPA's interpretation of "stationary source" in the Clean Air Act was valid.

The Supreme Court upheld the agency's interpretation. *Id.* at 842. In doing so, the Court ignored *Skidmore's* power-to-persuade test entirely and instead created a two-step deference framework, based in part on its holding in *Hearst Publications*.

By the way, you should get used to talking about *Chevron* using numbers if you want to be *au courant*. The Court framed the doctrine as having two distinct steps, which were soon named the "*Chevron* two-step." Legal academics, many of whom avoided business school because of math fears, have since argued the accuracy of this nomenclature. *See, e.g.*, Mathew Stephenson & Adrian Vermeule, Chevron *Has Only One Step*, 95 Va. L. Rev. 597 (2009); Thomas Merrill & Kristin Hickman, Chevron's *Domain*, 89 Geo. L.J. 833, 836 (2001) (noting that there is a third step: "Step Zero").

The Court described its two steps as follows. First, a court should determine "whether Congress has directly spoken to the precise question at issue." *Chevron*, 467 U.S. 842–43. In other words, is congressional intent clear—however clarity may be discerned—or is there a gap or ambiguity to be resolved? According to the Court, clarity was to be discerned by "employing traditional tools of statutory construction." *Id.* at 843 n.9. Under this first step, courts do not defer to agencies at all. Rather, "[t]he judiciary is the final authority on issues of statutory construction. . . ." *Id.* at 843. We will look at the two steps more closely in a moment.

In *Chevron*, the Court offered three reasons to justify its decision to defer to agency legal interpretations. First, the Court continued *Skidmore's* rationale that agency personnel are experts in their field while Judges are not. *Chevron*, 467 U.S. at 865. Congress entrusts agencies to implement law in a particular area because of this expertise. For example, scientists and analysts working for the Food and Drug Administration (FDA) are more knowledgeable about food safety and drug effectiveness than are judges. Because agencies are specialists in their field, they are in a better position to implement effective public policy. Courts are more limited in both knowledge and reasoning methods. While agencies can develop policy using a wide array of methods, courts are limited to the adversarial process. Hence, deferring to these experts makes sense.

Second, Congress simply cannot legislate every detail in a comprehensive regulatory scheme. Gaps and ambiguities are inevitable; an agency must fill and resolve these gaps and ambiguities. In *Chevron*, the Court presumed that by leaving these gaps and ambiguities, Congress impliedly delegated the authority to the agency to resolve them. *Id.* at 843–44.

Finally, administrative officials, unlike federal judges, have a political constituency to which they are accountable. "[F]ederal judges — who have no constituency — have a duty to respect legitimate policy choices made by those who do." *Id.* at 866.

Thus, in creating its new two-step deference framework, the Court provided three reasons: agency expertise, implied congressional delegation, and democratic theory. Deference, which had been earned by agencies through reasoned decision making under *Skidmore*, became essentially an all-or-nothing grant of power from Congress under *Chevron*. Either Congress was clear when it drafted the statute and the judiciary should not defer to an agency's interpretation that differed from congressional intent, or Congress was ambiguous or silent and the judiciary should defer completely to an agency's reasonable interpretation.

As an interesting aside, Justice Stevens did not think he was letting a new genie out of the bottle. He thought he was merely stating a familiar principle:

> We have long recognized that considerable weight should be accorded to an executive department's construction of a statutory scheme it is entrusted to administer, and the principle of deference to administrative interpretations has been consistently followed by this Court whenever decision as to the meaning or reach of a statute has involved reconciling conflicting policies, and a full understanding of the force of the statutory policy in the given situation has

depended upon more than ordinary knowledge respecting the matters subjected to agency regulations.

*Id.* at 844. And more than 25 years later, he expressed concern that *Chevron* has been read too broadly; he would prefer no deference on "pure" questions of law and *Hearst* deference on questions of law application. *Negusie v. Holder,* 555 U.S. 511 (2009) (Stevens, J., concurring and dissenting).

### b. Step One: Has Congress Spoken?

Let's now look at each of *Chevron*'s two steps. Step one seems too obvious to bother analyzing. Step one has been described as whether the statute is ambiguous. But in *Chevron,* Justice Stevens did not frame step one as a search for textual clarity; rather, he framed the step as "whether Congress has directly spoken to the precise question at issue." *Chevron,* 467 U.S. 842–43. These are different questions.

So, you might point out, if Congress really "has directly spoken to the precise question at issue," then there would have been no litigation in the first place. The statutes that are litigated are those in which Congress has *not* addressed the precise question at issue. Thus, you conclude, step one is meaningless: in every case involving an agency interpretation that comes before the court, the court should simply move to *Chevron*'s step two. Some would agree with you. Mathew Stephenson and Adrian Vermeule, Chevron *Has Only One Step,* 95 Va. L. Rev. 597 (2009). Those who agree would say that the only question is whether the agency's interpretation is reasonable and an agency's interpretation that is inconsistent with the statute is unreasonable. But others disagree. Kenneth Bamberger and Peter Strauss, Chevron*'s Two Steps,* 95 Va. L. Rev. 611 (2009) (there is independent value in both of *Chevron*'s steps).

This issue has not been resolved. A judge's approach to step one will vary as a function of that judge's theory of statutory interpretation. Judges who believe the statutory words have to speak for themselves and those who, by contrast, think legislative history and statutory purpose have to be factored in, will have different views on the clarity of any particular statute. *See, e.g., Cuomo v. Clearing House,* 557 U.S. 519 (2009) (in which five Justices found the statute clear enough to reject an agency's interpretation and four justices found the statute ambiguous and would have deferred to the agency).

After *Chevron* was decided, there was some debate about the appropriate analysis for step one. Some, like Justice Scalia, argued that step one was a search for textual ambiguity, while others countered that it was a search for congressional intent involving all of the traditional tools of statutory interpretation. *See MCI Telecommuns. Corp. v. AT&T,* 518 U.S. 218 (1994) (applying a textual first-step analysis to an agency's interpretation); *see generally,* Linda D. Jellum, Chevron*'s Demise: A Survey of* Chevron *from Infancy to Senescence,* 59 ADMIN. L. REV. 725, 761 (2007) (exploring the Supreme Court's approach to step one).

*Chevron*'s Footnote 9 seems to answer this question; step one is a search involving all the traditional tools of statutory interpretation, not a search solely based on text. Professors William Eskridge and Lauren Baer analyzed the Court's practice in this area and concluded, "it is all but settled that relevant legislative history is admissible in the *Chevron* inquiry." William N. Eskridge Jr. and Lauren E. Baer, *The Continuum of Deference: Supreme Court Treatment of Agency Statutory Interpretations from* Chevron *to* Hamdan, 96 GEO L.J. 1083, 1135 (2008).

While step one is not deferential to an agency at all, the agency's interpretation will still be upheld as valid at this step if the interpretation is consistent with congressional intent. Hence, agencies should consider arguing that the statute is clear at step one and means what they have said it means. There is, however, one drawback to an agency "winning" at step one: unlike an interpretation that is upheld at step two, an agency cannot later change an interpretation that is upheld at step one because the court has found that Congress has directly spoken to the precise issue and, thus, the agency's interpretation must stay consistent with that intent. *National Cable & Telecommuns. Ass'n v. Brand X Internet Servs.,* 545 U.S. 967, 982 (2005) (holding that a court's "prior judicial [interpretation] of a statute trumps an agency [interpretation] otherwise entitled to *Chevron* deference only if the prior court decision holds that its [interpretation] follows from the unambiguous terms of the statute and thus leaves no room for agency discretion."). We will return to *Brand X* in a moment.

### c. Step Two: Is the Agency's Interpretation Reasonable?

Assuming Congress's intent is not clear at step one, then, under step two, a court must accept any "permissible," or "reasonable," agency interpretation, even if the court believes a different policy choice would be better. *Id.* at 843. While Justice Stevens used the word *permissible* at step two, courts today typically use the word *reasonable* instead.

At step two, courts defer to agency interpretations that are reasonable, meaning they are within a range of possible statutory meanings. Deferring at step two is called *Chevron* deference, although sometimes courts describe the entire *Chevron* two-step analysis as *Chevron* deference. Do not make this rookie mistake.

Step two is supposed to be very differential to agencies, although it is becoming less so. *See* Orin S. Kerr, *Shedding Light on* Chevron: *An Empirical Study of the* Chevron *Doctrine in the United States Courts of Appeals*, 15 YALE J. REG. 1, 31 (1998) (finding that agencies win 42 percent of the time at step one and 89 percent of the time at step two). Note also that because there is generally more than one reasonable interpretation, agencies may change their interpretation at a later time if they wish (such as when a new president comes into office), which they can do so long as the new interpretation is reasonable.

Professors John Manning and Mathew Stevenson described *Chevron*'s second step with a visual similar to the one below. Note that an agency's interpretation will be reasonable so long as it stays within the range of reasonableness, even if the interpretation does not match the court's preferred interpretation. For example, if the language being interpreted is "black" and the agency interprets black to include dark grey, then that interpretation would likely be reasonable. But if the agency interprets "black" to include white or green, then that interpretation would likely be unreasonable. See Figure 6.3.

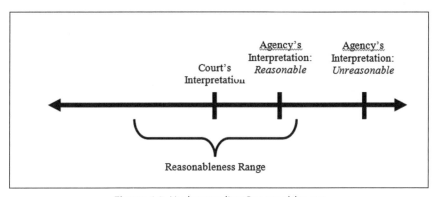

**Figure 6.3** Understanding Reasonableness

While some law professors and even court opinions have suggested that *Chevron*'s second step is simply arbitrary and capricious review, others disagree. *See, e.g., Michigan v. EPA*, 135 S. Ct. 2699, 2707 (2015) (using a one-step analysis that jumbled together *Chevron* and arbitrary and capricious review); Mark Seidenfeld, *A Syncopated* Chevron: *Emphasizing Reasoned Decision-Making in Reviewing Agency Interpretations of Statutes*, 73 TEX. L. REV. 83, 129– 30 (1994); Ronald M. Levin, *The Anatomy of* Chevron: *Step Two Reconsidered*, 72 CHI.-KENT L. REV. 1253, 1254–55 (1997). This argument has the advantage of making the two steps less redundant. Others agree, suggesting that this approach to step two ensures that all the standards of review in APA § 706(2) are fully met; in other words, the agency's interpretation meets that section's tests for legal, procedural, factual, and reasoning sufficiency. Kenneth Bamberger and Peter L. Strauss, *Chevron's Two Steps*, 95 VA. L. REV. 611, 621 (2009).

We will see below that arbitrary and capricious review is the standard that courts apply to review agency findings of fact and policy in informal rulemakings and adjudications. While arbitrary and capricious review and reasonableness review are similar, what the court is reviewing differs. For arbitrary and capricious review, a court reviews the record to determine whether there is a "rational connection between the facts found and the choice made." *Motor Vehicles Manufs. Ass'n v. State Farm*, 463 U.S. 29, 43 (1983); *see also Citizens to Preserve Overton Park v. Volpe*, 401 U.S. 402, 416 (1971) (describing such review as whether the agency's findings were based on a consideration of irrelevant factors or whether the agency made a clear error of judgment). For *Chevron* step two, a court compares the interpretation in the regulation or order to the statutory language, the legislative history, and the statutory purpose.

Finally, by way of warning, you will find the courts' application of *Chevron* inconsistent. Courts sometimes use a "strong" version, deferring frequently to most agency legal interpretations. Courts sometimes use a "weak" version, deferring less often and less deeply. Sometimes the doctrine is applied mechanically (Justice Scalia?) and sometimes the application varies in a case-by-case way (Justice Breyer?). In addition, sometimes, courts simply ignore *Chevron* entirely. Ann Graham, *Searching For* Chevron *in Muddy Waters— The Roberts Court and Judicial Review of Agency Regulations*, 60 ADMIN. L. REV. 229 (2008) (discussing eleven cases in which *Chevron* should have applied but was not mentioned). And, as indicated, there is considerable debate about application of each of the articulated steps. But never forget in all this variation that when a court makes an allocation decision the ultimate question is always this: which allocation of the senior/junior partner roles makes the most sense from the standpoint of legislative intent, expertise, and political accountability.

## 4. *Chevron* Step Zero

When *Chevron* was decided, it appeared to streamline deference analysis into two straightforward steps: first, a court looked to see if Congress had spoken on the specific issue before the court; if not, the court adopted the agency's interpretation so long as it was reasonable. But not long after *Chevron* was decided, the Court began to move away from a *Chevron*-only world. *Chevron* addressed the degree of deference to be given to a legislative rule, specifically one promulgated via notice and comment rulemaking procedures.

After *Chevron* was decided, the Court initially applied this two-step framework to all agency interpretations. In subsequent decisions, however, the Court resurrected *Skidmore*'s "power-to-persuade" test. *Skidmore* deference is thought to be less deferential than *Chevron*. Aaron-Andrew P. Bruhl, *Hierarchically Variable Deference to Agency Interpretations*, 89 NOTRE DAME L. REV. 728, 729 (2013) (describing *Skidmore* deference as only deferring "a bit"). As a result of later cases, *Chevron* no longer applies in every case involving an agency interpretation. *See, e.g., Christensen v. Harris County*, 529 U.S. 576 (2000); *United States v. Mead Corp.*, 533 U.S. 218 (2001). Hence, the question we address next is: when does *Chevron* apply?

Before a court can apply *Chevron*, the court must make sure that the interpretation is one deserving of *Chevron*. This step has become colloquially known as "*Chevron* Step Zero," and it is exceedingly complex. Cass R. Sunstein, Chevron *Step Zero*, 92 VA. L. REV. 187, 207–09 (2006) (naming this "new" step). But if you break the analysis into its subquestions, the analysis is at least approachable. Here are the sub-questions: (1) *What* did the agency interpret? (2) *Which* agency did the interpreting? (3) *How* did the agency do its interpreting? And (4) *Can* this agency interpret the statute? Below, each question is explored in more detail.

### a. What Did the Agency Interpret?

*Chevron* analysis is applicable only when an agency interprets a specific type of legal text: a statute. *Chevron* does not apply when agencies interpret the federal Constitution, court opinions, and legal instruments such as contracts. Similarly, *Chevron* does not apply when agencies interpret other agencies' regulations. Indeed, in these situations, courts do not defer at all.

Also, when an agency interprets its own regulation, a different deference standard applies: *Auer* deference. While judicial deference to agency interpretations of statutes has varied widely through time, judicial deference to an agency's interpretation of its own regulations has remained relatively constant. Traditionally, courts defer almost completely to an agency's interpretation of its own regulation. This high level of deference should come as no surprise; after all, it was the agency that drafted the regulation in the first place. And such interpretations owe much to the agency's expertise and experience. *Martin v. OSHRC*, 499 U.S. 144, 151 (1991) (explaining that the agency's continuing enforcement responsibilities give it special, practical insight into the interpretive problem).

Thus, in 1945, the Supreme Court held that an agency's interpretation of its own regulation has "controlling weight unless it is plainly erroneous or inconsistent with the regulation." *Bowles v. Seminole Rock & Sand Co.,* 325 U.S. 410, 414 (1945). The Supreme Court reasoned that when Congress delegates authority to promulgate regulations, it also delegates authority to interpret those regulations; such power is a necessary corollary to the former. This substantial level of deference is generally known as either *Seminole Rock* or *Auer* deference. The latter term refers to the Supreme Court case of *Auer v. Robbins,* 519 U.S. 452 (1997), which came after *Chevron* and confirmed that *Seminole Rock* deference had survived *Chevron. Id.* at 461–6.

*Auer* deference has recently been criticized on separation-of-powers grounds. For a true separation of powers, we should prevent the writer of a law from being the person who determines that law's final meaning. Hence, Congress cannot determine the final meaning of a statute; that task has been given to the courts. Granting such a high level of deference to an agency's interpretation of its own regulations allows agencies to function both as law writers and law expositors. This concern is not frivolous. Some commentators have worried that agencies could write very vague legislative rules, masking their true policy objectives, then announce those objectives in interpretations of the rule that would be effectively beyond judicial review. John Manning, *Constitutional Structure and Judicial Deference to Agency Interpretation of Agency Rules,* 96 Colum. L. Rev. 612 (1996). Beyond separation of powers considerations, undue deference to agency interpretation of their own regulations also has the practical effect of limiting public participation in new policy development because agencies need not use notice and comment procedures when issuing interpretative rules. APA § 553(b)(3)(A). Former Justice Scalia, and Justices Thomas and Alito seem to have adopted these concerns. *See, e.g., Perez v. Mortgage Bankers Ass'n,* 135 S. Ct. 1199, 1212 (2015) (Scalia, J. concurring) (stating that *Auer* deference should be jettisoned altogether as inconsistent with separation of powers).

There is at least one limitation on when an agency will receive this high level of deference. Assume an agency simply parrots statutory language in a regulation and then claims that it is interpreting the regulation rather than the statute. Here, the agency will not receive *Auer* deference because the agency is interpreting language from Congress, not from itself. *Gonzales v. Oregon,* 546 U.S. 243, 257 (2006) (refusing to defer to the Attorney General's interpretive rule that physician-assisted suicide was not a legitimate medical purpose for prescribing medication when the regulation merely paraphrased the statute).

In summary, *Chevron* applies only when an agency (1) *interprets a statute.*

### b. Which Agency Interpreted the Statute?

But it is not enough that an agency interprets the correct type of legal text, a statute. *Chevron* applies only when the agency that interprets the statute "administers" that statute. Agencies often interpret and apply statutes, including statutes that the agency does not administer. While the Court has never clearly articulated what it means to "administer" a statute, lower court cases that have addressed this issue suggest that agencies administer a statute when they have a special and unique responsibility for that statute. *See, e.g., Wagner Seed Co. v. Bush*, 946 F.2d 918, 925–26 (D.C. Cir. 1991) (Williams, J., dissenting) (arguing that the Environmental Protection Agency did not administer the reimbursement provisions of the Superfund Amendments and Reauthorization Act of 1986). Moreover, when more than one agency administers a statute, *Chevron* is generally inappropriate. *See Lawson v. FMR LLC*, 134 S. Ct. 1158, 1187 (2014) (Sotomayor, J., dissenting) (stating that "if any agency has the authority to resolve ambiguities in § 1514A with the force of law, it is the SEC, not the Department of Labor."); *Rapaport v. U.S. Dep't of the Treasury*, 59 F.3d 212, 216–17 (D.C. Cir. 1995) (declining to apply *Chevron* where the agency shared responsibility for the administration of the statute with another agency); *Illinois Nat'l Guard v. Fed. Labor Relations Auth.*, 854 F.2d 1396, 1400 (D.C. Cir. 1988) (declining to apply *Chevron* deference); *cf. CF Indus., Inc. v. FERC*, 925 F.2d 476, 478 n.1 (D.C. Cir. 1991) (stating in a footnote that there "might well be a compelling case to afford deference if it were necessary for decision [where] both agencies agree as to which of them has exclusive jurisdiction").

So, for example, although multiple agencies interpret the Internal Revenue Code, it is generally only the Department of Treasury that is authorized to administer those statutes; thus, only Treasury should receive *Chevron* deference for interpretations of federal tax statutes. *See, e.g., Mayo Found. for Med. Educ. & Research v. United States*, 562 U.S. 44, 55 (2011) (applying *Chevron* deference to review the Department of Treasury's interpretation of a tax statute). Note, however, that some statutes in the tax code are not just tax statutes. *See, e.g.,* the Affordable Care Act Patient Protection and Affordable Care Act, Pub. L. No. 111-148, 124 Stat. 119.

Agencies also must interpret generally applicable statutes, such as the Administrative Procedure Act (5 U.S.C. ch. 5, subch. I § 500 *et seq.*), the Regulatory Flexibility Act (5 U.S.C. §§ 601-12), and the Freedom of Information Act. (5 U.S.C. § 552). For such generally applicable statutes, no agency's interpretation is entitled to *Chevron* deference. *See, e.g., Association of Am. Physicians & Surgeons, Inc. v. Clinton*, 997 F.2d 898, 913 (D.C. Cir. 1993) (interpreting the Federal Advisory Committee Act); *FLRA v. U.S. Dep't of Treasury*, 884 F.2d 1446, 1451 (D.C. Cir. 1989) (refusing to apply *Chevron* to the Federal Labor Relation Authority's (FLRA) interpretation of the Freedom of Information Act (FOIA) or the Privacy Act because "FLRA is not charged with a special duty to interpret [these statutes]"); *Reporters Comm. for Freedom of the Press v. U.S. Dep't of Justice*, 816 F.2d 730, 734 (D.C. Cir. 1987) (stating that no deference would be given to an agency's interpretation of the FOIA because "it applies to all government agencies, and thus no one executive branch entity is entrusted with its primary interpretation"), *rev'd on other grounds*, 489 U.S. 749 (1989).

In summary, *Chevron* applies only when an agency (1) interprets a statute (2) *that the agency administers.*

### c. How Did the Agency Interpret the Statute: Force of Law?

It is not enough that an agency interpret a statute that it administers. As you have learned, agencies act in a variety of ways. Some of these ways require more procedural formality and deliberation than others.

For example, an agency might interpret a statute as part of a notice and comment rulemaking process, like the EPA did in *Chevron*. Also, an agency might interpret a statute during a formal adjudication. Or an agency might interpret a statute when drafting an internal policy manual or when writing a letter to a regulated entity. *See, e.g., Christensen*, 529 U.S. at 580–81, 586–89 (interpreting a statute in response to a letter inquiry from the county); *see also Mead Corp.*, 533 U.S. at 221–27 (2001) (interpreting a tariff classification ruling).

With the latter processes (non-legislative rulemaking), Congress has not given the agency the authority to act with the force of law. With the former processes (adjudication and notice and comment rulemaking), Congress has given the agency the authority to act with the force of law, and the agency has used that authority to implement change. If Congress has given the agency the authority to take action of that significance, Congress must have intended that agency legal interpretations should be respected by the courts. *See* Thomas Merrill and Kathryn Watts, *Agency Rules with the Force of Law*, 116 HARV. L. REV. 467, 472 (2002) (stating that "'Force of law' is not, of course, self-defining, but [means] quality of an agency action that is not subject to further challenge and which subjects a person who disobeys it to some sanction"). Moreover, the former processes are considered more formal, or procedurally prescribed, while the latter processes are thought to be less formal, or less procedurally prescribed. *See, e.g.*, Lisa Schultz Bressman, *How* Mead *Has Muddled Judicial Review of Agency Action*, 58 VAND. L. REV. 1443, 1447 (2005) (questioning "whether *Chevron* deference applies to interpretations issued through informal procedures").

If one purpose of administrative law is to attempt to cure procedural shortfalls that limit neutral and fair decision making, this approach to *Chevron's* applicability makes sense. If an agency chooses to make a determination informally where the protections of neutral and fair decision making are limited, then more intensive judicial review would seem appropriate. If, instead, the agency has followed a more formal procedure, one that facilitates neutral and fair decision making (such as notice and comment rulemaking or formal adjudication), then there is less need for intensive judicial review, and *Chevron* analysis seems appropriate.

In *Chevron*, the Supreme Court did not indicate, expressly or implicitly, whether the deliberateness of the agency's procedures affected the applicability of the two-step analysis. Linda D. Jellum, Chevron's *Demise: A Survey of* Chevron *from Infancy to Senescence*, 59 ADMIN. L. REV. 725, 774 (2007). Before the Court decided *Chevron*, however, the Court factored the deliberative nature of the agency's interpretive process into the analysis. Under *Skidmore* deference, interpretations that are made through a more deliberative process, such as notice and comment rulemaking, are considered more persuasive than interpretations made through a less deliberative process, such as non-legislative rulemaking.

Immediately after the Court decided *Chevron*, the Court did not distinguish between deliberative agency decision making and non-deliberative agency decision-making. Rather, the Court applied its two-step analysis to all types of agency interpretations, regardless of the deliberative nature of the procedure involved. So, for example, in *Reno v. Koray*, 515 U.S. 50, 61 (1995), the Court held that *Chevron* should apply to an interpretation contained in an agency's internal guideline, a non-legislative rule. And in *NationsBank of North Carolina v. Variable Annuity Life Insurance Co.*, 513 U.S. 251, 256–57, 263 (1995), the Court applied *Chevron* to an agency's decision to grant an entity's application to act as an agent and sell annuities, an informal adjudication. *See also National R.R. Passenger Corp. v. Boston & Me. Corp.*, 503 U.S. 407, 417 (1992) (applying *Chevron's* framework to an agency's interpretation made informally); *Federal Deposit Ins. Corp. v. Philadelphia Gear Corp.*, 476 U.S. 426, 439 (1986) (suggesting that *Chevron* should apply to an agency's long-standing "practice and belief"). But, with time, the formality of the procedure has gained importance.

Beginning in 2000, the Supreme Court decided a trilogy of cases that limited *Chevron's* application based on the procedures the agency used to make the interpretation. In *Christensen*, 529 U.S. at 576, *Mead Corp.*, 533 U.S. at 218, and *Barnhart v. Walton*, 535 U.S. 212 (2002), the Court substantially checked *Chevron*'s applicability based, in part, upon the formality of the procedure the agency had used to reach the interpretation being challenged. Let's start with *Christensen*.

With *Christensen*, the Supreme Court began its retreat from a *Chevron*-only deference world. At issue in *Christensen* was whether the United States Department of Labor's Wage and Hour Division (the Division) should receive *Chevron* deference for an interpretation the agency expressed in an opinion letter. 529 U.S. at 587. The defendant in the case, Harris County, had been concerned about the fiscal consequences of having to pay its employees for accrued but unused compensatory time. *Id.* at 578. For this reason, the County wrote to the Division and asked whether the County could require its employees to take, rather than continue to accrue, their unused compensatory time. *Id.* at 580–81. Responding by letter, the Division told the County that, absent an employment agreement to the contrary, the Fair Labor Standards Act of 1938 (FLSA) prohibited an employer from requiring employees to use accrued compensatory time. *Id.* at 581. The County ignored the letter and forbade its employees from accumulating more compensatory time than it deemed reasonable. *Id.* The employees sued, arguing that the County's policy violated FLSA. *Id.*

The issue for the Supreme Court was whether the agency's interpretation of FLSA, which was contained in an informal opinion letter, was entitled to *Chevron* deference. *Id.* at 586–87. For the first time since *Chevron* had been decided, the Court directly addressed whether the agency process mattered in the deference analysis; in other words, did a different deference standard apply when an agency acted with less deliberation and process?

The majority found the level of process to be determinative. The majority reasoned that the agency's opinion letter was not entitled to *Chevron* deference because it lacked the "force of law." *Id.* at 587. Agency interpretations have the "force of law" when "Congress has delegated legislative power to the agency and . . . the agency . . . exercise[d] that power in promulgating the rule." *American Mining Cong. v. Mine Safety & Health Admin.*, 995 F.2d 1106, 1109 (D.C. Cir. 1993) (defining "force of law"). In other words:

> An interpretation will have the force of law when the agency has exercised delegated power, as to both subject matter and format, reflecting congressional intent that such an interpretation is to bind. "Force of law" . . . merely connotes the binding effect given the kinds of agency interpretations that Congress through its delegations *intends*

to bind the courts. And that binding effect (force of law) means simply that the courts may not subject the interpretations to independent judicial review, but rather must accept them subject only to limited review for reasonableness and consistency with the statute. Thus, an interpretation carrying the force of law gets only limited review because by definition it is covered by delegation that contemplates only limited review.

Robert A. Anthony, *Which Agency Interpretations Should Bind Citizens and the Courts?*, 7 YALE J. ON REG. 1, 39 (1990) (footnotes omitted).

According to *Christensen*, procedurally prescribed actions, such as formal adjudication and notice and comment rulemaking, have the "force of law," while less procedurally prescribed actions, such as "opinion letters . . . policy statements, agency manuals, and enforcement guidelines . . . lack the force of law." *Christensen*, 529 U.S. at 587. The Court explained that "interpretations contained in [informal] formats such as opinion letters are 'entitled to respect' under our decision in *Skidmore* . . . , but only to the extent that those interpretations have the 'power to persuade.'" *Id.* at 587 (citation omitted). Thus *Christensen* seemingly divided agency interpretations into two well-defined categories: those subject to *Chevron* analysis—the "force of law" category—and those subject to *Skidmore* analysis—the no-"force of law" category.

*Christensen* appeared to present a simple, albeit, formalistic test: courts should apply *Chevron* deference to an agency's interpretation of a statute when an agency used relatively formal procedures (including formal adjudication, formal rulemaking, and notice and comment rulemaking), and courts should apply *Skidmore* deference when an agency used non-legislative procedures (including issuing interpretive rules, policy statements, ruling letters). This test would have been relatively simple for judges to apply: simply look to the agency action and apply the appropriate analysis, *Chevron* or *Skidmore*.

But alas, nothing remains so simple, and the Court refined *Christensen*'s force-of-law test a year later in *Mead Corp.*, 533 U.S. at 218. The issue in *Mead* was whether the U.S. Customs Service's ("Customs") informal ruling letters (which do not go through notice and comment or other formal procedures) were entitled to *Chevron* or *Skidmore* deference. *Id.* at 221. The plaintiff imported day planners. Although Customs had classified the planners as duty-free "day planners" for several years, it changed its interpretation and issued a ruling letter classifying them as "bound diaries." *Id.* at 225. Ruling letters were issued without any preliminary procedure, were not published, and were non-binding. The letters simply described the goods being imported and identified the amount of tariff to be paid. *Id.* at 223. The decision had financial consequences to both parties because bound diaries were subject to tariff, while day planners were not.

The majority held that *Skidmore* deference was appropriate, which should not be surprising or confusing given the absence of any formalized procedures. *Id.* at 227. In reaching its holding, the majority reaffirmed *Christensen* by explaining that *Chevron* applies when an agency acts with force-of-law, which occurs "when it appears that Congress delegated authority to the agency generally to make rules carrying the force of law and that the agency interpretation claiming deference was promulgated in the exercise of that authority." *Id.* at 226–27. Had *Mead* stopped at this point, it would not even warrant a footnote. Unfortunately, the Court did not stop at this point. The Court added a wrinkle to *Christensen*'s force of law test by saying that "[d]elegation of such authority may be shown in a variety of ways, as by an agency's power to engage in adjudication or notice-and-comment rulemaking, *or by some other indication of a comparable congressional intent.*" *Id.* at 227 (emphasis added). The Court added, "[A]s significant as notice-and-comment is in pointing to *Chevron* authority, the want of that procedure here does not decide the case, for we have sometimes found reasons for *Chevron* deference even when no such administrative formality was required and none was afforded." *Id.* at 231 (citing *NationsBank of N.C.,* 513 U.S. at 256–57, 263). The Court did not explain what these reasons were. But the Court did find that there were no such reasons in *Mead* because: (1) the face of the statute gave no indication that Congress intended to delegate authority to Customs to issue classification rulings with the force of law, (2) Customs regarded the classification decisions as conclusive only between itself and the importer to whom it was issued, and (3) forty-six different Customs offices issued 10,000 to 15,000 classifications each year. *Id.* at 233. There were simply too many classification rulings each year for Customs to be able to carefully consider the issue. Hence, the Court held that *Skidmore*, not *Chevron*, was appropriate.

Prior to *Mead*, the test was bright-lined: *Chevron* applied when the agency acted with more procedure, and *Skidmore* applied when the agency acted with less procedure. Now, the bright-line was blurring. The Court in *Mead* stated, without elaborating, that some agency actions might qualify for *Chevron* deference even though the agency used less formal procedures. Exactly what types of "other indications" would be sufficient to trigger *Chevron* was not readily apparent from this case alone. However, in the following year, the Court explained when *Chevron* deference should apply to agency interpretations arrived at without force of law procedures.

In *Barnhart*, 535 U.S. at 212, the Court explained what types of "other indications" might be sufficient to warrant *Chevron* deference. *Id*. In that case, the Social Security Administration (SSA) determined that the plaintiff, who was unable to work for 11 months, was not eligible for disability benefits. *Id*. at 215. The SSA enacted a regulation, using notice and comment procedures (apparently in response to the pending litigation), which stated that a claimant was not disabled if that claimant could engage in "substantial gainful activity." In doing so, the SSA codified an existing, nonlegislative rule. In addition to codifying the non-legislative rule, the SSA subsequently interpreted this new regulation to mean that the claimant was not disabled if "within 12 months after the onset of an impairment . . . the impairment no longer prevent[ed] substantial gainful activity." *Id*. at 217 (quoting 65 Fed. Reg. 42772 (2000)). All parties agreed that the second regulation, as an interpretation of the new regulation, was entitled to *Auer* deference. However, the parties disagreed about whether the new regulation governed because it was enacted in response to the litigation. If so, *Chevron* deference would be the appropriate deference standard under *Mead* and *Christensen*.

Writing for the majority, Justice Breyer held that the regulation controlled and thus *Chevron* deference was appropriate. *Id*. at 217. Given the level of procedure that was used (notice and comment rulemaking), that result should not be surprising. But once again, Justice Breyer did not stop when he should have; instead, he rejected the "force of law" formality dichotomy by saying that "the fact that the [SSA] previously reached its interpretation through means less formal than 'notice-and-comment' rulemaking does not automatically deprive that interpretation of the judicial deference otherwise its due." *Id*. at 221. *Mead* had made clear that there was no bright-line deference dichotomy based on how the agency made its interpretation. *Id*. Thus, *Barnhart* reaffirmed *Mead*, which had implied that some interpretations contained in nonlegislative rules might receive *Chevron* deference.

Whether the agency acted with force of law or whether there is some other indication that Congress intended the agency to have interpretive authority is colloquially known as either *Chevron* Step Zero or the *Mead* Mess. Cass R. Sunstein, Chevron *Step Zero*, 92 Va. L. Rev. 187, 211 (2006); Lisa Bressman, *How* Mead *Has Muddled Judicial Review of Agency Action*, 58 Vand. L. Rev. 1443 (2005) (coining the phrase "*Mead* Mess"). There is no doubt that determining which deference standard, if any, applies has become a complicated question. Justice Scalia was likely correct when he criticized the Court's decisions in *Mead* "as one of the most significant opinions ever rendered by the Court dealing with the judicial review of administrative action . . . and almost uniformly bad." *Mead*, 533 U.S. at

261 (Scalia, J., dissenting). The test is difficult to apply, leading to increased litigation.

Justice Breyer believes that *Skidmore* and *Chevron* simply articulated different rationales for judicial deference to agency interpretations. *Skidmore* deference is based on agency expertise, while *Chevron* deference is based on congressional delegation. In *Barnhart*, he explained that *Chevron* applies whenever Congress intended the courts to defer to an agency's interpretation. To determine whether Congress intended for courts to defer, a court must consider the following five factors: (1) the interstitial nature of the legal question, (2) the relevance of the agency's expertise, (3) the importance of the question to administration of the statute, (4) the complexity of the statutory scheme, and (5) the careful consideration the agency had given the question over a long period. *Barnhart*, 535 U.S. at 222. The test seems to meld factors from both *Skidmore* (agency expertise, careful consideration) and *Chevron* (implied delegation as shown by interstitial nature of the legal question and the importance of the question to administration of the statute), while adding an entirely new consideration: the complexity of the statutory scheme.

Professor Sunstein has put it bluntly: "force of law is a sufficient condition for *Chevron* deference, whether or not it is a necessary condition." Cass Sunstein, Chevron's *Step Zero*, 92 Va. L. Rev. 187, 218 (2006). Perhaps at this point, the best that can be said is that the appropriate level of deference rests on congressional intent. If Congress intends that an agency receive judicial deference for interpretations, then courts should apply *Chevron* regardless of how the agency reached the interpretation. In these situations, *Chevron* is appropriate because Congress intended for the agencies, not the courts, to develop this area of law. In contrast, if Congress does not so intend, then the agency is deserving of only *Skidmore* deference at best. In this situation, Congress intended the courts to be the final arbiters of these legal issues, but an agency's expertise can inform a court's decision.

Despite this five-factor test, since *Barnhart* was decided, the Supreme Court has not applied *Chevron* deference to an agency interpretation that was made without force-of-law procedures. However, some lower courts have done so. *Compare Schuetz v. Banc One Mortg. Corp.*, 292 F.3d 1004, 1011–13 (9th Cir. 2002) (holding that *Chevron* applied to a HUD Statement of Policy), and *Kruse v. Wells Fargo Home Mortg., Inc.*, 383 F.3d 49, 61 (2d Cir. 2004) (same), *with Krzalic v. Republic Title Co.*, 314 F.3d 875, 879 (7th Cir. 2002) (holding that *Chevron* did not apply to a HUD Statement of Policy).

In summary, *Chevron* applies only when an agency (1) interprets a statute (2) that the agency administers (3) *while using force of law procedures.*

### d. Can the Agency Interpret the Statute?

It is not enough that an agency interpret a statute that the agency administers while using force-of-law procedures. In the midst of deciding the *Christensen/Mead/Barnhart* trilogy, the Supreme Court issued another trilogy of cases in this area that only add to the complexity.

In *Chevron*, the Court rationalized deference to an agency's interpretation by suggesting that when Congress enacts gaps and creates ambiguities, Congress *implicitly* intends to delegate interpretive authority to the agency. But two cases, *FDA v. Brown & Williamson Tobacco Corp.*, 529 U.S. 120 (2000), and *King v. Burwell*, 135 S. Ct. 2480 (2015), the Court rejected, or at least narrowed, this rationale for some agency interpretations. In each of these cases, the Court reasoned that in some instances, despite ambiguity, Congress does not intend to delegate rulemaking authority to the agency at all. As the Court explained:

> Deference under *Chevron* to an agency's construction of a statute that it administers is premised on the theory that a statute's ambiguity constitutes an implicit delegation from Congress to the agency to fill in the statutory gaps. In extraordinary cases, however, there may be reason to hesitate before concluding that Congress has intended such an implicit delegation.

*Brown & Williamson*, 529 U.S. at 159 (internal citations omitted).

First, in *Brown & Williamson*, the majority rejected the Food and Drug Administration's (FDA) decision to regulate tobacco. *Brown & Williamson* is interesting historically. The FDA knew for years that tobacco was deadly. The FDA was authorized to regulate "drugs" and "devices," but chose not to regulate tobacco because it feared that Congress would reject its action. The tobacco companies had, and still have, an extremely powerful lobby in Washington. Moreover, Presidents Reagan and Bush would not have supported the FDA's attempt to regulate tobacco. In 1993, Bill Clinton assumed the office of president. President Clinton was anti-tobacco. He appointed Dr. David Kessler to head the FDA and indicated a willingness to support the FDA's attempt to regulate tobacco. Armed with Clinton's support, the FDA interpreted cigarettes and tobacco products to be "drugs." In response, the tobacco companies sued.

Under the relevant statute, the FDA was authorized to regulate "drugs," "devices," and "combination products." *Id.* at 126 (citing §§ 21 U.S.C. § 321(g)–(h) (1994 and Supp. III)). The statute defined these terms as "articles ... intended to affect the structure or any function of the body." *Id.* (quoting 21 U.S.C. § 321 (g)(1)(C)). The FDA interpreted this language as allowing it to regulate tobacco and cigarettes.

Despite the fact that the language of the statute alone was broad enough to support the agency's interpretation, the majority concluded, after applying *Chevron's* first step, "that Congress ha[d] directly spoken to the issue here and precluded the FDA's jurisdiction to regulate tobacco products." The majority supported its holding by noting that Congress had: (1) created a distinct regulatory scheme for tobacco products in subsequent legislation, (2) squarely rejected proposals to give the FDA jurisdiction over tobacco, and (3) acted repeatedly to preclude other agencies from exercising authority in this area. The majority suggested that this was "hardly an ordinary case," because of the importance of the tobacco industry to the American economy and Congress's oversight of this area. *Id.* at 159. Hence, while Congress may not have spoken to the precise issue when enacting the relevant statute, Congress had subsequently spoken broadly enough on related questions to prevent the agency from acting at all. *Id.* at 159–60. The Court resolved *Brown & Williamson* at *Chevron* step one and never reached step two. *See also, Gonzales,* 546 U.S. at 267 (applying *Skidmore* analysis rather than *Chevron* because "[t]he idea that Congress gave the Attorney General such broad and unusual authority through an implicit delegation in the [Controlled Substances Act] registration provision is not sustainable."); *Hamdan v. Rumsfeld,* 548 U.S. 557, 567 (2006) (refusing to apply *Chevron* or *Skidmore* analysis to an interpretation contained in an executive order); *Hamdi v. Rumsfeld,* 542 U.S. 507 (2004) (refusing to apply either *Chevron* or *Skidmore* analysis to evaluate the correctness of another executive order).

The Supreme Court would return to this "too important for the national economy" limitation on agency delegation fifteen years later in *King,* 135 S. Ct. at 2489. At issue in this case was whether language in the Affordable Care Act, "exchange established by the State" meant "exchange established by the State" only or whether it also included exchanges established by the Federal Government. *Id.* at 2487. The Department of the Treasury had issued a notice and comment regulation adopting the latter interpretation. *Id.* at 2487–88. Because the Treasury used force-of-law procedures, under *Christensen/Mead/ Barnhart, Chevron* should apply.

Had the Court applied *Chevron,* the majority likely would have found that the text pointed in one direction, while the statutory purpose pointed in another. Hence: Congress did not speak directly to the precise issue before the Court. Assuming the Court then reached step two, the Court likely would have found that Treasury's interpretation was reasonable given the conflict between the text and the statutory purpose.

But the Court refused to apply *Chevron.* The majority reasoned that the issue was simply too important for the agency to resolve. *Id.* at 2488–89. With this reasoning, the majority echoed *Brown & Williamson*'s "too important to the national economy" rationale. *Id.* at 2489. As you might imagine with such clear text, former Justice Scalia dissented loudly, calling the majority's opinion "absurd" and noting that "the Court's 21 pages of explanation make it no less so." *Id.* at 2496 (Scalia, J., dissenting).

In these cases—*Brown & Williamson* and *King*—the Supreme Court significantly limited the implied-delegation rationale. The Court held that Congress did not implicitly delegate interpretive power to the agency despite statutory ambiguity. The holdings in these cases are at odds with *Chevron*'s implicit-delegation rationale, which states that "[d]eference under *Chevron* to an agency's construction of a statute that it administers is premised on the theory that a statute's ambiguity constitutes an implicit delegation from Congress to the agency to fill in the statutory gaps." *Brown & Williamson*, 529 U.S. at 159. Notably, in none of the applicable statutes did Congress expressly say that it was not delegating to the agency. Rather, the Court inferred Congress's intent not to delegate based on other factors, including the existence of other legislation (*Brown & Williamson*) and the importance of the issue to the national economy (*Brown & Williamson* and *King*). Instead, the Court reviewed the agency's interpretation de novo.

In summary, *Chevron* applies only when an agency: (1) interprets a statute (2) that the agency administers (3) while using force-of-law procedures, (4) *so long as Congress intended to delegate interpretive power to the agency.* You have now mastered *Chevron* step zero.

### e. *Applying* Chevron*'s Step Zero*

At this point, you may well be wondering how to apply *Chevron*'s step zero. Let me suggest the following process: First, ask whether the agency is interpreting a statute and whether the agency has the sole or primary authority to administer that statute. If the agency is interpreting its own regulation, *Auer* deference is appropriate; if the agency is interpreting anything else, no deference is due.

Second, ask whether Congress intended to delegate the specific issue to the agency at all. If the issue is one of such major importance that Congress would never have intended to delegate authority, then the agency likely has no power to interpret the statute. Such a finding should be rare. This step is based on the holdings in *Brown & Williamson* and *King*. In such cases, de novo review is likely appropriate.

Third, if Congress intended to delegate interpretive authority to an agency, you should determine whether Congress intended courts to defer to that particular agency's interpretation. To do so, look first to the type of agency action at issue; in other words, look to see if the agency acted with force of law. If the agency interpreted the statute during notice and comment rulemaking, formal rulemaking, or formal adjudication, then *Chevron* analysis would be appropriate. This step is based on *Mead* and *Christensen*'s holdings.

Fourth, you should determine whether *Chevron* analysis is appropriate even though force of law procedures were not used. To do so, determine whether Congress intended *Chevron* to apply as shown by the *Barnhart* factors. Those factors include the following: (1) the interstitial nature of the legal question, (2) the relevance of the agency's expertise, (3) the importance of the question to administration of the statute, (4) the complexity of the statutory scheme, and (5) the careful consideration the agency has given the question over a long period. If these factors suggest that Congress did not intend for courts to defer, then *Chevron* analysis is inapplicable. If *Chevron* analysis is inapplicable, then you should apply *Skidmore*'s power-to-persuade test. This step is based on the holdings from *Mead* and *Barnhart*. But if the *Barnhart* factors suggest that Congress did intend for the courts to defer, you should apply *Chevron* analysis.

Fifth, apply the deference standard that you determined was appropriate. If you determined at step three or four that *Chevron* analysis should apply, then, using traditional tools of statutory interpretation, ask whether Congress has spoken to the precise issue before the court. This is *Chevron*'s first step. If Congress has so spoken, then your analysis is complete, for Congress has the authority to interpret its own statutes when it so chooses. But if Congress has not directly spoken to the precise issue, or if Congress has left a gap or impliedly delegated to the agency, then proceed to *Chevron*'s second step: Ask whether the agency's interpretation is reasonable in light of the underlying statute. Compare the interpretation with the language of the statute, the legislative history, and the purpose of the statute. If the agency's interpretation is unreasonable when compared to these sources, then no deference is due. If the agency's interpretation is reasonable, then full deference is due.

If, instead, you determined at step four that *Skidmore* analysis should apply, then apply *Skidmore*'s power-to-persuade factors to the agency's interpretation. An agency's interpretation is entitled to deference based on the following factors: (1) the consistency in the agency interpretation over time; (2) the thoroughness of the agency's consideration; and (3) the soundness of the agency's reasoning. Deference under this standard is earned, not automatic.

Understanding the difference between *Chevron* deference and *Skidmore* deference is not always so easy. However, Professor Gary Lawson has offered a way of thinking of the difference, which he defines as the difference between legal deference and epistemological deference. Gary Lawson,

*Mostly Unconstitutional: The Case Against Precedent Revisited*, 5 AVE MARIA L. REV. 1, 2–10 (2007). Legal deference is deference earned solely based on the identity of the interpreter and the method of interpretation. *Id.* at 9. For example, lower courts must defer to interpretations of higher courts within the same jurisdiction, but need not defer to interpretations from courts in other jurisdictions. The decision of whether to defer depends entirely on the identity of the interpreter. *Chevron* deference is a form of legal deference: agencies earn deference simply because they are agencies that interpreted statutes using a particular process.

In contrast, epistemological deference is deference earned because of the persuasiveness of the reasoning. *Id.* at 10. Courts in neighboring jurisdictions need not follow each other's opinions but can choose to do so because the reasoning is persuasive. The decision of whether to defer depends entirely on the persuasiveness of the reasoning; the identity of the interpreter is irrelevant. *Skidmore* deference is a form of epistemological deference: agencies earn deference based on the soundness of their reasoning, not because they are agencies interpreting statutes.

Not all academic administrative law experts would agree that this simplified, five-step process completely or even accurately captures *Chevron* Step Zero analysis. Rightly, they would note that the interaction of these cases is extremely complex and constantly changing. To illustrate, during listserv discussions, one scholar stated that the "force of law" phrase is one of the most confusing in administrative law. Another stated that *Mead* is not particularly coherent and raises tough issues regarding when *Chevron* should apply. These comments show that even the experts disagree on exactly how to understand and reconcile these cases. Unfortunately, *Chevron*'s Step Zero is a mess and may lead to *Chevron*'s demise.

## 5. Agency Interpretations that Conflict with Judicial Interpretations

In the last section, we addressed what level of deference, if any, a court should give to an agency interpretation when there are no preexisting judicial interpretations of the same statute. The next obvious question is: what if there is a prior judicial opinion? Should a court defer to an agency interpretation of a statute that varies from an existing judicial interpretation? Prior judicial interpretations exist when a court defers to an agency interpretation or interprets the meaning of a statutory provision when an agency has not yet interpreted it. The question is whether thereafter an agency is bound to follow this prior judicial interpretation or whether the agency is free to make its own interpretation. At issue is flexibility—the ability for an agency to adjust policy and statutory interpretations. On the one hand, flexibility is essential to the effective operation of administrative agencies as technology and economics advance and administrative priorities change with time and with a new administration. If agencies were unable to alter their interpretations over time, flexibility would be significantly hindered and agencies would be less effective at responding to changes. On the other hand, too much change can lead to unpredictability, uncertainty, and, potentially, unfairness. Similarly situated litigants expect the government to treat them similarly.

The Supreme Court addressed this issue in *National Cable & Telecommunications Ass'n. v. Brand X Internet Services*, 545 U.S. 967 (2005). In that case, the Court chose flexibility over certainty by holding that, if a prior court had determined that the statute was clear under *Chevron's* first step, then the agency would be bound by that judicial interpretation. *Id.* at 985. But if the court did not decide that the statute was clear under *Chevron's* first step, then the prior interpretation would not bind the agency. *Id.* In other words, a prior judicial interpretation does not eliminate a preexisting ambiguity. The prior interpretation merely reflects a determination that either there is no ambiguity or that there is ambiguity. If there is no ambiguity, then Congress has spoken and the agency, as well as the courts, must follow Congress's intent. But if there is ambiguity, then regardless of whether a court issues the first interpretation of an ambiguous statute or an agency does, the interpretation does not bind the agency.

This approach is intuitively appealing; however, judges have not always been so clear about whether an adopted interpretation rests on a finding that Congress was ambiguous at *Chevron's* first step, especially for cases that predate *Chevron*. Justice Scalia eloquently summarized this point in a 2012 case:

> In cases decided pre-*Brand X*, the Court had no inkling that it *must* utter the magic words "ambiguous" or "unambiguous" in order to (poof!) expand or abridge executive power, and (poof!) enable or disable administrative contradiction of the Supreme Court. Indeed, the Court was unaware of even the utility (much less the necessity) of making the ambiguous/nonambiguous determination in cases decided pre-*Chevron*, before that opinion made the so-called "Step 1" determination of ambiguity *vel non* a customary (though hardly mandatory) part of judicial-review analysis. For many of those earlier cases, therefore, it will be incredibly difficult to determine whether the decision purported to be giving meaning to an ambiguous, or rather an unambiguous, statute.

*United States v. Home Concrete & Supply*, 566 U.S. 478, 493–94 (2012) (Scalia, J., concurring in part).

In *Home Concrete*, the Court had to resolve the meaning of a tax statute. The statute allowed the IRS to assess a deficiency against a taxpayer within "3 years after the return was filed." *Id.* at 1839 (quoting 26 U.S.C. § 6501(a) (2000) (majority opinion). The statute further provided that the three-year period would be extended to six years when a taxpayer "omit[ed] from gross income an amount properly includible therein which is in excess of 25 percent of the amount of gross income stated in the return." *Id.* (quoting § 6501(e)(1) (A)). The question for the Court was "whether this latter provision applied (and extended the ordinary three-year limitations period) when the taxpayer overstated his basis in property that he had sold, thereby understating the gain that he received from its sale." Basis in property is generally the purchase price of an asset or its value. *Id.* In an earlier case, the Court had held that taxpayer statements overstating the basis in property did not fall within the scope of the statute. *Colony, Inc. v. Commissioner*, 357 U.S. 28, 32 (1958). Long after *Colony* was decided, the IRS enacted a regulation interpreting the relevant language in the statute to include basis misstatements. *Id.* at 1843.

When challenged in court, the IRS argued that it was entitled to *Chevron* deference for its interpretation pursuant to *Brand X* because the *Colony* Court had stated that the tax statute was "not unambiguous," meaning it was ambiguous. The majority disagreed. It observed that *Colony* had been decided long before *Chevron* and suggested that the *Colony* Court was not thinking in first step/second step terms. The *Home Concrete* Court noted that the *Colony* Court had said that the taxpayer had the better textual argument, had found that the legislative history supported the interpretation, concluded that the government's interpretation would create a patent incongruity in the tax law, and believed its interpretation to be in harmony with the 1954 Tax Code. *Id.* at 1843–44. For the majority, these findings resolved any ambiguity.

Not surprisingly, Justice Scalia vehemently disagreed. Because the *Colony* Court had stated that the statute was "not unambiguous," Scalia argued that the majority could only reject the agency's later interpretation under *Brand X* if the interpretation were unreasonable. *Id.* at 1847 (Scalia, J. dissenting). Calling for *Brand X*'s death, Scalia lamented, "*Colony* said unambiguously that the text was ambiguous, and that should be an end of the matter . . . . Rather than making our judicial-review jurisprudence curiouser and curiouser, the Court should abandon the opinion that produces these contortions, *Brand X*." *Id.* at 1848.

It looks like Justice Scalia got this one right. On July 31, 2015, Congress enacted H.R. 3236, Surface Transportation and Veterans Health Care Choice

Improvement Act of 2015. Section 2005 of the Act amended 26 U.S.C. § 6501(e)(1), which is the exception to the three-year statute of limitations at issue in *Colony* and *Home Concrete*. The amendment provides: "An understatement of gross income by reason of an overstatement of unrecovered cost or other basis is an omission from gross income." This amendment legislatively overruled both *Colony* and *Home Concrete & Supply*.

# C. Reviewing Agency Determinations of Fact and Policy

## 1. Defining Questions of Fact

Above, we defined a question of law as one in which the specific facts in a case are irrelevant. Now let's define a question of fact. A question of fact is one in which the resolution of the question does not require an application of or knowledge of the law. Thus, a statement of fact "is an assertion that a phenomenon has happened or is or will be happening independent of or anterior to any assertion as to its legal effect." LOUIS L. JAFFE, JUDICIAL CONTROL OF ADMINISTRATIVE ACTION 548 (1965). In short, the facts are mostly irrelevant when resolving pure questions of law, and the law is mostly irrelevant when resolving pure questions of fact.

Let's return to our non-agency example: the car accident. Assume that, during the investigation, the accident investigator noted that the skid marks on the pavement were 46 feet long. This assertion would be a statement of fact. The law is irrelevant. Ordinary facts answer questions about who did what, to whom, and with what effect.

For judicial review of questions of fact that do not involve agencies decisions, appellate courts use various standards to assess the sufficiency of a trial court or jury's findings, depending on the context. These standards include the following formulations: clear and convincing evidence, a preponderance of the evidence, substantial evidence, a scintilla of evidence, and so forth. Each of these standards involves a different level of intensity. You learned about these standards in criminal and civil procedure; we will not study them here.

Let's turn back to our world of agencies. Agencies must make factual determinations regularly. For example, the agency may have to determine whether one witness or another is truthful. The agency may have to determine whether someone was fired in the way he or she claimed. What is the scope of review for a court assessing the legality of an agency's finding of ordinary fact?

For judicial review of questions of fact that agencies resolve, appellate courts use two standards to assess the agency's findings. Those standards also depend on the context. First, and as noted above, you should begin with the enabling statute to see if Congress has provided a specific standard of review for such findings. Assuming that Congress has not done so, then section 706 of the APA applies. In section 706, there are only two standards of review for agency factual findings: the substantial evidence standard and the arbitrary and capricious standard.

Section 706(2)(E) provides that for *formal* proceedings (adjudications or rulemakings required to be conducted on the record under sections 556 and 557 of the APA), a reviewing court must apply the "substantial evidence" standard to review the factual adequacy of an agency's decision. Section 706(2) (A) provides that for *informal* proceedings (notice and comment rulemaking and informal adjudications), a reviewing court must apply the "arbitrary and capricious" standard. We will explore these two standards after we define questions of policy.

## 2. Defining Questions of Policy

Earlier we defined a mixed question of law and fact as one in which the agency applies the relevant law to the specific facts in an adjudication to reach a conclusion. A question of policy similarly involves resolution of both law and facts, but questions of policy generally arise during rulemakings rather than during adjudications. The relevant facts are not judicial facts (who said what, did what, did it when); rather, the facts are legislative in nature (are pesticides dangerous?).

For example, suppose an agency must decide on the location for the new highway, how many parts per million of a certain chemical will be injurious to human health, what kinds of safety features should be required in passenger cars, or what level of protection should be afforded workers in factories. Resolution of these kinds of issues involves policy decisions, decisions requiring value choices that are not fully resolved by the legislative facts or the legal standards. In making policy, the agency must consider the relevant facts in light of its delegated authority, e.g., "to make drinking water safe," to arrive at its policy choice. Usually, these policy choices involve complex and controverted scientific and technical issues. What level of intensity will a court use when reviewing an agency's policy decision?

To be sure, courts will be deferential here. The legislature that delegated its authority to the agency likely intended that agency to play the primary role in resolving the issues presented, not a court. Not only will agency policy decisions often turn on the agency's knowledge and experience, agencies are more likely to understand and be sympathetic to current legislative goals than the courts. Agencies have the expertise, were delegated the authority to make policy, and are accountable to the public.

Sections 706(2)(A) and (E) of the APA provides for judicial review of these kinds of agency determinations. The two standards are substantial evidence review and arbitrary and capricious review. When an agency makes a policy choice during a formal rulemaking (or through a formal adjudication if that is how the agency makes its policy decisions) or when Congress so provides, then substantial evidence is the appropriate standard. Otherwise, and more commonly, arbitrary and capricious is the appropriate standard. The next sections explain these two standards that apply to both questions of fact and questions of policy and explain how the standards differ, if at all.

## 3.  Substantial Evidence Review

The use of the substantial evidence standard to review agency factual findings predates the ABA. In 1913, the Supreme Court upheld a decision of the now-defunct Interstate Commerce Commission, saying that courts should review agency factual findings no further than to determine whether those findings are supported by substantial evidence. *ICC v. Louisville & N.R. Co.*, 227 U.S. 88, 93 (1913) (stating "it is necessary to examine the record with a view of determining whether there was substantial evidence to support the order."). Congress used the concept in 1914 in the Federal Trade Commission Act. Pub. L. No. 63-203, Section 5, 38 Stat. 717, 720 codified as amended at 15 U.S.C. § 45(c) (2012) (providing that the agency's findings of fact would be conclusive if supported by "testimony," later amended to "evidence"). This statutory language has been judicially interpreted to mean that the "substantial evidence" standard will be applied when a court reviews FTC fact-findings. *See Ash Grove Cement Co. v. F.T.C.*, 577 F.2d 1368, 1377–78 (9th Cir. 1978) *cert. denied*, 439 U.S. 982 (1978). Thus, when the APA then included substantial evidence in section 706(2)(E), the standard was already very familiar.

Justice Frankfurter, a former administrative law professor, described the meaning of substantial evidence as follows:

> [S]ubstantial evidence is more than a mere scintilla. It means such relevant evidence as a reasonable mind might accept as adequate to support a conclusion. . . . [It] must do more than create a suspicion of the existence of the fact to be established. . . . it must be enough to justify, if the trial were to a jury, a refusal to direct a verdict when the conclusion sought to be drawn from it is one of fact for the jury.

*Universal Camera Corp. v. NLRB*, 340 U.S. 474, 477 (1951) (internal citations omitted).

Substantial evidence is commonly thought of as a fairly deferential test placed somewhere in the middle of the intensity spectrum. A judge should not substitute his or her judgment for that of the agency. Notice that the Justice Frankfurter's description of this standard includes the word "reasonable." "Reasonable" in this sense applies to the agency's "reasoning" process. Thus, a judge should review the evidence in the record to confirm whether a reasonable person could make the same factual or policy finding that the agency made. In other words, the question is whether the evidence in the record supports the agency's findings, not whether the finding itself is reasonable in a more general sense. Thus, the task of the reviewing court is to examine each of the agency's findings of fact or policy to see if there is evidence in the record to support that finding. In making this determination, the reviewing court should take into account not only the evidence supporting the agency's findings, but also any evidence that "fairly detracts" from that finding. *Id.* at 487.

Let's look at an example of this standard as applied to review an agency's finding of fact. Suppose an agency denied a disability claim; in doing so, the agency relied on the testimony of its medical expert, who stated that the claimant could stand for seven or eight hours in a workday. Thus, the agency found that the claimant was not actually disabled. The claimant appealed and challenged the factual finding that he was not disabled. Assuming the substantial evidence standard applied, then a court would likely find the standard met. Because the agency's medical expert was the only expert to testify, the agency's factual finding that the individual was not disabled is supported by the evidence in this record. But what if there were other medical experts who testified that the claimant could stand no more than three or four hours per day? Assume further that these medical experts actually examined the individual, while the agency's medical expert merely reviewed the individual's medical records. In this case, the reviewing court would likely find that the agency's finding does not meet the substantial evidence standard.

Let's return to our hypothetical as amended. Assume that an ALJ first determined that the disability claimant was disabled. Then, the agency, using its de novo powers of review, reversed that finding. What is the significance of a disagreement between the agency and the ALJ on disputed factual questions? We discussed this topic in Chapter 3 and concluded that while section 557(b) gives the reviewing agency de novo review, the reviewing court will not ignore ALJ's factual findings that are based on the demeanor of witnesses. When reviewing the ALJ's decision, the agency may use its experience to evaluate the significance of evidence in the record and reject the ALJ's findings. But the agency had better explain its choice carefully, supporting the new finding with evidence in the record. In our hypothetical, the agency might explain that it is familiar with the claimant's medical experts who are all pediatricians and that they are unqualified to address this type of disability, for example.

If the agency had simply ignored the ALJ's findings and failed to explain why it was doing so, a court would view the agency's findings as less reasoned and, thus, less likely to survive the substantial review standard. In sum, a wise agency explains obvious contradictions between its factual findings and those of its ALJ.

Now let's look at an example of this standard used to review an agency's application of law to fact. Recall earlier that we learned that sometimes courts use the substantial evidence standard when reviewing these mixed questions. In *O'Leary v. Brown-Pacific-Maxon*, 340 U.S. 504 (1951), the Court applied the substantial evidence standard to review an agency's determination that an employee's death "arose out of and in the course of employment," entitling his dependents to file for workers' compensation benefits under the Longshoremen's and Harbor Workers' Compensation Act. *Id.* at 508. The facts were not disputed. The employee drowned during non-work hours when he attempted to rescue two men trapped on a reef. *Id.* at 505. The employer had maintained the recreation area for its employees. *Id.* After the employee's death, his mother filed for compensation, claiming the drowning arose out of the course of his employment. *Id.* at 505–06. The agency granted the petition; the employer sued in federal court; the district court denied the employer's petition to set aside the award; and the Ninth Circuit reversed. *Id.* at 506. The Supreme Court reversed the Ninth Circuit, concluding that the agency's decision was supported by substantial evidence. *Id.* at 506.

Three dissenters argued that because the facts were not in dispute, the substantial evidence standard did not apply. *Id.* at 509 (Minton, J. dissenting). The majority acknowledged that the issue was not primarily factual, but countered that it was not "of such a nature as to be peculiarly appropriate for independent judicial ascertainment as [a] 'question of law.'" *Id.* at 508 (majority opinion). Further, the majority noted that the substantial evidence standard was appropriate because that standard was more deferential to the agency than a de novo standard of review and allowed for the agency's expertise to be brought to the analysis. *Id.* Remember that this case predated *Chevron* and its replacement of de novo review for pure questions of law.

In sum, the substantial evidence standard is fairly deferential to the agency because the agency has expertise that the court does not. To be clear, the standard is not a preponderance of the evidence test; a reviewing court's job is to decide whether the agency's findings are reasoned, not whether they are right.

## 4. Arbitrary and Capricious Review

The substantial evidence standard is used to review the sufficiency of findings of fact or policy that agencies make during *formal* proceedings or when Congress specifies this standard of review in the enabling statute. For reviewing the sufficiency of findings of fact and policy made during *informal* proceedings, the reviewing court applies arbitrary and capricious review. APA § 706(2)(A). The APA provides that the reviewing court shall hold unlawful and set aside agency findings that are "arbitrary, capricious, [or] an abuse of discretion." *Id*. These three terms do not have independent significance; rather, combined, they are understood to mean arbitrary and capricious review.

Historically, courts used the arbitrary and capricious standard to determine whether laws affecting economic and social interests were unconstitutional. WILLIAM F. FUNK & RICHARD H. SEAMON, ADMINISTRATIVE LAW: EXAMPLES & EXPLANATIONS 313 (2009). Today, courts apply the rational relationship test instead. Pursuant to the rational relationship test, a law is unconstitutional only when there is no rational basis to believe the law will further a legitimate governmental interest—in other words, almost never. Likely then, this highly deferential standard of review was what the drafters of the APA intended arbitrary and capricious review to be: highly deferential. *Id*. Justice Brandeis stated as much in 1935:

> But where the regulation is within the scope of authority legally delegated, the presumption of the existence of facts justifying its specific exercise attaches alike to statutes, to municipal ordinances, and to orders of administrative bodies.

*Pacific States Box & Basket v. White*, 296 U.S. 176, 186 (1935).

By the late 1960s, however, the courts began to apply a more intensive version of review, especially when reviewing rulemaking. It is unclear why the standard became more intensive. Perhaps the change in intensity was, in part, a response to the new agencies being created in the 1960s and 1970s. Perhaps the change reflected a growing concern about agency "capture." Perhaps the change was the work of a few strong-minded judges in the D.C. Circuit. Whatever its cause, the feeling grew that firmer judicial oversight was warranted. As a result, the arbitrary and capricious test was pushed up the intensity scale a considerable distance from its 1930s position. *See generally* Peter L. Strauss, *Overseers or "The Deciders"—The Courts in Administrative Law*, 75 U. CHI. L. REV. 815, 821–23 (2008) (noting that arbitrary and capricious review has become considerably more intensive, especially for reviewing agency policy decisions (as distinguished from the review of fact findings) and most especially when agency discretion is exercised in high-stakes rulemaking).

Regardless of the reason for the change, in 1971, the Supreme Court gave the standard unexpected teeth in *Citizens to Preserve Overton Park, Inc. v. Volpe*, 401 U.S. 402 (1971). This case involved judicial review of an agency's policy decision made as part of an informal adjudication, but the standard applies for policy decisions made during notice and comment rulemaking as well.

In *Overton Park*, a law prohibited the Federal Highway Administration from providing public funds to build a highway through a public park unless no feasible and prudent alternative existed. *Id.* at 407. The State of Tennessee requested funds to build a highway that would cut through the middle of a local park in Memphis. The Secretary of Transportation approved the funds, stating that he agreed with the State that the highway should be built through the park. Local citizens sued, claiming that his approval was unlawful. *Id.* at 406.

The Supreme Court applied arbitrary and capricious review, describing it in the following way:

> To make [a finding that the actual choice made was not "arbitrary, capricious, an abuse of discretion, or otherwise not in accordance with law"] the court must consider whether the decision was based on a consideration of the relevant factors and whether there has been a clear error of judgment. Although this inquiry into the facts is to be searching and careful, the ultimate standard of review is a narrow one. The court is not empowered to substitute its judgment for that of the agency.

*Id.* at 416. Thus, for arbitrary and capricious review, courts must review the administrative record that was before the agency to determine whether "the decision was based on a consideration of the relevant factors and whether there has been a clear error of judgment." *Id.*

Similarly, in *Motor Vehicles Manufacturers Ass'n v. State Farm*, 463 U.S. 29 (1983), the Court struck down an agency's policy choice using arbitrary and capricious review. *State Farm* came about after President Reagan was elected and promised to roll back regulations. Under the Carter administration, the Department of Transportation had adopted a rule requiring car manufacturers to phase in passive restraints, such as automatic seatbelts and airbags. With the new administration, the newly appointed Secretary of Transportation undertook a new notice and comment rulemaking to rescind the phase-in rule. The evidence at the time was pretty clear: seat-belts save lives. So, the insurance industry sued, claiming that the new rule was unlawful. Oddly, although the relevant statute specifically required courts to apply the substantial evidence standard, the Court applied the arbitrary and capricious standard. It is unclear why.

In holding that the Department had acted arbitrarily and capriciously in revoking its prior rule requiring seatbelts or air bags in passenger cars, the Court reaffirmed that arbitrary and capricious review is "narrow" and that a court should not substitute its judgment for the agency's. Yet one might argue that the Court did just that: substituted its judgment for the agency's.

The Court specifically confirmed that arbitrary and capricious review is more intensive than the minimum rationality test used for statutes: "We do not view [arbitrary and capricious review] as equivalent to the presumption of constitutionality afforded legislation drafted by Congress." *Id.* at 43, n.9.

The Court then described arbitrary and capricious review of an agency's policy decisions as follows:

> [T]he agency must examine the relevant data and articulate a satisfac-tory explanation for its action including a "rational connection between the facts found and the choice made." In reviewing that expla-nation, we must "consider whether the decision was based on a consid-eration of the relevant factors and whether there has been a clear error of judgment." Normally, an agency rule would be arbitrary and capri-cious if the agency has relied on factors which Congress has not intended it to consider, entirely failed to consider an important aspect of the problem, offered an explanation for its decision that runs counter to the evidence before the agency, or is so implausible that it could not be ascribed to a difference in view or the product of agency expertise.

*Id.* at 43 (citations omitted). In short, "[the rule must be] the product of rea-soned decisionmaking." *Id.* at 52.

In *State Farm*, the agency had justified the rule change by claiming that the car manufacturers would choose to put in automatic seatbelts rather than air-bags and that individuals would then unhook those seatbelts; hence, safety would not be improved. *Id.* at 52–53. However, the Court reasoned that the agency had failed to consider an important aspect of the problem, namely the option of a rule that required the car manufacturers to include airbags only. *Id.* at 53. Further, the Court found that the agency offered an explanation for its decision that ran counter to the evidence: namely, the evidence did not sup-port the agency's finding that people detach automatic seatbelts at the same rate as they fail to use manual seatbelts. The agency had ignored inertia (otherwise known as laziness). *Id*. at 54.

It is difficult to see the review in this case as anything but high-level intensive review. The Court seems to reject the agency's policy conclusions as themselves unreasonable, rather than reject the agency's decision-making process. In sum, the Court substituted its policy choices for those of the agency. Perhaps the majority believed that the real reason for the change was the newly elected president's preference for deregulation. If true, then Justice Rehnquist had a response:

> The agency's changed view of the standard seems to be related to the election of a new President of a different political party. It is readily apparent that the responsible members of one administration may consider public resistance and uncertainties to be more important than do their counterparts in a previous administration. A change in administration brought about by the people casting their votes is a perfectly reasonable basis for an executive agency's reappraisal of the costs and benefits of its programs and regulations. As long as the agency remains within the bounds established by Congress, it is entitled to assess administrative records and evaluate priorities in light of the philosophy of the administration.

*Id*. at 59 (Rehnquist, J., concurring and dissenting).

Following up on Justice Rehnquist's "change in administration argument," the Court in *FCC v. Fox*, 556 U.S. 502 (2009), debated what the "obligation to explain" means when a rule changes because the president changes. *Fox* involved broadcasts with fleeting, indecent language. *Id*. at 510. Acting in the strong shadow of the First Amendment, the Federal Trade Commission had for many years prohibited fleeting expletives only when the offending words were used multiple times in one broadcast. *Id*. at 507–08. When President George W. Bush came to the White House, the Commission changed its rule to prohibit a single use of an offending word. *Id*. at 508. The Commission chose not to impose fines right away for violations because the rule was a new policy. *Id*. at 510. The Commission sent violation notices to Fox, which sued, claiming the rule was unlawful. The Second Circuit held that the Commission's change of policy was inadequately explained; hence, it was arbitrary and capricious. *Id*. at 511–12.

The Supreme Court reversed. *Id*. at 530. There were six different opinions in the case. Justice Scalia, writing for the majority, found the Commission's explanation for the change sufficient. *Id*. at 520–21. Applying *State Farm*'s articulation of arbitrary and capricious review, Justice Scalia said an agency can change policy but must explain why it is changing policy, *id*. at 513, but the agency is under no duty to prove to a court that the new policy is better than the old. *Id*. All the agency needs to do is establish that the new policy is rational and within its authority. *Id*. at 514. If the new policy results from changes in facts, laws, or policies on which the old policy rested, those changes should be identified and explained. *Id*. at 514–15. A court should "'uphold a decision of less than ideal clarity if the agency's path may reasonably be discerned.'" *Id*. at 513 (quoting *Bowman Transportation, Inc. v. Arkansas-Best Freight System, Inc.*, 419 U.S. 281, 286 (1974).

Dissenting, Justice Breyer defined the duty to explain as more encompassing:

> [T]he agency must explain why it has come to the conclusion that it should now change direction. Why does it now reject the considerations that led it to adopt that initial policy? What has changed in the world that offers justification for the change? What other good reasons are there for departing from the earlier policy?

*Id*. at 550 (Breyer, J., dissenting).

As in *State Farm*, the real explanation for the change was political; the new policy reflected the views of the current administration, rejecting the views of the administration in place when the original policy was announced. Should this alone be an acceptable explanation? For a useful analysis, see Kathryn Watts, *Proposing a Place For Politics in Arbitrary and Capricious Review*, 119 YALE L.J. 2 (2009) (proposing an expanded arbitrary and capricious review to include political influences).

Incidentally, *State Farm* is a case study of what happens when science (seatbelts and air bags unquestionably save lives) runs into: (a) public perceptions about the sanctity of the private automobile, (b) political attitudes about regulation, (c) stiff industry opposition, (d) insurance company interests, and (e) the normal complications of the legislative process. There are limits to what science can do. Even though we had seatbelt and airbag technology in the 1960s, these complicating factors resulted in 20 years of delay in regulations requiring their use, at a cost of 12,000 lives annually.

Today, we call this new intensive form of arbitrary and capricious review "hard-look" review. As originally understood, "hard-look review" focused on the competency of the agency's review of the record. Judge Leventhal said a court would overturn agency decisions "if the court becomes aware . . . that the agency has not really taken a 'hard look' at the salient problems and has not genuinely engaged in reasoned decisionmaking." *Greater Boston Television v. FCC*, 444 F.2d 841, 851 (D. C. Cir. 1970). Today, however, as a result of *Overton Park, State Farm*, and *Fox*, the phrase is now viewed as a requirement not just that a court should be sure the agency took a hard look at the problem, but that the court itself should take a hard look at the agency's policy choice and explanation for that choice. With this change, arbitrary and capricious review moved up on the intensity scale.

## 5. The Difference Between Substantial Evidence and Arbitrary and Capricious Review

Because both the substantial evidence and the arbitrary and capricious standards are framed in terms of the reasonableness of the agency's reasoning process and because arbitrary and capricious review has become more intensive, you might wonder whether they reflect different levels of review intensity. The academic and judicial debate over this question has raged for years. When former Justice Scalia was a circuit court judge, he claimed that the two tests were essentially identical because "it is impossible to conceive of a nonarbitrary factual judgment supported only by evidence that is not substantial in the APA sense." *Association of Data Processing Serv. Orgs. v. Board of Governors of Fed. Reserve Sys.*, 745 F.2d 677, 683 (D.C. Cir. 1984). While the Supreme Court has never resolved this issue definitively, the Court applied arbitrary and capricious review in *State Farm* even though the statute involved expressly provided that the agency's determination had to be supported by "[s]ubstantial evidence on the record considered as a whole." *State Farm*, 463 U.S. at 44 (quoting S. Rep. No. 1301, 89th Cong., 2d Sess., 8 (1966); H. R. Rep. No. 1776, 89th Cong., 2d Sess., 21 (1966)).

Others argue that the standards are different; substantial evidence requires the court to conduct a slightly more searching inquiry. There is support to this argument; after all, Congress specifically identified two different standards in the APA. Moreover, Congress sometimes requires the substantial evidence standard when the arbitrary and capricious standard would be the default. For example, the Occupational Safety and Health Administration, the Consumer Product Safety Commission, and the Federal Trade Commission all have enabling statutes requiring a court to apply the substantial evidence standard for reviewing informal proceedings. *See* 29 U.S.C. § 660(a); 15 U.S.C. § 2060(c); 15 U.S.C. § 45(c). The legislative history of these statutes suggests that Congress intended courts to more closely supervise the factual adequacy of decisions from these agencies. Peter L. Strauss, Administrative Justice in the United States 468–71 (3d ed. 2016).

In sum, whether the two standards truly reflect different intensity standards, the language used differs. And perhaps the mood with which courts approach their review responsibilities may also differ.

## 6. De Novo Review

One final point: the APA also provides that courts shall set aside agency findings found to be "unwarranted by the facts to the extent that the facts are subject to trial de novo by the reviewing court." APA § 706(2)(F). Notice that the court should apply the de novo standard of review in such situations.

When the APA was enacted, the House Report suggested that the provision should apply whenever the agency was enforcing a rule during an informal adjudication. FUNK & SEAMON, *supra* at 322. In contrast, the Attorney General's Manual argued the provision should apply only when some other statute or court decision requires it. *Id.* at 323. However, Professor John Duffy has argued that the Attorney General's Manual was often an attempt to undo the battles it lost during the legislative process. John Duffy, *Administrative Common Law in Judicial Review*, 77 TEX. L. REV. 113 (1998). And, in this case, the manual's description of the de novo review provision would be consistent with the Attorney General's preference for limiting judicial review entirely. FUNK & SEAMON, *supra* at 323. Hence, the House Report's view seems more credible.

However, the Supreme Court limited the de novo review provision out of existence in *Overton Park* and subsequent cases. In *Overton Park*, the Court refused to apply the de novo standard despite the fact that the agency proceeding involved the application of a rule during an informal adjudication. *Overton Park*, 401 U.S. at 415. The Court said that de novo review only applies in two situations. "First, such de novo review is authorized when the action is adjudicatory in nature and the agency factfinding procedures are inadequate." *Id.* Two years later, however, the Court refused to apply the de novo standard in just such a case. *Camp v. Pitts*, 411 U.S. 138, 142 (1973) (refusing to apply de novo review to an informal adjudication with arguable inadequate factfinding). As a result, courts rarely find an agency's factfinding procedures were inadequate. Second, the *Overton Park* Court said that de novo review would be appropriate "when issues that were before the agency are raised in a proceeding to enforce nonadjudicatory agency action." *Overton Park*, 401 U.S. at 415 (citing the House Report). Here, the Court suggested that de novo review applies only when an agency applies a rule in a court proceeding, not when an agency applies a rule in an adjudication. While that statement may be correct, such situations have no relevance to judicial review of agency action. In sum, the courts do not use the de novo standard in section 702(2)(F) for reviewing agency findings.

## 7. The Record for Fact and Policy Review

Once a court selects the correct standard of review, the next question to consider is what evidence that court should review. The answer to that question is simple. A court should review the record that was before the agency at the time it made its decision. For formal proceedings, the record will be the formal evidentiary record made as part of the trial-like process. For informal proceedings, the record will be whatever information was before the agency when it made its decision.

When an agency action is informal, the agency's record may not be as complete as when an agency action is formal. Where, then, is the judge to look for the evidence that would satisfy the arbitrary and capricious test?

For notice and comment rulemaking, we saw in Chapter 2 that this form of rulemaking generates a lot of information (in both paper and digital form), including public comment on the proposed rule, responses to those comments, drafts of the rule, etc. Indeed, as part of its notice and comment rulemaking process, agencies are required to disclose the studies and data upon which their analysis is based. *United States v. Nova Scotia Food Products*, 568 F.2d 240 (2d Cir. 1977). Where the factual sufficiency of an agency's notice and comment *rulemaking* is challenged, the courts will look at everything the agency had before it in making its decision. *See generally* William F. Pedersen, Jr., *Formal Records and Informal Rulemaking*, 85 YALE L. J. 38, 61 (1975) (highlighting the monstrous amounts of "unwieldy records" courts are confronted with as a result of reviewing an agency's notice and comment rulemaking). Thus, it is rare that a court will not have a sufficient record to review.

In contrast to the relatively complete record in notice and comment rulemakings, for informal *adjudications*, the agency may have little in the way of a record, making it difficult for courts to apply arbitrary and capricious review. If a court is unable to assess the factual adequacy of the order, the court may remand the case back to the agency for further proceedings. *Cf. Overton Park*, 401 U.S. at 406 (suggesting that the trial court had the power to remand). But courts prefer not to do so, and agencies prefer to provide explanatory and supporting documentation rather than be cross-examined after their decision-making process.

In sum, when courts are reviewing either informal rulemaking or informal adjudication for evidentiary sufficiency, the arbitrary and capricious standard of reasonableness requires that agencies explain and justify their decisions based on the factual record before them.

# E.  Summary

In summary, and as Figure 6.4 below shows, when determining which standard of review a court will apply to review an agency's finding, you must first determine what type of finding is involved: one of law, one of fact, one of application of law to fact, or one of policy. Then you must determine what procedure the agency used to reach its determination. For questions of law, the standard of review will vary based on what the agency was interpreting—a statute or its own regulation—and how the agency reached its interpretation, by legislative or non-legislative rulemaking. Remember that legislative rulemaking includes notice and comment rulemaking.

For questions of fact and policy, the standard of review will vary based on whether the agency used a formal procedure or informal procedure. For questions of law application, break the questions into parts and follow the appropriate standard for each subpart.

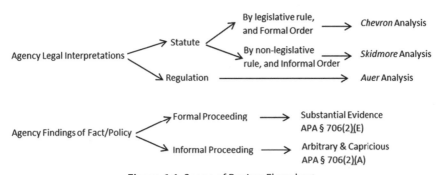

**Figure 6.4** Scope of Review Flowchart

But be aware that these standards of review are inexact. Even within a particular standard of review, the intensity of one court's review will vary from the intensity of another court's review. Let's return to Figure 6.1, which identified the scope of review intensity spectrum for conventional cases. Let's replace the conventional judicial standards of review with the standards of review used in administrative law. The revised figure might look something like Figure 6.5 below.

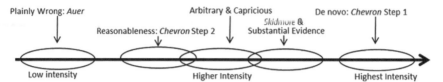

**Figure 6.5** The Scope of Review Intensity Spectrum in Administrative Law

Notice that the standards are not set points on the spectrum. Rather, courts apply varying levels of intensity even when applying the same standard of review. There are some factors that a court might consider in adjusting the intensity of its review upward or downward. Courts are not always explicit that these factors are playing a role in their decision to apply a more or less intense version of a particular standard; however, these factors may explain some of the inconsistency in these areas.

Here are a few such factors. Sometimes the legislature signals that it wants a more or less intense scope of review. A court might consider the following as indicators for a less intensive review: a delegation of especially broad powers, a requirement of formal procedures, or a setting in which the agency is given the first full crack at the decision. When the agency was active in proposing, drafting, or lobbying for a statute, then less intensive review may result.

The type of question itself may suggest a more or less intensive review. Review is likely to be more intensive if the question "feels" more like a question of law, i.e., is a general principle that will have broad effects, rather than when resolution of the case will affect only this one case. Review is likely to be less intensive when questions involve factual issues with which agency expertise is relevant.

The quality of the agency's decision-making process may suggest a more or less intensive review. Expect less intensive review of agency decision making that is thorough, fair, and complete. Further, an agency's reputation for objective policymaking and neutral factfinding can impact a court's choice. Agencies sometimes develop either favorable or unfavorable reputations in these areas.

Finally, a judge's view of the appropriate judicial role may affect this choice. Expect more intensive review (less *Chevron* deference) from judges who doubt the efficacy of political controls on agencies and who regard courts as effective and legitimate instruments for imposing such controls.

# Checkpoints

- Judicial review furthers separation of powers.

- Intensity is one way to measure judicial review. Different standards of review require different levels of intensity.

- Judges use different standards of review in administrative law, which depend on the type of issue involved.

- For questions of law, judges apply one of three standards: *Chevron*, *Skidmore*, or *Auer*.

- *Chevron* applies to most agency legal determinations made during relatively formal proceedings that have the "force of law," such as formal rulemaking, notice and comment rulemaking, and formal adjudication.

- At *Chevron* step one, a court should determine "whether Congress has directly spoken to the precise question at issue."

- At *Chevron* step two, if Congress has not so spoken, then a court should accept any "permissible," or "reasonable," agency interpretation.

- Under *Skidmore's* power-to-persuade test, an agency's interpretation of a statute made during non-legislative rulemaking is entitled to deference when (1) the agency consistently interprets the language over time, (2) the agency thoroughly considers the issue, and (3) the agency offers sound reasoning to support the interpretation.

- Under *Auer*, courts defer to an agency's interpretation of its own regulation unless the interpretation is "plainly wrong." This standard has been criticized as violating separation of powers.

- For questions of fact and policy, a court applies the substantial evidence standard when the agency reaches its finding via a formal proceeding. A court applies the arbitrary and capricious standard when the agency reaches its finding via an informal proceeding.

- Substantial evidence and arbitrary and capricious are similar, mid-level intensity standards with which judges evaluate whether the agency made reasoned findings.

# Chapter 7

# The Flow of Information

---

## Roadmap

---

This chapter explains legal problems that may arise as information flows from the public to the agencies and from the agencies to members of the public. Procedurally, this chapter should come much earlier in this text, certainly before the judicial review chapters, ideally as the second chapter. However, it is included here because traditionally law school courses cover it, if they cover it at all, at the end of the semester. But as you study this chapter, keep in mind that obtaining and providing information is something agencies do on a day-to-day basis, and their choices in this process may be subject to judicial oversight.

Both the Constitution and various statutes regulate this informational flow. We begin by exploring how and why information flows from the public to agencies, primarily through the methods of reports and inspections. We then turn to exploring how and why information flows from agencies to the public and the limits on that informational flow.

# A. Information Flowing to the Agencies

To effectively regulate, agencies need information and lots of it. National, state, and local codes set forth standards that regulated entities must meet to ensure that their businesses are healthy, safe, clean, and well-functioning. For agencies to enforce these codes, agencies require regulated entities to maintain and submit numerous compliance documents. In addition, agencies conduct thousands of inspections of businesses and even residences every year. Finally, in promulgating rules, agencies conduct research, draft reports, gather evidence, etc. Hence, millions of reports, documents, completed forms, and other pieces of paper and electronic documents are gathered every year. Much of this information flows to the agency from the entities it regulates.

Courts understand that agencies must have information if they are to perform the tasks the legislature has assigned to them. Hence, in the vast majority of cases, an agency is going to get the information it needs, whether it goes to court or not. There are statutory and constitutional limits on agencies' access to information, which the courts enforce. But because courts know how critical information is to an agency's mission, they are not likely to limit an agency's access to information without a clear and convincing showing that statutory or constitutional restrictions have been violated.

Generally, agencies obtain information from citizens and businesses in two ways. First, an agency may require that citizens produce information in documentary or testimonial form, either "voluntarily" through reports (such as your annual income tax return) or by compulsion in the form of an agency subpoena or investigative demand. Second, an agency may conduct a physical inspection of a residence or place of business to gather information relevant to some regulatory or enforcement standard. We will look at each method next, starting with documentary and testimonial information.

# 1. Documents and Testimony

The primary way agencies collect information is by obtaining documents (records and reports) and testimony directly from regulated parties. Regulated entities may be required by statute or subpoena to provide written reports or to complete forms. Because agencies' demand for such information has mushroomed in recent years, Congress has required agencies to maintain minimal standards of necessity, efficiency, non-duplication, and interagency coordination. *See, e.g.,* Paperwork Reduction Act, 44 U.S.C. § 3501 (2002); Information Quality Act, 44 U.S.C. § 3516 (2000). The Office of Management and Budget, which is located within the Executive Branch, oversees the Paperwork Reduction Act and the Information Quality Act.

## a. Voluntary Production

Agencies rely on "voluntary" disclosures of information for the most part. Every day, citizens provide information to the government on their tax returns, on license and permit applications, and in telephone inquiries, to name just a few. Most citizens provide such information, if not willingly, then at least without legal challenge. Why? One reason individuals willingly provide information is that they want something in return: a tax refund, a license to practice law, help with financial aid requirements, or a global entry pass, for example.

Another reason individuals provide information voluntarily is that if they did not, the government can generally compel disclosure of that information by issuing a subpoena. When the government turns to a subpoena, information disclosure is no longer voluntary.

## b. Involuntary Production

When agencies seek information that a citizen or business is unwilling to disclose voluntarily, the agency may seek that information by way of a subpoena or a subpoena *duces tecum*. A subpoena seeks testimony, while a subpoena *duces tecum* seeks documents. We will refer to both as subpoenas.

You should be aware that a federal agency does not have subpoena enforcement power, but must apply to a federal court for an order of compliance; by violating the court order, one risks a contempt citation, with its accompanying penalties.

So there is a sense in which noncompliance with an agency subpoena is penalty free. The client cannot be cited for resisting the subpoena. And in the court proceeding that the agency must bring to enforce the subpoena, the client will have an opportunity to raise any legal objections to the subpoena's issuance. A few statutes provide for a fine or even imprisonment for failure to comply with an agency subpoena, but courts typically refuse to enforce these penalties until the regulated entity fails to comply with a judicial compliance order.

Because noncompliance appears penalty free and you are a lawyer, your first instinct might be to recommend that your client resist the subpoena, which would require the agency to go to court to enforce it. Benefits of resistance include the following: (1) you might buy your client some time; (2) you might discourage the agency from pursuing the subpoena; (3) you might force the agency to limit or clarify the information it seeks; and (4) you might preserve your client's legal objection to providing the information, which may be waived when consent is given.

But an overwhelming majority of clients comply with the subpoena. Why? Because noncompliance has cost, including: (1) negative publicity (e.g., *"Joe's Restaurant Refuses to Provide Information to the Health Inspector"* may not be a headline your client would welcome), and (2) a lack of goodwill from the agency in both the short and long term when the information is not provided. The agency may have other ways of making your client's life uncomfortable or your client's business less profitable. For example, if an agency refuses to grant a permit or revokes a license, even if the denial is only temporarily, it could cost your client dearly. You should remember that your client will have a long-term regulatory relationship with the agency; good relationships with agency staff can be of considerable value. Thus, you might prefer to negotiate with the agency to narrow the subpoena's scope or request increased time for your client to comply.

If your client opts not to comply with a subpoena, on what grounds would a court "quash" the subpoena? We explore these challenges next.

### (1) Statutory Limits

First, you might question whether the agency has statutory authority. To issue a subpoena, an agency must have statutory authorization to do so. Such power relates to the agency's area of regulation. For example, Under the Employee Retirement Income Security Act (ERISA), the Department of Labor (DOL) has the power to investigate ERISA violations, including the power to subpoena books and records and compel witnesses to testify under oath. 15 U.S.C. § 49 (1975) ("the [DOL] shall have power to require by subpoena the attendance and testimony of witnesses and the production of all such documentary evidence relating to any matter under investigation."). If in the unlikely case the Department of Labor issued a subpoena seeking food safety information, DOL may well have exceeded its statutory authority to issue a subpoena. Second, the subpoena must comply with any limitations or procedures imposed by the statute, such as paying costs. Third, the agency must comply with any limitations in the agency's own rules.

Statutory authority is not usually a problem; statutory grants are usually quite broad, typically authorizing an agency to subpoena any documents or require any testimony relevant to the agency's authority. And generally the courts interpret an agency's subpoena authority broadly. For example, in *United States v. Sturm, Ruger Co., Inc.*, 84 F.3d 1 (1st Cir. 1996), the Occupational Safety and Health Administration (OSHA) brought an action to enforce a subpoena requiring the respondent-business to produce a myriad of documents concerning the manufacturing processes, employee training, and on-the-job injuries. Notably, OSHA issued this very broad subpoena when the business refused to complete a voluntary questionnaire. The respondent-business moved to quash the subpoena, arguing that issuing the subpoena was not within OSHA's statutory authority. *Id.* at 3. The First Circuit rejected the argument, saying "as long as the agency's assertion of authority is not obviously apocryphal, a procedurally sound subpoena must be enforced." *Id.* at 5–6. Indeed, the court found the attack on the subpoena in this case so lacking in merit that it dug deep into the English lexicon to reject it:

> Were we to succumb to the siren song that Sturmco sings and stop the subpoena for want of some sophisticated standard for systemically specifying ergonomic hazards, we would in effect be requiring OSHA to "charge first and investigate later." This tergiversation would stand the administrative enforcement process on its head and in the bargain would both defy the will of Congress and ignore the teachings of the Court. We will not encourage so resupinate an exercise.

*Id.* at 6 (citation omitted). Hence, most such challenges fail.

### (2) Constitutional Limits: Fourth Amendment

Assuming the agency has complied with its statutory authority, you might question whether the agency has acted constitutionally. The Fourth and Fifth Amendments are applicable to subpoenas. We will look at each.

In classic and elegant eighteenth-century language, the Fourth Amendment states both its proscriptions and their justification. Here is the Amendment in its entirety:

> The right of the people to be secure in their persons, houses, papers, and effects, against unreasonable searches and seizures, shall not

be violated, and no Warrants shall issue, but upon probable cause, supported by Oath or affirmation, and particularly describing the place to be searched, and the persons or things to be seized.

U.S. Const. Amend IV.

For most of our history, the Fourth Amendment was an important tool in defending citizens from responding to governmental requests for information. That was a time when Justice Holmes famously prohibited agency "fishing expeditions." *FTC v. American Tobacco Co.*, 264 U.S. 298, 305–06 (1924). But in the 1940s, the Supreme Court shifted its tone. Perhaps becoming more comfortable with the regulatory process as its novelty wore off or its inevitability became clear, the Court developed a very permissive approach to the Fourth Amendment in the administrative context. An agency need not show that it has probable cause to believe that the respondent was guilty of violating a statute or agency rule. Rather, the Court held that agency subpoenas were valid under the Fourth Amendment if the subpoenas sought information relevant to the exercise of the agency's power and were not written too broadly or indefinitely. *Oklahoma Press v. Walling*, 327 U.S. 186, 208–09 (1946).

To prevail on its action to enforce a subpoena, an agency must prove that: (1) the subpoena was issued for a congressionally authorized purpose, (2) the information sought is relevant to an authorized purpose, and (3) the information sought is adequately described. *Sturm, Ruger Co., Inc.*, 84 F.3d at 4. Courts broadly interpret relevance; a subpoena will be upheld if the evidence sought is "not plainly incompetent or irrelevant to any lawful purpose of the agency." *Endicott Johnson Corp. v. Perkins*, 317 U.S. 501, 509 (1943). Indeed, the Court has said that a subpoena enforcement action is not the place to raise questions about coverage of the agency's statute. *Oklahoma Press*, 327 U.S. at 214; *Endicott Johnson Corp.*, 317 U.S. at 507. The difference between a statute's coverage and an agency's jurisdiction is not altogether clear. At least one court has held that jurisdictional challenges can defeat a subpoena. For example, in *EEOC v. Karuk Tribal Housing Auth.*, 260 F.3d 1071, 1077 (9th Cir. 2001), the Ninth Circuit distinguished between coverage and jurisdiction, holding that because EEOC had no jurisdiction over a dispute between the Tribe and its members as a pure matter of law, the subpoena would not be enforced.

Similarly, courts have not readily embraced arguments that a subpoena was too broad or indefinite. On the one hand, if the agency knows the nature of the problem it seeks information about, the agency will draft its subpoena carefully, ensuring the subpoena passes judicial muster. On the other hand, if the agency does not yet fully know the extent of the problem, the court will allow the agency to provide general descriptions in the subpoena so that the agency's ability to find what it needs is not limited. Usually, the best a respondent can hope for is to make a careful and factual showing that the agency's informational need can be met with a narrower request, in which case the court may narrow the scope of the subpoena.

So if the Fourth Amendment does not provide much protection, what about the Fifth?

### (3)  Constitutional Limits: Fifth Amendment

The Fifth Amendment provides: "No person shall . . . be compelled in any criminal case to be a witness against himself." U.S. CONST., Amend. V. Because it is incorporated into the Fourteenth Amendment, the Fifth Amendment applies to federal, state, and local governments. *Andersen v. Maryland*, 427 U.S. 463, 470 (1976).

The prohibition against self-incrimination has historic roots in the field of criminal law, as is apparent from its text. While administrative agencies are not normally engaged in criminal law enforcement, the Amendment nevertheless may be relevant because administrative action may lead to criminal prosecution. While the agency may have only civil regulatory objectives when requesting oral or written information from a citizen or business owner, any information that is provided might later provide grounds for a criminal proceeding (think about a charge of tax evasion following a tax audit, for example).

The Fifth Amendment doctrine is very complex and in flux. In your courses in constitutional law and criminal procedure, you will explore some of its challenges in greater detail. Here, we touch briefly the doctrine's impact on administrative law, specifically as it protects against compelled testimony and production of documents.

In the administrative context, there are two important points to remember regarding the Fifth Amendment. First, the Fifth Amendment, like the Fourth, has been relaxed to meet the regulatory state's need for information. As with the Fourth Amendment, the trend of the cases has been unmistakably in the direction of reducing the protection the Fifth Amendment once provided, especially as it relates to the production of documents.

Second, the Amendment's historic roots go back to concerns about torture and coerced confessions. As a result, the Supreme Court has interpreted the Fifth Amendment to restrict principally the government's power to compel individuals to testify against themselves. Hence, if the Food and Drug Administration subpoenaed a business owner to testify about mislabeled drugs, that business owner may plead the Fifth Amendment if she believes that the answer to a question might lead to her criminal prosecution. The agency cannot penalize her for exercising her right, nor force her to testify absent a grant of immunity.

However, if the government grants immunity to a defendant, even over the defendant's objection, the Fifth Amendment's protection may be unavailable. The original 1893 statute granting such immunity protected a defendant from prosecution concerning the transaction about which the evidence related (transaction immunity). The Compulsory Testimony Act of 1893, 27 Stat. 443. The modern statute is much narrower, protecting the defendant only from the direct or indirect use of the evidence obtained in the document (use and derivative use immunity). 18 U.S.C. § 6002 (1994). If a prosecutor has evidence derived from a legitimate source wholly independent from the compelled testimony, the defendant may then be prosecuted. *See Kastigar v. United States*, 406 U.S. 441, 459 (1972) (reasoning that use and derivative use immunity are coextensive with the scope of the Fifth Amendment privilege).

In contrast, the Amendment is less protective of those individuals compelled to produce documents, no matter how incriminating those documents may be. Let's look more closely at the Fifth Amendment's requirements. Recall that the Fifth Amendment protects: (1) "persons" from being (2) "compelled" in (3) any criminal case to be a (4) "witness" against himself or herself. Let's look at each requirement in turn.

First, the term "persons" in the Fifth Amendment is interpreted literally. Because the Fifth Amendment was historically concerned with protecting individuals from forced confessions and torture, only natural persons can assert the right against self-incrimination. Although corporations have long been held to be "persons" for due process purposes, corporations are not "persons" within the meaning of the privilege against self-incrimination. *Wilson v. United States*, 221 U.S. 361, 390 (1911). The same is true of other so-called "artificial entities" such as partnerships, associations, and limited liability companies. In short, artificial entities cannot resist a subpoena on the ground that the documents or testimony sought could expose the entity to criminal prosecution. *Id.*

Moreover, when a business receives a subpoena *duces tecum*, a records custodian actually produces the documents on the business's behalf. Because these entities are not entitled to assert the privilege, the person who is the custodian of the business's records generally cannot assert the privilege either, even when disclosure of the documents would incriminate the custodian personally.

Because the owners of sole proprietorships are people, not artificial entities, you might think that their business and personal records would be protected. You would be wrong, as we will see as we explore the meaning of the other terms in the Amendment.

The second word in the Amendment that we will look at is "compelled." When applied to oral testimony, the Supreme Court has broadly interpreted "compelled." Although torture is not required, some form of forced compliance is, such as when the government threatens economic sanctions to obtain information. *Uniformed Sanitation Men Ass'n v. Commission of Sanitation*, 392 U.S. 280, 283–85 (1968) (holding that a government employee could not be prosecuted based on incriminating information that the employee gave under the threat of being fired); *Spevack v. Klein*, 385 U.S. 511, 515–16 (1967) (holding that someone holding a license to practice law could not be prosecuted based on information provided under threat of losing that license).

As it relates to the production of documents, the meaning of "compelled" has changed over time. Historically, when the government required a person to provide an incriminating document, the Court viewed such forced production as the equivalent of forcing someone to testify orally in a self-incriminating way. And the Fifth Amendment protected both. *Boyd v. United States*, 116 U.S. 616, 634–36 (1886).

With this background, the Supreme Court crafted the so-called "required records" doctrine, which is an exception to the Fifth Amendment's protections from disclosure. The required records doctrine denied Fifth Amendment protection to the production of "public records" that the government required an individual or an entity to keep. *Shapiro v. United States*, 335 U.S. 1, 34 (1948) (holding that various records a wholesaler of fruit and produce was obliged to keep under the Emergency Price Control Act were not protected from disclosure by the Fifth Amendment). Under the required records doctrine, an agency can obtain records an individual *involuntarily* created when the following three criteria were met:

> [F]irst, the purposes of the United States' inquiry must be essentially regulatory; second, information is to be obtained by requiring the preservation of records of a kind which the regulated party has customarily kept, and third, the records themselves must have assumed "public aspects" which render them at least analogous to public documents.

*Grosso v. United States*, 390 U.S. 62, 57 (1968) (holding that the doctrine did not apply to information sought from gamblers because the government cannot require recordkeeping of a selective group inherently suspected of criminal activity); *accord, Marchetti v. United States*, 390 U.S. 39, 57 (1968) (same regarding owners of sawed-off shotguns).

In crafting the required records doctrine, the Court reasoned that a person could not complain about being forced to produce a document that she was required as a member of a regulated industry to keep and to allow the government to access. *Shapiro*, 335 U.S. at 34. Because the individual created the document as a result of a lawful regulatory regime and voluntarily entered that regime, protection from self-incrimination was unnecessary. *See Smith v. Richert*, 35 F.3d 300, 301–02 (7th Cir. 1994) (describing this history).

But then the Supreme Court decided a new case, which held that the forced production of a self-incriminating document was not compulsion to testify unless the author had been forced to write the document. *Fisher v. United States*, 425 U.S. 391, 407–09 (1976). The Court reasoned that there was no compulsion because the government did not compel the author to give utterance to or record the information. Remember that the Fifth Amendment was concerned about the government beating confessions out of defendants. Under *Fisher,* then, the government could force individuals to produce *voluntarily* created documents, because the author voluntarily chose to create and include within them potentially self-incriminating information.

Because most information is voluntarily created, the Fifth Amendment does not protect their subsequent production. *United States v. Doe*, 465 U.S. 605, 610–11 (1984). For example, think of the many documents you create or keep to determine your tax liability. Other than W-2s, the government does not require much, if any, of this documentation, yet you create and maintain it anyway. And as Judge Posner has said, "A statute that merely requires a taxpayer to maintain records necessary to determine his liability for personal income tax is not within the scope of the required records doctrine." *Smith*, 35 F.3d at 303. To be created involuntarily, the statutory requirement to create the record must be more specific than that.

Hence, because most documents are voluntarily created, this "compulsion-equals-forced-drafting" interpretation greatly reduced the agency's need to resort to the required records exception. *CFTC v. Collins*, 997 F.2d 1230, 1232–34 (7th Cir. 1993). However, one time the exception came in handy was when an individual asserted that *the act of production* itself would be testimonial and, thus, should be protected.

The act of production exception provides that while the contents of a document may not be privileged because it was voluntarily produced, the very act of producing the document may be privileged. *United States v. Hubbell*, 530 U.S. 27 (2000); *Braswell v. United States*, 487 U.S. 99, 117–18 (1988). For example, assume that a subpoena demanded that someone produce all documents concerning a particular subject, like their tax liability. When a witness is required to produce a document (such as a W-2), the witness's act of production is an implied admission that the document exists, that it is authentic, and that it is in the witness's possession or control. By producing a W-2, the witness would be acknowledging three things: he received the W-2, it was a valid W-2, and that he thus should have reported at least the income identified in that W-2.

If these acknowledgments would be self-incriminating and the witness *voluntarily* created or maintained the documents (employers create W-2's, not taxpayers), then the witness could not be compelled to produce the documents under the Fifth Amendment's act of production doctrine. *Fisher*, 425 U.S. at 409–14; *Doe v. United States*, 487 U.S. 201, 209–10 (1984). Note that whether the act of producing documents in a particular case is testimonial will "depend on the facts and circumstances of particular cases or classes thereof." *Fisher*, 425 U.S. at 410; *see generally* Robert P. Mosteller, *Simplifying Subpoena Law: Taking the Fifth Amendment Seriously*, 73 VA. L. REV. 1 (1987) (noting that the lower courts have difficulty applying the law in this area consistently).

But if these acknowledgments would be self-incriminating and the witness *involuntarily* created or maintained the documents, then the witness could be compelled to produce the documents because they would fall within the required documents exception. The act of production exception would not apply because producing the documents would only show that that the regulatory program required that the records be created or maintained and that the business created or maintained the records as required. *In re Two Grand Jury Subpoena*, 793 F.2d 69, 73 (2d Cir. 1986) (holding that the W-2s are not shielded from production). Hence, the required documents exception is little used today.

The third phrase we will look at in the Fifth Amendments is "in any criminal case." The Supreme Court has interpreted this phrase broadly to include civil cases as well as criminal. Individuals cannot be compelled to testify in any proceeding when providing information could incriminate that individual in a future criminal proceeding. So, for example, prisoners can assert the Fifth Amendment so that they need not testify in prison disciplinary proceedings. *Lefkowitz v. Turley*, 414 U.S. 70, 77 (1973); *Spevack*, 385 U.S. at 515–16 (holding that attorneys could assert the privilege in disbarment proceedings).

The fourth phrase we will look at in the Fifth Amendment is "be a witness against himself." The Court has narrowly interpreted this phrase in two ways. First, one person cannot assert the privilege against self-incrimination on behalf of another. *Fisher*, 425 U.S. at 396 (holding that an accountant could not assert the Fifth Amendment on behalf of a client taxpayer).

Second, the privilege protects only the type of information a witness would traditionally provide, specifically, evidence that has some testimonial aspect. Most documents do not have a testimonial aspect. Documents do have a testimonial aspect when they communicate something that is in the mind of the person who produced them. For example, diaries are testimonial, for they convey the drafter's thoughts. In contrast, compulsory blood samples are not testimonial, because they communicate physical information about the owner's body, rather than what is in the owner's mind. *United States v. Patane*, 542 U.S. 630, 644 (2004) (holding that compulsory blood samples are not protected by the Fifth Amendment). Most documents contain information, not thoughts.

Summarizing the above information, the Fifth Amendment provides very limited protection in the administrative context. Regarding oral *testimony*, the Fifth Amendment provides the most protection. It protects individuals from being compelled to testify against themselves.

Regarding the production of *documents*, the Fifth Amendment provides very little protection: the Fifth Amendment does not protect artificial entities from producing incriminating business records; it does not protect the custodian of business records from producing incriminating records, even when the custodian would be implicated personally; it does not protect the owners of sole proprietorships from producing *involuntarily* created public records; and it does not protect the owners of sole proprietorships from producing *voluntarily* created documents unless the act of production itself would be incriminating.

We turn now to a discussion about physical inspections.

## 2. Physical Inspections

### a. Voluntary Compliance

Suppose you receive a phone call from a client who tells you there is an agency inspector at her door seeking entrance to her residence or place of business. In response to your question, you are told the inspector does not have a warrant. The client asks you whether she should allow if the inspector in.

As with subpoenas, a lawyer's first instinct might be to tell the client no, do not let the inspector in without a warrant. After all, the government should not be able to intrude on a private residence or a private place of business without a judge's conclusion that the intrusion is authorized and appropriate. A judge is a neutral arbiter in such situations and legitimizes any search. Shouldn't an agency inspector have a warrant? The answer is yes, but the probable cause supporting the warrant is significantly lessened in administrative searches, as we will see.

In the last section we discussed the benefits and costs of voluntary compliance with a subpoena. The benefits and costs are similar here. Benefits of resistance include the following: (1) you might buy your client some time;

(2) you might discourage the agency from pursuing the inspection, if the agency lacks legal authority; (3) you might force the agency to limit the scope of the inspection or clarify the information sought; and (4) you might preserve your client's legal objection to allowing the search, which is generally waived if consent is given.

But most clients comply with the inspection because non-compliance has costs, including: (1) negative publicity (e.g., *"Jane's Peanut Manufacturer Refuses to Allow Health Inspector In"* may not be a headline your client would welcome), and (2) a lack of goodwill in the future from the agency both short and long term, which may affect your client's profitability and ability to stay in business. Remember that your client will have a long-term regulatory relationship with the agency; good relationships with agency staff, including inspectors, can be valuable. Thus, you might prefer to negotiate with the agency to narrow the inspection's scope or request increased time for your client to comply.

### b. Involuntary Compliance

#### (1) Statutory Limits

If resistance seems a useful strategy, you will have to consider whether there are legal grounds for resistance. The first question, always, is agency statutory authority. Agencies have no inherent powers, so Congress must give the agency power to inspect in the enabling statute. An inspection that takes place must be consistent with any procedural requirements set out in the enabling statute or the agency's own rules. The statute and agency rules will let you know whether the agency has authority to conduct the inspection in this way, at this time, by this inspector, for this purpose, to this degree, and in this manner.

In addition to statutory grounds for resistance, there may be constitutional grounds, specifically the Fourth Amendment. In your courses in constitutional law and criminal procedure you will discuss this amendment in greater detail. Here we examine how this amendment is relevant to administrative searches.

#### (2) Constitutional Limits: Fourth Amendment

Recall that the Fourth Amendment provides as follows:

> The right of the people to be secure in their persons, houses, papers, and effects, against unreasonable searches and seizures, shall not be violated, and no Warrants shall issue, but upon probable cause, supported by Oath or affirmation, and particularly describing the place to be searched, and the persons or things to be seized.

U.S. Const. Amend IV. Recall further that it applies to the states by way of the Fourteenth Amendment. Note three things about the Fourth Amendment's language. First, the Amendment does not prohibit all searches; it only prohibits "unreasonable" searches. Second, the Amendment does not require that a warrant be issued in all cases. But the existence of a warrant is an important element in assessing the reasonableness of a search: in other words, a search pursuant to a warrant is presumed to be reasonable. Finally, the Amendment specifies the conditions for issuance of a warrant, namely: (1) that there be probable cause, and (2) that the warrant be relatively specific in its scope.

In 1959, the Supreme Court held that administrative inspections could be reasonable within the meaning of the Fourth Amendment even if there was no warrant. *Frank v. Maryland*, 359 U.S. 360, 366–67 (1959). The Court reasoned in *Frank* that Fourth Amendment protections were principally concerned with protecting citizens in a criminal rather than in an administrative context. As a result, the Amendment's requirements could be relaxed somewhat in the administrative sphere.

This holding did not last long, for it became clear to the Court that even absent criminal sanctions an individual could suffer serious disadvantages as a result of an administrative inspection. Hence, in 1967, the Court reversed itself and held that a search warrant was required before an administrative inspection of a residence or place of business. *See v. Seattle*, 387 U.S. 541, 545 (1967); *Camara v. Municipal Court*, 387 U.S. 523, 533 (1967).

However, the Court softened the "probable cause" requirement to make it easier for an agency to get a warrant. Specifically, the Court allowed agencies to obtain administrative warrants even when the agency did not have specific knowledge that the individual or business was violating the law. *See Marshall v. Barlow's, Inc.*, 436 U.S. 307, 320 (1978) (explaining that the "[p]robable cause justifying the issuance of a warrant [in the administrative context] may be based not only on specific evidence of an existing violation but also on a showing that reasonable legislative or administrative standards for conducting an . . . inspection are satisfied.").

Thus, an agency can request a warrant on the basis of a reasonable agency plan of periodic or area inspections. For example, in *Camara*, 387 U.S. at 538, the Court held that inspectors did have to get a warrant before they could search an apartment for violations of a city housing code; however, the inspectors did not have to show cause that they would find violations at the particular apartment they wanted to inspect. Instead, the inspectors had to show that the inspection complied with "reasonable legislative or administrative standards." *Id.* at 539. In other words, the inspection could occur without evidence of wrongdoing.

In sum, if the agency has a program that inspects businesses in a particular industry annually, a judge would issue a warrant to inspect a client's business if a year had passed since the agency's last inspection. The agency need not allege or show that it believes the business was violating the law. However, the agency's search must still be "reasonable"; that requirement remains. To be considered a reasonable search, the agency's program for searching businesses within an industry must be neutral and the agency's inspectors must be respectful of the regulated entity's convenience, privacy, and dignity concerns.

A warrant is not required for every search. There are several well-recognized exceptions to the warrant requirement, including: (1) searches of locations in plain view, (2) searches in emergency situations, (3) searches subject to consent, and (4) searches of "closely," or "pervasively," regulated businesses.

The first exception is that a warrant is not needed when the agency searches parts of a business that are open to the public or in "plain view." Government inspections of such places in plain view are not "searches" within the meaning of the Fourth Amendment. Such inspections are not searches because individuals do not have a reasonable expectation of privacy in the searched location. *See, e.g., Air Pollution Variance Bd. v. Western Alfalfa Corp.*, 416 U.S. 861, 864–65 (1974) (upholding an inspection of factory emissions from smokestacks when those emissions were visible from outside the factory).

The second exception is that a warrant is not needed when there is an emergency situation and the agency has statutory authority to conduct searches in emergencies. *See, e.g., North Am. Cold Storage Co. v. Chicago,* 211 U.S. 306 (1908) (allowing seizure of unwholesome food); *Jacobson v. Massachusetts,* 197 U.S. 11 (1905) (allowing compulsory smallpox vaccination); *Campagnie Francaise De Navigation À Vapeur v. Louisiana State Bd. of Health,* 186 U.S. 380 (1902) (allowing health quarantine). "Emergency" means that the agency reasonably believes that an immediate inspection is necessary to protect life, health, or property. As you might imagine, there has been considerable litigation over what constitutes an emergency sufficient to permit a warrantless search. For example, in *Michigan v. Tyler,* 436 U.S. 499, 509 (1978), the Supreme Court held that emergency officials could enter a burning building to extinguish the blaze and seize evidence of arson that was in plain view.

The third exception is that a warrant is not needed when the owner provides "informed" consent to the search. Indeed, as noted above, few inspections are actually based on a warrant because most individuals and businesses give consent to a search. Moreover, many trade and industry groups advise their members to consent to searches absent unusual circumstances that might justify refusal. Agencies prefer searches subject to consent, in part, because the inspector may be able to inspect more broadly with consent than with a warrant, which specifies the *what* and *where* of the search. Warrants tend to be more specific in scope and authority. However, in the situation in which a statute allows an agency to inspect a business when the agency receives complaints about that business, the scope of the search will generally be limited to the allegations in the complaint.

The Supreme Court has turned to the consent rationale to lessen the warrant requirements in specific situations in which the agency officials have special relationships to those being searched, such as prisons, hospitals, and schools. For example, in *Vernonia School District 47J v. Acton*, 515 U.S. 646, 664–65 (1995), the Court held that public school student athletes could be subject to urinalysis testing because they elected to participate in school activities. Then, in *Board of Education v. Earls*, 536 U.S. 822, 837–38 (2002), the Court extended *Vernonia School District*'s holding to all public school students who wished to participate in after-school activities. In *Pottawatomie*, the Court reasoned that students' privacy interests are limited when they attend public school and they voluntarily choose to participate in after-school activities. In addition, the Court reasoned that the degree of intrusion was minimal, while the government's interest in preventing children from using drugs was very strong. *Id.* at 833–35.

However, this implied consent rationale is not unlimited. The Court more recently held that the strip-search of a 13-year-old girl by public school officials who were searching for drugs violated the Fourth Amendment. *Safford Unified School District #1 v. Redding*, 557 U.S. 364, 376 (2009). The Court reasoned that in the public school setting, suspicion well short of probable cause would permit school officials to search a student's backpack and outer clothing, but school officials needed a substantially stronger suspicion before searching more deeply.

The fourth exception to the warrant requirement is that a warrant is not needed when the agency searches businesses that are "closely"—the Court also uses the term "pervasively"—regulated. *Colonnade Catering Corp. v. United States*, 397 U.S. 72 (1970) (allowing warrantless search of liquor licensee); *United States v. Biswell*, 406 U.S. 311 (1972) (allowing warrantless search of gun dealer). This exception is also known as the *Colonnade-Biswell* exception because of the two cases that developed the exception. In crafting this exception, the Court reasoned that such businesses have a long tradition of close government regulation and supervision and, thus, have a lower expectation of privacy than other businesses. The closely regulated business exception to the warrant requirement is essentially an outgrowth of the waiver/consent doctrine: by voluntarily engaging in a heavily regulated business, business owners give up their privacy expectations.

For the exception to apply, the business must be one that is subject to "pervasive regulation" and "long term government supervision." But these criteria are not very helpful. For example, warrants are still required in some industries despite extensive and detailed (pervasive?) regulation; for example, a manufacturing plant subject to quite detailed OSHA regulation. *See Marshall*, 436 U.S. at 323 (1978). Alternatively, some businesses have been subject to warrantless searches even though they have not been part of a long tradition of close government supervision. *See, e.g., Donovan v. Dewey*, 452 U.S. 594 (1981) (stone quarries); *New York v. Burger*, 482 U.S. 691, 707 (1987) (junkyards engaging in vehicle dismantling). To date, the following businesses have been found to be closely regulated: *Colonnade Catering Corp.*, 397 U.S. at 77 (liquor dealers); *Biswell*, 406 U.S. at 315 (weapon dealers); *Donovan*, 452 U.S. at 602–03 (stone quarries); *Burger*, 482 U.S. at 707 (junkyards engaging in vehicle dismantling). The Court appears to want to limit Congress's ability to authorize warrantless searches to settings where the business's legitimate expectations of privacy are outweighed by the government's need for prompt, even unannounced, searches. Consider Figure 7.1.

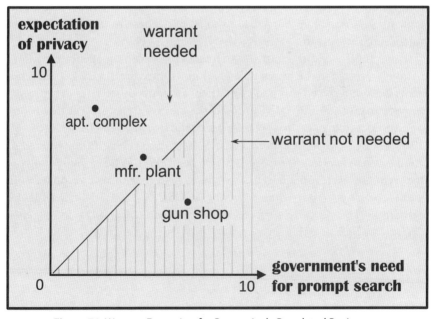

**Figure 7.1** Warrant Exception for Persuasively Regulated Businesses

Expectations of privacy are inferred from tradition, convention, history, and the absence of public notice that unannounced inspections are possible. Thus, one would normally have an expectation of privacy in the case of one's personal residence or rental home. However, one would not have an expectation of privacy in respect to that part of business premises already open to the public, such as a lobby in a hotel. And a quick inspection may be important where the danger risk is special or where frustration of the regulatory goals seems possible. Thus, a stone quarry might present risks of special physical danger where prompt inspection may be important. And an automobile junkyard may be a market for stolen vehicles and parts, where an unexpected search may be necessary to prevent destruction of incriminating evidence.

Warrantless searches are, of course, subject to abuse. Without a neutral arbiter issuing a warrant that specifies the place to be searched and the persons or things to be seized, there is little to restrain an inspector from abusing the power. For that reason, the Court has limited warrantless searches to situations where the authorizing law provides protection to the property owner that is somewhat equivalent to a warrant. The Court has said that the agency's inspection program must make it clear to the business owner that the inspector is performing the search according to law, and the program must limit the inspecting officer's discretion with respect to the time, place, and scope of the inspection. *Burger*, 482 U.S. at 691. These restrictions serve the function of the warrant.

If an unlawful administrative search takes place, can the agency use information it received in the search in later administrative hearings? The Supreme Court has not resolved this issue, and there are some differences in the lower courts. Because administrative proceedings are civil in nature, the exclusionary rule does not generally apply. *United States v. Janis*, 428 U.S. 433, 459–60 (1976); *see INS v. Lopez-Mendoza*, 468 U.S. 1032, 1033 (1984); *Pennsylvania Bd. of Probation & Parole v. Scott*, 524 U.S. 357, 363 (1998). When a civil penalty is involved, however, some lower courts have held that the exclusionary rule applies. *See, e.g., Trinity Industries, Inc. v. OSHRC*, 16 F.3d 1455, 1461–62 (6th Cir. 1994); *Lakeland Enters. of Rhinelander, Inc. v. Chao*, 402 F.3d 739, 744–45 (7th Cir. 2005).

# B. Information Flowing to the Public:

## 1. The Freedom of Information Act

### a. Requirements

All this information flowing into agencies has resulted in the accumulation of massive amounts of written and electronic material. The National Archives have three million cubic feet of documents and five billion electronic data records, and this amount is only going to increase. P. STEPHEN GIDIERE, THE FEDERAL INFORMATION MANUAL: HOW THE GOVERNMENT COLLECTS, MANAGES, AND DISCLOSES INFORMATION UNDER FOIA AND OTHER STATUTES 1–2 (2006). Often, individuals outside of the government would like to access the government's information. How do they do so?

Making information available to citizens is a complex process. Congress, the president, the regulatory agencies, the media, and special interest groups all take part. Multiple statutes are involved, including the Freedom of Information Act (5 U.S.C § 552), the Privacy Act (436 U.S. 499, 509 (1978), 5 U.S.C § 552a), the Paperwork Reduction Act (44 U.S.C. § 3501), the Classified Information Act (18 U.S.C. App.3 §§ 1–16), the Information Quality Act (44 U.S.C. § 3516), the Presidential Records Act (44 U.S.C. § 2111), and other acts with special disclosure provisions, such as the National Environmental Policy Act (42 U.S.C. § 4321) and the Clean Air Act (42 U.S.C. § 7401). Understandably, we cannot cover all of these in this book. So we will focus on the most commonly used statutes.

The broadest of these acts is the Freedom of Information Act (FOIA, pronounced "foy-uh."). FOIA's purpose is to ensure the citizenry is informed of government activity. One way FOIA accomplishes its purpose is to allow individuals, organizations, and businesses to obtain information from agencies for almost any reason, good or bad.

FOIA is part of the APA and is codified in section 552. Section 551 contains the APA's definitions, and sections 553–557 contain the APA's rulemaking and adjudication requirements. Additionally, the Privacy Act is codified in section 552a and the Government in Sunshine Act is codified in 552b. With so much statutory material between section 551 and the most important sections of the APA for your class in administrative law (sections 553–57), likely your statutory supplement relocated FOIA to follow the rulemaking and adjudication provisions; but in the code, FOIA comes before these provisions. Understanding FOIA's development will help you understand its odd location.

FOIA began life as a brief sentence in the section 3 of the original APA (codified in section 552; hence, its current placement). That section provided that except for records "requiring secrecy . . . or . . . relating to the internal management of the agency . . . matters of official record shall . . . be made available to persons properly and directly concerned, except information held confidential for good cause found." Pub. L. 89-554, § 1, 80 Stat. 383 (codified as amended at 5 U.S.C. § 552 (1966)). This section gave the agency tremendous discretion to withhold information, and courts were not anxious to interfere with this discretion.

But concerns about agency and executive branch secrecy began to emerge in the 1950s and 1960s. As a result, a number of disclosure statute drafts were introduced. FOIA was adopted in 1966; the Privacy Act and Sunshine Act were adopted in the 1970s. Since its enactment, FOIA has been amended several times, almost always to broaden disclosure requirements and withdraw agency discretion to withhold information. The amendments reflect the tension between Congress's wish for more executive branch disclosure and the executive branch's resistance to increased disclosure. For example, in 1974, Congress amended FOIA to address concerns about the excessive delays requesters (those requesting information from the government) experienced, the excessive user fees that agencies charged for providing information, and other implementation difficulties. President Ford vetoed the bill; however, Congress overrode his veto. Pub. L. 93-502, §§ 1–3, 88 Stat. 1561, 1563–1564 (codified as amended at 5 U.S.C. § 552 (1974)).

FOIA's basic principle is that secrecy is bad while openness and transparency are good; hence, maximum disclosure is required. But there are limits. Some information cannot be made public without jeopardizing national security, causing injury to citizens supplying the information, or invading personal privacy. To balance these concerns, the drafters chose a drafting strategy that would maximize disclosure while protecting specific information. The Act requires that agencies provide all information, subject to specific exemptions. Further, Congress drafted these exemptions narrowly to include only material whose disclosure would be dangerous or harmful.

So much for its purposes. What are the mechanics? FOIA makes agencies provide information to the public in three ways: (1) by publishing certain information in the Federal Register, (2) by making certain information available for inspection and copying, and (3) by responding to requests.

First, FOIA requires that agencies publish certain information in the Federal Register. APA § 552(a)(1). Such information includes agency descriptions, addresses, rules of procedure, and forms for all reports and examinations. In addition, this section directs the agency to publish "substantive rules of general applicability . . . and statements of general policy or interpretations." APA § 552(a)(1)(D). Thus, FOIA provides for publication of agency rules.

Second, FOIA also requires that agencies make certain information available for inspection and copying, including all final opinions and orders in adjudicated cases. APA § 552(a)(2). Full indexing is required for ease of access, and the act provides that matters not properly published or indexed are not binding on the public unless the persons have actual notice of them.

Third, the better known requirement in FOIA is that agencies must make records available upon request. The operative language of the Act provides: "[E]ach agency, upon request for records which . . . reasonably describe such records . . . shall make such records promptly available to any person." APA § 552(a)(3)(A). Notice the breadth of this statement: all "agencies" "shall" make "records" "promptly" available to "any person." Let's look at each of these terms.

FOIA contains its own definition of "Agencies." APA 552(f). This definition is broader than the one in APA § 551(1). FOIA's definition of agencies includes both executive branch and independent agencies. Additionally, the definition includes government-owned and government-controlled corporations and the Executive office; however, FOIA does not apply to the president, his or her personal staff, and to entities that exist solely to advise the president, such as the National Security Council and the Council of Economic Advisors. *See Kissinger v. Reporters Comm. for Freedom of the Press*, 445 U.S. 136 (1980). FOIA agencies do not include the many private organizations operating under federal contracts or supported by federal funds. Finally, the term does not cover Congress or the federal courts.

Additionally, FOIA says the agency "shall" make the records available. "Shall" is mandatory language, meaning that the agency has no discretion to withhold the information once it has been requested and assuming there is no exception prohibiting its disclosure. The exemptions are discussed below. The agency has twenty days to determine whether an exception applies and to notify the requester whether the agency will comply with the request. APA § 552(a)(6)(A)(i). Assuming the agency will comply, it must then "promptly" make the records available to the requester.

Despite these statutory deadlines, the reality is that agencies often do not respond promptly to FOIA requests. In 1996 and 2007, Congress amended FOIA to try to speed up agency response times. Specifically, in 1996, Congress allowed multitrack processing so that simple FOIA requests could leapfrog over more complex FOIA requests. APA § 552(a)(6)(D)(i). And in 2007, Congress amended FOIA to prohibit agencies from collecting fees when they fail to comply promptly. APA § 552(a)(4)(A)(vii). While the APA's text and amendments show congressional intent to require prompt compliance, courts have been understanding of agency delay caused by workload considerations and resource limits.

The Act does not define the term "records." Because the judicial enforcement provision for FOIA authorizes a court to order the agency to produce
"any *agency* records improperly withheld" from a requester (APA § 552(a)(4)
(B) (emphasis added)), the Supreme Court interpreted the provisions *in pari
materia* to hold that FOIA obligates an agency to produce only agency records.
Agency records are records in any format that the agency either has already
created or has obtained in the legitimate conduct of its official duties. *DOJ v.
Tax Analysts*, 492 U.S. 136, 144–45 (1989) (holding that FOIA required the
agency to provide copies of court opinions that it received in the course of litigating tax cases). Additionally, the agency must have the record in its possession at the time the request is made; the agency need not obtain information
if the agency no longer has the information or never had it to begin with. *Kissinger*, 445 U.S. at 139.

Further, private documents submitted to and within the control of an
agency are "records" under FOIA. However, the personal records of agency
officials (calendars, phone logs) that happen to be located in an agency office
are not FOIA records unless the documents were created for official use. *Kissinger*, 445 U.S. at 157.

FOIA is user-friendly. The requester need not identify the records precisely,
by providing, for example, the exact title and date it was created. The requester
need only "reasonably describe the record." Then, the agency must make a
good faith search of its files, including electronic files, for the requested records.
*See* APA §§ 552(a)(3)(C) & (D). Courts have not been especially generous
to agencies whose search efforts were perceived as inadequate. *Weisberg v. DOJ*,
705 F.2d 1344, 1348 (D.C. Cir. 1983) (affirming summary judgment as "fully
appropriate" after the plaintiff won four separate appeals due to the government's insufficient searches).

"Any person" may make a FOIA request. The Act defines the phrase "any
person" broadly, to include any "individual, partnership, corporation, association, or public or private organization other than an agency." APA § 551(2). The
phrase includes foreign governments and aliens, although since 9/11, Congress
has placed some limits on the ability of foreign governments to obtain records. APA § 552(a)(3)(E)(i). This broad definition replaced the narrow definition in the original section 3 ("persons properly and directly concerned"). In
addition, Congress removed the requirement that the person requesting the
records be motivated by a "proper" purpose. Subject to only a couple of narrow exceptions, the purpose of the requester is not relevant to the obligation
to disclose. Persons can compel disclosure simply because they are curious,
they are seeking information for competitive advantage, or they want to

embarrass or injure others. As the D.C. Circuit has said, "Congress granted the scholar and the scoundrel equal rights of access to federal records under the FOIA." *Durns v. Bureau of Prisons*, 804 F.2d 701, 706 (D.C. Cir. 1986).

As we close out what FOIA requires when information must be disclosed, there is one last thing to consider. In some situations, agencies may impose reasonable charges for their costs in searching and copying records. APA § 552(a)(4)(A)(ii). For example, agencies may charge reasonable fees for document search, duplication, and review, when records are requested for commercial use. APA § 552(a)(4)(A)(ii)(I).

### b. Exemptions

Not all information must be disclosed. FOIA contains nine types of information that have been exempted: (1) classified information; (2) internal agency personnel rules and practices; (3) matters that another statute specifically exempts from disclosure; (4) trade secrets and commercial or financial information that the agency obtained from someone other than the requester; (5) interagency or intra-agency memoranda and letters, not otherwise available through discovery in a civil action against the agency; (6) personnel files, medical files, and similar files, the disclosure of which would constitute a clearly unwarranted invasion of personal privacy; (7) records and information compiled for law enforcement purposes; (8) matters related to the regulation of banks and other financial institutions; and (9) geological and geophysical information. APA § 552(b)(1)-(9). With these exemptions, Congress attempted the difficult job of identifying the material whose disclosure would be dangerous or harmful. Let's look at each exemption, remembering that the government bears the burden of proving that an exemption applies.

Exemption 1 provides that agencies need not disclose "matters that are . . . specifically authorized under criteria established by an Executive order to be kept secret in the interest of national defense or foreign policy and . . . are in fact properly classified pursuant to such Executive order." APA § 552(b)(1). This exemption covers classified material where disclosure could impact national security. The exemption is worded in such a way as to make the decision whether to classify a document itself subject to judicial review. The only documents exempted are those properly classified under criteria established in advance by executive order. The judicial inquiry about the propriety of the classification extends to the question of whether the need for classification of a particular document still exists. Courts are specifically permitted to examine the disputed documents in camera both to review the propriety of the classification and to determine whether some parts of the document might be released. Despite this brave effort by Congress to enlist the courts as partners in the disclosure mission, courts have been reluctant—especially in recent times—to require disclosure of any material that plausibly could have a negative impact on national security.

Exemption 2 provides that agencies need not disclose information "related solely to internal personnel rules and practices" of the agency. APA § 552(b)(2). This exemption is not controversial when one is talking about purely internal matters, such as office decoration, computer use, and sick leave policies. But many matters of internal management can have a dramatic effect on the public, such as operating rules, guidelines, and procedural rules for adjudicating cases. The Supreme Court has required disclosure of such information where there is a significant public need for it and where there is no showing that disclosure would significantly risk circumvention of agency regulations (e.g., by disclosing agency investigative techniques). *Department of Air Force v. Rose*, 425 U.S. 352, 369–70 (1976). Lower courts continue to struggle with whether there is a public need for the information and tend not to require disclosure of law enforcement guides and manuals, for example. *Crooker v. Bureau of Alcohol, Tobacco & Firearms*, 670 F.2d 1051, 1703 (D.C. Cir. 1981) *abrogated in part by Milner v. Department of the Navy*, 562 U.S. 562 (2011).

Exemption 3 provides that agencies need not disclose "matters that are . . . specifically exempted from disclosure by [another] statute." APA § 552(b)(3). This exemption allows an agency to withhold information when a statute other than FOIA explicitly so authorizes. How explicit must the withholding statute be? This exemption only allows withholding if the statute on which the agency relies leaves the agency with no discretion in the matter ("the agency shall not release") or identifies specific criteria for withholding the information that the agency has followed. A number of statutes have been held to contain the necessary specificity, including statutes governing the CIA, the Census Bureau, and the Internal Revenue Service. *See generally* RICHARD PIERCE ET AL., ADMINISTRATIVE LAW & PROCESS 381–82 (6th ed. 2014).

Exemption 4 provides that agencies need not disclose "matters that are . . . trade secrets and commercial or financial information obtained from a person and privileged or confidential." APA § 552(b)(4). This exemption allows an agency to withhold certain types of information the agency obtains from a "submitter" who does not want the agency to disclose that information to others (e.g., to a "requester" who is a business competitor of the submitter). The exemption was drafted in a way that left many questions unanswered; it has a number of "ors" and "ands." A flow chart might look something like Figure 7.2.

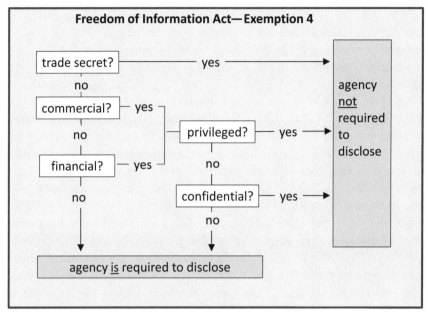

**Figure 7.2** The Fourth Exemption in the Freedom of Information Act

The courts have struggled with determining when commercial and financial information is confidential. Is the information confidential when the submitter claims the material is confidential? That would, of course, mean that the agency would disclose very little, because most submitters would make that claim. Or should a more objective test be used? In one leading case, the D.C. Circuit opted for an objective test: a matter is regarded as confidential within the meaning of Exemption 4 if (1) disclosing the information would impair the government's ability to obtain information in the future (e.g., by making later submitters less likely to volunteer information), or (2) if disclosure of the information would cause substantial competitive harm to the submitter. *National Parks v. Morton*, 498 F.2d 765, 768 (D.C. Cir. 1974).

In later cases, some courts have drawn a distinction between information submitted voluntarily and information obtained by compulsion. *Critical Mass Energy Project v. NRC*, 830 F.2d 278, 284 (D.C. Cir. 1987). If the information was obtained by compulsion, a court applies *National Parks'* objective test. But if the information was submitted voluntarily, the court applies a subjective test to determine whether the information is confidential. Pursuant to the subjective test, the agency has no obligation to disclose information the submitter itself regards and customarily treated as confidential. *Id.* at 281–83. Most agencies have rules that require submitters to identify any material they want kept confidential. Further, these rules require the agency to notify submitters if any material so identified has been requested and allow the submitter to participate in some fashion in the decision of whether to disclose the information.

An agency may wish to disclose material even if it is within one of the exemptions. May an agency do so? In other words, does the fact that there is an exemption in the FOIA for confidential records authorize a court to stop an agency from disclosing information that falls within the exemption? Such a suit is known as a "reverse FOIA" lawsuit. Under a reverse FOIA claim, a submitter would sue to stop an agency from disclosing material the submitter believed should be exempt.

But the Court rejected such lawsuits. The Court held that FOIA only requires disclosure and cannot be used to prohibit disclosure. *Chrysler v. Brown*, 441 U.S. 281, 285 (1979). So if a submitter provides trade secret information to an agency and a business competitor requests disclosure of that information from the agency, the agency need not disclose the information under Exemption 4. But the agency may choose to disclose the information if it wishes, and the submitter has no ability to sue under FOIA to stop disclosure. However, all is not lost. Possibly acts other than FOIA prohibit disclosure. For example, the Trade Secrets Act prohibits disclosure of trade secrets. 18 U.S.C. § 1905. The Court in *Chrysler* held that if another act prohibits disclosure, then the submitter can seek to prevent the agency's disclosure under the other act or under the Administrative Procedure Act. 441 U.S. at 285.

Exemption 5 provides that agencies need not disclose "matters that are . . . inter-agency or intra-agency memorandums or letters which would not be available by law to a party other than an agency in litigation with the agency." APA § 552(b)(5). This exemption exempts inter- or intra-agency memoranda that reflect the agency's internal decision-making processes. The exemption is premised on the belief that too much disclosure of the internal agency decision-making processes would reduce the candor and effectiveness of the agency's deliberation. Instead of trying to define this category of information in FOIA, Congress essentially adopted existing rules about disclosure that courts had developed to protect agency deliberations. Accordingly, Exemption 5 exempts information that would "fall within the ambit of a privilege against [disclosure] under judicial standards that would govern litigation against the agency that holds it." *DOI v. Klamath Water Users Protective Ass'n*, 532 U.S. 1, 8 (2001). Hence, an agency need not disclose information that would ordinarily be protected in litigation, such as government deliberations within the "executive privilege," certain attorney/client communications, and attorney work product.

For Exemption 5, judges distinguish between "pre-decisional" records and "post-decisional" records. Pre-decisional records are those made before the agency makes a decision and are protected from disclosure to further candid deliberations within the agency. Post-decisional records are those made after the agency makes a decision. They describe the rationale or interpretation of the decision that, being part of the agency's substantive law, are not protected from disclosure. *NLRB v. Sears*, 421 U.S. 132, 153–54 (1975).

Exemption 6 provides that agencies need not disclose "personnel and medical files and similar files the disclosure of which would constitute a clearly unwarranted invasion of personal privacy." APA § 552(b)(6). With this exemption Congress tried to protect the personal privacy of those whose information is submitted to the government. To decide whether a specific disclosure would be "clearly unwarranted," a court will balance the injury that disclosure would inflict on the individual with the public's interest in disclosure. In balancing these competing interests, the only relevant reason for disclosure is that disclosure would contribute to the public's understanding of the operations of government. Thus, if the requested disclosure shows nothing about the government's actions, there is nothing on the public interest side of the scale and disclosure will not be required. *Hertzberg v. Veneman*, 273 F. Supp. 2d 67, 86 (D.C. Cir. 2003) (disclosure of names of fire victims would shed no light on how government responded; hence, the names may be withheld). Note that the balancing test of Exemption 6 is one of the few places in FOIA where the identity and the motives *of the requester* may be relevant to the decision to disclose. Exemption 7 is another.

Exemption 7 provides that agencies need not disclose "records or information compiled for law enforcement purposes [in six specific situations identified below]." APA § 552(b)(7). This exemption seeks to protect legitimate law enforcement activities from unnecessary disclosure. An agency may withhold information compiled for law enforcement purposes if disclosure:

(A) could reasonably be expected to interfere with enforcement proceedings,
(B) would deprive a person of a right to a fair trial or impartial adjudication,
(C) could reasonably be expected to constitute an unwarranted invasion of personal privacy,

(D) could reasonably be expected to disclose the identity of a confidential source, . . .

(E) would disclose techniques and procedures for law enforcement investigations or prosecutions . . . if such disclosure would risk circumvention of the law, or

(F) could reasonably be expected to endanger the life or physical safety of any individual [law enforcement personnel, witnesses, etc.]

APA §§ 552(b)(7)(A)-(F). This important exemption has been amended multiple times. Originally, Exemption 7 was blessedly short; however, it gave the agencies tremendous discretion to withhold information. So, in 1974, Congress added the specific list to limit agencies' discretion. Also, in 1989, the words "or information" were added to the word "record," broadening what material might be exempt.

A few comments about this exemption: First, notice that the subsections shift between the word "could" and the word "would" in identifying when the consequences of disclosure warrant the exemption. "Would" requires a stronger showing on the agency's part than does "could." Notice also that the "clearly unwarranted" invasion of privacy, which is exempted in Exemption 6, becomes merely an "unwarranted" invasion of personal privacy in subsection C, an easier standard for the government to meet. For these reasons, the government may prefer to rely on Exemption 7(C) rather than Exemption 6. *See, e.g., Center for Nat'l Security Studies v. DOJ*, 331 F.3d 918 (D.C. Cir. 2003).

As noted, as with Exemption 6, Exemption 7(C) is one of the few places where the identity and motives of the requester are relevant. *National Archives & Records Admin. v. Favish*, 541 U.S. 157, 172 (2004) (holding that contrary to the usual rule for the other exemptions, "[w]here the privacy concerns addressed by exemption 7(C) are present, [the requester] . . . must show that the public interest sought to be advanced is a significant one [and that] the information is likely to advance that interest.").

Second, the Supreme Court has not limited the language "compiled for law enforcement purposes" to enforcement of criminal laws. The phrase encompasses criminal, civil, and administrative enforcement proceedings. Thus, such exempted information would include statements from witnesses that can be used in an administrative proceeding. *See NLRB v. Robbins Tire & Rubber Co.*, 437 U.S. 214, 242–43 (1978) (determining the NLRB was not required to disclose witness statements to a corporation because the production would interfere with enforcement proceedings). Further, the Court has held that the agency's compilation of the information at any time before the FOIA request is made constitutes "compilation" for law enforcement purposes. *See John Doe*

*Agency v. John Doe Corp.*, 493 U.S. 146, 155 (1990) (rejecting the distinction between information originally assembled for law enforcement purposes and information not originally gathered for that purpose when the information is later used for a law enforcement purpose).

Information that is (1) "compiled" (2) "for law enforcement purposes" must also fall within one of the six identified categories to be exempt. For example, after 9/11, the federal government arrested more than 1,000 individuals as part of its investigation of the attacks. Several organizations made FOIA requests seeking information about the detainees, including their names, the dates and locations of their arrest, and the reason therefor. The government rejected the request, citing Exemptions 7(A) and (C). *Center for Nat'l Security Studies*, 331 F.3d at 926. The majority and dissent agreed that the information was "compiled for law enforcement purposes," but disagreed whether the information fit within either of the two exemptions. *Id.* at 939–41, 945–46 (Tatel, J., dissenting).

Third, the Court may determine categorically that specific types of information will always be exempt, such as rap sheets detailing an individual's arrests and convictions. *DOJ v. Reporters Comm. for Freedom of the Press*, 489 U.S. 749, 780 (1989) (applying the balancing test and finding that the subjects of the rap sheets had a strong privacy interest in preventing disclosure while the public interest was low because their disclosure would not shed light on the government's activities).

Next, Exemption 8 provides that agencies need not disclose

> materials that are . . . contained in or related to examination, operating, or condition reports prepared by, on behalf of, or for the use of an agency responsible for the regulation or supervision of financial institutions.

APA § 552(b)(8). This exemption protects information relating to the regulation of financial institutions. The regulation of financial institutions has historically been an area where public disclosure of information has been greatly limited. So far, recent calls for more intensive regulation of these institutions have not changed the historic bias against disclosure.

Finally, Exemption 9 provides that agencies need not disclose "materials that are . . . geological and geophysical information and data, including maps, concerning wells." APA § 552(b)(9). This exemption is rarely invoked.

### c. Enforcement

Assuming a requester makes a FOIA request and the agency either fails to timely respond or cites an exemption and refuses to provide the information, what remedies does the requester have? This section explains the judicial enforcement provisions in FOIA.

Congress enacted FOIA in 1966 with high hopes for agency compliance, but experience quickly showed the need for more "teeth" in its enforcement provisions. After multiple amendments, FOIA is today regarded as a reasonably effective act, although it still falls short of congressional intent. Congress's clear desire for "prompt" agency response has been frustrated by agency workload. No one anticipated the tremendous volume of requests the Act would generate. To take only one example, the Social Security Administration received 18.6 million FOIA requests in fiscal year 2007. SUMMARY OF ANNUAL FOIA REPORTS FOR FISCAL YEAR 2006, UNITED STATES DEPARTMENT OF JUSTICE, OFFICE OF INFORMATION POLICY (2007), https://www.justice.gov /oip/blog/foia-post-2007-summary-annual-foia-reports-fiscal-year-2006.

While agency staff dedicated to handling record requests has grown greatly, few agencies are staffed to handle large and complex FOIA searches and analyses. Moreover, agencies are resistant to FOIA's goals of broad disclosure.

As a result, enforcement of the Act depends heavily on the courts. Courts have been understandably sympathetic to the agencies' cries of request overload. As a result, truly "prompt" agency responses are limited to relatively simple requests.

When a request for documents is made to an agency, the Act requires the agency to respond within twenty days. 5 USC § 552(a)(6). If the agency denies the request, the agency must provide an explanation and information about how to appeal internally. *Id.* Internal agency appeals are subject to a similarly short time frame. After the appeal, and assuming the agency has decided *not* to comply with the request, the requester may seek judicial review immediately in a federal district court. 5 USC § 552(a)(4)(B).

The judge will decide the issue "de novo," meaning the judge will give no deference to the agency's decision to withhold the document. 5 USC § 552(a) (B). It is the agency's burden to prove that its failure to disclose was legal. *Id.* The statute requires the agency to file a complete index that lists all of the documents within the scope of the request and identifies which exemption the agency is relying on to withhold the records. Further, the court may award a requester who "substantially prevails" in the judicial action attorneys' fees and costs. 5 USC § 552(a)(E).

In addition to the courts, the president also has an effect on FOIA compliance. Different presidential administrations have had different levels of enthusiasm for disclosure, and those differences have had major consequences.

Let's look at one example: suppose an agency is considering denying a request for records under a FOIA exemption. If the agency denies the request and litigation ensues, the agency needs the Department of Justice (DOJ) to defend it. But DOJ has a choice whether to do so. Shortly after 9/11 — and in part because of national security concerns — then-Attorney General John Ashcroft issued a memorandum indicating that DOJ would defend any agency decision to withhold information requested under the FOIA so long as the decision had a sound legal basis for doing so. Office of Att'y Gen., Memorandum on the Freedom of Information Act (October 12, 2001). With this statement, Attorney General Ashcroft was saying to agencies disposed to deny requests on technical, legal grounds, "I've got your back." Studies show that the memo resulted in fewer FOIA disclosures.

But when President Obama came to the White House, he rescinded the Ashcroft memo and promulgated a new executive order in its place. Regarding the issue of whether DOJ would provide litigation support for agencies denying FOIA requests, the order said that the DOJ will not defend every denial of a FOIA request. Office of Att'y Gen., Memorandum on the Freedom of Information Act (March 19, 2009). Instead, DOJ would defend the agency "only if . . . the agency reasonably foresees that disclosure would harm an interest protected by one of the statutory exemptions." *Id*. Under Obama's administration, an agency had to go beyond establishing a legal basis for withholding information to obtain litigation support. The agency also had to make a reasonable finding that disclosure would cause harm to relevant interests.

The Obama administration's memo confirmed the presumption of openness embodied in the FOIA. The memo instructed agencies to think of FOIA requests as raising questions about what can be released rather than what can be withheld. Further, it encouraged discretionary disclosure of exempt material where disclosure was lawful. Finally, it made other recommendations to improve speedy and coordinated implementation of FOIA.

It is unlikely that the Trump administration will maintain this approach to FOIA requests. But it is too soon to tell.

## 2. The Government in the Sunshine Act

FOIA is without a doubt the most important vehicle for citizens to obtain information from the government; however, it is not the only way. We will quickly examine three other relevant acts addressing public access to government information.

Congress enacted the Government in the Sunshine Act, or Sunshine Act, in 1976, during a time when Congress believed that government function should be open to public inspection. Pub. L. 94-409, 90 Stat. 1241, enacted

September 13, 1976, 5 U.S.C. § 552b. It is codified directly after FOIA at APA § 552b.

The Sunshine Act baldly requires that "every portion of every meeting of an agency shall be open to public observation." APA § 552b(b). It provides further that agencies must provide advance notice of meetings to ensure the public is aware of them. APA § 552b(b)(e). Note that the public has no right to participate, only to observe.

Although this operative language appears broad, the Act is much narrower in application. Specifically, the Act narrowly defines both "agency" and "meeting." First, the Sunshine Act defines "agency" as one "headed by a collegial body composed of two or more individual members, a majority of whom are appointed to such position by the President and with the advice of the Senate." APA § 552b(b). Thus, the Act applies only to the so-called independent agencies, such as the Federal Communications Commission, the Securities and Exchange Commission, and the Federal Trade Commission. It is these agencies that are generally headed by multi-member bodies. Because the executive agencies are typically headed by individuals, these individuals have no one with whom to deliberate; hence, their deliberations need not be public.

Second, the Sunshine Act defines "meeting" as "the deliberations of at least the number of individual agency members required to take action on behalf of the agency where such deliberations determine or result in the joint conduct or disposition of official agency business." APA § 552b(a)(2). Note that there is no requirement that the members meet in person. A telephone or video call would be sufficient if the requirements were met.

This definition of "meeting" includes three requirements for a gathering of agency members to be considered a meeting: (a) the number of agency members must constitute a quorum of the agency or a subpart that has power to act on behalf of the agency; (b) the agency members must deliberate; and (c) the deliberations must "determine or result in the joint conduct or disposition of official agency business." *Id.*

Despite the terms "determine" and "disposition" in the third requirement, the fact that the agency members do not actually decide issues at a meeting does not insulate it from the Sunshine Act open meetings requirement. A meeting can occur even when that meeting does not lead to an official agency action or decision. Rather, it is enough if the discussions are "sufficiently focused . . . as to cause or be likely to cause the individual participating members to form reasonably firm positions regarding matters pending or likely to arise before the agency." *FCC v. ITT World Communc'ns, Inc.*, 466 U.S. 463, 471 (1984). This last requirement excludes "informal background discussions [that only] clarify issues and expose varying views of official agency business." *Id.* at 470.

Like FOIA, the Sunshine Act allows an agency to hold a closed meeting when the discussion involves one of ten exempt matters and public interest does not require otherwise. Seven of those ten track FOIA (exemptions 1–4, 6–8), while three are unique to the Sunshine Act (5, 9–10). A covered agency may hold a closed meeting when the members are likely to

(1) disclose matters that are . . . to be kept secret in the interests of national defense or foreign policy . . . ;

(2) relate solely to the internal personnel rules and practices of an agency;

(3) disclose matters specifically exempted from disclosure by [another] statute;

(4) disclose trade secrets and commercial or financial information obtained from a person and privileged or confidential;

(5) involve accusing any person of a crime, or formally censuring any person;

(6) disclose information of a personal nature where disclosure would constitute a clearly unwarranted invasion of personal privacy;

(7) disclose investigatory records compiled for law enforcement purposes . . . ;

(8) disclose information contained in or related to . . . financial institutions;

(9) disclose information the premature disclosure of which would . . . be likely to significantly frustrate implementation of a proposed agency action . . . ; or

(10) specifically concern the agency's issuance of a subpoena, or the agency's participation in a civil action or proceeding . . . .

APA § 552b(c)(1)–(10).

Judicial enforcement of the Sunshine Act is similar to judicial enforcement of FOIA. "Any person" can bring suit in federal district court against an agency that fails to abide by the Act. APA § 552b(h). The agency carries the burden to prove that its decision to not open its meeting was legal. *Id.* Attorney fees and costs are also available. APA § 552b(j).

Timing is everything. A court cannot invalidate an agency action solely on the ground that the agency failed to abide by the Sunshine Act. *See* APA § 552b(h)(2). Thus, a litigant should sue before the meeting; otherwise, the only remedy may be to obtain a transcript of the illegally closed meeting. *Cf. Common Cause v. NRC*, 674 F.2d 921, 923 (D.C. Cir. 1982).

## 3. The Federal Advisory Committee Act

Federal advisory committees (including commissions, councils, task forces, boards, and working groups) are groups of individuals generally from the private sector. Such committees are established to help Congress and the executive branch make law and policy and to award grants. Congress, the president, or an agency head can establish an advisory committee to offer independent advice and expertise. These committees have offered advice on various topics from organ transplant practices to improving operations at the Department of Homeland Security. They have been around since the government's inception, but proliferated after World War II. In 2015, the Congressional Research Service noted that there were 1,009 active advisory committees with 72,200 members, costing the government close to $4 million annually. In short, there are many such committees that provide a wealth of information to the government, and there is a statute to regulate them.

Congress enacted the Federal Advisory Committee Act (FACA) in 1972 due to perceptions that some advisory committees were duplicative, inefficient, and dominated by special interests. *See* Pub. L. 92-463, § 1, Oct. 6, 1972, 86 Stat. 770. Further, Congress was concerned that such committees mostly operated secretly. Congress wanted to ensure that advice the various advisory committees provided to the government would be objective and open to the public. To accomplish its many goals, FACA mandates certain structural and operational requirements, such as reporting requirements, oversight responsibilities, and accessibility for meetings and records. It can be found at 5 U.S.C. App. 2, and its provisions will be cited here as FACA § X.

FACA defines a federal advisory committee broadly and contains two exceptions:

> The term "advisory committee" means any committee, board, commission, council, conference, panel, task force, or other similar group, or any subcommittee or other subgroup thereof (hereafter in this paragraph referred to as "committee"), which is—
> (A) established by statute or reorganization plan, or
> (B) established or utilized by the President, or
> (C) established or utilized by one or more agencies,
> in the interest of obtaining advice or recommendations for the President or one or more agencies or officers of the Federal Government, except that such term excludes (i) any committee that is composed wholly of full-time, or permanent part-time, officers or employees of the Federal Government, and (ii) any committee that is

created by the National Academy of Sciences or the National Academy of Public Administration.

FACA § 3(2).

This definition is, perhaps, the most litigated aspect of FACA. One litigated issue is FACA's application to the president. Unlike the other open-government laws, which exempt the president, FACA applies in full force to him or her. But the Supreme Court has expressed separation of powers concerns when Congress interferes with the president's constitutionally assigned functions. *See generally*, Michael J. Mongan, FIXING FACA: *The Case for Exempting Presidential Advisory Committees from Judicial Review Under the Federal Advisory Committee Act*, 58 STAN. L. REV. 895 (2005). It appears that FACA may implicate such concerns.

For example, in 1989, the Supreme Court held that the American Bar Association's Standing Committee on the Federal Judiciary ("ABA Committee") was not an advisory committee within the meaning of FACA. *Public Citizen v. DOJ*, 491 U.S. 440, 455 (1989). The ABA Committee evaluates individuals the president nominates for federal judgeships. The Court invoked the absurdity doctrine to avoid the ordinary meaning of the phrase "utilized by the President . . . in the interest of obtaining advice or recommendations." *Id.* at 451 (quoting FACA § 3(2)). Pursuant to the ordinary meaning of the statute, the ABA Committee was an advisory committee because the president routinely sought its recommendations regarding judicial nominees. However, because the statute was enacted to cure two specific ills—namely the wasteful expenditure of public funds for worthless committee meetings and biased proposals by special interest groups, the Court thought it unlikely that Congress intended the statute to cover every formal and informal meeting between the president and a group rendering advice. *Id.* at 466. Moreover, the Court expressed concern that if FACA applied, its requirements would interfere with the president's constitutional power to nominate federal judges. For these reasons, the Court held that the statute did not apply to the ABA Committee despite the ordinary meaning of the words of the statute. *Id.* at 455.

Assuming a committee meets the definition, FACA requires three things. FACA §§ 6–8. First, it controls the committee's operations to increase efficiency and effectiveness. Second, it places limits on the creation of new committees and renewal of existing committees. *See, e.g.*, FACA §§ 5(b)(3), 9, 10 & 14.

Third, and most important for our purposes, it enhances public scrutiny of and participation in advisory committees in several ways. Meetings must be announced in advance and open to the public. FACA §§ 10(a)(1) & (2). "Interested persons" must be given a chance "to attend, appear before, or file statements with any advisory committee." FACA § 10(a)(3). Relevant documents and minutes must be publicly available. FACA §§ 10(c) & (b). The exemptions that apply under the Government in the Sunshine Act and FOIA also apply here. FACA §§ 10(b) & (d).

FACA does not provide for judicial review; however, the courts have allowed plaintiffs who are personally injured to file an action for violations of some of the Act's provisions. Issues remain regarding which provisions are judicially enforceable and what remedies are available. *See, e.g., Center for Policy Analysis on Trade & Health v. Office of U.S. Trade Rep.*, 540 F.3d 940 (9th Cir. 2008) (affirming the district court's dismissal of plaintiff's complaint based on lack of standards for FACA's "fairly balanced" requirement as applied to the Trade Act of 1974); *Manshardt v. Federal Judicial Qualifications Comm'n*, 408 F.3d 1154, 1156 n.3 (9th Cir. 2005) (affirming the lower court's conclusion that the committee was not an advisory committee, and thus was outside the scope of FACA); *Cargill, Inc. v. United States*, 173 F.3d 323, 341–42 (5th Cir. 1999) (reversing trial court's holding that the defendants had met the FACA filing requirements and remanding to determine proper injunctive relief); *Alabama-Tombigbee Rivers Coalition v. DOI*, 26 F.3d 1103, 1107 (11th Cir. 1994) (finding injunctive relief an appropriate remedy when an agency failed to satisfy the requirements for committee meetings proscribed in FACA).

## 4. The Privacy Act

The Privacy Act is codified in APA § 552a and was enacted in 1974. Pub. L. 93-579, 88 Stat. 1896. The Act establishes rules for government collection, maintenance, use, and dissemination of personally identifiable information about individuals, not entities. On January 25, 2017, President Trump signed an executive order that limits the Privacy Act protections for U.S. citizens and permanent residents. Exec. Order No. 13,768, § 14, 82 Fed. Reg. 8799, 8802 (Jan. 25, 2017) (directing federal agencies to "ensure that their privacy policies exclude persons who are not United States citizens or lawful permanent residents from the protections of the Privacy Act regarding personally identifiable information").

The Act provides: "No agency shall disclose any record which is contained in a system of records by any means of communication to any person, or to another agency." APA § 552a(b). "Agency" is defined to include the same agencies FOIA covers: executive branch, independent agencies, the Executive office, and government-owned and government-controlled corporations. APA §552a(a)(1) (citing §552e).

In contrast, "record" is defined more narrowly in the Privacy Act than in FOIA. A Privacy Act record means "any item, collection, or grouping of information about an individual that is maintained by an agency." Further, such records include the individual's "education, financial transactions, medical history, and criminal or employment history and [records that] contain[] his name, or . . . other identifying particular assigned to the individual." APA §552a(a)(4). This definition is narrower because it focuses on personal information only.

Moreover, the Act prohibits disclosure of such records only when they are maintained in a "system of records." APA §552a(b) "System of records" is defined to include "records under the control of any agency from which information is retrieved by the name of the individual or by some identifying number, symbol, or other identifying particular assigned to the individual." APA §552a(a)(5). This definition reflects congressional intent to protect information stored on government computers and searchable using an individual's name or other identifier.

The Act has two other important safeguards. First, the Act allows individuals to access their own records and correct inaccurate, irrelevant, and incomplete information. APA §552a(d). Second, section 7(b) of the Privacy Act (located at 5 U.S.C. §552a note (Disclosure of Social Security Number)) requires "Any Federal, State or local government agency which requests an individual to disclose his Social Security account number shall inform that individual whether that disclosure is mandatory or voluntary, by what statutory or other authority such number is solicited, and what uses will be made of it." Sec. 7(b).

Despite the breadth of this language, two appellate courts have held that section 7 of the Privacy Act applies only to federal agencies and does not allow suits against state and local entities. *See Schmitt v. Detroit*, 395 F.3d 327, 329–30 (6th Cir. 2005) (holding that the Act applies only to federal agencies based on the definition section of the Act); *Dittman v. California*, 191 F.3d 1020, 1026 (9th Cir. 1999) (holding the Act provides no cause of action against a state licensing entity because the private right of action created in subsection (g) "is specifically limited to actions against agencies of the United States Government").

In contrast, two other appellate courts have held that individuals may enforce the Social Security number provisions via 42 U.S.C. §1983. *Gonzalez v. Village of W. Milwaukee*, 671 F.3d 649, 662 (7th Cir. 2012) (finding "no conflict between §§ 3 and 7 [of the Privacy Act]" as "it seems clear that when § 3(a)(1) defines agencies as *federal* agencies 'for purposes of *this section*,' it refers only to § 3 .... Accordingly, there is no need to look beyond the unambiguous text of § 7 to determine its applicability. By its express terms, § 7 applies to federal, state, and local agencies." ); *Schwier v. Cox*, 340 F.3d 1284, 1285 (11th Cir. 2003) (reasoning that "the remedial scheme of section 3 [in the Privacy Act] provides no basis for concluding that Congress intended to preclude private remedies under § 1983 for violations of section 7."); *See also Lanzetta v. Woodmansee*, 2013 WL 1610508, at *2 (M.D. Fla. Apr. 15, 2013) (following *Schwier* and stating "[a]n individual may also pursue enforcement of his privacy rights under Section 7 of the Privacy Act pursuant to [42 U.S.C. § 1983]" ).

In short, the Act prohibits agencies from disclosing information about individuals contained in searchable databases, provides a mechanism for individuals to obtain and correct their own information, and limits agency collection of Social Security information.

The disclosure prohibition is subject to a number of exceptions, including (1) when the individual provides written consent; (2) when the use is "routine"; (3) when the purpose for use involves law enforcement, census-taking, and statistical research; and (4) when disclosure is required under FOIA, meaning a FOIA exemption does not apply. APA § 552a(b). An agency may not rely on FOIA Exemption 6 to refuse to provide records about the individual requester: "No agency shall rely on any exemption contained in [FOIA] to withhold from an individual any record which is otherwise accessible to such individual under the provisions of [the Privacy Act]." APA § 552a(t)(1). Similarly, when an individual is entitled to records under FOIA, but not under the Privacy Act, the agency must disclose the records. "No agency shall rely on any exemption in [the Privacy Act] to withhold from an individual any record which is otherwise accessible to such individual under the provisions of [FOIA]." APA § 552a(t)(2). For the agency to withhold records about an individual from that individual, the records must fall within an exemption in both Acts, such as the law enforcement exemption.

When an individual believes an agency has violated the Privacy Act by (1) disclosing a record improperly, (2) refusing to make a record available, or (3) refusing to correct information, that individual may file an action in federal district court. *See* APA § 552a(g)(1). The available remedy varies according to the alleged injury. For improper disclosure, actual damages of at least $1,000 are available if the disclosure was "intentional or willful." APA § 552a(g)(4). Intentional and willful violations do not require the requester to prove that the agency official "set out purposely to violate the Act," rather, the official "commit(s) the act without grounds for believing [the disclosure] to be lawful (or) flagrantly disregard(s) others' rights under the Act." *Tijerina v. Walters*, 821 F.2d 789, 799 (D.C. Cir. 1987) (citation omitted).

For improper refusal to disclose or amend, a court can order disclosure or amendment, as appropriate. APA §§ 552a(g)(2) & (3). Attorneys' fees may also be available. APA §§ 552a(g)(2)(B), (3)(B), & (4)(B).

An interesting recent issue that has arisen in regard to failure to disclose involves the FBI's no-fly list. In 2004, the American Civil Liberties union filed a class action lawsuit, challenging the government's refusal to let individuals know whether and why they were included on the list. *Gordon v. FBI*, 388 F. Supp. 2d 1028 (N.D. Cal. 2005). The case settled in 2006; however, other suits were filed on behalf of specific individuals who were not permitted to fly. *See, e.g., Ibrahim v. Department of Homeland Security*, 62 F. Supp. 3d 909 (N.D. Cal. 2014) (holding that the government must inform the plaintiff whether she was on the no-fly list); *Mohamed v. Holder et al.*, No. 11-1924 2013 U.S. App. LEXIS 26340 (4th Cir. May 28, 2013) (refusing to dismiss lawsuit alleging that government's placing of an individual on the no-fly list caused him to be tortured and beaten for overstaying his visa in Kuwait). So far, the FBI appears to be losing the battle to withhold name and information about those included on the no-fly list.

## 5. Summary of these Acts

In summary, during the 1960s and 1970s, Congress generally moved in the direction of opening the executive branch up to public access. FOIA, the Government in Sunshine Act, and FACA all represent congressional attempts to make the government processes more open and accessible to the public. However, agencies as a whole have been less welcoming to the open approach and unable to comply with the voluminous requests for information in a timely manner. The courts have been largely understanding of agency work priorities.

The Privacy Act, in contrast, was a small step away from openness, for it protects information about individuals contained within searchable databases. With this Act, Congress gave individuals a way to correct misinformation and learn what the government knew about them. The Privacy Act also protects unwarranted disclosure of your Social Security information.

# Checkpoints

## Information flowing to the agencies

- Information is critical to agency work; courts respect that.

- Agencies obtain information from documents, testimony, and inspections.

- Citizens and business overwhelmingly provide information to agencies voluntarily.

- Agencies must have a statutory grant of authority to request information if a regulated entity is unwilling to provide the information voluntarily.

- Pursuant to the Fourth Amendment, an agency can subpoena records if it has statutory authority, the records are relevant, and the request is not oppressively broad.

- Regarding oral *testimony*, the Fifth Amendment provides the most protection; it protects individuals from being compelled to testify against themselves.

- Regarding the production of *documents*, the Fifth Amendment provides very little protection.

- The Fifth Amendment does not protect artificial entities from producing incriminating business records; it does not protect the custodian of business records from producing incriminating records, even when the custodian would be implicated personally; it does not protect the owners of sole proprietorships from producing *involuntarily* created public records; and it does not protect the owners of sole proprietorships from producing *voluntarily* created documents unless the act of production itself would be incriminating.

- Agencies must seek to enforce subpoenas in court.

- Most regulated entities comply with inspection requests.

- Agencies must have a statutory grant of authority to conduct an inspection if a regulated entity is unwilling to allow the inspection involuntarily.

- Pursuant to the Fourth Amendment, an agency needs a warrant to conduct an inspection; however, the agency need only show that the inspection complies with "reasonable legislative or administrative standards."

- One exception to the warrant requirement is that agencies do not need a warrant to inspect pervasively regulated businesses.

## Information flowing to the public:

- The Freedom of Information Act requires that agencies provide information to the public in three ways: (1) by publishing certain information in the Federal Register, (2) by making certain information available for inspection and copying, and (3) by responding to requests.

- FOIA contains nine types of information that have been exempted: (1) classified information; (2) internal agency personnel rules and practices; (3) matters that another statute specifically exempts from disclosure; (4) trade secrets and commercial or financial information that the agency obtained from someone other than the requester; (5) inter-agency or intra-agency memoranda and letters, not otherwise available through discovery in a civil action against the agency; (6) personnel files, medical files, and similar files, the disclosure of which would constitute a clearly unwarranted invasion of personal privacy; (7) records and information compiled for law enforcement purposes; (8) matters related to the regulation of banks and other financial institutions; and (9) geological and geophysical information.

- The Government in the Sunshine Act requires that meetings involving the deliberations of independent agency shall be open to the public, subject to ten exemptions.

- Federal advisory committees are groups of individuals generally from the private sector established to help Congress and the executive branch make law and policy and to award grants. The Federal Advisory Committee Act enhances public involvement in advisory committees and their meetings.

- Subject to four exceptions, the Privacy Act prohibits agencies from disclosing information about individuals contained in searchable databases, provides a mechanism for individuals to obtain and correct their own information, and limits agency collection of Social Security information.

# Mastering Administrative Law Master Checklist

**Chapter 1 • The Role of Administrative Law**
- ❏ Introduction and history
- ❏ The constitutionality of regulation
- ❏ Separation of powers problems with regulation
  - ○ The problem of authority
  - ○ The problem of unfairness
  - ○ The problem of unaccountability
- ❏ Administrative law defined

**Chapter 2 • Rulemaking**
- ❏ Why agencies use rulemaking
  - ○ Individualized decision making
  - ○ The use of general rules
- ❏ Rulemaking and the rule of law in a democracy
- ❏ A case study for modern rulemaking
- ❏ The legal framework for rulemaking
  - ○ The Administrative Procedure Act (APA) requirements
  - ○ Procedures in addition to those in the APA

**Chapter 3 • Adjudication**
- ❏ Understanding the nature of adjudication
- ❏ The APA's approach to adjudication
  - ○ Formal adjudication
  - ○ Informal adjudication
- ❏ The APA's procedural requirements
  - ○ Formal adjudication
  - ○ Informal adjudication

**Chapter 4 • Due Process Requirements for Administrative Proceedings**
- ❏ Introduction to the Due Process Clause
- ❏ Whether due process applies
  - ○ Issues protected by due process
  - ○ Interests protected by due process; property and liberty
- ❏ When due process applies: Pre-deprivation versus post-deprivation
- ❏ What process is due?
  - ○ The private interest
  - ○ The risk of error
  - ○ The public interest
  - ○ The right to a neutral decisionmaker

**Chapter 5 • The Availability of Judicial Review**
- ❏ Why judicial review is important
- ❏ When do courts have jurisdiction?
- ❏ Who is entitled to judicial review?
  - ○ Constitutional standing
  - ○ Prudential standing
  - ○ Statutory standing
- ❏ What is subject to judicial review?
  - ○ Agency action
  - ○ Express and implied preclusion
  - ○ Committed to agency discretion
- ❏ When is judicial review available?
  - ○ Finality
  - ○ Exhaustion of administrative remedies
  - ○ Administrative issue exhaustion
  - ○ Ripeness
  - ○ Primary jurisdiction

**Chapter 6 • Scope of Judicial Review of Agency Action**
- ❏ The importance of judicial review
- ❏ Reviewing agency determinations of law
  - ○ Defining questions of law
  - ○ Pre-*Chevron*: *Skidmore* and *Hearst*
  - ○ *Chevron*
  - ○ *Chevron* Step Zero
  - ○ Agency interpretations that conflict with judicial interpretations
- ❏ Reviewing agency determinations of fact and policy
  - ○ Defining questions of fact and policy
  - ○ Substantial evidence

# Appendix

## Select Sections of the Federal Administrative Procedure Act

### United States Code. Title 5

#### § 551. Definitions

For the purpose of this subchapter—

(1) "agency" means each authority of the Government of the United States, whether or not it is within or subject to review by another agency, but does not include—

(A) the Congress;

(B) the courts of the United States;

(C) the governments of the territories or possessions of the United States;

(D) the government of the District of Columbia; or except as to the requirements of section 552 of this title—

(E) agencies composed of representatives of the parties or of representatives of organizations of the parties to the disputes determined by them;

(F) courts martial and military commissions;

(G) military authority exercised in the field in time of war or in occupied territory; or

(H) functions conferred by sections 1738, 1739, 1743, and 1744 of title 12; chapter 2 of title 41; subchapter II of chapter 471 of title 49; or sections 1884, 1891–1902, and former section 1641(b)(2), of title 50, appendix;

(2) "person" includes an individual, partnership, corporation, association, or public or private organization other than an agency;

(3) "party" includes a person or agency named or admitted as a party, or properly seeking and entitled as of right to be admitted as a party, in an agency proceeding, and a person or agency admitted by an agency as a party for limited purposes;

(4) "rule" means the whole or a part of an agency statement of general or particular applicability and future effect designed to implement, interpret, or prescribe law or policy or describing the organization, procedure, or practice requirements of an agency and includes the approval or prescription for the future of rates, wages, corporate or financial structures or reorganizations thereof, prices, facilities, appliances, services or allowances therefor or of valuations, costs, or accounting, or practices bearing on any of the foregoing;

(5) "rule making" means agency process for formulating, amending, or repealing a rule;

(6) "order" means the whole or a part of a final disposition, whether affirmative, negative, injunctive, or declaratory in form, of an agency in a matter other than rule making but including licensing;

(7) "adjudication" means agency process for the formulation of an order;

(8) "license" includes the whole or a part of an agency permit, certificate, approval, registration, charter, membership, statutory exemption or other form of permission;

(9) "licensing" includes agency process respecting the grant, renewal, denial, revocation, suspension, annulment, withdrawal, limitation, amendment, modification, or conditioning of a license;

(10) "sanction" includes the whole or a part of an agency—
    (A) prohibition, requirement, limitation, or other condition affecting the freedom of a person;
    (B) withholding of relief;
    (C) imposition of penalty or fine;
    (D) destruction, taking, seizure, or withholding of property;
    (E) assessment of damages, reimbursement, restitution, compensation, costs, charges, or fees;
    (F) requirement, revocation, or suspension of a license; or
    (G) taking other compulsory or restrictive action;

(11) "relief" includes the whole or a part of an agency—
    (A) grant of money, assistance, license, authority, exemption, exception, privilege, or remedy;
    (B) recognition of a claim, right, immunity, privilege, exemption, or exception; or
    (C) taking of other action on the application or petition of, and beneficial to, a person;

(12) "agency proceeding" means an agency process as defined by paragraphs (5), (7), and (9) of this section;

(13) "agency action" includes the whole or a part of an agency rule, order, license, sanction, relief, or the equivalent or denial thereof, or failure to act; and

(14) "ex parte communication" means an oral or written communication not on the public record with respect to which reasonable prior notice to all parties is not given, but it shall not include requests for status reports on any matter or proceeding covered by this subchapter.

## [Open Government Provisions]

## § 552.  Public information; agency rules, opinions, orders, records, and proceedings

(a) Each agency shall make available to the public information as follows:

(1) Each agency shall separately state and currently publish in the Federal Register for the guidance of the public —

(A) descriptions of its central and field organization and the established places at which, the employees (and in the case of a uniformed service, the members) from whom, and the methods whereby, the public may obtain information, make submittals or requests, or obtain decisions;

(B) statements of the general course and method by which its functions are channeled and determined, including the nature and requirements of all formal and informal procedures available;

(C) rules of procedure, descriptions of forms available or the places at which forms may be obtained, and instructions as to the scope and contents of all papers, reports, or examinations;

(D) substantive rules of general applicability adopted as authorized by law, and statements of general policy or interpretations of general applicability formulated and adopted by the agency; and

(E) each amendment, revision, or repeal of the foregoing.

Except to the extent that a person has actual and timely notice of the terms thereof, a person may not in any manner be required to resort to, or be adversely affected by, a matter required to be published in the Federal Register and not so published. For the purpose of this paragraph, matter reasonably available to the class of persons affected thereby is deemed published in the Federal Register when incorporated by reference therein with the approval of the Director of the Federal Register.

(2) Each agency, in accordance with published rules, shall make available for public inspection and copying—

(A) final opinions, including concurring and dissenting opinions, as well as orders, made in the adjudication of cases;

(B) those statements of policy and interpretations which have been adopted by the agency and are not published in the Federal Register;

(C) administrative staff manuals and instructions to staff that affect a member of the public;

(D) copies of all records, regardless of form or format, which have been released to any person under paragraph (3) and which, because of the nature of their subject matter, the agency determines have become or are likely to become the subject of subsequent requests for substantially the same records; and

(E) a general index of the records referred to under subparagraph (D); unless the materials are promptly published and copies offered for sale. For records created on or after November 1, 1996, within one year after such date, each agency shall make such records available, including by computer telecommunications or, if computer telecommunications means have not been established by the agency, by other electronic means. To the extent required to prevent a clearly unwarranted invasion of personal privacy, an agency may delete identifying details when it makes available or publishes an opinion, statement of policy, interpretation, staff manual, instruction, or copies of records referred to in subparagraph (D). However, in each case the justification for the deletion shall be explained fully in writing, and the extent of such deletion shall be indicated on the portion of the record which is made available or published, unless including that indication would harm an interest protected by the exemption in subsection (b) under which the deletion is made. If technically feasible, the extent of the deletion shall be indicated at the place in the record where the deletion was made. Each agency shall also maintain and make available for public inspection and copying current indexes providing identifying information for the public as to any matter issued, adopted, or promulgated after July 4, 1967, and required by this paragraph to be made available or published. Each agency shall promptly publish, quarterly or more frequently, and distribute (by sale or otherwise) copies of each index or supplements thereto unless it determines by order published in the Federal Register that the publication would be unnecessary and impracticable, in which case the agency shall nonetheless provide copies of such index on request at a cost not to exceed the direct cost of duplication. Each agency shall make the index referred to in subparagraph (E) available by computer telecommunications by December 31, 1999. A final order, opinion, statement of policy, interpretation, or staff manual or instruction that affects a member of the public may be relied on, used, or cited as precedent by an agency against a party other than an agency only if—

(i) it has been indexed and either made available or published as provided by this paragraph; or

(ii) the party has actual and timely notice of the terms thereof.

(3)(A) Except with respect to the records made available under paragraphs (1) and (2) of this subsection, and except as provided in subparagraph (E), each agency, upon any request for records which (i) reasonably describes such records and (ii) is made in accordance with published rules stating the time, place, fees (if any), and procedures to be followed, shall make the records promptly available to any person.

(B) In making any record available to a person under this paragraph, an agency shall provide the record in any form or format requested by the person if the record is readily reproducible by the agency in that form or format. Each agency shall make reasonable efforts to maintain its records in forms or formats that are reproducible for purposes of this section.

(C) In responding under this paragraph to a request for records, an agency shall make reasonable efforts to search for the records in electronic form or format, except when such efforts would significantly interfere with the operation of the agency's automated information system.

(D) For purposes of this paragraph, the term "search" means to review, manually or by automated means, agency records for the purpose of locating those records which are responsive to a request.

(E) An agency, or part of an agency, that is an element of the intelligence community (as that term is defined in section 3(4) of the National Security Act of 1947 (50 U.S.C. 401a(4))) shall not make any record available under this paragraph to—

(i) any government entity, other than a State, territory, commonwealth, or district of the United States, or any subdivision thereof; or

(ii) a representative of a government entity described in clause (i).

(4)(A)(i) In order to carry out the provisions of this section, each agency shall promulgate regulations, pursuant to notice and receipt of public comment, specifying the schedule of fees applicable to the processing of requests under this section and establishing procedures and guidelines for determining when such fees should be waived or reduced. Such schedule shall conform to the guidelines which shall be promulgated, pursuant to notice and receipt of public comment, by the Director of the Office of Management and Budget and which shall provide for a uniform schedule of fees for all agencies.

(ii) Such agency regulations shall provide that—

(I) fees shall be limited to reasonable standard charges for document search, duplication, and review, when records are requested for commercial use;

(II) fees shall be limited to reasonable standard charges for document duplication when records are not sought for commercial use and the request is made by an educational or noncommercial scientific institution, whose purpose is scholarly or scientific research; or a representative of the news media; and

(III) for any request not described in (I) or (II), fees shall be limited to reasonable standard charges for document search and duplication . . . .

(iii) Documents shall be furnished without any charge or at a charge reduced below the fees established under clause (ii) if disclosure of the information is in the public interest because it is likely to contribute significantly to public understanding of the operations or activities of the government and is not primarily in the commercial interest of the requester . . . .

(B) On complaint, the district court of the United States in the district in which the complainant resides, or has his principal place of business, or in which the agency records are situated, or in the District of Columbia, has jurisdiction to enjoin the agency from withholding agency records and to order the production of any agency records improperly withheld from the complainant. In such a case the court shall determine the matter de novo, and may examine the contents of such agency records in camera to determine whether such records or any part thereof shall be withheld under any of the exemptions set forth in subsection (b) of this section, and the burden is on the agency to sustain its action. In addition to any other matters to which a court accords substantial weight, a court shall accord substantial weight to an affidavit of an agency concerning the agency's determination as to technical feasibility under paragraph (2)(C) and subsection (b) and reproducibility under paragraph (3)(B) . . . .

(E)(i) The court may assess against the United States reasonable attorney fees and other litigation costs reasonably incurred in any case under this section in which the complainant has substantially prevailed.

(ii) For purposes of this subparagraph, a complainant has substantially prevailed if the complainant has obtained relief through either—

(I) a judicial order, or an enforceable written agreement or consent decree; or

(II) a voluntary or unilateral change in position by the agency, if the complainant's claim is not insubstantial . . . .

(6)(A) Each agency, upon any request for records made under paragraph (1), (2), or (3) of this subsection, shall—

(i) determine within 20 days (excepting Saturdays, Sundays, and legal public holidays) after the receipt of any such request whether to comply with such request and shall immediately notify the person making such request of such determination and the reasons therefor, and of the right of such person to appeal to the head of the agency any adverse determination; and

(ii) make a determination with respect to any appeal within twenty days (excepting Saturdays, Sundays, and legal public holidays) after the receipt of such appeal. If on appeal the denial of the request for records is in whole or in part upheld, the agency shall notify the person making such request of the provisions for judicial review of that determination under paragraph (4) of this subsection.

The 20-day period under clause (i) shall commence on the date on which the request is first received by the appropriate component of the agency, but in any event not later than ten days after the request is first received by any component of the agency that is designated in the agency's regulations under this section to receive requests under this section. The 20-day period shall not be tolled by the agency except—

(I) that the agency may make one request to the requester for information and toll the 20-day period while it is awaiting such information that it has reasonably requested from the requester under this section; or

(II) if necessary to clarify with the requester issues regarding fee assessment. In either case, the agency's receipt of the requester's response to the agency's request for information or clarification ends the tolling period . . . .

(b) This section does not apply to matters that are—

(1) (A) specifically authorized under criteria established by an Executive order to be kept secret in the interest of national defense or foreign policy and (B) are in fact properly classified pursuant to such Executive order;

(2) related solely to the internal personnel rules and practices of an agency;

(3) specifically exempted from disclosure by statute (other than section 552b of this title), provided that such statute (A) requires that the matters be withheld from the public in such a manner as to leave no discretion on the issue, or (B) establishes particular criteria for withholding or refers to particular types of matters to be withheld;

(4) trade secrets and commercial or financial information obtained from a person and privileged or confidential;

(5) inter-agency or intra-agency memorandums or letters which would not be available by law to a party other than an agency in litigation with the agency;

(6) personnel and medical files and similar files the disclosure of which would constitute a clearly unwarranted invasion of personal privacy;

(7) records or information compiled for law enforcement purposes, but only to the extent that the production of such law enforcement records or information (A) could reasonably be expected to interfere with enforcement proceedings, (B) would deprive a person of a right to a fair trial or an impartial adjudication, (C) could reasonably be expected to constitute an unwarranted invasion of personal privacy, (D) could reasonably be expected to disclose the identity of a confidential source, including a State, local, or foreign agency or authority or any private institution which furnished information on a confidential basis, and, in the case of a record or information compiled by criminal law enforcement authority in the course of a criminal investigation or by an agency conducting a lawful national security intelligence investigation, information furnished by a confidential source, (E) would disclose techniques and procedures for law enforcement investigations or prosecutions, or would disclose guidelines for law enforcement investigations or prosecutions if such disclosure could reasonably be expected to risk circumvention of the law, or (F) could reasonably be expected to endanger the life or physical safety of any individual;

(8) contained in or related to examination, operating, or condition reports prepared by, on behalf of, or for the use of an agency responsible for the regulation or supervision of financial institutions; or

(9) geological and geophysical information and data, including maps, concerning wells.

Any reasonably segregable portion of a record shall be provided to any person requesting such record after deletion of the portions which are exempt under this subsection. The amount of information deleted, and the exemption under which the deletion is made, shall be indicated on the released portion of the record, unless including that indication would harm an interest protected by the exemption in this subsection under which the deletion is made. If technically feasible, the amount of the information deleted, and the exemption under which the deletion is made, shall be indicated at the place in the record where such deletion is made.

(c)(1) Whenever a request is made which involves access to records described in subsection (b)(7)(A) and—

(A) the investigation or proceeding involves a possible violation of criminal law; and

(B) there is reason to believe that (i) the subject of the investigation or proceeding is not aware of its pendency, and (ii) disclosure of the existence of the records could reasonably be expected to interfere with enforcement proceedings,

the agency may, during only such time as that circumstance continues, treat the records as not subject to the requirements of this section.

(2) Whenever informant records maintained by a criminal law enforcement agency under an informant's name or personal identifier are requested by a third party according to the informant's name or personal identifier, the agency may treat the records as not subject to the requirements of this section unless the informant's status as an informant has been officially confirmed.

(3) Whenever a request is made which involves access to records maintained by the Federal Bureau of Investigation pertaining to foreign intelligence or counterintelligence, or international terrorism, and the existence of the records is classified information as provided in subsection (b)(1), the Bureau may, as long as the existence of the records remains classified information, treat the records as not subject to the requirements of this section.

(d) This section does not authorize withholding of information or limit the availability of records to the public, except as specifically stated in this section. This section is not authority to withhold information from Congress.

## § 552a.  Privacy Act [omitted]

## § 552b.  The Government in Sunshine Act

(a) For purposes of this section —

(1) the term "agency" means any agency, as defined in section 552(e) [1] of this title, headed by a collegial body composed of two or more individual members, a majority of whom are appointed to such position by the President with the advice and consent of the Senate, and any subdivision thereof authorized to act on behalf of the agency;

(2) the term "meeting" means the deliberations of at least the number of individual agency members required to take action on behalf of the agency where such deliberations determine or result in the joint conduct or disposition of official agency business, but does not include deliberations required or permitted by subsection (d) or (e); and

(3) the term "member" means an individual who belongs to a collegial body heading an agency.

(b) Members shall not jointly conduct or dispose of agency business other than in accordance with this section. Except as provided in subsection (c), every portion of every meeting of an agency shall be open to public observation.

(c) Except in a case where the agency finds that the public interest requires otherwise, the second sentence of subsection (b) shall not apply to any portion of an agency meeting, and the requirements of subsections (d) and (e) shall not apply to any information pertaining to such meeting otherwise required by this section to be disclosed to the public, where the agency properly determines that such portion or portions of its meeting or the disclosure of such information is likely to —

(1) disclose matters that are (A) specifically authorized under criteria established by an Executive order to be kept secret in the interests of national defense or foreign policy and (B) in fact properly classified pursuant to such Executive order;

(2) relate solely to the internal personnel rules and practices of an agency;

(3) disclose matters specifically exempted from disclosure by statute (other than section 552 of this title), provided that such statute (A) requires that the matters be withheld from the public in such a manner as to leave no discretion on the issue, or (B) establishes particular criteria for withholding or refers to particular types of matters to be withheld;

(4) disclose trade secrets and commercial or financial information obtained from a person and privileged or confidential;

(5) involve accusing any person of a crime, or formally censuring any person;

(6) disclose information of a personal nature where disclosure would constitute a clearly unwarranted invasion of personal privacy;

(7) disclose investigatory records compiled for law enforcement purposes, or information which if written would be contained in such records, but only to the extent that the production of such records or information would (A) interfere with enforcement proceedings, (B) deprive a person of a right to a fair trial or an impartial adjudication, (C) constitute an unwarranted invasion of personal privacy, (D) disclose the identity of a confidential source and, in the case of a record compiled by a criminal law enforcement authority in the course of a criminal investigation, or by an agency conducting a lawful national security intelligence investigation, confidential information furnished only by the confidential source, (E) disclose investigative techniques and procedures, or (F) endanger the life or physical safety of law enforcement personnel;

(8) disclose information contained in or related to examination, operating, or condition reports prepared by, on behalf of, or for the use of an agency responsible for the regulation or supervision of financial institutions;

(9) disclose information the premature disclosure of which would—

> (A) in the case of an agency which regulates currencies, securities, commodities, or financial institutions, be likely to (i) lead to significant financial speculation in currencies, securities, or commodities, or (ii) significantly endanger the stability of any financial institution; or
>
> (B) in the case of any agency, be likely to significantly frustrate implementation of a proposed agency action,
>
>> except that subparagraph (B) shall not apply in any instance where the agency has already disclosed to the public the content or nature of its proposed action, or where the agency is required by law to make such disclosure on its own initiative prior to taking final agency action on such proposal; or

(10) specifically concern the agency's issuance of a subpoena, or the agency's participation in a civil action or proceeding, an action in a foreign court or international tribunal, or an arbitration, or the initiation, conduct, or disposition by the agency of a particular case of formal agency adjudication pursuant to the procedures in section 554 of this title or otherwise involving a determination on the record after opportunity for a hearing . . . .

(e)

    (1) In the case of each meeting, the agency shall make public announcement, at least one week before the meeting, of the time, place, and subject matter of the meeting, whether it is to be open or closed to the public, and the name and phone number of the official designated by the agency to respond to requests for information about the meeting. Such announcement shall be made unless a majority of the members of the agency determines by a recorded vote that agency business requires that such meeting be called at an earlier date, in which case the agency shall make public announcement of the time, place, and subject matter of such meeting, and whether open or closed to the public, at the earliest practicable time . . . .

(h)

    (1) The district courts of the United States shall have jurisdiction to enforce the requirements of subsections (b) through (f) of this section by declaratory judgment, injunctive relief, or other relief as may be appropriate . . . .

(i) The court may assess against any party reasonable attorney fees and other litigation costs reasonably incurred by any other party who substantially prevails in any action brought in accordance with the provisions of subsection (g) or (h) of this section, except that costs may be assessed against the plaintiff only where the court finds that the suit was initiated by the plaintiff primarily for frivolous or dilatory purposes. In the case of assessment of costs against an agency, the costs may be assessed by the court against the United States . . . .

### [APA Procedural Rules]

### §553. Rule making

(a) This section applies, according to the provisions thereof, except to the extent that there is involved—

    (1) a military or foreign affairs function of the United States; or

    (2) a matter relating to agency management or personnel or to public property, loans, grants, benefits, or contracts.

(b) General notice of proposed rule making shall be published in the Federal Register, unless persons subject thereto are named and either personally served or otherwise have actual notice thereof in accordance with law. The notice shall include—

(1) a statement of the time, place, and nature of public rule making proceedings;

(2) reference to the legal authority under which the rule is proposed; and

(3) either the terms or substance of the proposed rule or a description of the subjects and issues involved.

Except when notice or hearing is required by statute, this subsection does not apply—

(A) to interpretative rules, general statements of policy, or rules of agency organization, procedure, or practice; or

(B) when the agency for good cause finds (and incorporates the finding and a brief statement of reasons therefor in the rules issued) that notice and public procedure thereon are impracticable, unnecessary, or contrary to the public interest.

(c) After notice required by this section, the agency shall give interested persons an opportunity to participate in the rule making through submission of written data, views, or arguments with or without opportunity for oral presentation. After consideration of the relevant matter presented, the agency shall incorporate in the rules adopted a concise general statement of their basis and purpose. When rules are required by statute to be made on the record after opportunity for an agency hearing, sections 556 and 557 of this title apply instead of this subsection.

(d) The required publication or service of a substantive rule shall be made not less than 30 days before its effective date, except—

(1) a substantive rule which grants or recognizes an exemption or relieves a restriction;

(2) interpretative rules and statements of policy; or

(3) as otherwise provided by the agency for good cause found and published with the rule.

(e) Each agency shall give an interested person the right to petition for the issuance, amendment, or repeal of a rule.

## § 554. Adjudications

(a) This section applies, according to the provisions thereof, in every case of adjudication required by statute to be determined on the record after opportunity for an agency hearing, except to the extent that there is involved—

(1) a matter subject to a subsequent trial of the law and the facts de novo in a court;

(2) the selection or tenure of an employee, except an administrative law judge appointed under section 3105 of this title;

(3) proceedings in which decisions rest solely on inspections, tests, or elections;

(4) the conduct of military or foreign affairs functions;

(5) cases in which an agency is acting as an agent for a court; or

(6) the certification of worker representatives.

(b) Persons entitled to notice of an agency hearing shall be timely informed of—

(1) the time, place, and nature of the hearing;

(2) the legal authority and jurisdiction under which the hearing is to be held; and

(3) the matters of fact and law asserted.

When private persons are the moving parties, other parties to the proceeding shall give prompt notice of issues controverted in fact or law; and in other instances agencies may by rule require responsive pleading. In fixing the time and place for hearings, due regard shall be had for the convenience and necessity of the parties or their representatives.

(c) The agency shall give all interested parties opportunity for—

(1) the submission and consideration of facts, arguments, offers of settlement, or proposals of adjustment when time, the nature of the proceeding, and the public interest permit; and

(2) to the extent that the parties are unable so to determine a controversy by consent, hearing and decision on notice and in accordance with sections 556 and 557 of this title.

(d) The employee who presides at the reception of evidence pursuant to section 556 of this title shall make the recommended decision or initial decision required by section 557 of this title, unless he becomes unavailable to the agency. Except to the extent required for the disposition of ex parte matters as authorized by law, such an employee may not—

(1) consult a person or party on a fact in issue, unless on notice and opportunity for all parties to participate; or

(2) be responsible to or subject to the supervision or direction of an employee or agent engaged in the performance of investigative or prosecuting functions for an agency.

An employee or agent engaged in the performance of investigative or prosecuting functions for an agency in a case may not, in that or a factually related case, participate or advise in the decision, recommended decision, or agency review pursuant to section 557 of this title, except as witness or counsel in public proceedings. This subsection does not apply—

    (A) in determining applications for initial licenses;

    (B) to proceedings involving the validity or application of rates, facilities, or practices of public utilities or carriers; or

    (C) to the agency or a member or members of the body comprising the agency.

(e) The agency, with like effect as in the case of other orders, and in its sound discretion, may issue a declaratory order to terminate a controversy or remove uncertainty.

## § 555. Ancillary matters

(a) This section applies, according to the provisions thereof, except as otherwise provided by this subchapter.

(b) A person compelled to appear in person before an agency or representative thereof is entitled to be accompanied, represented, and advised by counsel or, if permitted by the agency, by other qualified representative. A party is entitled to appear in person or by or with counsel or other duly qualified representative in an agency proceeding. So far as the orderly conduct of public business permits, an interested person may appear before an agency or its responsible employees for the presentation, adjustment, or determination of an issue, request, or controversy in a proceeding, whether interlocutory, summary, or otherwise, or in connection with an agency function. With due regard for the convenience and necessity of the parties or their representatives and within a reasonable time, each agency shall proceed to conclude a matter presented to it. This subsection does not grant or deny a person who is not a lawyer the right to appear for or represent others before an agency or in an agency proceeding.

(c) Process, requirement of a report, inspection, or other investigative act or demand may not be issued, made, or enforced except as authorized by law. A person compelled to submit data or evidence is entitled to retain or, on payment of lawfully prescribed costs, procure a copy or transcript thereof, except that in a nonpublic investigatory proceeding the witness may for good cause be limited to inspection of the official transcript of his testimony.

(d) Agency subpoenas authorized by law shall be issued to a party on request and, when required by rules of procedure, on a statement or showing of general relevance and reasonable scope of the evidence sought. On contest, the court shall sustain the subpoena or similar process or demand to the extent that it is found to be in accordance with law. In a proceeding for enforcement, the court shall issue an order requiring the appearance of the witness or the production of the evidence or data within a reasonable time under penalty of punishment for contempt in case of contumacious failure to comply.

(e) Prompt notice shall be given of the denial in whole or in part of a written application, petition, or other request of an interested person made in connection with any agency proceeding. Except in affirming a prior denial or when the denial is self-explanatory, the notice shall be accompanied by a brief statement of the grounds for denial.

### § 556. Hearings; presiding employees; powers and duties; burden of proof; evidence; record as basis of decision

(a) This section applies, according to the provisions thereof, to hearings required by section 553 or 554 of this title to be conducted in accordance with this section.

(b) There shall preside at the taking of evidence—
    (1) the agency;
    (2) one or more members of the body which comprises the agency; or
    (3) one or more administrative law judges appointed under section 3105 of this title.
This subchapter does not supersede the conduct of specified classes of proceedings, in whole or in part, by or before boards or other employees specially provided for by or designated under statute. The functions of presiding employees and of employees participating in decisions in accordance with section 557 of this title shall be conducted in an impartial manner. A presiding or participating employee may at any time disqualify himself. On the filing in good faith of a timely and sufficient affidavit of personal bias or other disqualification of a presiding or participating employee, the agency shall determine the matter as a part of the record and decision in the case.

(c) Subject to published rules of the agency and within its powers, employees presiding at hearings may—
    (1) administer oaths and affirmations;
    (2) issue subpoenas authorized by law;
    (3) rule on offers of proof and receive relevant evidence;
    (4) take depositions or have depositions taken when the ends of justice would be served;
    (5) regulate the course of the hearing;

(6) hold conferences for the settlement or simplification of the issues by consent of the parties or by the use of alternative means of dispute resolution as provided in subchapter IV of this chapter;

(7) inform the parties as to the availability of one or more alternative means of dispute resolution, and encourage use of such methods;

(8) require the attendance at any conference held pursuant to paragraph (6) of at least one representative of each party who has authority to negotiate concerning resolution of issues in controversy;

(9) dispose of procedural requests or similar matters;

(10) make or recommend decisions in accordance with section 557 of this title; and

(11) take other action authorized by agency rule consistent with this subchapter.

(d) Except as otherwise provided by statute, the proponent of a rule or order has the burden of proof. Any oral or documentary evidence may be received, but the agency as a matter of policy shall provide for the exclusion of irrelevant, immaterial, or unduly repetitious evidence. A sanction may not be imposed or rule or order issued except on consideration of the whole record or those parts thereof cited by a party and supported by and in accordance with the reliable, probative, and substantial evidence. The agency may, to the extent consistent with the interests of justice and the policy of the underlying statutes administered by the agency, consider a violation of section 557(d) of this title sufficient grounds for a decision adverse to a party who has knowingly committed such violation or knowingly caused such violation to occur. A party is entitled to present his case or defense by oral or documentary evidence, to submit rebuttal evidence, and to conduct such cross-examination as may be required for a full and true disclosure of the facts. In rule making or determining claims for money or benefits or applications for initial licenses an agency may, when a party will not be prejudiced thereby, adopt procedures for the submission of all or part of the evidence in written form.

(e) The transcript of testimony and exhibits, together with all papers and requests filed in the proceeding, constitutes the exclusive record for decision in accordance with section 557 of this title and, on payment of lawfully prescribed costs, shall be made available to the parties. When an agency decision rests on official notice of a material fact not appearing in the evidence in the record, a party is entitled, on timely request, to an opportunity to show the contrary.

## § 557. Initial decisions; conclusiveness; review by agency; submissions by parties; contents of decisions; record

(a) This section applies, according to the provisions thereof, when a hearing is required to be conducted in accordance with section 556 of this title.

(b) When the agency did not preside at the reception of the evidence, the presiding employee or, in cases not subject to section 554(d) of this title, an employee qualified to preside at hearings pursuant to section 556 of this title, shall initially decide the case unless the agency requires, either in specific cases or by general rule, the entire record to be certified to it for decision. When the presiding employee makes an initial decision, that decision then becomes the decision of the agency without further proceedings unless there is an appeal to, or review on motion of, the agency within time provided by rule. On appeal from or review of the initial decision, the agency has all the powers which it would have in making the initial decision except as it may limit the issues on notice or by rule. When the agency makes the decision without having presided at the reception of the evidence, the presiding employee or an employee qualified to preside at hearings pursuant to section 556 of this title shall first recommend a decision, except that in rule making or determining applications for initial licenses—

(1) instead thereof the agency may issue a tentative decision or one of its responsible employees may recommend a decision; or

(2) this procedure may be omitted in a case in which the agency finds on the record that due and timely execution of its functions imperatively and unavoidably so requires.

(c) Before a recommended, initial, or tentative decision, or a decision on agency review of the decision of subordinate employees, the parties are entitled to a reasonable opportunity to submit for the consideration of the employees participating in the decisions—

(1) proposed findings and conclusions; or

(2) exceptions to the decisions or recommended decisions of subordinate employees or to tentative agency decisions; and

(3) supporting reasons for the exceptions or proposed findings or conclusions.

The record shall show the ruling on each finding, conclusion, or exception presented. All decisions, including initial, recommended, and tentative decisions, are a part of the record and shall include a statement of—

(A) findings and conclusions, and the reasons or basis therefor, on all the material issues of fact, law, or discretion presented on the record; and

(B) the appropriate rule, order, sanction, relief, or denial thereof.

(d)(1) In any agency proceeding which is subject to subsection (a) of this section, except to the extent required for the disposition of ex parte matters as authorized by law—

> (A) no interested person outside the agency shall make or knowingly cause to be made to any member of the body comprising the agency, administrative law judge, or other employee who is or may reasonably be expected to be involved in the decisional process of the proceeding, an ex parte communication relevant to the merits of the proceeding;
>
> (B) no member of the body comprising the agency, administrative law judge, or other employee who is or may reasonably be expected to be involved in the decisional process of the proceeding, shall make or knowingly cause to be made to any interested person outside the agency an ex parte communication relevant to the merits of the proceeding;
>
> (C) a member of the body comprising the agency, administrative law judge, or other employee who is or may reasonably be expected to be involved in the decisional process of such proceeding who receives, or who makes or knowingly causes to be made, a communication prohibited by this subsection shall place on the public record of the proceeding:
>
> > (i) all such written communications;
> >
> > (ii) memoranda stating the substance of all such oral communications; and
> >
> > (iii) all written responses, and memoranda stating the substance of all oral responses, to the materials described in clauses (i) and (ii) of this subparagraph;
>
> (D) upon receipt of a communication knowingly made or knowingly caused to be made by a party in violation of this subsection, the agency, administrative law judge, or other employee presiding at the hearing may, to the extent consistent with the interests of justice and the policy of the underlying statutes, require the party to show cause why his claim or interest in the proceeding should not be dismissed, denied, disregarded, or otherwise adversely affected on account of such violation; and
>
> (E) the prohibitions of this subsection shall apply beginning at such time as the agency may designate, but in no case shall they begin to apply later than the time at which a proceeding is noticed for hearing unless the person responsible for the communication has knowledge

that it will be noticed, in which case the prohibitions shall apply beginning at the time of his acquisition of such knowledge.

(d)(2) This subsection does not constitute authority to withhold information from Congress.

## § 558.  Imposition of sanctions; determination of applications for licenses; suspension, revocation, and expiration of licenses

(a) This section applies, according to the provisions thereof, to the exercise of a power or authority.

(b) A sanction may not be imposed or a substantive rule or order issued except within jurisdiction delegated to the agency and as authorized by law.

(c) When application is made for a license required by law, the agency, with due regard for the rights and privileges of all the interested parties or adversely affected persons and within a reasonable time, shall set and complete proceedings required to be conducted in accordance with sections 556 and 557 of this title or other proceedings required by law and shall make its decision. Except in cases of willfulness or those in which public health, interest, or safety requires otherwise, the withdrawal, suspension, revocation, or annulment of a license is lawful only if, before the institution of agency proceedings therefor, the licensee has been given—

(1) notice by the agency in writing of the facts or conduct which may warrant the action; and

(2) opportunity to demonstrate or achieve compliance with all lawful requirements.

When the licensee has made timely and sufficient application for a renewal or a new license in accordance with agency rules, a license with reference to an activity of a continuing nature does not expire until the application has been finally determined by the agency.

## § 559.  Effect on other laws; effect of subsequent statute

This subchapter, chapter 7, and sections 1305, 3105, 3344, 4301(2)(E), 5372, and 7521 of this title, and the provisions of section 5335(a)(B) of this title that relate to administrative law judges, do not limit or repeal additional requirements imposed by statute or otherwise recognized by law. Except as otherwise required by law, requirements or privileges relating to evidence or procedure apply equally to agencies and persons. Each agency is granted the authority necessary to comply with the requirements of this subchapter through the issuance of rules or otherwise. Subsequent statute may not be held to supersede or modify this subchapter, chapter 7, sections 1305, 3105, 3344, 4301(2)(E), 5372, or 7521 of this title, or the provisions of section 5335(a)(B) of this title that relate to administrative law judges, except to the extent that it does so expressly.

## [Judicial Review]

### § 701. Application; definitions

(a) This chapter applies, according to the provisions thereof, except to the extent that —
  (1) statutes preclude judicial review; or
  (2) agency action is committed to agency discretion by law.

(b) For the purpose of this chapter —
  (1) "agency" means each authority of the Government of the United States, whether or not it is within or subject to review by another agency, but does not include —
    (A) the Congress;
    (B) the courts of the United States;
    (C) the governments of the territories or possessions of the United States;
    (D) the government of the District of Columbia;
    (E) agencies composed of representatives of the parties or of representatives of organizations of the parties to the disputes determined by them;
    (F) courts martial and military commissions;
    (G) military authority exercised in the field in time of war or in occupied territory; or
    (H) functions conferred by sections 1738, 1739, 1743, and 1744 of title 12; chapter 2 of title 41; subchapter II of chapter 471 of title 49; or sections 1884, 1891–1902, and former section 1641(b)(2), of title 50, appendix; and
  (2) "person", "rule", "order", "license", "sanction", "relief", and "agency action" have the meanings given them by section 551 of this title.

### § 702. Right of review

A person suffering legal wrong because of agency action, or adversely affected or aggrieved by agency action within the meaning of a relevant statute, is entitled to judicial review thereof. An action in a court of the United States seeking relief other than money damages and stating a claim that an agency or an officer or employee thereof acted or failed to act in an official capacity or under color of legal authority shall not be dismissed nor relief therein be denied on the ground that it is against the United States or that the United States is an indispensable party. The United States may be named as a defendant in any such action, and a judgment or decree may be entered against the United States: *Provided*, That any mandatory or injunctive decree shall specify the Federal officer or officers (by name or by title), and their successors in office, personally responsible for compliance. Nothing herein (1) affects other limitations on judicial review or the power or duty of the court to dismiss any action or deny relief on any other appropriate legal or equitable ground; or (2) confers authority to grant relief if any other statute that grants consent to suit expressly or impliedly forbids the relief which is sought.

## § 703.  Form and venue of proceeding

The form of proceeding for judicial review is the special statutory review proceeding relevant to the subject matter in a court specified by statute or, in the absence or inadequacy thereof, any applicable form of legal action, including actions for declaratory judgments or writs of prohibitory or mandatory injunction or habeas corpus, in a court of competent jurisdiction. If no special statutory review proceeding is applicable, the action for judicial review may be brought against the United States, the agency by its official title, or the appropriate officer. Except to the extent that prior, adequate, and exclusive opportunity for judicial review is provided by law, agency action is subject to judicial review in civil or criminal proceedings for judicial enforcement.

## § 704.  Actions reviewable

Agency action made reviewable by statute and final agency action for which there is no other adequate remedy in a court are subject to judicial review. A preliminary, procedural, or intermediate agency action or ruling not directly reviewable is subject to review on the review of the final agency action. Except as otherwise expressly required by statute, agency action otherwise final is final for the purposes of this section whether or not there has been presented or determined an application for a declaratory order, for any form of reconsideration, or, unless the agency otherwise requires by rule and provides that the action meanwhile is inoperative, for an appeal to superior agency authority.

## § 705.  Relief pending review

When an agency finds that justice so requires, it may postpone the effective date of action taken by it, pending judicial review. On such conditions as may be required and to the extent necessary to prevent irreparable injury, the reviewing court, including the court to which a case may be taken on appeal from or on application for certiorari or other writ to a reviewing court, may issue all necessary and appropriate process to postpone the effective date of an agency action or to preserve status or rights pending conclusion of the review proceedings.

## § 706.  Scope of review

To the extent necessary to decision and when presented, the reviewing court shall decide all relevant questions of law, interpret constitutional and statutory provisions, and determine the meaning or applicability of the terms of an agency action. The reviewing court shall—

(1) compel agency action unlawfully withheld or unreasonably delayed; and

(2) hold unlawful and set aside agency action, findings, and conclusions found to be—

(A) arbitrary, capricious, an abuse of discretion, or otherwise not in accordance with law;

(B) contrary to constitutional right, power, privilege, or immunity;

(C) in excess of statutory jurisdiction, authority, or limitations, or short of statutory right;

(D) without observance of procedure required by law;

(E) unsupported by substantial evidence in a case subject to sections 556 and 557 of this title or otherwise reviewed on the record of an agency hearing provided by statute; or

(F) unwarranted by the facts to the extent that the facts are subject to trial de novo by the reviewing court.

In making the foregoing determinations, the court shall review the whole record or those parts of it cited by a party, and due account shall be taken of the rule of prejudicial error.

### [Administrative Law Judges]

## § 3105.  Appointment of administrative law judges

Each agency shall appoint as many administrative law judges as are necessary for proceedings required to be conducted in accordance with sections 556 and 557 of this title. Administrative law judges shall be assigned to cases in rotation so far as practicable, and may not perform duties inconsistent with their duties and responsibilities as administrative law judges.

## § 7521.  Actions against administrative law judges

(a) An action may be taken against an administrative law judge appointed under section 3105 of this title by the agency in which the administrative law judge is employed only for good cause established and determined by the Merit Systems Protection Board on the record after opportunity for hearing before the Board.

(b) The actions covered by this section are—

    (1) a removal;

    (2) a suspension;

    (3) a reduction in grade;

    (4) a reduction in pay; and

    (5) a furlough of 30 days or less;

but do not include—

        (A) a suspension or removal under section 7532 of this title [national security];

        (B) a reduction-in-force action under section 3502 of this title [RIF]; or

        (C) any action initiated under section 1215 of this title [special counsel proceedings].

# Index